Books are to be returned ⌐
tho lⸯ

WITHDRÁWN

The Development of Higher Education in the United Kingdom since 1945

SRHE and Open University Press Imprint

Current titles include:

The Development of Higher Education in the United Kingdom since 1945

Malcolm Tight

 Society for Research into Higher Education
& Open University Press

Open University Press
McGraw-Hill Education
McGraw-Hill House
Shoppenhangers Road
Maidenhead
Berkshire
England
SL6 2QL

email: enquiries@openup.co.uk
world wide web: www.openup.co.uk

and Two Penn Plaza, New York, NY 10121–2289, USA

First published 2009

A catalogue record of this book is available from the British Library

ISBN–13: 978–0–33–521642–0 (hb)
ISBN–10: 0–33–5–21642–0 (hb)

Library of Congress Cataloging-in-Publication Data
CIP data applied for

Typeset by RefineCatch Limited, Bungay, Suffolk
Printed in the UK by Bell and Bain Ltd, Glasgow

Fictitious names of companies, products, people, characters and/or data that may be used herein (in case studies or in examples) are not intended to represent any real individual, company, product or event.

The McGraw·Hill Companies

Contents

Abbreviations

Note that some of these abbreviations are historic, as the bodies or practices referred to have been superseded.

AAU	Academic Audit Unit
ABRC	Advisory Board for the Research Councils
ACACE	Advisory Council for Adult and Continuing Education
ACARD	Advisory Council for Applied Research and Development
ACOST	Advisory Council on Science and Technology
ACP	Association of College Principals
ACSP	Advisory Council on Scientific Policy
ACSTT	Advisory Committee on the Supply and Training of Teachers
ACU	Association of Commonwealth Universities
AEC	Association of Education Committees
AFE	Advanced Further Education
AFEC	Advanced Further Education Council
AGCAS	Association of Graduate Careers Advisory Services
AHRC	Arts and Humanities Research Council
AHUA	Association of Heads of University Administration
APL	accreditation of prior learning
APR	Age Participation Ratio
APT	Association of Polytechnic Teachers
ARC	Agricultural Research Council
AS	Advanced Supplementary
ASTMS	Association of Scientific Technical and Managerial Staffs
ATCDE	Association of Teachers in Colleges and Departments of Education
ATO	Area Training Organization
ATTI	Association of Teachers in Technical Institutions
AUBC	Association of the Universities of the British Commonwealth (later ACU)
AUT	Association of University Teachers

BBSRC	Biotechnology and Biological Sciences Research Council
BEC	Business Education Council (later part of BTEC)
BTEC	Business and Technician Education Council (now EdExcel)
CAT	College of Advanced Technology
CATE	Council for the Accreditation of Teacher Education
CBI	Confederation on British Industry
CCLRC	Council for the Central Laboratory of the Research Councils
CDP	Committee of Directors of Polytechnics
CEI	Council of Engineering Institutions
CETL	Centre for Excellence in Teaching and Learning
Cert Ed	Certificate of Education
CGLI	City and Guilds of London Institute
CI	Central Institution
CIHE	Council for Industry and Higher Education
CLEA	Council of Local Education Authorities
CNAA	Council for National Academic Awards
COSHEP	Committee of Scottish Higher Education Principals
CPD	continuing professional development
CSP	Council for Scientific Policy
CSR	Comprehensive Spending Review
CSU	Careers Services Unit
CSUP	Committee of Scottish University Principals
CTE	Council for Tertiary Education
CUCO	Commission on University Career Opportunity
CVCP	Committee of Vice-Chancellors and Principals
DEL	Department for Employment and Learning
DENI	Department of Education for Northern Ireland
DES	Department of Education and Science
DfEE	Department for Education and Employment
DfES	Department for Education and Skills
DipHE	Diploma in Higher Education
DIUS	Department for Innovation, Universities and Skills
DPS	Diploma in Professional Studies
DSIR	Department of Scientific and Industrial Research
DTI	Department of Trade and Industry
ECTS	European Credit Transfer System
EHE	Enterprise in Higher Education
EPSRC	Engineering and Physical Sciences Research Council
ESRC	Economic and Social Research Council (formerly SSRC)
EU	European Union
FD	foundation degree
FEFC	Further Education Funding Council
FETS	Further Education and Training Scheme
FTEs	full-time equivalents
GCE	General Certificate of Education
GCSE	General Certificate of Secondary Education
GNVQ	General National Vocational Qualification

GTC	General Teaching Council
HEA	Higher Education Academy
HEFCE	Higher Education Funding Council for England
HEFCW	Higher Education Funding Council for Wales
HEQC	Higher Education Quality Council
HERDF	Higher Education Regional Development Fund
HEROBAC	Higher Education Reach-out to Business and the Community
HESA	Higher Education Statistics Agency
HESDA	Higher Education Staff Development Agency
HMI	Her Majesty's Inspector(ate)
HNC	Higher National Certificate
HND	Higher National Diploma
ILEA	Inner London Education Authority
ILTHE	Institute for Learning and Teaching in Higher Education
JIF	Joint Infrastructure Fund
JISC	Joint Information Systems Committee
LEA	Local Education Authority
LSC	Learning and Skills Council
LTSN	Learning and Teaching Support Network
MRC	Medical Research Council
MSC	Manpower Services Commission
NAB	National Advisory Body for Local Authority (later Public Sector) Higher Education
NACEIC	National Advisory Council on Education for Industry and Commerce
NACTST	National Advisory Council on the Training and Supply of Teachers
NAO	National Audit Office
NATFHE	National Association of Teachers in Further and Higher Education
NCTA	National Council for Technological Awards
NCTET	National Council for Teacher Education and Training
NCVQ	National Council for Vocational Qualifications
NERC	National Environment Research Council
NIACE	National Institute for Adult Continuing Education
NQF	National Qualifications Framework
NTFS	National Teaching Fellowship Scheme
NUS	National Union of Students
NVQ	National Vocational Qualification
OECD	Organization for Economic Co-operation and Development
OFSTED	Office for Standards in Education
ONC	Ordinary National Certificate
OND	Ordinary National Diploma
PCAS	Polytechnics and Colleges Admissions Service
PCFC	Polytechnics and Colleges Funding Council
PEVE	Post-experience vocational education

PGCE	Postgraduate Certificate of Education
PICKUP	Professional, Industrial and Commercial Updating Programme
PPARC	Particle Physics and Astronomy Research Council
PSBR	public sector borrowing requirement
PSHE	Public Sector Higher Education
QAA	Quality Assurance Agency for Higher Education
QCA	Qualifications and Curriculum Authority
QPI	qualified participation index
RAC	Regional Advisory Council
RAE	Research Assessment Exercise
RDA	Regional Development Agency
RSA	Royal Society for the encouragement of Arts, Manufactures and Commerce
SCDPCIHE	Standing Conference of Directors and Principals of Colleges and Institutes of Higher Education
SCOP	Standing Conference of Principals
SCOTVEC	Scottish Vocational Education Council
SCUE	Standing Conference on University Entrance
SED	Scottish Education Department
SEDA	Staff and Educational Development Association
SERC	Science and Engineering Research Council (formerly SRC)
SHEFC	Scottish Higher Education Funding Council
SNVQ	Scottish National Vocational Qualification
SQA	Scottish Qualification Authority
SRC	Science Research Council
SRHE	Society for Research into Higher Education
SSA	Student Support Agency
SSRC	Social Science Research Council
STEAC	Scottish Tertiary Education Advisory Council
STFC	Science and Technology Facilities Council
SVQ	Scottish Vocational Qualification
TA	Training Agency
TAA	test of academic aptitude
TEC	Technician Education Council (later part of BTEC); Training and Enterprise Council
THES	Times Higher Education Supplement
TLTP	Teaching and Learning Technology Programme
TQA	teaching quality assessment
TTA	Teacher Training Agency
TUC	Trades Union Congress
TVEI	Technical Vocational Education Initiative
UCAS	Universities and Colleges Admissions Service (formerly UCCA)
UCCA	Universities Central Council on Admissions
UCEA	Universities and Colleges Employers Association

UCET	Universities Council for the Education of Teachers
UCoSDA	Universities and Colleges Staff Development Agency
UFC	Universities Funding Council
UGC	University Grants Committee
UKCOSA	UK Council for Overseas Student Affairs
UKGCE	United Kingdom Council for Graduate Education
UoA	Unit of Assessment (in the Research Assessment Exercise)
USR	Universities Statistical Record
USS	Universities Superannuation Scheme
UUK	Universities UK (formerly the CVCP)
WAB	Welsh Advisory Body for Local Authority (later Public Sector) Higher Education
WEA	Workers' Educational Association
YTS	Youth Training Scheme

Preface and dedication

Putting together a single volume account of the development of a sector as complex as higher education in the UK over a period of 60+ years has been an interesting, perhaps foolhardy, undertaking. I did it because there was no such, up-to-date, account in existence, yet I was convinced of the importance of making one accessible. It would be truly remarkable if, in producing this book, I had made no errors of fact, though hopefully I will have kept these to a minimum. Readers will also have different interpretations of aspects of the story to offer, and other ideas about which elements should have been given more or less prominence. I would welcome any communications along these lines.

This book is dedicated to all of those higher education researchers and writers who have gone before, and whose work I have made extensive use of. Reading and rereading their work was a salutary exercise in showing not just how some issues rise and fall in significance, but also that many concerns remain consistently important and have been extensively considered on many occasions.

Malcolm Tight
September 2008

1
Introduction

Even at the end of the twentieth century many historians engaging with higher education were mostly at home revising accounts of medieval Oxford and Cambridge, while others were in pursuit of later Oxbridge and its colleges, or the idea of a university and liberal education in the eighteenth, nineteenth and twentieth centuries, prompted by a landscape filling out with new institutions, purposes, contexts and policies. (Silver 2006: 121)

This book aims to provide an accessible, up-to-date, comprehensive, single-volume guide to the development of higher education in the UK since 1945. While dozens of books and hundreds of articles are published on higher education every year in the UK, including a goodly number focusing on the history of particular institutions of higher education, no comprehensive account of this nature has been published since 1989 (Stewart 1989).

Yet the need for an accessible, single-volume account is arguably greater than it has ever been. The UK higher education system, in common with most others, has grown and changed enormously during the post-war period, and the pressures for further development do not look like diminishing in the foreseeable future. Many of those of us who work or study within our universities and colleges, or who are otherwise affected by them as parents, employers, policy makers or interested citizens, would surely welcome a guide to how the system has developed in the way that it has.

The need for a guide is strengthened by the many misconceptions that exist about the ways in which higher education has changed. It is common, for example, to read or hear of practices in universities or colleges being described as 'traditional', as if they had been handed down essentially intact from the Middle Ages, when what is really meant is that this was how it was done here in recent memory, and in some cases only last year. That many of the same issues have cropped up time and again to challenge those working in higher education, and that earlier responses might still have some relevance today, is often not appreciated.

To provide such a guide is the broad and ambitious task I have set for myself in writing this book.

The approach taken

The obvious approach to take in providing a historical account is, of course, a sequential one. Start at the beginning or, as in this case, at a given year, and summarize what happened year by year. Arguably, it is impossible to avoid this strategy in compiling a book of this nature, but in this case I have opted to give it a secondary role.

My main approach will, instead, be thematic. Drawing on a survey I recently undertook of the state of contemporary research into higher education (Tight 2003, 2004), I have identified seven key themes in the story of UK higher education in the post-war period. These are: policy and funding, institutional diversity, institutional management and relationships, course design, research and knowledge, the student experience and the staff experience. These themes form the foci for the main body of the book, Chapters 4–11, with the discussion of the student experience occupying two chapters (9 and 10). Within each of these chapters, which are cross-referenced, the treatment of each topic is then organized in terms of sub-themes.

Key documents have been identified for some of the themes for extended consideration. For example, in the chapter on policy and funding, the Robbins and Dearing reports (Committee on Higher Education 1963a; National Committee of Inquiry into Higher Education 1997a), as the two major national reports on higher education in the post-war period, clearly merit close attention. These two inquiries also commissioned research to inform their deliberations, and the reports of these projects have provided key documents for a number of other chapters. For these and other themes, further contemporary research reports, and classic and current writings, have also been used.

To balance the thematic approach, three chapters adopt a predominantly sequential strategy. One of these (Chapter 2) provides a brief overview of the history of higher education in the UK up until 1945. Another (Chapter 3) offers a tabular summary of post-war higher education developments, together with a list of current UK universities and their origins, and key statistics on student numbers. A final chapter (Chapter 12) concludes the book with a discussion of the changing idea of the university in the UK, and the international influences on this.

Sources

There are a multitude of potential sources for a project like this, which is both a strength and a challenge. These sources include, most obviously:

government documents; documents and statistics produced by national agencies; institutional documents and histories; histories of particular disciplines and sectors of provision; contemporary research on higher education; newspapers, especially the professional press; and auto/biographical accounts by those involved. As the post-war period covers the time during which higher education research has 'come of age' in the UK, the accumulated body of research on higher education carried out during the period – particularly from the 1960s onwards – which once was contemporary but is now historical, has been of particular significance.

In managing these sources, my main aim has been to try and ensure that key documents were identified and referred to. In doing so, I have also endeavoured to acknowledge differences in opinion and key debates.

Continuity and change

Of course, if we were simply to compare the state of UK higher education in 1945, when this account starts, and 2008, the date at which I delivered it to the publishers and it, therefore, ends, the immediate impression would be one of enormous change. A glance at the tables in Chapter 3 is all that is required to confirm the huge increase in the scale of activity since 1945, whether measured in terms of the numbers of students, staff or institutions. An observer who was able to travel back in time to visit the universities and colleges of 1945, as well as noting their relatively small size, would also be struck by other apparent 'oddities' of practice. For example: universities then had their own MPs (no less than 13 of them!); the universities were crammed with lots of ex-service men studying; women students were a small minority, taught in separate colleges at Oxford, Cambridge and London, and housed in single-sex halls of residence elsewhere; continuous assessment was virtually unheard of; and there were no business schools. Indeed, and perhaps more fundamentally, no one in 1945 spoke of the UK as having a higher education 'system', or even, for that matter, of 'higher education'.

But, to put all the emphasis on the changes that have undeniably taken place would be to ignore the considerable continuities in practice that reach across the 63-year period under review. For example, the structure of our degrees, and indeed of the academic year (semesterization notwithstanding), remains essentially the same. The hierarchies of students or institutions (whether we approve of them or not) are still pretty much intact, though now further extended. And, arguably more importantly, our underlying values – of academic freedom and institutional autonomy, of the importance of teaching and research – remain; though, as so often, under threat. So, it is important to try and balance an account of development with a recognition of what has been more constant.

2

Higher education before 1945

Introduction

Higher education in the UK looked very different before the Second World War to the way it does today, not least, of course, in terms of the scale of the activity. Nevertheless, most of the institutions we know now were already in existence in some form before 1945, and most of the issues that we face today – for example, over institutional and student funding, the organization of the curriculum, the linkages between higher education and work, the role of research – were already evident.

While the history of universities in the UK can be traced back to the twelfth century, and at least the aspiration towards some form of higher education even earlier than that, it makes sense, in a book that focuses on the post-war period, to concentrate in this chapter on the latter part of the pre-war period. The emphasis here will, therefore, be on the nineteenth century and the first half of the twentieth century. It was during this period that the number of institutions involved in higher education began to multiply, and the development of a national system of provision – with the increasing involvement of government in establishing policy, and providing funding, for higher education – became an important concern.

This chapter starts, therefore, by examining the range of institutions involved in higher education during the nineteenth and early twentieth centuries, in rough order of antiquity:

- the 'ancient' institutions (Oxford and Cambridge, the 'ancient' Scottish universities, Trinity College);
- the nineteenth-century foundations (the University of London, the English civic universities, the University of Wales, the Irish universities);
- pre-war twentieth-century foundations;
- non-university institutions (teacher training colleges, colleges of art and design, technical colleges, the Scottish central institutions).

A series of key themes, cross-cutting the provision made by these institutions, are then briefly considered – the development of state funding and policy, the relation between higher education and work, and the development of postgraduate studies and research – before the progress made towards a national system by the start of the Second World War is assessed.

The 'ancient' institutions

Prior to the nineteenth century, the history of higher education in the UK is essentially the story of a small number of relatively small institutions – only some of them designated as universities – in a handful of towns and cities. There was nothing that might be termed a system of higher education in existence then; nothing was formally available for women; much of what was offered was either vocationally directed (producing clerics, doctors, lawyers, teachers, etc.) or intended as a kind of finishing school for the well-to-do (for whom actually gaining a degree was not that important); and research, such as it was, was only a minority interest among academics.

Given the relative underdevelopment of higher education prior to the second half of the nineteenth century – when compared to the present day or even the immediate pre-war period – it should be no surprise that some seemingly contradictory patterns were in evidence. Thus, higher education in Scotland was significantly more developed than it was in England (or in Ireland, for that matter, then still part of the British kingdom; or in Wales, which was then totally lacking in formal higher education provision). And, in England, a substantial part of what we would now regard as higher education – that concerning the legal and medical professions – took place outside the then existing universities of Oxford and Cambridge, and was run by the appropriate professional bodies and employers based in the capital city, London.

Oxford and Cambridge

> At the opening of the nineteenth century, Oxford and Cambridge Universities were the English universities. As the only such institutions in England, this was, of course, a truism but, over centuries of hegemony, they had acquired uniquely privileged roles in the life of the nation.
> (Vernon 2004: 9)

Of all the higher education institutions in the UK, the universities of Oxford and Cambridge have been, by far, the most studied. In virtually any university library, one can find shelves full of books, not just on the two universities, but, more particularly, on each of their component colleges. The attention devoted to the minutiae of college politics, and to the lives of leading dons and students, in past centuries at these two universities far outstrips study of the development of higher education in general, even in more recent periods. While this is, arguably, out of all proportion to their contemporary contribution, it is understandable given their historical dominance and elite appeal.

Seen from a national perspective, for Oxford and Cambridge much of the nineteenth and twentieth centuries were spent in a, at times painfully slow, reform process, designed to make them more relevant to the developing needs of an expanding and industrializing nation. Thus, for Oxford:

> The University Reform Act of 1854 was . . . a watershed in Oxford's history. College life was to experience a steady reorientation as senior common rooms slowly lost their clerical character and received infusions of fresh blood. A fellowship could no longer be regarded as a prize which the fortunate recipient could hope to enjoy for the remainder of his life without serious duties. Henceforth it became more and more a responsible tutorial office whose holder was expected to engage in advanced study and research. Major changes occurred with the creation of new honour schools, with a more effective professoriate and with a more efficient, theoretically more democratic, form of self-government. (Green 1974: 149)

And at Cambridge: 'The great revolution of the late nineteenth century saw college teaching become very much more effective, and a whole structure of university institutions and laboratories grow up beside the colleges' (Brooke 1993: 20). A further University Reform Act was passed in 1877, which abolished religious tests and the celibacy rule for academics, and then another in 1923: 'by 1926 the process of reform was completed: Oxford and Cambridge had new constitutions and the statutes of both universities and all the colleges had been revised' (p. 341). Women were finally admitted to all degrees at Oxford, except in theology, in 1920, with theology finally succumbing in 1935.

The expansion of the curriculum away from the classics, and the development of research capacity, were slow processes, resisted all of the way by many Oxbridge academics:

> The later-Victorian ancient universities present much the same picture as the public schools. Socially of less significance (most public school boys did not go on to university), they too witnessed a 'conservative revolution' beginning in mid-century that revivified them and increased their contribution to the life of the nation, while preserving the essentials of traditional gentry culture. In the eighteen-fifties and sixties, 'modern' subjects were scarcely in evidence in the Oxbridge curriculum . . . As with the public schools, very few undergraduates came from business backgrounds. Oxford and Cambridge, even more than the public schools, were precincts reserved for the sons of gentry, clergy, and the more distinguished professions. (Wiener 1981: 22)

By the end of the nineteenth century, several other universities and university colleges (soon to become universities in their own right) had been established in England, yet:

. . . Oxford and Cambridge were still the English national universities, although the nature and meaning of the role had changed. Previously the universities' national position rested on their privileged relationships to the national Church and informal, though still highly political, ties to the state. Now, the national function of Oxford and Cambridge meant that they accepted students from all constituencies of the nation (apart from women) and, while no longer the only universities in the country, they were undoubtedly the largest, wealthiest and most prestigious, propelling their students, much as they had before, into the elites of Church, state and the professions. (Vernon 2004: 49)

They were to remain the largest universities in the country until overtaken by London in the 1930s, and are still the wealthiest and most prestigious. Curriculum change and expansion continued, however, to be only gradual:

> Given the intimate connection between the public school and Oxbridge, it is not surprising that the ethos and curricula of the two ancient universities even up until the Second World War should also have been inspired by the victory won by the Victorian liberal-education men. Both universities for long successfully defended the medieval disciplines of the classics and philosophy against the encroachments of science; and for longer still the encroachments of technology. Greek remained a compulsory subject at Cambridge even for scientists until 1919; at Oxford until 1920. (Barnett 1986: 218)

It was only well into the twentieth century that Oxford and Cambridge became defined in their present sense in distinction from the other universities and colleges that were being established:

> All in all, Oxbridge gradually became a real entity within the British university system after 1914. It was not only the ritual of competitive solidarity in the annual boat-race. It was an intricate network of institutional and individual exchange, born of common interest in perpetuating the Oxbridge ideal within a growing system that might otherwise have engulfed the ancient universities. (Halsey 1995: 70)

That ideal remains an immensely strong – if slowly diminishing – influence, though some would say liability, in the contemporary British higher education system (see also Chapter 12).

One other, perhaps ultimately more important, way in which Oxford and Cambridge influenced the development of higher education, at least in England, was through their involvement in university extension. Cambridge led the way here, with the first extension lecture courses organized in 1873, with Oxford following suit in 1878, offering courses in towns and cities in many parts of the country (Goldman 1995; Harrop 1987; Jepson 1973). This then established a pattern or service, which built on a much longer tradition, and led other universities and university colleges to offer adult education provision as they became established (Blyth 1983; Fieldhouse 1996; Kelly

1970; Marriott 1981, 1984). A sustained tradition of extension lecture or extramural courses was an important factor in the development of a number of university colleges, such as Reading (originally an Oxford extension college), Exeter and, after the Second World War, Keele (with which Oxford was also closely connected).

The ancient Scottish universities

The early Scottish university foundations were established by papal authority – while those in England owed their charters and privileges to the English crown – at a time when travelling to the continent to study was difficult, and going to Oxford or Cambridge unpopular. St Andrews, Glasgow and Aberdeen (which had two separate foundations until they eventually combined in 1860) were all set up in the fifteenth century, with Edinburgh – established and controlled by the town council, a position only changed by an 1858 Act – following in the late sixteenth century (Scotland 1969a).

It has been argued, reasonably convincingly, that the Scottish higher education tradition was in many ways more 'democratic' (Davie 1961) and advanced than that in England, and some would claim that it remains so to this day. One of the key Scottish educational historians – the appropriately named Scotland – has pointed out that the nineteenth-century Scottish universities differed from those in England in several respects:

> First, the Scottish universities were essentially local, not national institutions, having strong ties with the region in which they were located. In this they contrasted strongly with Oxford, Cambridge and London, though one of the effects of the 1858 Act was to make them more national in outlook and appeal. Second, instruction was very cheap, because classes were large and the session lasted no more than half the year . . . the third feature [was] the diffusion of a desire for knowledge throughout the country . . . A fourth characteristic rose from the numbers in attendance. Many students who finished their course found no opening in the older professions . . . There was no matriculation examination, and this depressed the standard of instruction immediately before and after entrance . . . the elementary standard of the first two university years was notorious. (Scotland 1969a: 332)

This is not to claim, of course, that the standards of instruction at Oxford and Cambridge were particularly high either at the beginning of the nineteenth century.

While philosophy was a key part of the curriculum at both English and Scottish universities, the latter offered a broader range of subjects to a wider proportion of the population, as well as engaging to a greater extent with the professions. Being more local in focus, the Scottish institutions did not, however, concern themselves much with the residence or welfare of their students:

... the Scottish universities offered another model that was ... in clear contrast to Oxbridge, most notably in their greater accessibility. The universities of Edinburgh, Glasgow, Aberdeen and St Andrews took students direct from the parochial schools at a young age and offered a wide-ranging course with a philosophical basis. Tuition was by professorial lecture and qualification by certificate of attendance. There was some emphasis on professional subjects, and the University of Edinburgh especially had created a renowned medical school. Students were not required to live in residential colleges, but could seek accommodation to suit their pockets. Altogether, there were far fewer costs attached to a university education in Scotland than in England, and, in principle, a boy of quite modest means could acquire a sound general education preparatory to training as a minister, schoolteacher or entering a profession. (Vernon 2004: 17)

Many of these differences are still evident in contemporary Scottish practices (see also Chapter 5).

Trinity College

It might seem strange, in a book focused on the UK, to mention, if only briefly, what is now an Irish institution. However, Ireland did not become an independent state until 1937, so it has a long – and to some extent shared – higher education history with the rest of the British Isles.

Trinity College was founded in Dublin in the late sixteenth century to serve the needs of the then protestant ruling class. It had been closely modelled on Trinity College Cambridge, and, like Oxbridge, emphasized the residential undergraduate experience. This tradition was diluted somewhat in the nineteenth century, such that, by 1852, half the undergraduates were non-resident, some of them even living in England (McDowell and Webb 1982). They were provided with a syllabus and annual tests in what was arguably an early external examination system. Indeed, it has been suggested that this 'complex but clearly defined process influenced developments at the London University' (Foden 1989: 17).

The nineteenth-century foundations

While the newer universities and colleges, which were founded in the UK – or rather the British Isles – from the nineteenth century onwards were intended to spread the benefits of higher education more widely, they took key elements of their organizational form from existing institutional examples, most notably Oxford and Cambridge (but also, as Foden indicates, more widely as well). Instead of the contemporary idea of the self-contained unitary university, what emerged were alliances of colleges in relation with one another under the auspices of a university constructed as an examining body:

> . . . the college as a teaching institution, and the federation of colleges as modelled on Oxford and Cambridge and embodied in London and Victoria Universities and the provincial colleges . . . preceded the emergence of the university, which granted degrees. Indeed, the 'university' in the UK was and is the degree-granting body, as over against the colleges, which have been agencies for teaching. (Trow 1993: 283)

In the case of Durham, founded in 1832, the Oxbridge template was mimicked much more closely, with the colleges also co-located, enabling a smooth transition into a more modern university form (Whiting 1932). The federal university model established by London, founded in 1836, and which exists to this day, albeit under some stress, was copied in other parts of the British Isles and throughout the then Empire (Bell and Tight 1993; Harte 1986). The federal University of Wales, founded in 1893, also still exists, though also under some strain.

The Victoria University, on the other hand, based on Owens College in Manchester, barely survived the nineteenth century as a fully functioning body before its other component colleges – in Liverpool, Leeds and Sheffield – had become free-standing universities. Some functions, however, such as the Joint Matriculation Board examining system, continued for much longer. A further federal establishment, the Royal University of Ireland (which itself replaced the federal Queen's University of Ireland), also disbanded before the First World War, but was partially replaced in the south of the island by the federal National University. In Northern Ireland, Magee College in Londonderry remained subject to the examining authority of the University of Dublin until 1970.

The nineteenth-century foundations (Durham excepted) were very different from the ancient universities, with which they were scarcely in competition. For decades they remained relatively small, local institutions, focused on survival as much as expansion, with students living locally rather than in residence, and many of them studying part time. Much of their focus was vocational in nature:

> After 1870 the civic university colleges reacted very sharply against Oxford and Cambridge – as Durham and Manchester had earlier tried to follow them – and asserted the vocational, professional and technological nature of their education. In colleges such as Birmingham and Sheffield literary arts subjects were kept very constrained and subordinate in the nineteenth century, and indeed in the former college were specifically excluded by the wishes of the founder. (Sanderson 1975: 4)

Yet, though they were founded to serve local industrial and technical needs, they were alert to the model provided by Oxbridge, at which many of their staff would have studied, and aspired to 'greater things'. Over time, therefore, they succumbed to what later authors (Pratt and Burgess 1974), studying the development of the polytechnics in the 1970s, would refer to as academic drift:

> In the case of those provincial colleges which had been distinctly intended by their founders to be overwhelmingly technical in character, such as Mason's College, Birmingham (now Birmingham University), Leeds, Sheffield and Nottingham, powerful outside factors compelled them eventually to conform to the prevailing British pattern of a 'liberal education'. The first of these factors lay in London University's examination requirements for external degrees (for which initially the new provincial colleges had to enter their students), which demanded literature and the classics as a necessary part even of a science degree. In the second place, the new 'Victoria University' of 1880, a federation of northern colleges dominated by Manchester, insisted that purely technological institutions like Sheffield and Leeds should broaden their coverage to the arts if they wished to be admitted. Then again, when the state in Britain at last began to give financial support to university education in 1889, the body which dispensed the funds, being weighty with Oxbridge high minds, required that remaining overly technical institutions like Birmingham and Southampton should strengthen their teaching in unuseful knowledges if they wanted government money. And finally there was the pressure of demand for the arts from students intending to become school-teachers, wherein was manifested another aspect of the wider influence exerted by the triumphant 'liberal education' lobby; indeed the operation of a closed loop. (Barnett 1986: 222)

Thus, the liberal/vocational tension was deeply embedded in the emergent UK higher education system before the end of the nineteenth century, and has remained as a key issue ever since.

The University of London

The direct and indirect influence of the University of London on higher education (as well as secondary education), both within the UK and overseas, has been enormous. As, effectively, the British 'Imperial' University of the nineteenth and twentieth centuries, its impact in establishing the pattern and standards of provision, in institutional and curricular terms, is much underrated. While the university has now largely shrunk back to its metropolitan core – though it is still by far the largest conventional university in the country, the Open University now has more students, although almost all of them are part-time and studying at-a-distance – an understanding of its origins and development is arguably of greater importance to an appreciation of the contemporary state of UK higher education than an immersion in the history of Oxbridge:

> London was precedent and exemplar as well as certifying agency for the new colleges. It had been founded in a major city by members of the

intellectual and professional middle classes; it survived without significant endowment; it offered new types of education and catered to new
demands; it was relatively cheap and entirely non-denominational. The
curriculum set the standard for the Victorian foundations: matriculation and degrees would both require a wide range of knowledge of
classical and modern letters, history, mathematics, and science. (Jones
1988: 16)

But, of course, it need not have worked out that way. For the University
of London was initially established in 1836 as a means of meeting the competing aspirations of two new foundations in London – University College
and King's College:

> The first two university colleges of the University of London are remark-
> able examples of the new social forces at work in England in the third
> and fourth decades of the nineteenth century. The early educational
> policies adopted by both were strongly oriented to the local market and
> were in this respect, as in so many others, conscious departures from
> the historic model offered by the ancient universities. Yet we must be
> prepared for a paradox. Despite these undeniable facts, the subsequent
> development of the University of London is a history of 'upward
> academic drift'. (Rothblatt 1988: 130)

This upward drift was in no small part due to the subsequent use made of the
University of London by the state, the developing educational establishment
and the university itself. Always an awkward amalgam of examining body and
conventional university colleges, the University of London was used to draw
together and regulate not just the university level institutions in the London
area – many of which, most notably the teaching hospitals, had been in
existence in some form for centuries – but those not already of independent
university status elsewhere, first in the British Isles, and then throughout the
Empire. And, because of the importance of the university's matriculation or
entrance examination, this influence was extended downward to regulate
practices throughout the school sector:

> Despite its confusing and controversial nature, the University of
> London, in conjunction with its principal London outlets, pioneered
> modern university education in England. They severed the connection
> between religion and university degrees, developed new subjects rele-
> vant to a modern urban society, removed the requirement of residence,
> even of attendance, and, eventually, admitted women to degrees.
> Although a remote device, the exacting requirements of London Uni-
> versity examinations came to serve as a guardian of university standards
> and, effectively, a monitor of higher education throughout the Empire.
> (Vernon 2004: 52)

In emphasizing its national and international role – because they are so often
overlooked – we should not, however, underestimate the achievement of the

University within London itself. This was in part steered, as was the development of most British universities at the time, by the recommendations of successive royal commissions:

London became almost the embodiment of Haldane's dream: a great imperial university covering every aspect of human knowledge. Though the Davey Commissioners [who completed their work in 1900] had not included the four schools of music, nor the four Inns of Court, they had re-constituted twenty-four other colleges as schools of the University of London. These were University College, King's College, six colleges in the Faculty of Theology, two women's colleges (Holloway and Bedford), the Royal College of Science, the South East Agricultural College, the ten medical schools of the great London Hospitals, the Central Technical College, and the London School of Economics. To these twenty-four were added another eleven during the period 1902–25: Westfield (1902), the London School of Tropical Medicine (1905), the East London College (1909), University College Hospital Medical School (1909), the London Day Training College (1910), the Royal Dental Hospital School (1911), Birkbeck College (1920), and the School of Pharmacy (1925). (Armytage 1955: 256–7)

London, like Oxford and Cambridge, was also closely involved in the university extension movement, introducing three or four year diploma courses in a range of subjects in 1910. More coordinated provision for adults throughout the country followed after the First World War, with the foundation of extramural departments by many of the English civic universities.

The English civic universities

In a broad sense the university colleges were a somewhat belated response to the needs created by the industrial revolution. (Mountford 1966: 21)

The English civic university colleges, established in the large industrial cities of Birmingham, Bristol, Leeds, Liverpool, Manchester and Sheffield by local interests during the nineteenth century, did not become free-standing, independent universities until the first decade of the twentieth century:

Not until Birmingham University was chartered in 1900 did England gain a college-university on something like the Scottish pattern. Earlier, in England and Wales there developed a clutch of 'redbrick' or provincial university colleges (not college-universities) which, in the later nineteenth century, offered teaching for degrees which were conferred elsewhere – by London University from 1836 onwards, by the federal Victoria University in Manchester from 1880 onwards, and by the new federal University of Wales from 1893. (Carter and Withrington 1992: 2)

As well as the desire to spread university provision throughout the country – or at least to the main population centres: a Victorian, private sector version of the contemporary UK 'widening participation' policies – the civic university colleges were closely linked to the needs of industry for higher level training for workers and applied research:

> The character of the provincial universities thus derives from the convergence of two nineteenth-century movements. One was local – a desire to bring the perceived benefits of metropolitan liberal culture to civic life, and this was supported by the University Extension movements of the ancient English universities. The other was a national movement which aimed to bring higher technological education into the service of industry. It was inspired by fear of industrial competition from the Continent, appreciation of the industrial benefits gained by Germany, France and Switzerland from their polytechnics and admiration of the American land grant colleges. (Halsey et al. 1971: 54)

As such, the civic university colleges placed themselves in the developing higher education institutional hierarchy in a position similar to that which would later be adopted, in the post-war period, by first the colleges of advanced technology and then the polytechnics (see Chapter 5). That is, they were 'not yet universities' but higher education providers, with both a vocational focus and broader aspirations:

> What these civic colleges did achieve was to distance themselves from the technical colleges, although in many instances their curricula encroached upon the preserves of those colleges. Equally, they were unable to achieve recognition as first-grade institutions of higher education – this accolade was reserved for Oxbridge, and never truly threatened. Thus, by 1914, a rigidly hierarchical system of higher education had emerged in England. (Lowe 1987: 165)

But, as those comparisons suggest, once established, the civic university colleges did not remain in stasis, but sought both new markets – indeed, almost any markets at first in the struggle to establish themselves – and greater status. In short, they were, necessarily, innovative, taking their lead from the University of London:

> The civic colleges constituted a new form of higher education in England. Their response to demands produced new curricula in which Classics and Mathematics lost their primacy, though they remained important, other Arts subjects including English Literature, History and Economics became prominent, the physical sciences were assiduously cultivated, and technology made its somewhat tentative entry into higher education. Professional education also assumed a new importance. Faced with little competition in the newer fields, the colleges quickly distinguished themselves as centres of scientific, historical and social studies. (Jones 1988: 3)

This adaptive behaviour soon led the colleges away from an emphasis on primarily serving industrial needs:

It is not the picture of many technical courses and predominantly industrially-based demand which has often been painted. Social and economic demands for Arts subjects were substantial. The demand for pure science came as much from the medical students and those seeking general education as from industry. The colleges prepared more professionals than technologists. The middle classes were the principal consumers of the civic colleges' offerings, and the financial and social rewards of liberal education and white collar and professional employments were their primary goal. (Jones 1988: 65–6)

The civic university colleges, later to become the civic universities, were thus able, alongside London, to play a major role in the development of new disciplines and new audiences for higher education: 'they placed a strong emphasis on the development of new disciplines, particularly those like chemistry, and later engineering, for which there was a growing demand' (pp. 167–8). In so doing, they were immeasurably helped by the decision of the government in the late nineteenth century to begin to put public funds into higher education:

... the parliamentary grant provided much-needed regular income for the university colleges; it also thereby confirmed the distinctiveness of a particular set of institutions, despite the differences between them. Bolstered by official recognition, the colleges expanded during the last decade of the nineteenth century, and consolidated their positions as centres of higher education. (Vernon 2004: 123)

Progress remained slow, however, and: 'it was not until after the First World War that the total number of students in all the provincial universities put together (not counting London) first exceeded the total of Oxford and Cambridge' (Watts 1972: 138).

The University of Wales

Wales was the fourth British federal university established in the nineteenth century, following London, the Queen's University of Ireland (later reconstituted as the Royal University of Ireland) and the Victoria University. It benefited from the nationalist sentiment in the principality, while suffering from the topography. Its establishment in 1893 was preceded by the three university colleges at Aberystwyth (founded in 1872), Cardiff (1883) and Bangor (1884), and was intended to make greater sense of the higher education provision in Wales. The college at Lampeter, founded as early as 1822, for long remained outside of the University of Wales set-up (Swansea was not founded until 1920).

Higher education in Wales was clearly not developing as smoothly as its promoters had hoped:

> The evidence with regard to facilities for Higher Education in Wales, as tendered to the Aberdare Committee [1881], was not particularly encouraging. There seemed to be a general dissatisfaction regarding Aberystwyth: yet the Committee felt that any such feeling should not be taken to be conclusive against the successes of such colleges in Wales. They therefore recommended that a college similar to Aberystwyth should be founded in South Wales, either at Cardiff or Swansea, and that no provision should be made at the cost of the foundation for boarding and lodging the students . . . With respect to North Wales, they recommended that its needs be met by the College at Aberystwyth, whether retained on its present site or removed to Caernarvon or Bangor. (Ellis 1935: 52)

Like both London, which had a much wider role and still survives, and Victoria, which broke up relatively quickly, the power exercised by the University of Wales was soon resented by its component colleges:

> in spite of the almost passionate desire evinced to be free from the external limitations imposed by the study for London University degrees that marked the early period, it appears that soon after the granting of the Charter the Colleges grew to feel themselves somewhat tied by the regulations made by the University Senate. (p. 68)

But, despite the continuing disputes, the University of Wales, like London, still survives, albeit in modified and less powerful form.

Ireland

Ireland, along with London, Wales and the Victoria University, provides a further example of a nineteenth-century university foundation on federal lines. In this case, however, its progress was hampered by the religious divisions it was partly intended to overcome.

A Queen's University, with colleges at Belfast, Cork and Galway, was founded in 1845 to supplement the existing protestant institution of Trinity College, Dublin, but suffered from financial and ecclesiastical problems. It was replaced by a Royal University of Ireland, following the London model, in 1881. The colleges at Belfast, Cork and Galway continued, preparing students for the examinations of the Royal University (and others, including London), in which they were joined by a newer University College in Dublin and Magee College in Londonderry. The Royal University was then itself replaced by the National University of Ireland in 1909. As part of the same negotiations, the Queen's University of Belfast was chartered in 1908 as a separate institution (Bell and Tight 1993; Moody and Beckett 1959).

The larger part of the island of Ireland gained internal self-government in 1921, with independence declared in 1937. This left Queen's as the only university in what then became Northern Ireland, and orienting itself towards comparable British rather than Irish institutions.

Pre-war twentieth-century foundations

The next wave of university colleges after the civic institutions, sometimes referred to as the 'new civics', were also founded in the nineteenth century, in the smaller English cities of Exeter, Hull, Leicester, Nottingham, Reading and Southampton. In the case of Exeter, a small cathedral city, the aim was to provide university provision for the south-west of England; while for Reading, the local influence of Oxford was apparent. The other four cities were all substantial ports and/or manufacturing centres. Only one of these foundations, Reading, made it to independent university status before the Second World War (in 1926): the others remained 'apprenticed' to the University of London into the post-war period.

Alongside the University of London, the other main influence on these university colleges was the developing University Grants Committee (UGC: see also the discussion later in this chapter of 'The development of state funding and policy'). Indeed, their development may be seen as early evidence of an increasing degree of national planning in British higher education:

> The UGC played a cardinal role in the development of the three university colleges at Nottingham, Reading and Southampton. That Committee had a particularly crucial involvement with all three colleges until 1921 when the decision was reached to retain them on the grant list. From that point their development was directed and encouraged towards university status. (Shinn 1986: 96)

Through its deliberations, the UGC developed its own notion of what a university should be, thus articulating what the nascent higher education system was aspiring towards:

> The UGC directed its influence in order to create, out of the colleges, institutions which met all the criteria of an English university. The UGC may never have produced a document which discussed and defended these criteria but, after negotiations with Reading, Nottingham and Southampton they had been crystallized and identified. Universities were to be:
>
> (a) *centres of academic excellence* but not necessarily of comprehensive learning . . .
> (b) *sustained by sound finances*, adequate remuneration and equitable and appropriate organization.
> (c) *a minimum size of institution* should be stipulated, and academic and intellectual values reasoned that a high proportion of such a

student population should be full-time scholars engaged on post-graduate, first degree or equivalent studies . . .
  (d) *located within the community* . . .
  (e) *places of freedom of thought,* disseminated freely through writing and teaching. (Shinn 1986: 96–7, original emphasis)

Not surprisingly, given the influence of Oxbridge on the Committee, these criteria can be read as a contemporary distillation of an older idea of the nature of the university, largely based on an idealized version of Oxford and Cambridge (see also Chapter 12).

The 'new civic' universities, along with the older civic establishments, were also key centres in the further development of university adult education. Nottingham University College was the first British higher education institution to set up an extramural department, immediately after the First World War. This pattern was then adopted by most of the other universities and university colleges (Fieldhouse 1996).

Non-university institutions

Alongside the 'ancient' foundations, and the newer universities and university colleges established in the nineteenth and early twentieth centuries, there were a range of other higher education providers in existence before the Second World War. Indeed, some of these were of greater antiquity than all but the 'ancient' universities, and many had nineteenth-century roots. For convenience, they are often lumped together under the label of 'the colleges':

> The evolution of the colleges is the story of three main streams of evolution . . . which have their sources in the early years of the nineteenth century . . . The three streams led to the evolution of the colleges of education, the development of the colleges of art and design and to the slow rise of the technical college . . . The colleges of education were generally small and 'collegiate' in that the courses offered were based on the college as a whole; a high priority was accorded to community life and to the pastoral care of students . . . There was little or no educational co-operation or common interest between them and the other public colleges. The colleges of art and design were usually also small and the full-time staff faculty was usually particularly small because, as a matter of educational policy, much teaching was done by active practitioners on part-time teaching contracts . . . The technical colleges tradition, numerically by far the largest, arises from their initial purpose as places to which people in employment went to learn new skills, to secure qualifications and hence to secure advancement at work or entry to one of the professions. Courses were originally offered entirely on a part-time basis to meet the needs of people at work and the requirements of industry and commerce. (Matterson 1981: 12–13)

Each of these three main streams – many of the members of which have subsequently become the basis for independent universities or university colleges – will be considered in turn, before the development of their Scottish variant, the central institution, is also reviewed.

Teacher training colleges

The training of school teachers, in a national and formal sense, began to be a major public concern during the first part of the nineteenth century, stimulated by the same concerns that underlay the establishment of the new universities and university colleges in the major cities: that is, the need for a better educated workforce. Teacher training was also closely associated with religion, an association which has continued, though in increasingly diluted form, up until the present day:

> Teacher training in England originated in the 1840s, in early industrialism. By 1845 there were twenty-two church training colleges, and after the introduction of the pupil-teacher system and the establishment of the Teacher's Certificate in 1846 the pattern was virtually set for the rest of the century. Colleges were small, residential and rarely co-educational. They were State-aided, inspected, and certificated, but were denominationally controlled. Their regime was frugal and austere . . . Their curricula, similarly, were severely functional. (Craft 1971: 7)

By the end of the nineteenth century, with a national educational system being established, the expectations of teacher training had grown. A linkage between the teacher training colleges and the newer universities and university colleges – useful to many of the latter in terms of finance, if sometimes regarded as inappropriate business for an established university (which was to be a continuing theme throughout the twentieth century) – was made in order to ensure academic credibility and standards:

> The Royal Commission on Elementary Education in 1888 recommended that the university colleges take on responsibilities for training school teachers, and in 1890, a new initiative, the Day Training College, was authorised by the Education Department. DTCs had to be attached to a university or college of university rank, but were, formally, separate institutions and did not offer degree courses in education. Students followed a syllabus laid down by the Education Department leading to a professional qualification, but took academic subjects as well, alongside other students studying arts and science subjects. (Vernon 2004: 127; see also Dobson 1973)

This association was to grow, though the precise nature of the relationship was subject to regular review, particularly as regards the link between teacher training and degree studies: 'By 1922 nearly 5000 intending teachers were following a four-year course, spending the first three years on the degree followed by a one-year course of professional training' (Niblett et al. 1975: 24). Then:

> In 1925, the Departmental Committee on the Training of Teachers for Public Elementary Schools . . . recommended an association between the universities and their local colleges . . . and this led to the establishment of Joint Boards which gave the universities a co-ordinating and examining role. (Craft 1971: 8)

Eleven Joint Boards had been established by 1930, formal regional groupings of colleges with particular universities, with a Central Advisory Committee set up as a standardizing body.

Colleges of art and design

The present-day colleges of art and design, some now amalgamated into larger institutions, trace their origins to the mid-nineteenth century. The so-called Normal School of Design was established in London in 1837 with government funding. It was eventually renamed the Royal College of Art in 1896, by which time it had formed the template for colleges of art and design throughout the country. Branches of this school, and then further independent schools, were set up across the country from the 1840s. Provision for the training of art and design teachers soon followed, and the basis of a national system of instruction had been established by the 1850s (Bell 1963; Frayling et al. 1987; Macdonald 1970).

The colleges of art and design were set up as – and for much of their history most of them remained as – small independent institutions. In their size and focus, they were similar to the teacher training colleges. They differed from them, however, in not having, or seeking, a close relationship with the universities until much later in their history; and in their extensive use of art and design practitioners as part-time teaching staff.

Technical colleges

Organized technical education dates back chiefly to the numerous mechanics' institutes founded from 1823 onwards (the original one, the London Mechanics' Institute, later became Birkbeck College, and in 1920 part of the University of London). These were often associated with literary institutes, lyceums, adult schools, evening classes and other forms of voluntarily organized adult education.

The demand for higher levels of technical education was, as already indicated, one of the key stimuli behind the development of the civic universities and university colleges. As they diversified their provision and moved more 'upmarket', and as the demand for technical education grew with increasing industrialization, there was a need for more extended provision, leading to the growth of the technical colleges. Demand and the availability of funding were less then desired, however, and the provision made was partial:

> ... by 1851, the separation between theory and practice established by the mechanics' institutes had provided a model for the subsequent provision of further education of a vocational nature, until it became an established tradition that instruction outside the workshop should be limited to theoretical instruction and should exclude the teaching of the trade itself. (Cotgrove 1958: 34)

Once again, then, the academic/vocational split, which many have argued has worked to the detriment of the British economy, was evident.

In the London area, technical education took a particular form, with the development of the polytechnics (anticipating, by the best part of a century, their nationwide development in the 1960s). The first polytechnic was opened in Regent Street in 1882 (in the previous year the first English technical college had been opened, in Finsbury by the City & Guilds Institute: Argles 1964). Subsequent development was fast, such that 'by 1897, there were nine polytechnics with an enrolment of 26,000 students, a large proportion of them manual workers' (Cotgrove 1958: 60).

The London polytechnics soon moved into degree-level work, teaching for University of London degrees, and with increasing numbers of their staff enjoying 'recognized university teacher' status:

> In spite of the prevailing view that technical instruction and the polytechnics should provide trade classes and elementary instruction, there was strong pressure from the large student body in London for more advanced studies in both day and evening, including university work. By 1904, six polytechnics were providing complete degree courses, fifty of their teachers were recognised university teachers, instructing 500 undergraduates. By 1908–9, this had increased to 100 recognised teachers, and 836 matriculated students, four-fifths of whom were evening students. (Cotgrove 1958: 64)

Nationally, there was rapid growth in technical education between 1880 and 1905, helped by the provisions of a series of Acts enabling local authorities to raise funds for this purpose (Argles 1964; Cotgrove 1958). Subsequently, there was then little growth in enrolments until after the Second World War: 'the future pattern of technical education had been set: it was one of part-time evening instruction, combined with practical experience in industry' (Argles 1964: 65).

National and Higher National Certificate (for part-time students) and Diploma (full-time) courses were introduced from 1921 (Millerson 1964):

> The requirements combined both theoretical and practical competence in technology and the courses were sponsored jointly between the Board of Education and the professional associations . . . The Ordinary National Certificate required three years of successful study at certain technical colleges and schools and the Higher National a further two,

and these qualifications were the best available from 1921 for over thirty years. (Stewart 1989: 34)

The Scottish central institutions

In Scotland, as with university education, other forms of higher education have always been organized somewhat differently from the patterns in England, Wales and Ireland. Not surprisingly, Scottish politicians and commentators have long argued that their arrangements are preferable to and ahead of those in the rest of the UK. For example, as regards Scottish teacher education:

> Legally, organizationally and intellectually the English and Scottish traditions of teacher education are far apart . . . as early as 1905, the responsibility for teacher education was placed upon four Provincial Committees connected to the universities . . . In 1920 the administration of the training of teachers was delegated to a National Committee for the Training of Teachers . . . and Scotland had achieved a national system of teacher education which has not yet been achieved in England . . . Scottish Colleges of Education thus became, and have remained, national institutions. (Lynch 1979: 16–17)

In Scotland, applied and vocational provision was further developed during the early twentieth century, mainly outside of the universities in separate, specialized institutions, termed 'central institutions'. These were essentially the equivalent of the London polytechnics or the better technical colleges, but, unlike in England, and as with the Scottish provision of teacher education, organized on a national basis:

> . . . while there were university faculties of engineering, a distinctive feature of the educational system was the 'central institution', offering higher courses up to degree and diploma level in technology, applied science, art, music, drama, commerce and other studies . . . Ten were recognised between 1901 and 1909 and one more before 1939. Five others were controlled by the Department of Agriculture . . . In 1938, 2,500 . . . Scottish students were working at a level comparable with the standard in universities; the corresponding figure for the whole of England and Wales was only 4,000. (Scotland 1969b: 137)

Many of these central institutions were to become universities, particularly in the latter part of the post-war period.

Themes: continuity and change

While the period of a century and a half considered in this chapter may be viewed as a time of great change in British higher education – that is, a period of expansion and diversification underpinning the creation of the national system of higher education – there was also considerable resistance to that change. Thus, it was only in 1871 that universities and colleges were barred from applying religious tests to those seeking entry. And, while the University of London led the way by opening its provision to women on equal terms to men in 1878, Oxford held out until 1920 (Robertson 1944).

As this resistance to change implies, there was a good deal of continuity in the 'system' as well as change, and often it was arguably for good reasons. This continuity resided mostly in attitudes about what a university or a college was, and what they should do, which enabled institutions to retain a clear sense of their purpose as they grew (see also Chapter 12).

Three cross-cutting themes, affecting all the institutions considered in differing ways, and reflecting in their different ways the importance of both change and continuity, will be briefly considered in this section:

- the development of state funding and policy;
- the relation between higher education and work;
- the development of postgraduate studies and research.

Each of these will be further considered, for the post-war period, in subsequent chapters (see, in particular, Chapters 4, 6, 7 and 8).

The development of state funding and policy

While the initial nineteenth-century development in England and Wales of an alternative university system to that offered by the medieval foundations of Oxford and Cambridge was dependent on local and private financing, by the end of the century the state had become inextricably involved in higher education funding and policy. The most obvious evidence of this close involvement was the continuing series of commissions and inquiries set up from the mid-nineteenth century onwards:

> Oxford and Cambridge were investigated by commissions in the 1850s, over the [religious] Tests Acts in the 1860s and again over their finances and statutes in the 1870s and 1880s. The Scottish universities endured successive inquiries to examine the possibility of anglicising reform in the 1820s, the 1850s, the 1870s and by reform commissioners after 1889. Durham has its own commission in the 1860s and the tangled problems of London were interminably thrashed over by Selborne in the 1880s, Cowper in the 1890s and Haldane in the 1900s while Wales too received the Aberdare and Raleigh commissions in the 1880s and 1900s. At the same time most universities were investigated by bodies concerned with other subjects – the commissions of Devonshire and Samuelson on science in the 1870s and 1880s, the Royal Commission on the Civil Service in the 1910s. Far from being institutions operating in some

non-accountable independence of the state they were subject to an almost perpetual detailed public investigation and cross-examination from the 1850s onwards. (Sanderson 1975: 12–13)

By the Second World War, the state would become the dominant funder of universities and colleges, and this would remain the position, despite repeated attempts to reduce dependency on the state, thereafter:

> From the turn of the century to the First World War, the scale of state involvement in university education expanded dramatically . . . there was a substantially increased level of state funding, which, in turn, demanded more stringent accountability. Pervading this . . . was a growing appreciation of the importance of the universities to the nation, which meant that they deserved greater state resources. (Vernon 2004: 134)

Increased state involvement in university funding led to the eventual establishment, in 1919, of the University Grants Committee (UGC), under the auspices of the Treasury but effectively under the control of the vice-chancellors (Berdahl 1959):

> The UGC was established on 14 July 1919 by a Treasury Minute. It had no statutory basis or powers, no bank account, no income-generating capacity, and no grant was made to it. And so it was to remain for the next 70 years . . . From this inauspicious beginning the UGC was to evolve into one of the dominant influences in British higher education. Though its terms of reference were to change they remained fundamentally vague. (Salter and Tapper 1994: 104–5)

This vagueness clearly suited the needs of the universities and university colleges, however, as the UGC, through its deliberations and funding, led the development of the emerging university system:

> The foundations laid in the early years of the UGC's work found a basis for the steady expansion of university work between the wars. This had as its basis a greater awareness of the benefits of university education, a policy of giving grants to the clever poor, a considerable enlargement of research facilities – mirrored in the growing number of higher degrees instituted and awarded, and a growing number of subjects for university teaching – economics, modern languages, and the newer natural sciences, for example. Government grants gradually increased to provide the means to finance the expansion, and so did private benefaction – though not on the 'generous American scale'. (Vaizey 1963: 170–1)

Until well into the post-war period, the UGC, from the universities' perspective, served as an ideal 'buffer' body between the state and the universities: in receipt of increasing state funds, under the control of the universities, and able to allocate funds to individual institutions in a supportive fashion:

Up to 1939 the universities dictated the terms of the ideological climate within which any discussion of the universities took place. Academics, civil servants and politicians alike considered it perfectly natural that the state should be very much the subordinate partner in its relationship with the universities and that the administrative arrangements should reflect that subordinate position. As a result, the UGC was able to propagate without interference, albeit through suggestion rather than direction, its own values regarding the appropriate direction of university development. (Salter and Tapper 1994: 107)

The post-war development, and eventual demise, of the UGC is considered in Chapter 6.

The relation between higher education and work

One of the great debates, perhaps the great debate, that has continued as state funding for higher education has grown, has been about what the nation was getting back for its investment. For one of the main functions of higher education has always been preparing its students, directly and indirectly, for their future employment. Initially, many students would literally have a 'vocation': for the priesthood, then for medicine, the law, engineering, or teaching and, latterly and perhaps less commonly seen as vocations, for a whole range of public sector occupations.

Conversely, the link with industry and commerce in a broader sense, as the driving force of economic productivity – now so commonly regarded as a key, and often the key, purpose of higher education – was historically evident by its absence: 'For some six hundred years before the nineteenth century the universities of England and Scotland had fulfilled a variety of changing roles, none of which had much bearing upon industry' (Sanderson 1972: 1).

The nineteenth- and early twentieth-century university foundations attempted to address this absence by emphasizing, at least initially, their local industrial links (in both teaching and research). There were, however – as has already been commented upon on a number of occasions – conflicts between industry and education, and within the educational curriculum, as to the appropriate place in which to teach (or train) theory or academic content, on the one hand, and practical or vocational content, on the other. And, as these universities and colleges grew, their functions and audiences multiplied, their aspirations grew, and their link to industry weakened:

In the inter-war years, there was a rise in the number of university graduates entering industry, but this occurred more out of necessity (as a mounting number of graduates confronted a scarcity of openings in the overseas civil service and the traditional professions) than choice. The better students on the whole found more gentlemanly employment, and the number of industrialists' and engineers' sons leaving behind their fathers' sort of life continued to exceed the number of graduates entering it. On balance, the universities were still, as earlier, an avenue out of, not into, industry. (Wiener 1981: 133)

This debate was to continue, with renewed force, in the post-war period (Aldcroft 1992; Barnett 1986).

The development of postgraduate studies and research

Both postgraduate studies and research, nowadays considered as key parts of university activity, developed rather late in the UK. Thus, the PhD, long offered in the USA and Germany, was only introduced in Britain in 1917, though various other research degrees had been introduced before then – London introduced a DSc and DLitt by thesis in the 1880s, and the Scottish universities introduced the DSc, DLitt and DPhil in 1895 (Simpson 1983). Postgraduate students remained a small minority of the total student population until after the Second World War.

While limited private and state sponsorship for academic research had been made available before, substantive state funding also only arrived during the First World War, stimulated by the needs of the armed forces:

> In 1916, the scientific advisory council established early in the war was upgraded into the Department of Scientific and Industrial Research (DSIR), with an annual vote from Parliament and £1 million of additional funds to give its work a firm foundation. Although it made grants for some work during the war and kept a watching brief on what was happening throughout the country, its objects were longterm. It was to provide grants for postgraduate training and research, co-ordinate and sponsor research either through grants for independent researchers or in its own facilities, and encourage and initiate industrial research. (Vernon 2004: 182: see also Melville 1962)

The Medical Research Council – or the Medical Research Committee and Advisory Council as it was originally titled – had been established a few years earlier, in 1913 (Thomson 1973, 1975). The Agricultural Research Council was chartered in 1931, but the spread of state funding to all fields of academic research had to wait until after the Second World War (see Chapter 8).

The struggle towards a system of higher education

All of the developments discussed in this chapter were to lead, by the time of the outbreak of the Second World War, to the development of, if it could not yet be termed 'a fully fledged system of higher education', then at least something that was clearly well on its way to becoming one:

By 1930 the elements of a system were in place, with increasing numbers of institutions, government funding to the universities and university colleges and scholarship support for a limited number of students. Nevertheless, commentators still found it difficult to see a 'system'. (Silver 2003: 23)

This was, in part, because there were many contradictions embedded in this emerging system. Most notably, perhaps, Oxbridge remained a world apart: 'It was rare in these early decades of the [twentieth] century for any vision of a system of higher education to incorporate Oxford and Cambridge – they were present but off limits for discussion of integration or co-ordination' (p. 22).

The emergent system was also very different from what it was to become in the post-war period. Thus, to the present eye, it remained very open and relatively uncompetitive: 'Until 1945 virtually any student who could pass a relatively easy matriculation examination could go to a university if he could find the money, and if he wished to do so' (Furneaux 1961: xii). From then on, as subsequent chapters will make clear, matters were to become both more competitive and more egalitarian.

3

A tabular summary of post-war developments

Introduction

This chapter consists of four tables providing detailed factual information to underpin the discussion in the chapters that follow.

Table 3.1 lists key developments in, or effecting, higher education in the UK between 1945 and 2008. The table is organized in four columns, noting:

- dates and changes in national governments;
- relevant acts and reports;
- national agencies dealing with higher education, and major changes in practice;
- higher education institutional developments.

Table 3.2 contains an alphabetical listing of current UK universities, their dates of foundation or chartering as universities, and brief notes (where relevant) on their former histories.

Table 3.3 lists multi-faculty universities in the UK by their date of foundation.

Table 3.4 provides statistics on the number of higher education students in the UK post-war.

Table 3.1 A timeline of post-war developments

Date and Governments	Acts and Reports	Agencies and Practices	Institutions
1945 First post-war Labour (Attlee) government	Education Act Percy Report, *Higher Technological Education*		
1946	Barlow Report, *Scientific Manpower*		
1947		Advisory Council on Scientific Policy (ACSP) established	
1948		National Advisory Council on Education for Industry and Commerce (NACEIC) established Regional Advisory Councils (RACs) for further education established	Nottingham achieves university status
1949		National Advisory Council on the Training and Supply of Teachers (NACTST) established	
1950 Labour (Attlee) government re-elected			

(*Continued overleaf*)

Table 3.1 (continued)

Date and Governments	Acts and Reports	Agencies and Practices	Institutions
1951 Conservative (Churchill) government elected	White Paper, *Higher Technological Education*		
1952			Southampton achieves university status
1954			Hull achieves university status
1955 Conservative (Eden, later Macmillan) government re-elected		National Council for Technological Awards (NCTA) established	Exeter and UMIST achieve university status
1956	White Paper, *Technical Education*	Diploma in Technology established	Colleges of Advanced Technology (CATs) established in Birmingham, Edinburgh (Heriot–Watt), London (Battersea) and Salford
1957			Leicester achieves university status
			CATs established in Bradford, Cardiff, London (Chelsea and Northampton Polytechnics) and Loughborough
			25 regional colleges designated

1958		Sussex University approved (opens 1961)
1959 Conservative (Macmillan later Douglas Home) government re-elected	Crowther Report, *15–19*	
1960	Anderson Report, *Grants to Students*	3-year teacher education course introduced in England and Wales
1961	White Paper, *Better Opportunities in Technical Education*	East Anglia and York Universities approved (both open in 1963) CAT established in Bristol
1962		Universities Central Council on Admissions (UCCA) established
1963	Robbins Report, *Higher Education*	Essex (opens 1964), Kent (1965), Lancaster (1964) and Warwick (1965) Universities approved Keele achieves university status Brunel designated a CAT
1964 Labour (Wilson) government elected	Crick Report, *A Higher Award for Business Studies*	4-year BEd degree starts Council for National Academic Awards (CNAA) established Newcastle separates from Durham and achieves university status Colleges of Education designated Strathclyde achieves university status

(*Continued overleaf*)

Table 3.1 (continued)

Date and Governments	Acts and Reports	Agencies and Practices	Institutions
Department of Education and Science replaces Ministry of Education, assuming responsibility for UGC and research councils	Report of the UGC Committee on *University Teaching Methods*	Society for Research into Higher Education (SRHE) founded	Stirling University approved (opens 1967)
1965	Crosland announces binary policy in Woolwich speech	Science, Natural Environmental and Social Science research councils established	New University of Ulster approved (opens 1968) London and Manchester Business Schools founded
1966 Labour (Wilson) government re-elected	White Paper, *A Plan for Polytechnics and Other Colleges*	General Teaching Council established in Scotland	Aston (Birmingham), Bristol (later Bath), Bradford, Brunel, City (Northampton), Heriot–Watt (Edinburgh), Loughborough and Surrey (formerly Battersea) Universities established from CATs
1967			Dundee separates from St Andrews and achieves university status Royal College of Art achieves university status

1969			Salford (former CAT) University established. Cardiff (former CAT) becomes part of University of Wales as UWIST
			Open University established (opens 1971)
			Cranfield Institute of Technology granted university status
			Bristol, Hatfield, Leicester, Newcastle, Portsmouth, Sheffield, Sunderland and Wolverhampton Polytechnics established
1970	Conservative (Heath) government elected		Committee of Directors of Polytechnics (CDP) established
			Brighton, Central London, City of London, Huddersfield, Kingston, Lanchester (Coventry), Leeds, Liverpool, Manchester, North East London, North Staffordshire, Oxford, Plymouth, South Bank, Teesside, Thames, Trent (Nottingham) and Wales (later Glamorgan) Polytechnics established
1971		Rothschild Report, *A Framework for Government Research and Development*	*Times Higher Education Supplement* first published
			Chelsea (former CAT) becomes part of the University of London
			Birmingham, North London and Ulster Polytechnics established

(*Continued overleaf*)

Table 3.1 (continued)

Date and Governments	Acts and Reports	Agencies and Practices	Institutions
1972	White Paper, *Education: A Framework for Expansion* James Report, *Teacher Education and Training*	Advisory Board for the Research Councils (ABRC) established	
1973		Association of Polytechnic Teachers (APT) established Advisory Council on the Supply and Training of Teachers (ACSTT) established	Buckingham University College established (opens 1976) Preston (later Lancashire) and Middlesex Polytechnics established
1974 Labour (Wilson, later Callaghan) government elected		Manpower Services Commission (MSC) established Diploma of Higher Education (DipHE) introduced Advisory Board for the Research Councils (ABRC) replaces ACSP	
1975		CNAA Report, *Partnership in Validation*	
1976		National Association of Teachers in Further and Higher Education (NATFHE) established through amalgamation	

1977	Standing Conference of Directors and Principals of Colleges and Institutes of Higher Education (SCDPCIHE) established
1978	Green Paper, *Higher Education into the 1990s: A Discussion Document*
	Oakes Report, *Management of Higher Education in the Maintained Sector*
1979 Conservative (Thatcher) government elected	Council for Tertiary Education in Scotland (CTES) established
1980	Education Act
	Business Education Council (BEC) and Technician Education Council (TEC) established
	Finniston Report, *Engineering our Future*
	Advisory Committee for the Supply and Education of Teachers (ACSET) set up
1981	Selectivity exercise cuts university recurrent grants

(*Continued overleaf*)

Table 3.1 (continued)

Date and Governments	Acts and Reports	Agencies and Practices	Institutions
1982	Chilver Report, *Future of Higher Education in Northern Ireland*	National Advisory Body for Local Authority Higher Education (NAB) and Welsh Advisory Body for Local Authority Higher Education (WAB) established	
1983 Conservative (Thatcher) government re-elected		Business and Technician Education Council (BTEC) established through amalgamation of BEC and TEC	Buckingham gains university status
1984		Council for the Accreditation of University Teaching (CATE) established	Ulster University established through amalgamation of Ulster Polytechnic and New University of Ulster
		NAB Report, *A Strategy for Higher Education into the Late 1980s and Beyond*	
		University Grants Committee (UGC). Report, *A Strategy for Higher Education into the 1990s*	
		Social Science Research Council (SSRC) renamed as Economic and Social Research Council (ESRC)	
1985	Green Paper, *The Development of Higher Education into the 1990s*	Jarratt Report, *Efficiency Studies in Universities*	

1986	Lindop Report, *Academic Validation in Public Sector Higher Education*	Scottish Tertiary Education Advisory Council (STEAC) Report, *Future Strategy for Higher Education in Scotland* NAB's remit is extended to include voluntary sector, and NAB is renamed National Advisory Body for Public Sector Higher Education	London Business School achieves university status
1987 Conservative (Thatcher, later Major) government re-elected	White Paper, *Higher Education: Meeting the Challenge* Croham Report, *Review of the University Grants Committee*	Reynolds Report, *Academic Standards in Universities*	
1988	Education Act Consultative Paper, *Top-up Loans for Students*	ABRC Report, *A Strategy for the Science Base* MSC launches *Enterprise in Higher Education* NAB Report, *Management for a Purpose*	
1989		UGC and NAB abolished. Universities Funding Council (UFC) and Polytechnics and Colleges Funding Council (PCFC) established	Designated polytechnics and colleges receive corporate status
1990	Education (Student Loans) Act		Bournemouth and Humberside Polytechnics established

(*Continued overleaf*)

Table 3.1 (continued)

Date and Governments	Acts and Reports	Agencies and Practices	Institutions
1991	White Paper, *Higher Education: A New Framework*		Anglia and West London Polytechnics established
1992 Conservative (Major) government elected. Department for Education and Science succeeded by Department for Education. ABRC and science responsibilities transferred to Office of Science and Technology	Further and Higher Education Act	UFC and PCFC abolished. Higher Education Funding Councils for England, Wales and Scotland (HEFCE, HEFCW, SHEFC) established. CNAA abolished	Anglia Polytechnic, Bournemouth, Brighton, Central England (Birmingham), Central Lancashire (Preston), Coventry, De Montfort (Leicester), Derby, East London, Glamorgan, Greenwich (Thames), Hertfordshire (Hatfield), Huddersfield, Humberside, Kingston, Leeds Metropolitan, Liverpool John Moores, London Guildhall (City of London), Manchester Metropolitan, Middlesex, Napier, North London, Northumbria (Newcastle), Nottingham Trent, Oxford Brookes, Paisley, Plymouth, Portsmouth, Robert Gordon (Aberdeen), Sheffield Hallam, South Bank, Staffordshire, Sunderland, Teesside, Thames Valley (West London), Westminster (Central London), West of England (Bristol) and Wolverhampton Universities (mostly former polytechnics) established

1993			Glasgow Caledonian, London Institute and Luton granted university status
1994			Abertay Dundee established
1995	Department for Education merged with Employment to become Department for Education and Employment.		Teacher Training Agency established, replacing Council for the Accreditation of Teacher Education
1996		Education (Student Loans) Act	
1997	Labour (Blair) government elected	Dearing Report, *Higher Education in the Learning Society*	
2000			CVCP renamed Universities UK
2001	Labour (Blair) government re-elected	Department for Education and Skills replaces Department for Education and Employment		Gloucestershire gains university status

(*Continued overleaf*)

Table 3.1 (continued)

Date and Governments	Acts and Reports	Agencies and Practices	Institutions
2002			London Guildhall and North London universities combine as London Metropolitan University
2003	White Paper, *The Future of Higher Education*	Arts and Humanities Research Council established	
2004	Higher Education Act		Manchester and UMIST amalgamate. Cardiff separates from the University of Wales
2005 Labour (Blair) government re-elected			Bath Spa, Bolton, Canterbury Christ Church, Chester, Chichester, Liverpool Hope, Northampton, Roehampton, Southampton Solent, Winchester and Worcester achieve university status
2006		GuildHE replaces Standing Conference of Principals (SCOP)	Edge Hill achieves university status
2007 Brown takes over from Blair as Prime Minister Department of Innovation, Universities			St Martins College achieves university status as University of Cumbria. Buckinghamshire Chilterns College becomes Buckingham New University. Queen Margaret University College

and Skills established, taking over part of the responsibilities of the Department for Education and Skills	(Edinburgh) becomes Queen Margaret University. Imperial College separates from the University of London
2008	Glyndwr and Swansea Metropolitan achieve university status within University of Wales

Note: It is not uncommon to find disparities between, and sometimes within, sources regarding dates. In some cases these are readily explicable – for example, a university may receive its charter in a given year but only admit students a few years later; or a report might be submitted in one year but only published during the following year – in others less so.

Table 3.2 An alphabetical listing of contemporary UK universities

The major, multi-faculty colleges of the Universities of London and Wales are also identified separately under their 'parent' universities. The date given for foundation relates to the date when university status was achieved.

University	Foundation	Notes
Aberdeen	1495	King's College, the original foundation, and Marischal College (founded in 1593), combined in 1860
Abertay	1994	In Dundee
Anglia Ruskin	1992	Two main sites: Cambridge and Chelmsford, Formerly Anglia Polytechnic (established 1991), Anglia Higher Education College (formed in 1989 by merger of Essex Institute of Higher Education and Cambridgeshire College of Arts and Technology).
Aston	1966	Formerly Birmingham College of Advanced Technology (established 1956), with its origins in the Birmingham and Midland Institute established in 1854
Bath	1966	Formerly Bristol College of Advanced Technology (established 1960), moved site, origins in the British Diocesan Trade School established in 1851
Bath Spa	2005	
Bedfordshire	1993	Formerly Luton University, Luton College of Higher Education (established 1976 through merger of colleges of technology and education), origins in Luton Modern School (1908)
Belfast	1908	Established as Queen's College in 1845
Birmingham	1900	Originated in Mason Science College, founded in 1880
Birmingham City	1992	Formerly University of Central England, Birmingham Polytechnic (established 1971: amalgamation of existing colleges of technology, commerce, art and education)
Bolton	2005	Formerly Institute of Technology
Bournemouth	1992	Formerly Bournemouth Polytechnic (established 1990), Dorset Institute of Higher Education (founded 1976 from part of Bournemouth College of Technology)

Bradford	1966	Formerly Bradford College of Advanced Technology (established 1957), origins in schools of weaving, design and building in the 1860s, and a mechanics' institute founded in 1832
Brighton	1992	Formerly Brighton Polytechnic (established 1970: amalgamation of existing colleges of technology, art, education and higher education)
Bristol	1909	University College Bristol had been founded in 1876
Brunel	1966	In Uxbridge. Formerly Brunel College of Advanced Technology (established 1962), having moved site, origins in Acton Technical College, opened in 1928, and in late nineteenth-century Chiswick Polytechnic
Buckingham	1983	Only UK private university, founded as University College in 1973 (opened 1976)
Buckinghamshire New University	2007	Formerly Buckinghamshire Chilterns College (established 1975)
Cambridge	Thirteenth century	
Canterbury Christ Church	2005	Established as a College in 1962
Cardiff	1893	Founded in 1883, became part of the University of Wales in 1893. Merged with University of Wales Institute of Science and Technology (UWIST) in 1988, became independent from University of Wales in 2004
Central Lancashire	1992	In Preston. Formerly Lancashire (Preston) Polytechnic (established 1973)
Chester	2005	Formerly Chester College of Higher Education, originally established as a teacher training college in 1839
Chichester	2005	Formerly part of West Sussex Institute of Higher Education
City	1966	Formerly Northampton (after Northampton Square in London) College of Advanced Technology (established 1957), origins in Northampton Institute (founded 1894)

(*Continued overleaf*)

Table 3.2 (continued)

University	Foundation	Notes
Coventry	1992	Formerly Coventry (Lanchester) Polytechnic (established 1970 through merger of colleges of technology and art)
Cranfield	1969	Formerly Cranfield Institute of Technology, with origins in College of Aeronautics founded in 1946
Cumbria	2007	Created from amalgamation of St Martins College (Lancaster) with smaller specialist colleges in Cumbria
De Montfort	1992	Multi-site: in Leicester and Milton Keynes, formerly Leicester Polytechnic (established 1969 through merger of colleges of technology, art and education)
Derby	1992	Formerly Derby College of Higher Education (founded 1977 through merger)
Dundee	1967	Founded as University College in 1881, became part of the University of St Andrews in 1897, renamed Queen's College in 1954
Durham	1832	
East Anglia	1960	In Norwich, opened in 1963
East London	1992	Formerly North East London Polytechnic (established 1970 through merger of colleges of technology and art)
Edge Hill	2006	In Ormskirk, formerly College of Higher Education
Edinburgh	1582	
Essex	1961	In Colchester, opens in 1964
Exeter	1955	Formerly University College of the South West (founded in 1922)
Glamorgan	1992	Formerly Wales Polytechnic (established 1970 from college of technology)
Glasgow	1451	

Glasgow Caledonian	1993	
Gloucestershire	2001	In Cheltenham. Formerly Cheltenham and Gloucester College of Higher Education, established through merger in 1990
Greenwich	1992	Formerly Thames Polytechnic (established 1970), origins in Woolwich Polytechnic (founded 1890)
Heriot–Watt	1966	In Edinburgh. Formerly Edinburgh College of Advanced Technology (established 1956), origins in School of Arts opened in 1821
Hertfordshire	1992	In Hatfield. Formerly Hatfield Polytechnic (established 1969), origins in Hatfield Technical College (founded 1951)
Huddersfield	1992	Formerly Huddersfield Polytechnic (established 1970: amalgamation of colleges of technology and education), origins in 1840s
Hull	1954	Established as a University College in 1927
Imperial College	1907	Component parts date back to 1845. Absorbs Wye College (founded as South-Eastern Agricultural College in 1893, School in 1945) in 2000, separates from University of London in 2007
Keele	1962	Founded in 1949 as the University College of North Staffordshire
Kent	1961	In Canterbury, opened in 1965
Kingston	1992	Formerly Kingston Polytechnic (established 1970: merger of colleges of technology, art and design, and education)
Lancaster	1961	Opens in 1964
Leeds	1904	Formerly Yorkshire College of Science and Technology, origins in 1874
Leeds Metropolitan	1992	Formerly Leeds Polytechnic (established 1970: amalgamation of colleges of technology, art, commerce and education)
Leicester	1957	Founded as University College in 1921
Lincoln	1992	Formerly Humberside Polytechnic (established in 1990 in Hull), moved site. Formerly Hull College of Higher Education (founded 1976 through merger)

(Continued overleaf)

Table 3.2 (continued)

University	Foundation	Notes
Liverpool	1903	Founded as University College in 1881
Liverpool Hope	2005	Formerly Liverpool Institute of Higher Education (established in 1980 through merger)
Liverpool John Moores	1992	Formerly Liverpool Polytechnic (established in 1970 through merger of colleges of art, commerce, technology and building)
London Birkbeck College	1836 1920	Founded in 1823 as the London Mechanics' Institute, admitted as School in 1920
Goldsmiths' College	1904	Founded in 1891, becoming part of the University in 1904, a School in 1988, Chartered in 1990
King's College London	1829	Absorbed Chelsea College (founded as South West London Polytechnic Institute 1896, Chelsea Polytechnic 1922, becomes a School in 1969) and Queen Elizabeth College (founded as King's College for Women 1908, School in 1953) in 1985
London School of Economics	1895	A School of the University in 1900
Queen Mary College	1915	Origins in 1880s, absorbed Westfield College (founded 1882) in 1989
Royal Holloway College	1900	Founded in 1886, became a School in 1900, absorbed Bedford College (founded 1849) in 1985
Royal Veterinary College	1949	Founded in 1791, becomes School of University in 1949
School of Hygiene & Tropical Medicine	1924	Founded in 1899

Institution	Year	Notes
School of Oriental & African Studies		Founded in 1916
School of Pharmacy	1925	Founded in 1842, becomes School of University in 1925
University College London	1826	
London Business School	1986	Founded in 1965
London Metropolitan	2002	Amalgamation of University of North London (chartered 1992, formerly Polytechnic of North London, established 1971) and London Guildhall University (chartered 1992, formerly City of London Polytechnic, established 1970 through merger)
London South Bank	1992	Formerly South Bank Polytechnic (founded 1970 through merger), origins in Borough Polytechnic (1892)
London, University of the Arts	1993	Formed in 1986 through amalgamation as London Institute
Loughborough	1966	Formerly Loughborough College of Advanced Technology (established 1957), origins in Loughborough Technical Institution, founded in 1905
Manchester	1880	Founded as Owen's College in 1851. Manchester and UMIST (University of Manchester Institute of Science and Technology, origins in 1824 mechanics' institution, incorporated in University in 1905, separately chartered in 1955) re-amalgamate in 2004
Manchester Metropolitan	1992	Formerly Manchester Polytechnic (established 1970: merger of colleges of technology, art and design, commerce and education)
Middlesex	1992	Multi-site in north London, formerly Middlesex Polytechnic (established 1973 through merger of colleges of technology, art, education and speech and drama)
Napier	1992	In Edinburgh

(*Continued overleaf*)

Table 3.2 (continued)

University	Foundation	Notes
Newcastle	1963	Formerly part of Durham, origins dating back to 1834
Northampton	2005	Formerly Nene College (established through merger of colleges of art, technology and education in 1975)
Northumbria	1992	In Newcastle, formerly Newcastle Polytechnic (established 1969 through merger of colleges of technology, art and design, commerce and education)
Nottingham	1948	University College founded in 1903, dates to 1881
Nottingham Trent	1992	Formerly Trent Polytechnic (established 1970: merger of colleges of technology, art and design, and education)
Open	1969	Based in Milton Keynes, a distance education provider, opens in 1971
Oxford	Twelfth century	
Oxford Brookes	1992	Formerly Oxford Polytechnic (established 1970), Oxford College of Technology (1963), origins in 1865
Plymouth	1992	Formerly Plymouth Polytechnic (established 1970 from college of technology)
Portsmouth	1992	Formerly Portsmouth Polytechnic (established 1969: merger of colleges of technology, art and design, and education)
Queen Margaret	2007	In Edinburgh, formerly university college
Reading	1926	Origins in extension college established in 1892
Robert Gordon	1992	In Aberdeen
Roehampton	2005	Roehampton Institute of Higher Education formed in 1975 through amalgamation of four colleges of education

Royal Academy of Music	1930	
Royal College of Art	1967	Founded in 1837 as the School of Design
Royal College of Music	1883	
Royal Northern College of Music	1973	
St Andrews	1410	
Salford	1967	Formerly Salford College of Advanced Technology (established 1956), dates to 1895
Sheffield	1905	University College established in 1897, dates to 1879
Sheffield Hallam	1992	Formerly Sheffield City Polytechnic (established 1969 through merger of colleges of technology, art and education)
Southampton	1952	University College established in 1902, origins in Hartley Institution in 1862
Southampton Solent	2005	Formerly Southampton Institute of Higher Education (established through merger in 1984 of colleges of art and technology)
Staffordshire	1992	In Stoke, formerly Staffordshire Polytechnic (established 1970 through merger of colleges of technology and education)
Stirling	1964	Opens in 1967
Strathclyde	1964	Origins in 1796. Royal College of Science and Technology and Scottish College of Commerce merge in 1964
Sunderland	1992	Formerly Sunderland Polytechnic (established 1969 through merger of colleges of technology, art and education)
Surrey	1966	In Guildford, formerly Battersea College of Advanced Technology (established 1956, origins dating back to 1891), moved site
Sussex	1958	Near Brighton. Opened in 1961

(Continued overleaf)

Table 3.2 (continued)

University	Foundation	Notes
Teesside	1992	In Middlesbrough. Formerly Teesside Polytechnic (established 1970 from college of technology)
Thames Valley	1992	Formerly West London Polytechnic (established 1991 through merger)
Trinity Laban		Founded in 1872
Ulster	1984	Multi-campus: Belfast, Coleraine, Derry, formed from amalgamation of Ulster Polytechnic (established 1971) and New University of Ulster (founded in 1965, opened in 1968)
Wales	1893	
Aberystwyth	1893	Founded in 1872
Bangor	1893	Founded in 1884
Cardiff Institute		
Glyndwr	2008	In Wrexham, formerly North East Wales Institute, origins in School of Science & Arts in 1887
Lampeter	1961	Founded in 1822, in receipt of UGC funds from 1961
Newport	2003	Formerly Gwent College of Higher Education, origins in mechanics' institute, 1841. Admitted to University of Wales as a university college in 1996
Swansea	1920	Founded in 1920
Swansea Metropolitan	2008	Formerly Swansea Institute, origins in School of Art 1853
Warwick	1961	In Coventry, opened in 1965
West of England	1992	In Bristol, formerly Bristol Polytechnic (established 1969 through merger of colleges of technology, commerce, art and education)

West of Scotland	1992	Formerly Paisley University
Westminster	1992	Formerly the Polytechnic of Central London (established 1970 through merger), origins in Royal Polytechnic Institute (1838)
Winchester	2005	Formerly King Alfred's College, origins dating back to 1840
Wolverhampton	1992	Formerly Wolverhampton Polytechnic (established 1969: merger of colleges of technology, art and education)
Worcester	2005	Former Worcester College of Higher Education
York	1960	Opened in 1963

Note: It should be evident that most of the universities named have lengthy and convoluted histories, often involving several name changes and reorganizations, and not infrequently moves of site. For more details, consult individual university histories and/or websites.

Table 3.3 Universities by date of foundation

Date	No. Universities	Universities Founded
Pre-1900	10	Aberdeen, Cambridge, Durham, Edinburgh, Glasgow, London,[1] Manchester, Oxford, St Andrews, Wales
1900	11	Birmingham
1903	12	Liverpool
1904	13	Leeds
1905	14	Sheffield
1908	15	Belfast
1909	16	Bristol
1926	17	Reading
1948	18	Nottingham
1952	19	Southampton
1954	20	Hull
1955	22	Exeter, UMIST[2]
1957	23	Leicester
1958	24	Sussex
1960	26	East Anglia, York
1961	30	Essex, Kent, Lancaster, Warwick
1962	31	Keele
1963	32	Newcastle[3]
1964	34	Stirling, Strathclyde
1965	35	New Ulster
1966	43	Aston, Bath, Bradford, Brunel, City, Heriot–Watt, Loughborough, Surrey
1967	45	Dundee,[4] Salford
1969	47	Cranfield, Open
1983	48	Buckingham[5]
1984	48	Ulster[6]

---

[1] For convenience, the separate component parts of the University of London are not listed here.

[2] UMIST (University of Manchester Institute of Science and Technology) re-amalgamated with the University of Manchester in 2004.

[3] Formerly part of Durham.

[4] Formerly part of St Andrews.

[5] The only private university based in England.

[6] Established through amalgamation of New University of Ulster (established 1965) and former Ulster Polytechnic.

Date	No. Universities	Universities Founded
1992	86	Anglia Ruskin, Birmingham City, Bournemouth, Brighton, Central Lancashire, Coventry, De Montfort, Derby, East London, Glamorgan, Greenwich, Hertfordshire, Huddersfield, Kingston, Leeds Metropolitan, Lincoln, Liverpool John Moores, London Guildhall,[7] London Metropolitan, London South Bank, Manchester Metropolitan, Middlesex, Napier, Northumbria, Nottingham Trent, Oxford Brookes, Paisley, Plymouth, Portsmouth, Robert Gordon, Sheffield Hallam, Staffordshire, Sunderland, Teesside, Thames Valley, West of England, Westminster, Wolverhampton
1993	89	Bedfordshire, Glasgow Caledonian, London Arts
1994	90	Abertay Dundee
2001	91	Gloucestershire
2002	90	London Guildhall and London Metropolitan amalgamate
2004	90	Cardiff separates from University of Wales. Manchester and UMIST re-amalgamate
2005	101	Bath Spa, Bolton, Canterbury Christ Church, Chester, Chichester, Liverpool Hope, Northampton, Roehampton, Southampton Solent, Winchester, Worcester
2006	102	Edge Hill
2007	106	Buckinghamshire New, Cumbria, Queen Margaret. Imperial College separates from University of London

Note: Only multi-faculty institutions have been included in this table. In addition to the above, a number of specialist institutions of agriculture, art, business and music have been granted university status.

University names have changed in some cases: their current names are used in this table.

---

[7] Merged with London Metropolitan University in 2002.

Table 3.4 Numbers of higher education students in the UK post-war

Unfortunately, no consistent and reliable data source is available over the period as a whole that enumerates all higher education students in the UK. The periodic changes in status of institutions, the different methods and definitions used in the collection of data, changes in responsibilities for data collection, and the different countries to which the data collected refers (England, England and Wales, Great Britain, the UK) all bedevil the presentation of a simple and consistent table. But we must do what we can!

Table 3.4a provides data on the numbers of university students over the period, splitting the overall figures down in terms of students' gender, level and mode of study. Sudden jumps in numbers (notably between 1990 and 1995) reflect the designation of additional universities. The statistics refer to Great Britain for 1945, and to the UK thereafter. The source for the statistics is Carpentier (2004, updated). This was an ESRC-funded project, part of the aim of which was to compile a consistent set of statistics.

There were, however, substantial numbers of higher education students studying outside of the universities throughout the post-war period. Tables 3.4b and 3.4c provide some details for different periods. Table 3.4b provides statistics on the numbers of higher education students by mode, level and sector between 1954 and 1984. The sources for this table are the *Reports from Universities and University Colleges in Receipt of Grant* and *Statistics of Education: Further Education*, both published annually by HMSO. Note, however, that while the university statistics are for the UK, the further education statistics only cover England and Wales, and, for 1984, only England. The 1974 and 1984 figures for further education also include teacher training establishments, which were previously excluded. Open University students are not included. The jump in university student numbers between 1964 and 1974 is due partly to the transfer of several institutions from the further education to the university sector. Table 3.4b demonstrates a number of trends, including the rapid growth in provision in the advanced further education sector, when compared to the universities, and the greater concentration there on both part-time provision and provision at 'other' than first degree level (mostly sub-degree).

Table 3.4c provides statistics on the numbers of higher education students in the UK by mode of study between 1971 and 1991. It includes both university and advanced further education (or, as it was by then known, public sector) students. The source is *Social Trends*, published annually by HMSO. Comparing this table with Table 3.4a shows how, over this period, the public sector grew to be more important than the university sector in terms of the numbers of students accommodated, and particularly so for part-time students.

Table 3.4a Numbers of university students in the UK post-war

Date	Total	FT UG	PT UG	FT PG	PT PG	Men	Women
1945	49,809	36,837	10,976	1,002	994	32,873	16,936
1950	103,081	78,064	13,580	7,357	4,080	80,514	22,567
1955	100,560	71,591	11,476	12,312	5,181	74,687	29,533
1960	123,500	90,200	10,600	16,800	5,900	92,339	32,164
1965	180,820	131,796	14,813	25,966	8,245	115,460	65,360
1970	250,680	186,217	5,128	39,852	19,483	176,169	75,186
1975	283,057	209,078	3,405	48,606	21,968	191,313	91,744
1980	331,938	251,990	4,381	48,536	27,031	211,613	120,325
1985	345,760	254,819	8,806	50,189	31,946	208,237	137,523
1990	404,831	290,285	10,558	60,696	43,292	230,355	174,476
1995	1,534,369	817,788	413,660	128,894	174,027	767,477	766,892
2000	1,816,360	902,750	544,490	150,700	218,440	820,610	995,750
2005	2,287,545	1,165,445	589,465	226,060	306,570	979,180	1,308,365

Table 3.4b Numbers of higher education students by mode, level and sector, 1954–1984

Sector	Mode	1954	1964	1974	1984
University	FT first degree	64,778	109,058	205,491	249,410
	FT other	16,927	29,653	52,192	55,598
	Total FT	81,705	138,711	257,683	305,008
	PT first degree	1,576	1,376	1,666	5,479
	PT other	14,570	16,711	23,710	35,273
	Total PT	16,146	18,077	25,376	40,752
Further education	FT first degree	2,700	21,450	54,278	137,664
	FT other	6,960	32,000	153,960	100,449
	Total FT	9,660	53,450	208,238	238,113
	PT first degree	4,790	2,730	4,894	15,895
	PT other	22,320	101,970	111,137	156,018
	Total PT	27,110	104,700	116,031	171,913

Table 3.4c Higher education students in the UK by mode, 1971–1991

Date	Total	Full time	Part time
1971	621,500	432,400	164,700
1976	733,200	514,900	218,300
1981	827,400	534,900	292,500
1986	936,800	600,000	336,800
1991	1,175,000	747,000	428,000

4

Policy and funding: from elite to mass participation

Introduction

This chapter focuses on what have inevitably been the key issues in higher education in the post-war period: in particular, perhaps, for politicians and senior institutional managers, but also for academics and students, and, in so far as they have been concerned with higher education, the general public. These issues have to do with changing policies on higher education, and, especially, those effecting the funding of higher education institutions and students. The main trend underlining post-war higher education policy and funding – as the tables included in Chapter 3 demonstrate – has been the growth in participation (though this growth has at times been spasmodic rather than steady). Over the post-war period, this has radically altered the nature of UK higher education, changing it from a small-scale system serving the needs of an elite sector of the population to a mass system seeking to serve the majority at some point (and, increasingly, repeatedly) during their lives.

Starting from the position at the end of the Second World War, this chapter outlines and discusses the key policies and events, decade by decade. The decadal organization is, of course, a convenience, as policies do not simply change with the beginning of a new decade; though, looking back, it does appear as if particular decades had particular characteristics.

Links are made throughout to later chapters, which focus on specific themes in greater detail. Special attention is given to the two major national reports published during the period – the Robbins Report of 1963 and the Dearing Report of 1997 – and their impact. The chapter closes with a comparative discussion of the different emphases of the two reports, and then considers 'where are we now?' (i.e. currently) in terms of higher education policy and practice in the UK.

The aftermath of the war

The new, sustained relationship of the universities with government and other bodies . . . put the CVCP and the universities generally on a different footing. Their graduates were in demand for science, technology and public administration. The expectations and requirements of both university and state determined new priorities, but also new methods of working. (Silver 2003: 34)

Even such cataclysmic events as the Second World War do not necessarily provide precise and neat dividers in human activities and policies, whether concerned with higher education or other issues. In the case of higher education, as in many other areas of economy and society, planning for the post-war world started well before the war itself ended. The policies developed were, however, influenced by the experience of the war, and the desire to improve living and working conditions thereafter. Thus, the Education Act 1944 sought to establish a comprehensive national educational system, one which would impact upon the higher education sector in terms of increasing demand:

The Education Act of 1944 was particularly significant for the universities in at least three main ways: Educationally, it promised to greatly increase the number of students qualified for university matriculation. Administratively, by completing the long transition from the laissez-faire beginnings of state involvement in education in 1833 to a national system of education, it lent support to those who were urging increased state coordination of developments in higher education. And politically, by means of its proposed 'alternate ladder' to scientific status, involving 'parity of esteem' for those who ascended via new secondary modern or technical schools and then technical colleges, it added to the controversy over 'social equality' and the universities. (Berdahl 1959: 71)

The pressures towards higher education expansion came from a number of complementary sources. Perhaps the most obvious, at least initially, came from the series of reports commissioned towards the end of the war, focusing on what were then called 'manpower' needs, and with a particular concern for science and technology employment:

The closing months of the war saw a growing consensus that expansion was necessary . . . This expansionism was sustained by several official reports. The McNair Report, calling in 1944 for three-year courses of training for teachers and the establishment of more advanced courses in technical colleges for intending youth workers, foresaw an annual need for 15,000 newly trained teachers and 300 youth workers. But it was the 1945 Percy Report of *Higher Technological Education* which crystallised the contemporary debate on the nature of the expansion that was needed

... the Percy committee was led to reject the idea of a technological university ... but went on to suggest the promotion of a small number of technical colleges ... The case for expansion was strengthened by the appearance of the Barlow Report on *Scientific manpower* in 1946. This anticipated a doubling of the output of science graduates within a decade, and went well beyond the Percy Report in calling for the upgrading of the five university colleges and the foundation 'of at least one new university' (Lowe 1988: 57–9)

Of these last two proposals, the first did happen, though it took until the end of the 1950s. The response to the second was rather more immediate, with the establishment of the University College of North Staffordshire (later Keele University) in 1949; though this proposal had been under consideration for some time, and was not particularly oriented towards science and technology. This foundation was unusual in a number of ways, not least in offering a four rather than three-year degree, with the first year passed following a common foundation course (Gallie 1960; Mountford 1972). It anticipated the new foundations of the 1960s in that the institution was created from scratch and immediately funded by the University Grants Commission (UGC); and also harked back to older practices, as the college was placed under the oversight of Oxford, Birmingham and Manchester Universities, the last example of an apprenticeship being served in this fashion: 'Keele was the first of the new university institutions in financial and administrative as well as academic terms' (Stewart 1989: 56).

Of the three reports identified by Lowe, the second, the Percy Report, came in for particular criticism:

The Percy Committee was a disappointment to the Ministry of Education. It did identify many of the problems – the need for new forms of training, the high failure rates in technical colleges, above all the lack of focus and direction in technical education – but was less fruitful of solutions. The damaging consequences of the inferior status of technical education, the need for a national award and for a new sandwich course was accepted. The principle of parity of esteem was acknowledged but then not granted. (Davis 1990: 123)

The official reports were not limited to those identified by Lowe, but went on to cover a whole range of specialist areas, implying a doubling in the number of students admitted to higher education compared to the pre-war position. The universities and colleges were faced with the question of:

... how to respond to a stream of government reports on the needs of the professions; the advancing shadow of a planned society: the Barlow report (1946) which recommended that the output of scientists and technologists should be doubled; and reports on medical schools (1944), dentistry (1945), agriculture (1945), veterinary education (1944), oriental, Slavonic, East European and African studies (1947), and social and economic research (1946). From these committees and other sources the Nuffield College group estimated that the annual intake for a score of the commoner professions must rise from 14,000 to 22,000. The university grants committee foresaw an expansion of the student population from 50,000 in 1938 to 90,000. (Ashby and Anderson 1966: 231; see also Nuffield College 1948)

A second sort of pressure towards expansion came from the backlog of those who might have gone into higher education during the war years, but instead served in the armed or auxiliary services. In response to this demand, the government, following the precedent of practice after the First World War, set up the Further Education and Training Scheme (FETS). While not all awards under this scheme were concerned with higher education, a total of 86,425 awards were made (93 per cent of them to men). At the peak of the scheme in 1948, some 10,000 new entrants to university were ex-service personnel with FETS awards, representing about half of their total intake (Peston and Peston 1974: 56, 60). A related initiative channelled 37,000 men and women into accelerated teacher education programmes between 1945 and 1951, with about 29,000 successfully completing (Stewart 1989: 68; see also Dent 1954: chapter 1; Ministry of Education 1950).

A third pressure on the universities and colleges was more general, stemming from the enhanced expectations of a growing population:

> The initial expansion of the 1940s was clearly due to the return of men after the war, but after a slight pause the upward movement continued with the 'trend' to staying on in the sixth form in the 1950s providing the dynamic behind expansion even before the post-war birth 'bulge' reached the universities. (Sanderson 1972: 351)

The UGC, having noted that in its last pre-war report it had wished for a period 'in which "quantitative growth will be less rapid" ', described the expansion of the system as 'revolutionary':

> The desired increase of numbers by something like 80 per cent within a decade represents an expansion out of all proportion to anything which has previously been attempted in the universities of Britain. The accompanying need for the rapid expansion of staffs and for the building of new accommodation impose upon the universities a task which is unparalleled in their earlier development. (University Grants Commission 1948: 26, 28)

As this expansion had the general support of both government and opposition politicians, it led to a substantial increase in the resources made available by the state to the universities: 'The annual recurrent grant to the universities rose from the pre-war figure of £2.25 million to £8 million in 1945–6 and £16.6 million by 1950–1' (Benn and Fieldhouse 1993: 305). But, with this increased financial support came not only increased expectations but a closer interest in influencing, though not yet by any means directing, the work of the universities and colleges:

> It was inevitable in these circumstances that the position of the UGC and the formal relationship between the state and the universities should be modified to reflect the increasing interest and investment of the former. In July 1946 the terms of reference of the UGC were extended so as to define the position of the Committee more explicitly. (Gosden 1983: 139–40)

The changing role of the UGC and other such intermediary bodies is discussed in more detail in Chapter 6.

Alongside the increased state financial support given to the universities and colleges, and influenced by the experience of FETS, came increasing pressure to improve and regularize the provision of financial support for students:

> The growth in the total number of students was closely related to increasingly generous provision of student awards for undergraduates. At the end of the war the awards available to those who were not ex-servicemen remained much as they had been in 1939. About 300 state scholarships were awarded on the basis of Higher School Certificate results while LEAs [local education authorities] each had their own schemes. Many of the awards they offered covered fees but often only part or even none of the cost of maintenance. The undergraduate was still expected to live at home with his parents and to attend a university within daily travelling distance. Many LEAs only paid part of an award in the form of a grant, the remainder – typically up to 50 per cent – was available as a loan to be repaid once the student had completed his course and started work. Entrance scholarships were also available on a competitive basis from universities and colleges. In 1946 the state introduced university supplemental awards which enabled students who won entrance scholarships and exhibitions to have the value of their award brought up to the level of state scholarships – which met fees and full residential maintenance. (Gosden 1983: 147–8)

While the provision of student awards by both the state and local authorities did, therefore, steadily improve, it was not until the early 1960s that a standardized, national system of student support was finally established.

The 1950s

The 1950s can appear to be something of an interregnum, so far as higher education is concerned, between the sweeping policy changes of the immediate post-war period and the massive institutional expansion of the 1960s. Yet they were a period of continuing steady growth (see Table 3.4) –

excepting a slight dip in student numbers in the early 1950s when the post-war FETS awards came to an end – characterized by a building up of the newer parts of the system:

> Most of the increase [in full-time university students in the 1950s] took place in universities other than Oxbridge and London . . . It was thought in most quarters that no further substantial increases would be possible without seriously reducing standards. (Argles 1964: 100)

That misgiving, however, was later overcome. In hindsight, the later 1940s, 1950s and 1960s, taken together – and when compared with what was to follow – can be seen as a period of growth based on confidence in the higher education sector:

> The period between 1950 and 1970 in Britain was one of unprecedented expansion of the university system. The reasons behind this growth are clear: (1) 'the trend' (an increase in the proportion of the age group seeking higher education); (2) 'the bulge' (an increase in the birth rate, which peaked in 1947); and (3) a desire on the part of society, reflected by governments of both parties, to expand the opportunities for higher education and to support university research efforts. (Heyck 1987: 213)

If there ever was a 'golden age' of British higher education, then the 1950s, rather than the 1960s, have a fair claim to being it (see also the discussion in Chapter 11). Increases in student numbers were matched by new staff appointments, so workloads remained manageable; funding for both institutions and students was improving; institutions of higher education and individual academics were left largely alone to get on with their work; the pressures to engage in both teaching and research had not yet gathered much strength; remuneration was reasonable and academe was held in high esteem:

> . . . in the mid-twentieth century the academy enjoyed exceptional prestige. The old power of the dons within a university system intimately related to the nation's elite was reinforced by the new power of the code-breakers, atom scientists and social engineers of the post-war great and good. No longer dependent on student fees or on civic and industrial support but subsidized, at arm's length, by the state, universities, and to a lesser extent other higher education institutions, were more autonomous than ever before (or since?). (Scott 1989: 9)

The number of universities was also increasing. Leicester, the last of the university colleges founded in the first half of the twentieth century to be given independent status, finally received its charter in 1957 (only a year before the first of the new campus universities, Sussex, which gained so much attention in the 1960s, received its).

As in the 1940s, most policy attention in the 1950s focused on technical, technological and vocational education:

Technical education was completely restructured nationally in the non-university sector in the 1950s and the UGC planned with the universities that two-thirds of their increases in student numbers should be in the sciences with an emphasis in the applied sciences wherever possible. (Stewart 1989: 90)

As Stewart indicates, this involved changes in the non-university, or advanced further education, sector at least as much as in the university sector.

In 1952 the Government made the first move towards establishing a hierarchy of institutions [of further education]. A special 75 per cent grant was introduced, payable to colleges undertaking a high proportion of advanced work, especially teaching and research at graduate and postgraduate levels. By 1956 twenty-four English and Welsh colleges were receiving this distinctive accolade and assistance. (Regan 1977: 168)

A National Council for Technological Awards (NCTA) was set up in 1955 to further promote higher technological education. It introduced, and exercised oversight over, a new Diploma in Technology award, designed as equivalent to a first degree in standing:

... the NCTA's main purpose [was] ... to provide the means to produce graduate engineers from sources which had hitherto produced few ... The NCTA ... simply encouraged growth in the colleges, provided that the courses came up to its rather exacting standards. (Burgess and Pratt 1971: 30)

Diploma students mainly followed full-time sandwich courses, typically incorporating both liberal studies and project work. The NCTA was thus primarily responsible for the widespread introduction, at least in particular kinds of institution, of the sandwich 'principle' within British higher education (see also the discussion in Chapter 7).

More radical policy changes were to come in 1956, with the creation of the colleges of advanced technology (CATs). Eleven were eventually established from among 24 existing colleges (Ministry of Education 1956). While the CATs were given greater independence, they were to remain under local authority control until 1962. In recognition of the disproportionate financial load CATs placed on the local education authorities in which they were located, a system of pooling of costs among LEAs was introduced in 1959.

The CATs were to concentrate on advanced full-time and sandwich courses ... A year after the White Paper, the Ministry of Education issued Circular 305 explaining a further evolution of government thinking. The technical colleges outside the CATs were ranked into three grades: regional colleges, area colleges, local colleges. Thus there was established a complete hierarchy of the institutions of further education based on the two criteria of level of work and extent of full-time attendance. (Regan 1977: 168–9)

The 1960s

In England [and throughout the United Kingdom] the crucial feature of the system in the early 1960s was expansion. The seven new universities were being planned before the Robbins committee on higher education was appointed in 1961, and they were opening either before it reported or soon afterwards. The CATs were rapidly increasing their degree-level work under the auspices of the NCTA. The teacher training colleges were raising their entry standards and turning their two- into three-year courses. (Silver 2003: 177)

This continuing expansion was, however, viewed as a mixed blessing by those who believed in the existence of a fixed 'pool of ability', from which students suited for higher education could be selected: a view famously summed up by the author Kingsley Amis in the phrase 'more means worse' (Amis 1960). These doubters included senior figures in the established universities, but the UGC, recognizing the increasing role played by considerations of national needs, took a more measured view:

We feel . . . that we may be reaching the end of a phase . . . The number of places to be provided in the universities is no longer simply decided, on the one hand, by the number of boys and girls who wish to enter the universities and who would benefit by a university education and, on the other hand, by the ability of the country to meet the necessary expenditure. Other considerations, such as the demand for graduates and in particular for certain types of graduates, are coming into the picture. Moreover, the universities are no longer the sole institutions in which courses of university standard are now available. (UGC 1964a: 2)

The 'golden age', and the regard in which higher education was held, lasted for a while longer into the 1960s, buoyed by continuing, state-supported expansion in a relatively stable economy: 'The period 1963–67 marked a high point in the public esteem for higher education both in the Government and the country at large' (Shattock 1994: 6). This state of grace could only last for so long, however, as the pressures of shifting away from an elite system towards mass provision made themselves felt.

The changes that took place in the 1960s dwarfed anything that had taken place before: 'The student expansion of the late 1950s only heralded the explosion of the 1960s . . . The build-up and expansion of higher education had by now become a social trend having wide popular support' (Simon 1991: 225).

Whereas, at the end of the 1950s, there had been only 24 universities in the UK, by 1969 this figure had doubled to 47 (see Table 3.3). This increase was a result of the establishment of the new campus universities, the transfer of the CATs to the university sector, the division of some existing universities and the granting of charters to some long-established specialist institutions (for a fuller discussion of these institutional developments, see Chapter 5). At the same time, the size of individual universities was increasing, something which the UGC expressed reservations about:

The general view of the British universities is that great size can entail the loss of cohesion, with disadvantages both academic and social . . . we think that there are advantages in this country in a wide distribution of institutions of higher education throughout the country rather than their concentration in a few places. (UGC 1964a: 7)

This growth, unlike that in the 1940s and 1950s, when the emphasis was very much placed on science and technology, was also associated with the arts and humanities, and, most notably, with the burgeoning social sciences, for which the 1960s represented a 'coming of age':

For some of the second half of the 1960s the expansion in higher education was accompanied by a flight from the sciences . . . and a flight to the social sciences . . . The UGC returns for *undergraduates* show that between 1961 and 1966 the pure sciences increased by 53%, the applied sciences . . . by 120% and the social sciences by 181% . . . This extraordinary leap forward for the social sciences showed particularly in economics, sociology and business studies. (Stewart 1989: 110–11, original emphasis)

This was to lead to a decline in the perceived relevance and engagement of the universities:

. . . overall it is fair to say that the new universities were not especially committed to industry and much of what involvement there was lay in management and economics rather than applied science and tech-nology. In this there was a sharp contrast with the civic universities of Victorian times. (Sanderson 1999: 95)

For higher education, the 1960s is indelibly associated with the name of Robbins, who chaired the national Committee on Higher Education that reported in 1963. As the discussion that follows makes clear, however, the impact of the Robbins Report is easily exaggerated, as many of its recommendations were not acted upon while others were already effectively under way. But there was also another key report, that of the Anderson Committee (Ministry of Education 1960), which preceded Robbins and arguably had more long-term impact in establishing the principle of a standardized, national support system for students in higher education:

Robbins persuaded the world at large, and the university world in particular, that there was a pool of young talent capable of benefiting from higher education which was substantially larger than the three and a half per cent of the 18 year old age cohort then entering higher education. However, credit for making expansion possible should also go to the earlier report of the Anderson Committee. In accepting the Anderson recommendations, the government bestowed a means-tested maintenance grant upon all young people who were admitted to a full time university degree place. (Booth 1999: 106–7)

While the Anderson Report was critical in establishing this principle, it, like Robbins, was also only recognizing and regularizing long-established trends. The numbers of students receiving full or partial awards from national or local government had been increasing steadily since the war. Thus, in 1958–9, 65,422 out of 79,000 home students (83 per cent) following full-time first degree courses were in receipt of awards from public funds. The Anderson Report estimated that giving them all full awards, even without any parental contribution, would only increase public expenditure by £8.2m, from £16.8m to £25.0m (Ministry of Education 1960: 92–3). That, of course, was then, when the higher education system recruited a relatively small proportion of the age cohort: as this proportion rose, the pressure on public funds would inevitably increase, reaching its breaking point in the 1980s.

The Robbins Report

The decisive factors in causing the Macmillan Government to set up the Robbins Committee were both the enormous increase in the number of secondary school pupils achieving the minimum standard or better for university admission and the increasing awareness of the lack of any coherent overall plan for the rapidly exploding higher education scene. (Gosden 1983: 150)

What the Robbins Report was about was . . . the need to remove . . . barriers to higher education, but also the structures and strategies most appropriate for the new and extended categories of students to be attracted into the system, once the concept of a restricted 'pool of ability' had been abandoned. (Silver 1983: 183)

The Robbins Committee was appointed in 1961 to 'review the pattern of full-time higher education' and 'on what principles its long-term development should be based' (Committee on Higher Education 1963a: 1). Having noted the lack of a British system of higher education, 'if by system is meant a consciously co-ordinated organisation' (p. 4), the committee went on to identify:

. . . four objectives essential to any properly balanced system . . . instruction in skills suitable to play a part in the general division of labour . . . what is taught should be taught in such a way as to promote the general powers of the mind . . . the advancement of learning . . . the transmission of a common culture and common standards of citizenship. (Committee on Higher Education 1963a: 6–7)

They then propounded what came to be known as the Robbins' principle, influencing higher education policy for at least the next two decades: 'courses of higher education should be available for all those who are qualified by ability and attainment to pursue them and who wish to do so' (p. 8). Much of the committee's work then focused on determining how many satisfied this principle, and how the system that would educate them should best be organized.

The committee estimated that, on the basis of their principle, the minimum number of home students in full-time higher education would rise from 195,000 in 1962/3 to 312,000 in 1970/1 and 507,000 in 1980/1 (p. 65). Including overseas students, the figures would rise from 216,000 to 344,000 and 558,000 (p. 69). They recommended that:

. . . 2,000 students or thereabouts is probably the upper limit for a single-purpose institution, and about 4,000–5,000 for an institution . . . whose main preoccupations will be in the faculties of science and technology . . . many of the multi-faculty universities of this country should expand to accommodate 8,000 or even 10,000 students. (Committee on Higher Education 1963a: 153–4)

Even though these numbers would imply a substantial expansion of most existing higher education institutions – and of both the campus universities, then being established, and the colleges of advanced technology (recently removed from local authority control), which the committee recommended should become universities – they would not enable the estimated demand to be satisfied. Hence, the committee went on to 'recommend the foundation of six new universities in addition to those now in the process of formation. One of them will be a Special Institution for Scientific and Technological Education and Research [SISTER]' (p. 155).

Expansion was also recommended for the colleges of education, as the teacher training colleges – with their newly designated BEd degrees – were now to be called (so that colleges with less than 750 students would become the exception), and for further education. This would entail a rise in public expenditure on full-time higher education, assuming that the state remained the major funder of both institutions and students, from £206m in 1962/3 to an estimated £742m in 1980/1 (p. 202).

Other recommendations of the committee included:

- the creation of further 'SISTERs' from Imperial College in London and the Colleges of Science and Technology in Manchester and Glasgow;
- the creation of two postgraduate business schools: a proposal developed

further that year in the Franks Report (Franks 1963), with the two Business Schools, in London and Manchester, duly founded in 1965;
- giving university status to the major Scottish central institutions;
- the replacement of the National Council for Technological Awards by a Council for National Academic Awards (CNAA);
- the bringing of the Royal College of Art and the College of Aeronautics within the ambit of the Grants Commission (which was to replace the UGC).

Responses to Robbins

The government immediately issued a brief statement following the publication of the Robbins Report (Prime Minister 1963). It accepted the Robbins principle and the student number forecasts, and pledged to make the resources available to cope with them, even though this implied 'more than doubling the annual cost of higher education in 10 years' (p. 4). The general tenor of the Robbins Report was widely accepted by politicians and academics alike, despite minority reservations. Some went so far as to argue that it did not go far enough:

> There was nothing really revolutionary about the Robbins Report. Apart from the crisis measures to cope with the bulge it virtually recommended the slowing up of the rate of growth of full-time higher education. The envisaged rate of expansion – 5.4 per cent per annum at compound interest – was rather less than that achieved over the previous eight years. (Armytage 1968: 95–6)

Indeed, Robbins' (admittedly conservative) predictions on the likely growth in student numbers soon proved to be underestimates: 'From 1962–3 to 1967–8 the number of students in full-time higher education in Britain grew from 217,000 to 376,000, and the increase over these five years was greater than over the preceding twenty-five' (Layard et al. 1969: 13).

Others were not so positive in their judgements, though they were, admittedly, often to make them with the benefit of hindsight. Thus, looking back 20 years later, Carswell, a former senior civil servant, argued that:

> The weaknesses of the Report lie not in its proposals but in its omissions. Some of these could be perceived at the time, others only by hindsight . . . Perhaps the biggest anxieties came from over-optimism about the wider consequences of expanding the system quickly and by an order of magnitude . . . the problems of managing large institutions with thousands of employees and tens of thousands of students received little attention. (Carswell 1985: 39)

Carswell also critiqued the report for convoluting suggested increases in the number of women students and the numbers studying science and technology, for the lack of serious consideration given to medical education, for ignoring that the rapid expansion in student numbers would inevitably mean the recruitment of a lower standard of staff, and for its devotion to a particular autonomous model of the university:

> Robbins was not done on the cheap. Building standards were generous, staffing ratios were maintained or even allowed to improve, postgraduate support was rapidly extended, and the growth of ancillary services (health, counselling, placement, sport) was faster than the growth of student numbers. (Carswell 1985: 63)

Carswell carried out a statistical analysis of the higher education system's performance against the growth planned by Robbins. He found that 'overall performance came within 6 per cent of programme, and at mid-term considerably exceeded it' (p. 169). In two important respects, however, there was considerable statistical divergence from the Robbins' plans. First, far more growth took place outside the university sector – that is, in advanced further education institutions – than had been intended (see the discussion of 'other developments' that follows). Second, the emphasis on the expansion of student numbers in science and technology subjects (to be achieved partly through the inclusion of the former CATs within the university system, and partly through encouraging the new universities to engage closely with industry; see also Archer 1979) was not realized.

The expansion of the colleges of education also garnered a mixed assessment, as it resulted in an almost complete change in the character of the institutions involved:

> Following the Robbins Report, teacher education in the 1960s was . . . massively expanded and relocated within the higher education system proper and the new BEd degree was born. The increased size of the institutions, the reduction in tutor and student residence and the coeducational nature of the institutions meant that relationships were less personal. In addition, the curriculum became more differentiated, academic and removed from the direct world of the school. Moreover, in order to satisfy the demands for academic rigour of the validating universities, new disciplinary specialists in sociology, psychology, philosophy and history were recruited to replace generalist education tutors. (Furlong et al. 2000: 99–100)

Of course, many of the developments recommended by Robbins, such as the upgrading of the colleges of advanced technology to university status, were widely expected at the time. Others proved relatively uncontroversial; for example, the CNAA was established in place of the NCTA, and the Royal College of Art and the College of Aeronautics (the forerunner of Cranfield University) were given university status. However, many other detailed recommendations were not acted upon. Thus, no further tranches of universities or SISTERs were created, though Imperial College and UMIST continued their roles, and the University of Strathclyde was recognized in Glasgow. Robbins' ideas on the maximum desirable size for universities and other institutions of higher education were also ignored and soon overtaken.

Neither was the UGC replaced, though its relation to government was irrevocably altered by a transfer of its oversight from the Treasury to the new Department of Education and Science (DES):

> On 1 April 1964 the UGC became the responsibility of the newly created DES. Thereafter, its ability to define the ideological and administrative nature of the middle ground between universities and the state was never to be the same again. (Salter and Tapper 1994: 120)

Robbins, therefore, served to establish the growing significance of higher education as an activity within the UK to justify its continuing reliance on state funding, and to kick-start the development of further, and more detailed, government policy in this area: 'In retrospect the main significance of the Robbins Report appears above all to have been the effect it had in securing for higher education a much more prominent position in the public and political consciousness' (Gosden 1983: 151).

Robbins himself, reflecting, like Carswell, nearly two decades later on the impact of the committee he had chaired, also seemed to feel that they had perhaps not been radical enough. He indicated that his main regret was that little had been done to ensure that there were 'adequate facilities for studies in breadth as well as depth' in the universities (Robbins 1980: 106).

Other developments

> The period 1963–66 was crucial in establishing the modern structure of British higher education, culminating in the creation of the poly-technics. Once this burst of decision-making was over, neither major political party seems to have had a policy on higher education. (Shattock 1994: 9)

The other key development of the 1960s, which Robbins neither recommended nor really foresaw, was the creation of the polytechnics (Department of Education and Science 1966). They formed the other half of what was termed the binary policy, counterbalancing the university sector, and focusing more on applied and vocational forms of study. The binary policy was – to the surprise of many (e.g. Lukes 1967) – instigated by the then minister, Richard Crosland, and led to the creation of 31 polytechnics in the late 1960s and early 1970s:

> Each new polytechnic would be formed from an existing technical college, or more usually, several adjacent colleges. To secure the advantages of scale it was envisaged that each should aim at an eventual minimum of 2,000 full-time students plus part-timers. (Regan 1977: 171)

The creation of a whole new higher education sector, so soon after the expansion of the university and teacher education sectors recognized and recommended by Robbins, not surprisingly received 'a very mixed reception':

> The universities, for instance, were hardly likely to agree that they were not responsive to social needs, as Crosland clearly implied. The CVCP feared that the cost of building up the local authority sector would lead to a denial of funds to universities. The larger regional colleges which in terms of the Robbins policy might have hoped to have joined the ex-CATs as universities were clearly disappointed. The majority of technical college people, on the other hand, welcomed the speech. (Gosden 1983: 179)

There was also, though, a prevalent feeling that what was being established was only temporary and, in some senses, was bound not to live up to its aims:

> The principal objection levelled at the binary system by its critics is that it divides higher education into superior and inferior leagues. The polytechnics have no chance of being accepted as equal to, though different from, the universities. (Regan 1977: 183–4)

The polytechnics, like the CATs before them, would, it was widely accepted, inevitably aspire to university status (see also the discussion in Chapter 5). However, the binary system established in the late 1960s proved to be surprisingly robust, forming 'the basis of planning in higher education from 1965 until 1992, under governments of both the main parties' (Pratt 1997: 7).

The final major institutional development of the 1960s was the establishment of the Open University as a national provider of higher education at a distance. It was given the go-ahead in 1969 and – despite some early reservations resulting from the change of government in 1970 – enrolled its first students two years later, in 1971 (Perry 1976).

One other event indelibly associated with higher education in the late 1960s, both in the UK and internationally, was student (and, to a lesser degree, staff) rebellion. Compared with other countries, such as France and the USA, however, this rebellion was not as far reaching, and nor, partly for this reason, did it attract the same strong responses. Sit-ins and demonstrations were common, particularly in certain institutions, but they were generally short-lived and readily resolved. While some at the time may have thought, or wished, that the revolution was imminent (Cockburn and Blackburn 1969; Crouch 1970, 1972; Rooke 1971), when examined with hindsight (and I was an undergraduate myself at the time in London) the student rebellions of the 1960s and early 1970s in the UK do not seem so significant.

The late 1960s, partly because of the demands on academic staffing caused by expansion, and partly because of the attractions of other systems (notably, of course, in North America), was also a period of considerable concern about 'brain drain'; that is, the emigration of highly trained young people:

> There is a serious brain drain of young engineers, technologists and scientists from the United Kingdom. The right solution is to create more challenging opportunities, particularly in industry, for talented people. (Committee on Manpower Resources for Science and Technology 1967: vii)

This concern was associated with more general worries about the production of adequate numbers of science and engineering graduates by universities and colleges (Committee on Manpower Resources for Science and Technology 1968), itself linked to the declining proportion of students following these subjects (Council for Scientific Policy 1968). Increased efforts at recruitment, prioritization of employment and a greater emphasis on shorter periods of postgraduate study were among the main recommendations made in response.

The 1970s

If the 1960s were the high watermark of post-war UK higher education development, with continuing public confidence in the system, a generous funding regime for both institutions and students, and substantial growth in numbers, types and sizes of institution, then the 1970s represent the start of the slide. While growth continued, internal and external problems and issues began to manifest themselves.

A major contextual concern was that the economy, subject to oil crises and other global developments, was not growing as fast as it had been: 'From the late 1960s an increasing number of difficulties arose as national expectations appeared likely to outrun any probable increase in the rate of growth of the gross national product' (Gosden 1983: 155).

At the same time, the legacy of the student rebellions of the late 1960s, combined with the increased scale of the management challenges faced by larger and larger institutions of higher education, had begun to raise questions about how universities and colleges were being run: 'By the 1970s, confidence in the objectives and operational capacities of higher education had begun to decline' (Kogan and Hanney 2000: 56).

These trends resulted in increased scrutiny of the operation of the higher education sector by politicians, and greater demands for information:

> The isolation of the university sector from the normal procedures of public accountability meant that it had never had to construct or justify its internal arrangements on a basis logically comprehensible to a parliamentary committee. (Salter and Tapper 1994: 44)

This was now to change.

At first, however, even with a change of government, higher education policy and funding seemed to be continuing on much the same trajectory as in the 1960s. The 1972 education White Paper was bullish, but the government's plans were undone by demography and student choice, which, given the declining state of the economy, was perhaps not such a bad thing:

> The 1972 White Paper was . . . called *Education: A Framework for Expansion*. It reaffirmed the Robbins principle and expected full-time higher education places to grow from 463,000 in 1971/72 to 750,000 by 1981. The absolute expansion in the number of places over the nine years to 1981 was expected to be greater than the increase that had occurred in the nine years since Robbins. The reality has been very different. Fewer students wanted to come. Or, more precisely, the age participation rate having doubled in the decade following Robbins then began to decline. The effect on enrolment was mitigated by population growth within the 18–21 age group and continued growth in the numbers of mature students and overseas students which ensured some rise in overall numbers. (Wagner 1982: 8–9)

Potential students were increasingly opting for employment, when they could find it, rather than higher education:

> While the 1972 white paper . . . assumed that participation would reach 21 per cent of the relevant age group by 1981 and still be rising, in practice it peaked at 14.2 per cent in 1972/73, falling to 12.4 per cent in 1979/80 before recovering to 12.7 per cent in 1980/81 and 12.9 per cent in 1981/82, the highest level since the mid-1970s. (Booth 1982: 34)

The optimism of the post-Robbins period was gone:

> The result of the adoption of the Robbins principle by successive governments and of the chronic over-estimation of demand in projections of the APR [age participation rate] was that government plans for higher education were capable of being trimmed back progressively as part of the general retrenchment of public expenditure in a way that, in the early stages, was relatively painless. Furthermore, the increase in the size of the age group meant that absolute demand was rising . . . Because student numbers were expanding, albeit slowly, for much of the 70s, particularly in large public sector institutions, it was possible to increase 'efficiency' as measured by student staff ratios and cut unit costs while maintaining academic standards in teaching if not in research. (Booth 1982: 34–5)

The unforeseen direction of these trends led to continuing concerns about demography and participation rates, which were reflected in a series of official and discussion documents (e.g. Department of Education and Science 1978). Questions were asked about who was not participating in higher education, and why, and about who might replace the declining proportions and/or numbers of conventional age students when the post-war 'baby boomers' had been through the system. Specific initiatives were designed to better engage such 'non-standard' or 'non-traditional' groups, including mature and working class students (see also the discussion in Chapter 10).

Thus, the late 1970s saw the beginnings of the 'access' movement, at first ostensibly targeted at ethnic minority groups:

> In 1978, the Department of Education and Science used higher educa-tion as part of an incorporating and socialising process by inviting seven local authorities, including the Inner London Education Authority, to establish access courses (special pilot courses for entry to higher education) with a view to increasing the opportunities for members of ethnic minorities to enter higher education. (Benn and Fieldhouse 1993: 308)

The 1970s was also a period of rapid and radical change in teacher education, again linked to demography and demand, as well as to changing ideas as to how teacher education should best be provided (see also Chapter 5). The James Report (Department of Education and Science 1972) recommended a reconfiguring of the arrangements for teacher educa-tion and training, but its suggestions were not acted upon. It also suggested that a new, two-year, full-time award, the Diploma in Higher Education (DipHE), should be introduced for those students who did not wish to undertake a full degree course. This was acted upon, but did not prove that popular.

Having experienced rapid expansion, and re-designation, in the late 1960s to cope with a shortage of trained teachers, a downturn in demand in the mid-1970s led to equally rapid cutbacks in provision in the colleges of education. The long-standing tradition of providing teacher education in relatively small, single-purpose, institutions was ended, and the only recently created college of education sector effectively disappeared:

> Large numbers of colleges of education were closed and amalgamated and there were substantial job losses. Following what many considered to be the 'rape' of the teacher education system, initial teacher educa-tion increasingly took place in highly diversified institutions – the monotechnic college gave way to the polytechnic and institutes of higher education. (Furlong et al. 2000: 100; see also Hencke 1978)

At the same time, teacher education was made more academic as quality was ratcheted up:

> Entry qualifications to teacher education were raised to two 'A' levels, the same minimum as for the universities . . . A new BEd degree was introduced, at first alongside the Certificate, and later, when entry qualifications to teacher education were raised, for all who wished to

pursue concurrent courses. Teacher education became a responsibility of the new colleges and institutes of higher education, based upon previous college of education foundations; of polytechnics, with which many of the colleges had merged, and of universities. Changed institutional settings, a stronger academic emphasis, and a shift towards more conservative, subject-centred, instrumental education purposes weakened and diversified what had been the core values of teacher education. (Taylor 1984: 19)

Underlying everything, however, were the continuing problems with the national economy. For higher education, as for other parts of the public sector, difficult decisions were increasingly having to be made, but those running the system were often not best placed to make or act upon such decisions:

> The policy led expenditure programmes of successive governments in the 1960s and early 1970s not only increased the university sector's dependence on Exchequer grants, they diverted attention away from the need to develop systematically and implement plans for raising funds from non-public sources, and also for the universities to increase the flexibility of their staffing arrangements. (Sizer 1988: 80)

Under this strain, the university funding system stuttered:

> From 1974 to 1977 every kind of university grant, whether for buildings, furniture, equipment or general supplementation, was withheld wholly or in part at some point . . . This was generally agreed to be the worst financial crisis experienced by all universities in peacetime and it came when sixteen new ones were hoping to build strength . . . when the Open University was taking its first innovative steps, and when the polytechnics in their new form were finding their way. (Stewart 1989: 162)

And, to emphasize the problems and the extent of the changes required, the time-honoured quinquennial funding arrangements themselves ceased part-way through 1972/77 period. Worse was, however, to come.

The 1980s

The Robbins vision ended with the 1981 White Paper which avoided numerical estimates of places and gave warning of a 10 per cent cut in expenditure over the following two years. (Brooks 1991: 41–2)

The nadir of government support for higher education was probably reached in the early 1980s . . . when a new government took over in 1979 with a determination to cut public expenditure, higher education was in a particularly vulnerable position. (Fulton 1990: 151–2)

The late 1970s saw the voting in to power of the first Thatcher government, and a sea change in the dominant political attitudes towards not only higher education, but the whole of the public sector. Efficiency savings, increased entrepreneurial activities, stronger institutional management and the adoption of private sector practices were the order of the day. The policies and directives became so relentless that some saw them as a coordinated 'attack' on higher education, its practices and what it stood for: 'The 1979–83 government attacked higher education without real thought about the consequences, and the UGC implemented government policies too loyally and on particularly narrow and socially unresponsive criteria' (Kogan and Kogan 1983: 110). Others interpreted the changes in policy as an attempt to 'privatize' higher education (e.g. Walford 1988).

Consequently, the 1980s began, as the 1970s had ended, with cuts in the state finances made available to higher education:

> Two successive changes in Government policy followed a period of expansion of the university sector of higher education until May 1979. The first, made in Autumn 1979, was a decision to withdraw subsidy progressively from overseas students coupled with a policy of 'level funding' for home students. The second, in the period December 1980 to March 1981, was a decision to reduce annual expenditure on home students by amounts totalling 8.5 per cent by 1983–84 . . . The impact of the two successive changes varied significantly between institutions. Firstly, the number and percentages of overseas undergraduate and postgraduate students in universities in 1979–80 varied considerably between institutions. Secondly, the UGC adopted a highly selective approach in implementing the reductions in grant. (Sizer 1988: 79)

The impact of these cuts on individual universities could be severe, as in the case of Aston, a former CAT in Birmingham, but they also offered an opportunity for institutional remodelling:

> In July 1981 the University Grants Committee announced its allocation of government financial support for each of the universities for the following three years. The University of Aston in Birmingham was informed that it was to lose more than a third of its funding and that it would have to reduce its student numbers by more than a fifth within three years. The announcement marked the beginning of a long and often bitter internal political struggle as the university accommodated to these demands and reorganized itself, such that by 1985 it was in a strong position to face the anticipated problems of the late 1980s and early 1990s. By the end of 1985 more than half of the academic staff of 1981 had left and not a single new permanent academic staff member had been appointed. Many courses had been cut and over half the departments within the university had either been closed or merged with others. Yet at the same time the university had spent over £5 million

on physical restructuring and campus development, had established a rapidly expanding Science Park with venture capital of over £2 million, had ensured that the average 'quality' of student in terms of A level entry grades was higher than the national average of all universities in every subject, and had developed a unique Education Extension Centre based on Tutored Video Instruction. (Walford 1987: 1)

Perhaps the most significant longer-term impact of the 1981 cuts in funding was, however, the establishment of the principle of more selective funding of research by the UGC, which led directly to the research assessment exercise (RAE), first carried out in 1985/6, and then again in 1989 (Universities Funding Council 1989), and every five or six years thereafter. Using 'informed peer review', a series of subject panels assessed and graded the research performance of those university departments and academics that submitted documentation, which then formed the basis for differential funding (the RAE is discussed further in Chapter 8). From the mid-1980s onwards, the UGC also established a wide series of disciplinary subject reviews of teaching provision (some of which were trans-binary in scope), leading to the concentration and rationalization of provision (Hoare 1991).

Apart from their desire to cut costs, however, the Thatcher government initially appeared to offer little in the way of higher education policy:

So far as we have in Britain any policy for higher education it is the binary policy. For the division of higher education into a university and a polytechnic and college sector not only establishes the political, administrative and financial context in which detailed decisions about both educational and resource priorities are made, but also serves as an influential metaphor about the future shape and direction of the system. The binary policy is the nearest thing we have to an authoritative statement about the purposes of higher education. (Scott 1982: 166)

Policy development subsequently began to proceed at some pace. The UGC and the new National Advisory Body (NAB) for Local Authority Higher Education (later Public Sector Higher Education) – which had been established in 1982 as the intermediary body between the government and the English polytechnics and colleges of higher education, following the report of the Oakes Working Group (Secretary of State for Education and Science 1978) – were asked to give advice.

In their responses, the UGC and the NAB went so far as to make a joint statement. This included a reformulation of the Robbins axiom to read 'courses of higher education should be available for all those who are able to benefit from them and who wish to do so', and the addition of a fifth objective to the four identified by Robbins: 'the provision of continuing education in order to facilitate adjustment to technological, economic and social change and to meet individual needs for personal development' (UGC 1984b: 2). The growing interests of the NAB and the UGC in continuing

education had been signalled earlier the same year in the publication of a brace of reports (National Advisory Body 1984a; UGC 1984a).

Perhaps more significantly in the longer term, another review set in place in that year, this time by the Committee of Vice-Chancellors and Principals (CVCP), acting before its hand was forced, focused on the efficiency of university management. This resulted in the publication of the Jarratt Report in the following year (CVCP 1985; discussed in more detail in Chapter 6). In addition it recommended that the government should review the operation of the UGC; which led to the Croham Report two years later (Secretary of State for Education and Science 1987), and the replacement of the UGC, after 70 years of service, with a Universities Funding Council (UFC) – 'to expose the universities to market forces' (Swinnerton-Dyer 1991: 205) – in 1989.

Jarratt also suggested that the state should provide the funds necessary to meet the costs of reductions in university staff, urged universities to adopt strategic planning practices from private sector organizations, and paved the way for the introduction of an increasingly managerial approach. At the same time, the Lindop Committee was reviewing the validation of degree courses in the public sector by the CNAA and the universities, and recommending improvements and greater coordination in practice (Committee of Enquiry into the Academic Validation of Degree Courses in Public Sector Higher Education 1985).

Not surprisingly, having consulted widely among the institutions they funded, the advice on higher education strategy provided by the NAB and the UGC to the government emphasized the need to provide for higher levels of student recruitment and to ameliorate the resourcing situation (NAB 1984b; UGC 1984b). The government's response to this advice came in a Green Paper published in the following year, and in the White Paper, *Higher Education: Meeting the Challenge*, that followed in 1987 (DES 1985, 1987). The Green Paper was clear about the underlying priority:

> The economic performance of the United Kingdom since 1945 has been disappointing compared to the achievements of others. The Government believes that it is vital for our higher education to contribute more effectively to the improvement of the performance of our economy . . . The Government is particularly concerned by the evidence that the societies of our competitors are producing, and plan in the future to produce, more qualified scientists, engineers, technologists and technicians than the United Kingdom. (DES 1985: 3)

The paper went on to condemn the perceived 'anti-business' snobbery among academics, and to urge institutions to develop closer links with industry, commerce and their local communities. Continuing diversity among institutions was to be encouraged, but with attention given to adjustment in subject balance and choice in the light of the decline in student numbers anticipated in the 1990s. Clearly the perspectives of the government, the UGC and the NAB were rather different: the alignment of interests between academe and government that had existed for the first part of the post-war period had gone for good.

Future projections in student numbers were being given particularly close attention, as the post-war baby boom had now passed through higher education. The demography suggested a reduced recruitment ahead (DES 1984, 1986), with a 'projected fall in the number of 18-year olds from 778,000 in 1985 to 551,000 in 1995' (Benn and Fieldhouse 1993: 308). While the institutions hoped to at least make good reduced numbers of young home, full-time entrants with increased numbers of older, part-time and foreign students, the government's predictions were more pessimistic:

> In Projection P total numbers increase to 700,000 full-time equivalents by 1989, followed by a decrease of 84,000 to 616,000 by 1996 and then a small increase to 633,000 by the end of the century. In Projection Q numbers increase to 726,000 in 1990, followed by a much smaller decrease of 35,000 to 691,000 by 1996, and a subsequent increase of 32,000 by the year 2000. (DES 1986: 15)

In the light of these projections, the institutions' desire to ease their financial pain by recruiting more 'non-traditional' students was further undermined by the changing graduate labour market:

> . . . the market for graduates began to weaken in the early 1970s, slipped to a historic low in the early 1980s, and has recovered substantially since then. The reasons are not hard to find. The expansion of the 1960s, huge though it was in relative terms, was absorbed to a substantial degree cannibalistically by growth in employment within the education system itself; and the expansion in the early 1970s was swallowed up by a wide range of other jobs in the expanding public sector . . . while the first signs of rising graduate unemployment occurred – and were commented on – in the early 1970s, it was not until the sharp recession following 1979 that the problem of total output seemed to demand urgent attention from policy-makers. (Fulton 1990: 149–50)

Some comfort – inevitably qualified – was, however, to come. The 1987 White Paper (DES 1987) reiterated the primary economic purpose of higher education, along with the need to further improve quality and efficiency. Yet it also, in a seeming reversal of the 1981 cuts and the earlier pessimism on student numbers, committed the government to a policy of increasing participation in higher education by both young and older people. The policy shift was associated with a change of minister:

> [The Conservatives] . . . took office with one series of policies and then suddenly and radically reversed field in the mid-1980s . . . Policy A was based firmly in an economy drive, and apparently supported by demographic projections showing a large potential reduction in the numbers of 18 and 19-year olds applying for places . . . This policy reached its apogee in Joseph's Green Paper of 1985, *The Development of*

Higher Education into the 1990s. Broadly the government proposed a reduction in reliance on the taxpayer, stronger links with business and industry, and rationalization into a smaller number of institutions . . . Policy B was kick-started by Kenneth Baker's White Paper of 1987 (*Higher Education: meeting the challenge*) . . . [and] included a profound transformation of the post-Robbins inheritance, especially in demographic terms . . . What is more, in keeping with at least one priority of Policy A, much of this expansion and change had been achieved through huge efficiency gains. (Watson and Bowden 1999: 244–5)

The subsequent expansion was to be in a changed system, where costs had been driven down and a greater proportion of provision was made in the newly designated (and cheaper) polytechnics and colleges sector. This was partly because the UGC, while implementing the cuts in funding, had done what it could to protect the unit of resource (i.e. the amount of money provided to support each student): 'This meant that from 1981 to 1985 the universities admitted fewer students than the government might have wished, and, in consequence, the polytechnics and colleges were able to expand to absorb the increased demand' (Walford 1988: 49).

The government now proposed to remove the polytechnics and colleges from the control of the local authorities, granting them corporate status in 1989. By the end of the decade, the UGC had been replaced by the UFC, with a parallel Polytechnics and Colleges Funding Council (PCFC) replacing the NAB to oversee funding of the polytechnics' and colleges' sector. Funding of universities through block grants based on historical norms was being replaced by formula funding and contracts. Attempts were even made to encourage institutions to undercut each other in making provision for students in particular subject areas, though these were largely unsuccessful (Johnes 1992):

The mechanism for funding by UFC and PCFC was intended to be by contract based on formulae. Higher education institutions would be contracted to run courses and be paid on a per capita basis. They would also be contracted to do research. This was a monumental change in the relationship between the government and higher education (especially the universities). (Lawton 1992: 56)

Closer control was still, however, exercised over the polytechnics' and colleges' sector:

The histories of the National Advisory Body for Higher Education (NAB) and the Polytechnics and Colleges Funding Council (PCFC), although sequential, constitute quite different stages in the expansion of DES power and in its ability to manage change in what became known as the Public Sector of Higher Education (PSHE). In many ways the NAB was simply a neutral arena in which the plurality of interests then extant in PSHE could apply their lobbying skills in the hope of influencing the outcome of its deliberations . . . By contrast, the PCFC was clearly a colony of the DES. (Salter and Tapper 1994: 133)

Throughout the decade, the government's increasing attempts to steer higher education in particular directions was evidenced through the creation of a variety of short-term, semi-competitive funding initiatives (the pattern was to continue in the decades that followed). Two such schemes were PICKUP and Enterprise in Higher Education. PICKUP (Professional, Industrial and Commercial Updating Programme) was introduced at the beginning of the 1980s. Its intention was to pump-prime the provision of short, post-experience vocational updating courses by universities, polytechnics and colleges, which would then – hopefully – become profitable and self-supporting activities (DES 1980, 1989).

The Enterprise in Higher Education initiative, introduced in 1987, was rather more ambitious. Its intention was to encourage higher education institutions to better develop enterprising skills and attitudes among all their students, and hopefully many of their staff as well (Manpower Services Commission 1987; Training Agency 1989, 1990). While official evaluations were relatively positive (Her Majesty's Inspectors 1992), the programme was much critiqued by academics (Coffield 1990; Tasker and Packham 1994).

While most attention was initially given to institutional funding, another financial issue that began to absorb increasing amounts of attention at this time was student funding. With further increases in the numbers of students in higher education, and a continuation of the student grants policies established in the early 1960s, it quickly became apparent to most parties that alternative funding arrangements would have to be developed (Barr and Crawford 2005). The 1988 White Paper that introduced a policy for top-up loans for students (Department of Education and Science 1988) was, however, widely criticized: 'The [1988] White Paper is fundamentally flawed . . . its cost calculations just do not add up; the costs are so huge that they rule out any prospect of expanding higher education, even in the very long run' (Barr 1989: 50).

Barr argued instead for a repayment loan scheme operating through national insurance contributions (or income tax), using private sector start-up funds. However, with back-bench opposition from its own party, concerned that the policy would impact on their middle-class voters, the government abandoned introducing significant changes for the time being.

The 1990s

In the space of just 7 years, between 1988 and 1994, the participation rate for young people doubled from 15 to around 30 per cent, and the number of higher education students in the English system increased by more than half. It was also a largely unplanned episode, with the abolition of the binary system and the introduction of unified quality assurance arrangements following rather than leading the expansion. (Parry 2006: 393)

For much of the 1990s, the trends established in the 1980s continued, as conservative governments continued in power. Participation in higher education continued to grow, more and more ambitious targets were set, and the funds provided to institutions were steadily reduced on a per capita basis:

> In the 1992 general election the government's target for growth in higher education, to cater for one third of 18–21 year olds by the year 2000, was accepted by all parties. In Scotland indeed, this target had already been met, so that country aims for half of all its 17–21 year olds in HE by that date. (Ainley 1994: 11)

With more and more young people achieving first degrees, credential inflation began to impact, and there was an increasing need for a greater proportion of the labour market to gain postgraduate qualifications, either immediately following their undergraduate studies or after a period in employment:

> In England, as in other parts of the United Kingdom, the recent expansion of numbers in higher education has been general to all types of institution and across most levels and modes of study, with growth fastest in postgraduate education and at first degree level but much slower and more uneven in other kinds of undergraduate education. (Parry 1997: 6)

1991 saw a flurry of white papers, with two volumes focusing on education and training for 16–19 year olds (DES 1991a), and a further volume dealing with higher education (DES 1991b). The former represented another attempt to raise the status of vocational qualifications, and signalled the removal of sixth forms and further education colleges (following the polytechnics and higher education colleges) from local authority control. The latter presaged the end of the binary system, with the introduction of 'a single funding structure for teaching in universities, polytechnics and colleges' (DES 1991b: 14). The UFC and PCFC were to be replaced by a united Higher Education Funding Council for England (HEFCE), with equivalent bodies in Scotland and Wales. A national system for the assessment of the quality of teaching and courses was also to be introduced.

The 1992 Act removed the binary policy, which had been established in the mid-1960s, with the polytechnics and some larger colleges of higher education raised to university status. This was the greatest single period of university creation so far in UK history (see Table 3.3). It represented the continuation of a trend of favouring the polytechnics and freeing them from other controls, while at the same time exerting greater controlling influence over the universities:

In important respects, the former polytechnics became more free than they were before incorporation under the 1988 Act; the controls exercised by their local authorities were removed, as were those of the Council for National Academic Awards by the 1992 Act. The 'old' universities, however, experienced more external pressure than hitherto. (Kogan and Hanney 2000: 47)

Quality, efficiency and productivity remained the focus of government policy on higher education, with performance indicators the 'principal technical means' (Peters 1992: 127) used to measure compliance. The market rhetoric and associated behaviours were by now firmly embedded among senior academic managers and central university staff, even though the sector hardly behaved like a conventional market:

> Government in the UK employs the rhetoric of the market in connection with higher education, but since government controls the price universities can place on their services, and the amount and variety of services they can sell, universities currently operate not in a market but in something more like a command economy. (Trow 1996: 310)

In response to governmental concerns about the quality of teaching provision, the CVCP established an Academic Audit Unit (AAU) in 1990 to assess universities' mechanisms for the quality assurance of teaching provision (Williams 1992). This established – in a way analogous to the approach taken by the research assessment exercise (which continued, with another two exercises held in 1992 and 1996) – a pattern of institutional self-evaluation, a brief but intense visit to departments (only in selected cases at first), and a follow-up report. This included a simple assessment of provision as satisfactory or excellent, or, in a few cases, unsatisfactory.

This approach did not entirely satisfy the government, however, and, following the 1992 Act and the reorganization of higher education, the AAU was supplanted in England (arrangements for the other parts of the UK were devolved) by the Higher Education Quality Council (HEQC), and by practices modelled more on those developed in the former polytechnics. While the quality assurance process continued to follow the same general lines, the documentation required increased, all departments were visited by review teams, and the assessment was broken down by theme and made numeric.

While its main role was quality assurance, the HEQC also became involved in related matters like the recognition of access courses (Davies and Parry 1993), the dissemination of good practice, the development of credit frameworks, widening participation and the notion of graduate standards (Higher Education Quality Council 1994, 1995, 1996a, 1997). It also sought to extend its influence beyond taught courses to research degrees (HEQC 1996b). While widening access to, and participation in, higher education continued to be a concern, it was recognized that under-representation was now mostly an issue as regards lower socio-economic groups and the disabled, though the performance of individual institutions in this respect varied widely (Higher Education Funding Council for England 1996a).

In a fast-moving world, the HEQC was itself superseded by the Quality Assurance Agency (QAA) in 1997 (the quality 'movement' in higher education is discussed in more detail in Chapter 7).

The Dearing Report

The Dearing Report, which was issued in 1997 at the time when the long period of Conservative government was finally giving way to a (New) Labour administration, served as a summation of official thinking on higher education of its time. Unlike the earlier Robbins Report, the terms of reference of the Dearing Report made explicit mention of funding, and in particular student funding:

> To make recommendations on how the purposes, shape, structure, size and funding of higher education, including support for students, should develop to meet the needs of the United Kingdom over the next 20 years, recognising that higher education embraces teaching, learning, scholarship and research. (National Committee of Inquiry into Higher Education (NCIHE) 1997a: 3)

Indeed, the Dearing Committee had been established before the 1997 election, in an agreement between the then Conservative government and the Labour opposition, at least in part to remove the issue of higher education funding from the election campaign. Higher education funding (and particularly student funding) was, necessarily, a key issue as all major parties were supportive of the policy of further widening participation.

The Dearing Report started, like the Robbins Report, by considering the main purposes of higher education, which it defined – rather similarly, but in more up-to-date and wordy language – as:

- to inspire and enable individuals to develop their capabilities to the highest potential levels throughout life, so that they grow intellectually, are well-equipped for work, can contribute effectively to society and achieve personal fulfilment;
- to increase knowledge and understanding for their own sake and to foster their application to the benefit of the economy and society;
- to serve the needs of an adaptable, sustainable, knowledge-based economy at local, regional and national levels;
- to play a major role in shaping a democratic, civilised, inclusive society. (NCIHE 1997a: 72)

The report went on to consider many of the same kinds of issue that Robbins had focused on, including demand, participation, learning, research, staff, institutions and management. But the final third of the main report was devoted to a close analysis of the key issue of funding. Dearing's argument on funding proceeds in four stages. First, the case is made that higher education is underfunded:

We are particularly concerned about planned further reductions in the unit of funding for higher education. If these are carried forward, it will have been halved in 25 years . . . In summary, over the last 20 years: the number of students has much more than doubled; public funding for higher education has increased in real terms by 45%; the unit of funding per student has fallen by 40%; public spending on higher education, as a percentage of gross domestic product, has stayed the same. (NCIHE 1997b: 3, 11)

Second, it is recognized that the costs of higher education are already shared:

The taxpayer meets a large part of the costs through grants to universities and colleges and through support to individual students. Individual students may pay part or all of their own tuition costs if they are studying part-time or at postgraduate level, and employers may pay their employees' fees or allow them paid leave to pursue higher education. Students . . . may, over time, repay loans for their living costs. Commercial and public sector bodies may pay for contract research, consultancy or other specific services from higher education. (NCIHE 1997a: 85)

Third, if the deficit in higher education funding is to be made good, the need for new sources of funding, or at least a rearrangement in the shares of funding provided by the different parties, is clear. The shift is to be away from public and towards private sources. However, a market solution is not proposed; rather, the need for continuing state oversight is argued:

Firms and individuals are most likely to engage primarily in training specific to their immediate needs. There is therefore a danger that, if left to employers or individuals, the nature and level of higher education will not best serve the long term needs of the economy as a whole; and there will be under-investment. The state alone is able to ensure that tomorrow's workforce is equipped with the widest range of skills and attributes. (NCIHE 1997a: 288)

Fourth, and finally, within this framework, the solution to the funding problem is presented: shift a greater proportion of the increasing costs onto the students:

The costs of higher education should be shared among those who benefit from it. We have concluded that those with higher education qualifications are the main beneficiaries, through improved employment prospects and pay. As a consequence, we suggest that graduates

. in work should make a greater contribution to the costs of higher education in future. (NCIHE 1997b: 28–9)

The Dearing Report had plenty to say on matters other than student funding, though that was its key focus. There were many detailed recommendations designed to encourage further recruitment of students from disadvantaged groups, and better preparation of students for their subsequent working lives, to broaden the work of the Quality Assurance Agency, and exploit developing information and communication technologies. Attention was also given to the training of academics, the future funding of research, institutional governing bodies and institutional titles.

Responses to Dearing

So how is the HE system in the UK to be depicted in 1997? An optimistic assessment would point to a much enlarged and diversified system which is in comparison with most systems notably cost-effective, with relatively short study periods, low drop-out rates, high levels of graduate output, and a popular choice for foreign students who generate substantial earnings. A more critical evaluation would describe a system, mass in size but still elite in its values, crowded and under-funded, largely traditional in its pedagogy, with staff untrained in effective learning, senior management unskilled in introducing change and with too many of the pre-1992 universities espousing a culture unsympathetic to non-traditional groups. Both portrayals are caricatures, of course, but both also contain elements of welcome as well as disturbing accuracy. (Coffield and Vignoles 1997: 5)

While the higher education system was far larger in 1997 than it had been at the time of the Robbins Report in 1963, and a much greater proportion of the population had direct or indirect experience of it, the Dearing Report, in some ways, still had a lesser impact. Like the Robbins Report, Dearing was replete with appendices and commissioned research, but it had more of the feel of a rushed job, and it did not come across so readily as an authoritative contemporary statement on the condition of higher education (perhaps because it was neither chaired by an academic, nor was its membership dominated by academics). And Dearing was, of course, much more focused on a single issue of political concern; that is, what to do about student funding.

In the event, the Labour government, which was in office by the time that Dearing reported, opted for a somewhat different student funding model than that recommended (Department for Education and Employment 1998a, 1998b; Wagner 1998), and there has been quite a bit of further tinkering done since. The Dearing Report had, nevertheless, done its job, in serving to legitimate one of the most significant higher education policy changes in the post-war period. The Anderson Report of 1960 (Ministry of Education 1960), which itself had been a milestone in establishing the principle of mandatory grants for undergraduate students, was finally undone.

The 2000s

As their cooperation over the establishment of the Dearing Committee indicated, the higher education policies of the new Labour government and its predecessor were not radically different. The early years of the twenty-first century, like the 1970s, have, therefore, been largely a period of consolidation (and tweaking) of policy and practice after a time of significant change.

The 2003 White Paper, *The Future of Higher Education* (Department for Education and Skills 2003) announced above-inflation increases in funding for higher education, both for institutions and students (with the reintroduction of grants for those from lower-income families). Maintaining international competitiveness, further enhancing quality of provision, collaboration at all levels, and continuing to expand access were key themes. The government's vision for higher education was described in the following terms:

> We see a higher education sector which meets the needs of the economy in terms of trained people, research and technology transfer. At the
> · same time it needs to enable all suitably qualified individuals to develop their potential both intellectually and personally, and to provide the necessary storehouse of expertise in science and technology, and the arts and humanities which defines our civilisation and culture.
> (Department for Education and Skills 2003: 21)

Note the continuing echo of Robbins in the use of 'suitably qualified', the rather old-fashioned notion of a 'storehouse of expertise', and the way in which 'the arts and humanities' are tagged on at the end almost as an afterthought. The reference to technology transfer, by contrast, highlights the continuing concern with engaging higher education with industry, by now known as the 'third mission' (Lambert 2003; see also Chapter 6).

Quality continued to be a concern in the first decade of the twenty-first century, but in a much less overweening fashion:

> Over the past eight years, there has been a comprehensive programme of external peer review at subject level, covering all main subject areas in all higher education institutions in England. That programme was completed in December 2001. It demonstrated that, in general, the quality of higher education programmes is very high, with only a small minority of programmes found to be failing or in need of substantial improvement . . . We are now therefore in a position where the future quality assurance approach can be much more selective. It can rely more than previously on internal HEI [higher education institution]

quality procedures. (Quality Assurance Agency for Higher Education 2002: 1)

Audit was henceforth to be 'lighter touch' and to focus at the institutional level. All of the resource – largely the time of academic and administrative staff – that had been invested in meeting the requirements of quality audits had, in effect, been largely wasted. The research assessment exercise continued, however, with two further RAEs administered in 2001 and 2008. Here again, though, the future seems to promise less demanding and time-consuming forms of assessment, with plans to make more use of 'metrics' – that is, existing quantitative data on research funding, publication citation rates, and the like – alongside more limited panel assessments.

One frequently overlooked aspect of the 2000s has been the continued expansion in the number of recognized universities. Up until the present time, 16 new universities had been recognized, typically former colleges of education based in smaller cities and towns, which had diversified their provision and grown significantly since the traumas of the 1970s.

Another aspect of the new century has been the growing impact of the devolved governments in Scotland and Wales on higher education (currently the devolved Northern Ireland government had not had much time to make much impact). The Scottish Executive (2003, 2004) emphasized a shared commitment to 'responsiveness, relevance, quality and coherence' among policy makers, the funding agency and the 20 Scottish higher education institutions. The Welsh Assembly Government (2002), promoting Wales as the 'learning country', sought to emphasize diversity and networks in the provision of higher education.

Both devolved governments, however, continued to contextualize their achievements, and to seek to differentiate their policies (notably as regards student funding), by comparison with England. Thus, the Scottish Executive identified that: 'The key perceived competitive threat to Scotland is legislation to change the system of university funding, contained in the UK Government's Higher Education Bill' (Scottish Executive 2004: 9). How well distinctly different systems will thrive, and further develop, in Scotland, Wales and Northern Ireland is an interesting question for the future. England, of course, has the key advantage of size, and therefore the greater ability to maintain one or more 'world class' universities.

Conclusions

The concluding section of this chapter will attempt to, albeit briefly, do two things. First, a comparative assessment of the orientations and achievements of the two major national reports on higher education in the post-war period – Robbins and Dearing – will be attempted. Second, an overview of the state of play at the time of writing (i.e. the early twenty-first century) will be offered.

Robbins and Dearing compared

Not surprisingly, as the two key national reports on British higher education produced during the post-war period, the Robbins and Dearing Reports have been the subject of comparative analyses before. For example, Barnett produced an analysis focusing on how the reports addressed a range of issues – student participation and access, international contexts, quality and standards, curricula, teaching and academic freedom – noting that:

> In relation to their intended positioning of higher education, Robbins conveys a sense of higher education somewhat external to the wider society . . . For Dearing, on the other hand, higher education should be much more integrated with the wider society, especially the economy, than it has been. (Barnett 1999: 296)

Barnett also usefully draws a distinction between the perceived purposes and intended audiences of the two reports:

> I . . . suggest that we should understand the Robbins Report as the view of the academic community – of its age – speaking largely to government with, accordingly, an agenda of the academic community. We should, in turn, see the Dearing Report as a more complex text speaking to multiple audiences and carrying multiple agendas, crucial amongst which is that arising from the emergence of 'the global age'. (Barnett 1999: 293–4)

The 34 years that passed between the publication of the Robbins and Dearing Reports undoubtedly witnessed a major change in perceptions of the roles of higher education. Thus, Robbins, appearing in the guise of the guardian of the values of a small, but developing, higher education sector, presents universities as independent but, by right, publicly funded, organizations. Dearing was charged with sorting out the funding of a much expanded higher education sector, and took a perspective as much from the outside as from within the university. It saw the universities as much more subject to central oversight, given the demands they made on public funds, but as needing to increase the amount and proportion of funding they received from students and other sources.

Where are we now?

Very different perceptions of the development of higher education in the UK since the Second World War may be, and have been, offered. The most conventional approach is simply to record the expansion that the system has undergone over the period, as in this recent comment:

> The expansion has not been evenly paced. It was rapid between 1960–1961 and 1972–1973 – from 5% to a peak of nearly 14% [age

participation index]. Thereafter the participation rate changed little until a sustained rise started in the early 1980s. By 1988–1989 it had reached 17%. In the subsequent four years the rate shot up to 30%. The index peaked at 34% in 1997–1998, but since then has altered little, standing at 33% in 2000–01 ... The expansion of the 1960s, which occurred before and after the publication of the Robbins Report, was met in large part by an increase in the number of universities ... This expansion was well funded. The second rapid expansion coincided with the end of the binary divide between polytechnics and universities, though there was also internal growth within individual institutions, particularly the ex-polytechnics. It was this second wave of developments that resulted in Britain acquiring what might be called a mass higher education system. In comparison to the expansion of the 1960s, it was not well funded. (Mayhew et al. 2004: 65–6)

Note that an element of policy critique creeps in here towards the end, as the more recent expansion is contrasted unfavourably with the earlier period in terms of funding.

An alternative, and also popular, approach – at least among academic commentators – is to regret what has been lost in terms of academic power and influence (rather than just funding), and the shift towards greater and greater state interference in the operation of higher education, as in this example:

After decades of incremental progress, the state has acquired powers which mark a qualitative shift in its relationship with the institutions of higher education. It is now in the position to orchestrate change on a scale and in a manner which knows no precedent. (Salter and Tapper 1994: 1)

A third evaluation of the post-war development of higher education in essence combines these two themes, of expansion and loss, and argues that there is 'unfinished business' that the system still has to accommodate itself to:

The transformation of British higher education during the past two decades has been intense, but remains curiously incomplete. The number of universities has doubled; they have become large and complex organisations; and they have taken on new roles. The number of students has quadrupled; as a result, novel academic programmes, course structures and learning strategies have been developed. The proportion of young people going on to higher education has risen from fewer than one in ten to almost a third ... Yet, despite these rapid and radical changes in the 'public life' of higher education, the rhythms of its 'private life' are less regular. In its broad cultural intentions there seems to be an underlying continuity. Many universities and colleges still embrace notions of education, rooted in subtle and stealthy socialisation and acculturation rather than explicit intellectual formation and skills development, which are recognisably elitist. (Scott 1995: 1–2)

In other words, while the system may have moved from catering for the elite to involving the mass of the population, there are still many working within it who harbour or practise elite attitudes. The system is not uniform or standardized – an issue that forms the focus for the following chapter – but diverse and hierarchical, with an elite sub-system within it.

While there can, of course, be no such thing as a balanced perspective on such a potentially emotive question as 'where are we now?', it is perhaps, then, most realistic to view the post-war period in UK higher education simultaneously as a time of both great achievement (for the greater number) and great loss (for a lesser number). One interesting issue would be just who the lesser number who have lost are: almost certainly not those in the most elite institutions.

But the most interesting question, perhaps, is whether the former gain could have been achieved without the latter loss. In other words, could the higher education sector have been expanded to the extent that it has been with no loss in academic sovereignty or the higher education experience? I would suggest that the answer is probably 'no', as well as doubting that the general public would have been prepared to bear the additional costs of doing so for very long.

5

Institutions: continuing diversity?

Introduction

The tables in Chapter 3 and the discussion in Chapter 4 both indicate that the post-war period has witnessed a continuing, if periodic, expansion of the UK higher education system through the creation and/or incorporation of successive waves of new universities (and new institutions of higher education more broadly). Thus, we have seen:

- the recognition of the remaining 'new civic' university colleges as universities in the 1940s and 1950s;
- the creation of the 'campus' universities in the early 1960s;
- the incorporation within the university sector of the former colleges of advanced technology in the late 1960s;
- the creation of the polytechnics, and the binary system of universities and 'public sector' institutions of higher education, in the late 1960s and early 1970s;
- the end of the binary divide, and the re-designation of the former polytechnics and some larger colleges as universities in the early 1990s;
- the recognition of the remaining larger colleges of higher education as universities in the 2000s.

Alongside these major trends, additional new universities have occasionally been created through the division or amalgamation of existing institutions, and a number of 'odd' or unusual universities have been established. Existing universities have also been enlarged by the absorption of activities, mostly notably teacher and nurse education, formerly undertaken in other institutions. In this way, the UK higher education system has expanded from a total of just 17 universities immediately after the war to 106 in 2007 (note that this figure counts the federal universities of London and Wales as just one each).

This chapter considers each of these successive institutional developments, in addition to, more briefly, the continuing development of those institutions that were already in existence in 1945 (see also Chapter 2). Attention is also given to the small, specialist colleges that still exist within the system, and to the different institutional patterns that are, and have been, evident in the component parts of the UK. Finally, the issue of institutional diversity itself – long held to be an essential and defining characteristic of the UK higher education system – is critically addressed.

Universities already in existence in 1945

The ancient universities

> Oxford and Cambridge are thought of spontaneously when universities are mentioned. If a young man, talking to an educated stranger, refers to his university studies, he is asked 'Oxford or Cambridge?' And if he says Aberystwyth or Nottingham, there is disappointment on the one side and embarrassment on the other. It has always been that way. (Shils 1955: 11–12)

The medieval English foundations of Oxford and Cambridge, and the slightly later Scottish establishments at St Andrews, Glasgow, Aberdeen and Edinburgh, loomed large on the British university landscape in 1945. Not only was this literally the case – leaving aside the complex federal structure of London, the universities of Cambridge, Oxford, Glasgow and Edinburgh were by some distance the largest in the country – but it also applied to the influence they wielded throughout society:

> Oxford and Cambridge have provided 87 per cent of permanent sec-retaries, 72 per cent of the cabinet, nearly 40 per cent of members of parliament, and 71 per cent of the vice-chancellors of other universities. In 1959 Oxford and Cambridge provided all but one of the successful candidates (by examination and interview) for the Senior Civil Service and Foreign Service. The 18,000 students of Oxbridge make up, from the outside, at least, one of the most elite elites in the world. (Sampson 1962: 198)

Perhaps unsurprisingly, given their elite position, Oxford and Cambridge remained relatively slow in adapting to the demands of the modern world:

> Oxford and Cambridge had one great peculiarity still in the 1960s: they were male universities. There were indeed distinguished colleges of women attached to them; and since 1948 Cambridge had recognised that the women were full members of the university . . . [yet] in Oxford and Cambridge . . . a woman applicant had only a one in ten chance against a man. Furthermore, they were still in large measure segregated. (Brooke 1993: 527)

While Oxford and Cambridge are nowhere near as numerically dominant within the university system today as they were in 1945, and have now fully opened their doors to women as well as men students, their influence remains strong. Leading politicians, civil servants and academics are still more likely to have studied at Oxbridge than any other university, Oxford and Cambridge are typically the first two universities in any meaningful contemporary university league table, and Oxbridge remains at the core of the English idea of a university (see Chapter 12).

The ancient Scottish universities were in some ways in an even more dominant position within Scotland immediately after the war. For, while Oxford and Cambridge between them accounted for about one-quarter of the students in English universities at this time, in Scotland higher education provision remained largely the business of the ancient universities, with Glasgow and Edinburgh alone enrolling about two-thirds of the total students (University Grants Committee 1958: 82). The Scottish universities also differed in having a narrower recruitment focus: 'Except for St Andrews, the vast majority of students at Scottish universities were native Scots' (Scotland 1969b: 249).

This tendency is exacerbated by the differences between the Scottish and English educational systems, and has, if anything, been increased by recent Scottish devolution. Given the relatively small size of the Scottish system of higher education, the universities of Glasgow and Edinburgh, in particular, still loom large, accounting for nearly one-quarter of all students in Scotland (though the University of Strathclyde has now become the largest Scottish university in these terms: www.hesa.ac.uk).

The universities of London and Wales

The two federal universities that remain to this day, London and Wales, formed major parts of the UK higher education system by 1945. London, a complex set of institutions in and around the capital city, became the largest university in the country in 1908, exerting a major influence on higher education both in the UK and overseas. The University of Wales, for its part, while rather smaller and not quite so complex, has continued to dominate the higher education landscape in the principality.

A major trend in the internal organization of the University of London in the post-war period has been to shift power from the federal university towards the major constituent colleges (somewhat confusingly termed 'schools'). Thus, as a result of a review set in train after the Robbins Committee had reported in 1963:

> A number of important changes resulted. In various ways the Schools were given more control over their own teaching arrangements. 'School-based' degree syllabuses were approved. There had already been some moves in this direction, and in the Faculty of Science a new degree structure based on 'course units' was introduced [cf. the much

more recent and widespread moves nationally towards modularisation].
(Harte 1986: 264)

The same issues of greater school autonomy, as well as the – somewhat
contradictory – need to strengthen the central operation of the university
were returned to in the 1970s by the Murray Committee (Committee of
Enquiry into the Governance of the University of London 1972), and, in the
1980s, by the Swinnerton–Dyer Committee. Since then, the trend towards
greater independence for the schools has continued, with Imperial College
finally severing its links in time for its centenary celebrations in 2007, after
many years of receiving its grant separate from the rest of the university.

All through this period, the scale of operations of the university and its
colleges was expanding, for much of the time faster than in the nation as
a whole:

> The University of London underwent a boom that made the develop-
> ment of the new universities elsewhere in the country look small-scale
> . . . All constituent parts of the University grew. University College,
> King's College and Imperial College in particular remained bigger in
> themselves than many of the provincial universities. (Harte 1986: 269)

Thus, the numbers of internal students doubled from 26,762 in 1960–1 to
51,965 in 1984–5 (p. 269). In the 1980s, the amalgamations of Bedford and
Royal Holloway Colleges, and of Queen Mary and Westfield Colleges, turned
them into substantial higher education institutions alongside University,
King's and Imperial Colleges. At the same time, Chelsea (a former polytechnic, and then a college of advanced technology) and Queen Elizabeth
Colleges joined up with King's.

The University of London initially went to great lengths to sustain and
develop its external study system after the Second World War (Bell and Tight
1993). In its evidence to the Robbins Committee, the university identified
three phases of post-war expansion: a rapid growth between 1945 and 1952,
from 11,000 to 29,000 students registered, in response to the immediate
post-war demand; a slight decline between 1953 and 1957, caused by the
introduction of higher entry standards, the demise of the intermediate
degree examination, and the independence of the remaining English university colleges; and an upward trend thereafter, though with rising failure
rates (Committee on Higher Education 1963d, evidence 1237).

Throughout this period, the University itself only made limited support
available for its external students – through the Commerce Degree Bureau
and a more general advisory service, and latterly through an independent
guided study system. UK-based students could either register with the
University as independent students, perhaps following a course provided
by a correspondence college, or enrol to study for the University's degrees
at one of the university colleges, polytechnics or technical colleges that
taught their syllabuses. This role went into decline after the creation of
the CNAA in 1964, but, even as late as 1976, there were still 6230 London

external candidates studying at polytechnics and colleges. Until 1970, the University of London, along with a number of other UK universities, also played a major role in developing universities in the former British Empire (see Chapter 6 for further discussion).

External registrations peaked again in 1969/70 at 35,198 students, after which another decline set in. The university seemed to doubt that there was a continued need for this service, with the growth in the number of independent higher education institutions in the UK, the creation of the Open University to serve students who could not attend institutions, and the end of the Empire. More recently, however, the external system has begun to revive: 36,759 students were registered in 2003/4, mostly now overseas, and mostly studying law, computing or management (Jones 2008; Tight 2005).

The University of Wales, while smaller than London, has been much more dominant within the Welsh higher education system than the University of London is, even within the London area. Indeed, for many years the University of Wales was effectively Welsh higher education. It has, however, experienced similar post-war trends to the University of London, with growth being matched by increasing demands for autonomy from the main component colleges (Pritchard 1994).

Thus, University College Cardiff, despite having been forcibly combined with the University of Wales Institute of Science and Technology (UWIST) to overcome its financial management problems as recently as 1988 (Shattock 1988), left the university in 2004 in order to assume the title of the University of Cardiff on combining again with another Welsh institution, the College of Medicine. It remains to be seen how the University of Wales will fare with the leading Welsh higher education institution now outside the federation.

The 'old civic' universities

The 'old civic' or 'redbrick' universities – Birmingham, Bristol, Leeds, Liverpool, Manchester and Sheffield – founded in the latter part of the nineteenth century, were all reasonably substantial institutions, at least by the standards of the time, at the start of the post-war period (Noble 1956). Including Durham, which then still incorporated what was later to become Newcastle University, they together enrolled about one-third of the students in the English university system. While they were, therefore, both established and successful, their position in the institutional hierarchy was clear:

> The division between Oxbridge and Redbrick . . . is essentially a class one. While 50 per cent of Oxbridge undergraduates come from public schools, less than 10 per cent of Redbrick do: many public school boys would rather go straight into business, into the services or to a foreign university like McGill, Grenoble or Harvard, than go to a Redbrick university: they prefer no degree to a Redbrick degree. (Sampson 1962: 206)

Such preferences, however, and the civic universities' relative position in the institutional pecking order, were to change as more and different universities and colleges were founded. Excluding London and the Open universities, the old civic universities now rank, alongside the former polytechnics in the same cities, as the largest universities in the country. Indeed, the re-amalgamation of the University of Manchester with the University of Manchester Institute of Science and Technology (or UMIST as it was more popularly known) in 2004 – after their separation in 1955 – created the largest conventional university in the country, with an enrolment currently close to 40,000 students.

The 'new civic' universities

The 1950s saw the 'new civic' universities – Exeter, Hull, Leicester, Nottingham, Reading and Southampton – which were set up as university colleges in the first half of the twentieth century, and which had taught their students for University of London external degrees, all finally recognized as independent universities in their own right. At the beginning of the post-war period, though, they remained relatively small, with a typical enrolment of only about 1000 students each.

Following their recognition came that for three other universities in the 1960s, two at least of which are commonly thought of as civic universities. Keele, which had only been established in 1949, and underwent a period of sponsorship by the universities of Birmingham, Manchester and Oxford, received its charter in 1962. In character, however, it is more what might be called a proto-campus university. Both Newcastle, which separated from Durham in 1963, and Strathclyde, which parted from Glasgow in 1964, are much more clearly civic in their nature.

While much greater expansion was to come, the UGC could, therefore, look back on the 1950s and early 1960s as a period of considerable development:

> The last ten years have seen the addition of 14 new universities to our grant list. Seven of these were evolved from existing institutions. Five were university colleges which were granted their Charters as fully autonomous institutions – Southampton (1952), Hull (1954), Exeter (1955), and Leicester (1957). The University College of North Staffordshire became the University of Keele in 1962. In 1963 the federal University of Durham resolved into two separate parts and the University of Newcastle upon Tyne came into existence. In the same year the Royal College of Science and Technology, Glasgow, in which students followed courses for degrees of the University of Glasgow, was authorised to apply to the Privy Council for a Charter as a fully autonomous institution. (University Grants Committee 1964a: 90)

The campus universities

The creation of the campus or 'plateglass' universities in the 1960s and 1970s really began to shake up the institutional hierarchy:

> . . . the post-1960 'Plateglass' universities, the first to seriously challenge the social supremacy of Oxbridge, were closer in many ways to the ancient than to the Victorian foundations. Despite their self-conscious modernity, largely expressed in a great emphasis on the social sciences, they by and large shared Oxbridge's lack of interest in technology and business. The 'Plateglass' universities, significantly, were located away from large centers of population, in the cathedral town–country estate setting that had become typical of elite schools. In these cases, physical form followed social and psychological function – the embodiment of an ideal of 'civilization' bound up with preindustrial, preurban models – forming an amalgam of an idealized medieval church and a similarly idealized eighteenth-century aristocracy. (Wiener 1981: 23)

Unlike the 'new civic' universities, the nine campus universities were not formed from pre-existing institutions, which had undergone an apprenticeship to an older university for a period before they were enabled to award their own degrees. Instead, in a reversal of existing policy and practice – and one which would still be unprecedented but for the creation of the Open University in the same way a few years later – they were established from the early 1960s as fully fledged universities from scratch. Seven were located in England, and one each in Scotland and Northern Ireland.

The UGC was responsible for setting the parameters for the campus universities, and for selecting which of the many proposals advanced to proceed with:

> We . . . gave careful thought to the minimum size for a university site. It should, if possible, provide space within its limits for all university activities. If, as we were prepared to advise, these new universities were to accommodate not less than 3,000 students, and some might even rise to 7,000 or 8,000, an initial site of not less than 200 acres was desirable. (UGC 1964a: 99)

The UGC also stressed the importance of local interest and enthusiasm, the presence of industries in the area to provide 'a useful association', a supply of local lodgings and the necessity of 'the attractiveness of the area to academic staff' (p. 99).

While the creation of the campus universities may have owed something to the optimism of the times (Sandbrook 2006), it was mostly a particular form of response to a generally accepted need for the expansion of university education (see Chapter 4). While there were those, including members of the Robbins Committee (Committee on Higher Education 1963a), who argued in favour of the expansion of existing universities in the large cities – which happened as well anyway – an alternative view held sway in this instance.

Why these new foundations were located in (or, rather, on the edges of) smaller, attractive cathedral cities and country towns – Brighton, Canterbury, Colchester, Coleraine, Coventry, Lancaster, Norwich, Stirling and York – is, however, a matter of some debate. There are those who have argued that this is just the way it happened to work out, given the options that were presented at the time to the UGC, and the criteria they used in reaching their decisions:

> It was, though, no nostalgic impulse that prompted the UGC's choice of sites. Indeed, once regional considerations had been taken into account, it was almost fortuitous that new universities were planted in cathedral cities. The University of East Anglia could have been at Bury St Edmunds, not Norwich. Lancaster could have been at Blackpool, Kent at Folkestone or Margate, Warwick at Cheltenham, Worcester or Gloucester, Essex at Chelmsford or Clacton . . . Cost-effectiveness rather than a sense of history dominated the argument. The new universities needed at least two hundred acres apiece if they were to have integrated campuses with a potential for expansion in future decades . . . A good supply of accommodation was another necessity. (Beloff 1968: 28–9)

Interestingly, some of the alternative sites listed by Beloff, including Bury St Edmunds, Worcester and Gloucester, were also cathedral cities; while the seaside resorts of Blackpool, Margate and Clacton would have certainly had a 'good supply of accommodation' outside the summer holiday season (rather more than there was at Lancaster or Colchester). A number of these sites – Worcester, Gloucester and Chelmsford – have also, more recently, become hosts to universities. But the point is that Lancaster was chosen at the time rather than Blackpool, and Canterbury rather than Folkestone, adding to the attraction of the new universities for both staff and students, and enabling the almost immediate continuation of an old-fashioned, and very English, university tradition (see also Chapter 12):

> It says much for the power of a particular model of university life within England, deeply influenced by Oxbridge, that the seven [English] proposals which did emerge as the basis of new universities during the 1960s all resulted in semi-rural campuses associated with townships which were remarkable as much for their historical associations as for their links with British industry. (Lowe 1988: 162; see also Cross and Jobling 1969; Marks 2005)

The two characteristics of the campus universities that attracted most attention at the time were their perceived insularity or isolation and, more particularly, their apparent innovativeness.

The former could be a problem:

> At Warwick, Essex and East Anglia the physical separation of town and gown has at times been matched by social distance, lack of mutual understanding, and on occasion open hostility – especially when

university 'radicals' have been seen to be 'outsiders' interfering in 'local affairs'. (Jobling 1972: 331)

This 'difference' was particularly strong in the late 1960s and early 1970s, the period of student revolt, but some resentments still linger, especially – as in the cases of Canterbury and Lancaster – when the local economy and social life is so dependent on the student population.

The latter was seen as a 'breath of fresh air' when compared to the stuffy traditions of the existing universities: 'Easily the most important character-istic of the New Universities is their readiness to experiment with what is taught, in what combinations, and with different methods of teaching and assessment' (Perkin, 1969b: 30).

Innovation was evident in their architectural form (Birks and Holford 1972; Edwards 2000; Muthesius 2000) as well as their internal organization and curricula. Some of the campus universities (e.g. Kent, Lancaster) were organized in terms of a series of colleges, like Oxford and Cambridge (and Durham), hoping to develop within themselves a series of smaller, inter-disciplinary communities. Some (e.g. Sussex: as Keele had previously attempted) dispensed with the conventional departmental/disciplinary form of organization, preferring to establish schools that covered a broader subject area and demanded of students a more general engagement. New disciplines and degrees were also pioneered, particularly in the social sciences.

Forty years on, while the campus form and relative isolation of these universities remains largely intact, many of their innovations have been steadily unpicked, as more conventional forms of organization and competi-tion with the older universities have taken hold. A more recent evaluation of the achievements of the campus universities would, therefore, also be more measured:

> The New Universities were an ambitious attempt to shake up English higher education, to make a new start away from the elitism, narrow academicism and conservatism of the old university system, to stake out intellectual territory closer to the needs of mass higher education in a rapidly changing, high-tech world. They caught a tide of faith in the miraculous powers of higher education to produce economic growth and solve social problems not only in Britain but in the world at large. When the tide ebbed, through disappointment with the promise of instant economic growth and the 'ingratitude' of student unrest, the backlash against the New Universities took the form of a myth: they were, it seemed, the opposite of their dream, a nostalgic retreat into the pro-verbial ivory tower. Finally, they were seen, for better or worse, to be harbingers of the 'enterprise culture' of the 1980s. (Perkin 1991: 294–5)

An examination of contemporary university league tables would, however, typically show a number of the campus universities in the 'top 20' UK institu-tions, challenging older institutions as attractive alternatives for students, particularly in their subject specialisms. The campus universities have succeeded, therefore, in shaking up the university hierarchy; indeed, they have played a major role in helping to establish a system of higher education in the UK. Arguably, though, a more significant role was played by the colleges of advanced technology and, especially, the polytechnics.

The colleges of advanced technology

> In the Beginning was the Mechanics Institute . . . and the Mechanics Institute begat the Bradford Technical School and the Bradford Technical School begat the Bradford Technical College. The Bradford Technical College had dual offspring – the Bradford College of Art and Technology and the Bradford Institute of Technology. The Bradford College of Art and Technology begat Bradford College which grew mighty in stature and became the Bradford and Ilkley Community College . . . but from the Bradford Institute of Technology issued forth the UNIVERSITY OF BRADFORD. (McKinlay 1991: 3 emphasis in original)

The story of the 11 Colleges of Advanced Technology (CATs) is a brief one, lasting little more than a decade. There is, though, a continuing postscript, as all but two of them went on to become independent universities – these two, Cardiff (as UWIST, the University of Wales Institute of Science and Technology) and Chelsea, became parts of the federal universities of Wales and London respectively, and later amalgamated with University College Cardiff and King's College London – forming the so-called technological universities group. And there is also a pre-history, as the quotation opening this section makes clear, as most could trace their origins to the technical education movement in the nineteenth century:

> With the exception of Brunel, which began as Acton Technical College in 1928, the Technological Universities stem from part-time classes which started in the nineteenth century, and the earliest of the technological institutions derive from the Mechanics' Institutes originating in the period 1820–35. (Venables 1978: 15)

The story of the CATs is the story of one of those repeated attempts – see also the discussion of the polytechnics in the next section – to establish technical education on a similar footing to academic university education. In this case, it was the White Paper on *Technical Education* published in 1956 (Ministry of Education 1956) that paved the way for a reorganization of the technical education system, including the recognition of the CATs: nine of them in England, and one each in Wales and Scotland (Heriot–Watt in Edinburgh):

> Early in 1957 the Minister designated the following as colleges of advanced technology: Birmingham College of Technology; Bradford

Institute of Technology; Loughborough College of Technology; the Royal Technical College, Salford; Battersea College of Technology; Chelsea College of Science and Technology; Northampton College of Advanced Technology (London); and the Welsh College of Advanced Technology, Cardiff. Bristol was added in 1960, and Brunel College (Acton) a little later. In 1961 it was announced that all the CATs were to be direct-grant establishments (under the Minister of Education) with independent governing bodies. (Argles 1964: 109)

While, at the time, the details of the policy were the subject of some critique, the underlying aim to create a national system of technical higher education was clear:

At first sight, the geographical distribution of the ten colleges seems arbitrary. There is a concentration of four in the London area (Battersea, Chelsea, Northampton and Brunel). There are two in the Midlands (Birmingham and Loughborough), and two in the North Midlands (Bradford and Salford). The other two are in the South-West (Bristol and Cardiff). Large and industrially important areas such as the North-East of England contain no CAT, despite the existence of colleges well qualified for the status. With these exceptions, however, the allocation of advanced college status represents an attempt to encourage higher technological education in the parts of England and Wales most likely to benefit from it. Separate provision is made for Scotland and Northern Ireland. (Buchanan 1966: 71)

In one sense, the CATs experiment – if it can be called an experiment – failed, while in another it succeeded. It failed because the CATs gave less emphasis to the lower-level and part-time work they had been renowned for before their designation, and more to degree-level study and above, full-time education and non-technical education. And this transition happened rapidly: 'nobody in 1956 thought of the CATs as becoming universities. Yet by 1962 this transformation was largely thought to be inevitable, and it was complete by 1966' (Burgess and Pratt 1970: 172).

Conversely, the CATs experiment succeeded in that it gave renewed emphasis to technical studies in higher education, and embedded the sandwich principle (discussed further in Chapter 7) of course organization within the system. At the time, though, some of the judgements involved appeared to have been made more on political than academic grounds:

No tests of academic quality or potential were applied to the Colleges of Advanced Technology, which, in 1963, were in widely different stages of development from their technical college past, to decide which should be granted university status as recommended by Robbins. The decision to transfer them from the public to the university sector was taken *en bloc*; yet, if even the tests applied to the colleges of education after the 1972 White Paper regarding location, relative size and proximity to other higher education institutions had been applied, some choices would have had to be made. (Shattock 1994: 9)

One particularly interesting aspect of the CATs story is that it involves three of the limited number of post-war examples of institutional migration, in each case to enable subsequent expansion on a single site:

The move from Battersea to the site of the University of Surrey at Guildford took two long years. For the Bristol College there was the abortive plan to move from Ashley Down to King's Weston in Bristol, partially begun in 1960, but abandoned after an invitation had been received to become the University of Bath, a move which was finally completed in 1975 with the transference there of management studies. Brunel's move from Acton to Uxbridge/Hillingdon took three years, having been extended distressingly by bitter labour disputes. (Venables 1978: 39)

In the first two of these cases, the universities of Bath and Surrey, the resultant institutions, while maintaining their emphases on science and technology, assumed more of the locational and residential characteristics of the campus universities.

The polytechnics

The fourth main wave of post-war expansion of higher education institutions in the UK was, and is, arguably the most significant. The creation of the polytechnics was the second major post-war attempt, after that of the CATs, to address the nation's needs for higher-level technical and vocational education. The so-called binary policy, spelt out in the speeches given in the mid-1960s at Woolwich and Lancaster by the then Minister of Education, Anthony Crosland, was intended to establish, alongside the existing university sector, a polytechnic sector of similar size and status (see also Chapter 4).

The White Paper that formalized this policy was remarkably thin on detail (Department of Education and Science 1966). It amounted to little more than a list of the 29 new institutions it was then proposed to establish from existing colleges of technology, art and commerce (most subsequently also absorbed colleges of education) – 28 in England and one in Wales – with a brief covering note. In the London area, the existing polytechnics, founded from the nineteenth century onwards, were to be incorporated in this new national system.

However, if it was short on detail, the impact of the White Paper, and the policy it adumbrated, was to be immense: 'Thirty polytechnics are to be formed by the amalgamation of some 68 colleges including 36 polytechnics and colleges of technology, 18 colleges of art, 10 colleges of commerce and four specialist colleges' (Robinson 1968: 92). With a much larger number of institutions being (re-)designated, the polytechnic policy had a much wider reach than that of the CATs:

The geographical spread was fair, at least so far as centres of population were concerned. (The north-east, which had failed to get a CAT, got three polytechnics). But there were places where the new polytechnics seemed to be replacing the 'lost' CATs. Manchester (Salford), Birmingham, Bristol, Treforest (Cardiff) and other places where the polytechnics were alongside new universities – Coventry (Warwick) and Brighton (Sussex). (Burgess and Pratt 1971: 91)

While the polytechnics lasted twice as long as the CATs, expanding substantially over the period, evaluations of their success are similarly mixed. Doubts were already being voiced by some at the time of their foundation:

Public debate about the 'binary' system has been confused for three reasons. First, it was never made clear whether the system was considered to be an 'ideal' or an acceptance, largely for economic reasons, of historical fact, involving the 'systematization' of what had hitherto been unsystematic dualism or polycentrism in higher education. Second, the bare economics of the systematization were never clearly set out – relative costs, for example, in universities and polytechnics. Third, the implementation of policy was determined largely by civil servants in discussion with local authorities, and much that was happening was hidden from public view. (Briggs 1969: 106)

Alongside such doubts about the intent of the policy and its cost-effectiveness, the other main line of criticism was similar to that made about the CATs; namely that it would result in 'academic drift', with the polytechnics seeking to become independent universities as quickly as possible:

The spectrum of work in the polytechnics is thus developing from predominantly part-time, both advanced and non-advanced, towards full-time and sandwich advanced, a pattern of growth which is in marked contrast with that of the constituent colleges hitherto . . . We had every reason to suspect that the historical process of aspiration of colleges created specifically to be different from universities would overwhelm their best intentions, and they would increasingly aspire to university status and increasingly resemble university institutions. (Pratt and Burgess 1974: 76, 172)

Donaldson went even further in identifying 'pluralistic drift', arguing that:

The local nature of the polytechnics is limited and declining . . . Close and detailed contact with local industry seems to be decreasing . . . The student body of at least some of the polytechnics is as high in social class composition as is that of the universities . . . The supposedly comprehensive nature of the polytechnics has been called into question. (Donaldson 1975: 199–200)

A later assessment, dating from the time of their demise (all of the poly-technics and several larger colleges were given university status in 1992), recognized the strengths of the policy, and what it brought into higher education more generally:

> The polytechnics opened the way to many developments to which the universities were not, at least at first, hospitable: more open access; part-time degrees; modular curricula; courses which were more formally planned, validated and monitored; a wider range of subjects and a much larger proportion of part-time students. (Becher and Kogan 1992: 31)

Ultimately, one's judgement of whether the polytechnic policy was essen-tially a success or a failure probably depends on one's view of what higher education is for. Thus, while the polytechnics enabled many more people to participate in higher education, they also dramatically changed the nature of the higher education they were participating in. Pratt, the foremost histor-ian of the 'polytechnic experiment', comes to a balanced assessment:

> There is no doubt that in many ways the polytechnic experiment in England and Wales can be regarded as a success . . . The polytechnics maintained and developed the open tradition of the non-university sec-tor and expanded access to new kinds of students . . . There are, how-ever, significant ways in which the policy can be regarded as having failed. The polytechnics did, after all, become universities; in this sense the polytechnics were the most monumental example of 'academic drift' in British education history . . . The polytechnics could also be said to have fulfilled the worst fears of the conservatives and elitists of the 1960s. They came to offer higher education on the cheap, and worse still obliged the universities to follow suit. (Pratt 1997: 306–8)

Booth, by then a former polytechnic director (and university vice-chancellor), not surprisingly, comes up with a more, but still not overwhelmingly, positive verdict:

> I think it is possible to write a 'score card' for the new universities (and the polytechnics which preceded them) which records their successes as follows:
>
> - large and effective institutions developed from very small beginnings which made higher education accessible to a wide range of people
> - introduced a much more varied range of courses appropriate to a more diverse student body
> - opened up new routes into higher education
> - encouraged ethnic minority and mature students to participate
> - introduced advanced study in a wider range of subjects
> - developed new course patterns
> - enabled expansion to take place at affordable cost.
>
> These are remarkable achievements for which the academic and other

staff have received far too little recognition. But there were also short-comings. Parity of esteem – given much prominence by Crosland – was not to be achieved. The idea of a stable pillar of higher education under democratic local government control came to nought. Some institutions suffered excesses of managerialism and a few, failures of governance. Costs may have been driven down too far. And finally, the diversity of the higher education system may have been more difficult to maintain than under the binary system. (Booth 1999: 121–2; see also Robinson 2007)

The role of the former polytechnics in the contemporary UK higher education system is substantial, as they currently recruit a similar number of students to the universities chartered before 1992, with particular emphases on undergraduate, part-time and local (Brown 1972) students. While 'academic drift' has seen the polytechnics become universities, developing a greater interest in postgraduate studies and research, at the same time the older universities have taken on some of the characteristics of the former polytechnics, as they too have adapted to the demands of expanded student numbers.

The colleges of higher (and further) education

In Chapter 2, three streams of non-university higher education were recognized in the pre-war period: the teacher training colleges, the colleges of art and design, and the technical colleges (the work of which was carried out in Scotland by the so-called central institutions). This section focuses on the post-war development of these institutions, providing a further reflection of the trends already noted in the history of other types of higher education institution: that is, on the one hand, pressures for inclusion or amalgamation within the university sector; and, on the other, the continuing need to redevelop both non-advanced and advanced technical, or, as it now became known, further education.

The post-war period has also seen the emergence and increased significance of a fourth stream – the colleges of nursing. This will also be briefly commented upon, though its development seems less well studied to date.

Teacher education

The reasons why the training colleges needed reform – their poverty, isolation and low standards – were, of course, reasons why the universities should regard their proposed responsibility with a somewhat jaundiced eye. (Niblett et al. 1975: 152, referring to the immediate post-war period)

The teacher training college of the 1950s was typically small, single sex, and physically and intellectually isolated – all factors which enhanced its capacity for creating a moral community . . . experiential knowledge was held to be of prime importance. This was a view which legitimated the authority of the staff whose claims to expertise derived, for the most part, from years of successful school teaching experience. (Bell 1981: 5–6)

The place of teacher education within the higher education system, and its relationship with other institutions, has been the subject of much debate, and of varied 'solutions', since the end of the Second World War (as it was before – see Chapter 2). In the period up until the 1970s, it became established as a third sector, alongside the universities and advanced further education (from which both the CATs and the polytechnics, discussed earlier, had sprung). The colleges of education, as they had by then become known, were then subjected to a period of massive upheaval, with many closed, others amalgamated with other institutions, and others set on a course of diversification and expansion that would see them becoming universities in their own right in the early twenty-first century.

Immediately after the Second World War, the relations between teacher training colleges and the universities were formalized:

> After the Education Act 1944 and following the somewhat divided recommendations of the McNair Committee, the teacher training colleges became associated academically with a university through membership of the university Institute of Education normally centred on the University School or Department of Education. The Institute was the basis of the Area Training Organisation through which, for example, the administrative arrangements for training in the schools were made. (Matterson 1981: 45)

The National Advisory Council on the Training and Supply of Teachers (NACTST) was 'set up in 1949 to provide the Minister of Education with the means of obtaining advice on national policy relating to the training, qualification, recruitment and distribution of teachers' (Hicks 1974: 249). It lasted until 1965.

Under this system of guidance, the colleges went through successive curricular developments. Up until 1960, trainee teachers followed a two-year certificate course. This was then extended to three years, with a further year leading to a BEd degree for some, and more emphasis placed on the study of an academic 'main subject' (Bell 1981).

As new universities were established in the 1960s, many of them also began to develop relationships with their local colleges of education:

> At the present time all the universities established up to 1950 have departments of education, one or two of which offer a course that runs concurrently with the undergraduates' degree studies. Of the newer universities – York, Sussex, Essex, East Anglia, Lancaster, Warwick and Kent – not all have yet established such departments. Lancaster and Warwick have entered into special relationships with near-by colleges,

whereby these undertake the graduate training that elsewhere takes place in the university itself. Several of the technological universities have appointed professors of education and are in process of establishing post-graduate courses. (Taylor 1969: 72)

While these colleges typically only had a few hundred students each, there were large numbers of them across the country, and many, though a decreasing proportion, were 'voluntary', religious foundations:

At the beginning of the academic year 1968–9 there were 166 colleges of education in England and Wales, and twenty-eight university departments of education. One hundred and thirteen colleges were provided by local education authorities, twenty-seven by the Church of England and the Church in Wales, seventeen by the Roman Catholic Church, and nine by the Methodists, Free Churches and undenominational bodies. During the post-war period the most notable change in the pattern of organization and control of teacher education has been the increase in the number of local authority colleges, which now constitute 68 per cent of the total, as compared with 29 per cent in 1938. (Taylor 1969: 78)

In response to a sharp increase in the demand for teachers, the late 1960s and early 1970s witnessed an expansion in both the size and numbers of colleges of education. This, combined with the move to coeducation and away from a shared residential experience, the changing curriculum and the growing emphasis on degree status, almost completely changed the character of the colleges:

The combined effect of . . . three virtually simultaneous phenomena – the acute shortage of teachers, the introduction of a three-year course, and the institution of a four-year course for some – was a massive expansion of the numbers of students in training and fundamental changes in the nature of the colleges and the work they undertook. A later development, the requirement that all graduates wishing to teach in maintained schools should have a professional qualification [the Post-graduate Certificate of Education, or PGCE], added impetus to the movement already in train by vastly increasing the number of post-graduates in the colleges. In 1956 there were 26,000 in the colleges (13,000 annual intake). In 1971 there were 110,000 students (39,000 annual intake). (Hewett 1972: 22)

By the mid-1970s, however, and partly in response to further shifts in demand (this time downwards), the picture was to change again, and even more radically:

. . . the 1972 White Paper initiated the upheaval of more than 200 institutions of further and higher education. Never before had Government created so much turmoil for so many colleges. Twenty-five colleges of education closed: 12 were integrated with universities; 37 were amalgamated with polytechnics; from 78 colleges of education together with

34 colleges of further education emerged 59 colleges of higher education, a new creature on the education landscape. (Locke et al. 1985: 35)

Over a period of a few years, the third sector of the teacher training colleges
was dismantled and, in its place, a new third sector of colleges of higher
education was emerging (Hencke 1978; Raggett and Clarkson 1976). This
new college sector strove to broaden its provision away from teacher education, in many cases incorporating a substantial amount of further education
activity. The more successful of these new, diversified colleges would form
the basis for the latest university foundations in the early twenty-first century.

The next major bout of government intervention in teacher education,
however, came in the mid-1980s (Galvin 1996). This involved both a shift
to greater central control of provision, under the auspices of first the Council
for the Accreditation of Teacher Education (CATE), and then the Teacher
Training Agency (TTA), and a move back from academic content to a greater
emphasis on practical, in-school training. As a consequence, a greater proportion of the funds available were channelled towards the participating
schools, which led many universities to question their commitment in this
area. At the present time, teacher education is concentrated in a more
limited number of higher education institutions than previously, with many
of the major providers the new university descendants of the former colleges
of education.

Technical and further education

As the discussion in Chapter 2 indicated, the relationship between technical,
latterly further, education colleges and universities has been both varied and
of long standing. In several cases it has resulted in a close affiliation:

> The closest relationship between university and technical college has
> long existed at Manchester, where the College of Technology is the
> Faculty of Technology for many subjects . . . At Sunderland, the tech-
> nical college is affiliated to the University of Durham in the Schools
> of Engineering, enabling many of its students to proceed to internal
> degrees. Similar arrangements exist at Leeds. Provision for affiliation
> has been made at Sheffield and Liverpool, but little use has, so far, been
> made of the provision . . . Seven London technical colleges are affiliated
> to the University . . . Collaboration and affiliation between technical
> college and university is, however, the exception. (Cotgrove 1958: 143–4)

The technical and further education colleges have always been the most
disparate group of institutions within the UK higher education system, especially as higher education has typically only constituted a minor part of their
offerings. They have been defined as much by their difference from other,
more closely delineated, higher education institutions – universities, polytechnics, colleges of education – as by their similarity with each other. Their

membership has also been volatile, as groups of colleges have successively become, or been amalgamated into, universities or polytechnics at different times. Other colleges, as with many of the colleges of education, have simply been closed when demand for their specialist offerings has collapsed. So the sector has had to continually reinvent itself in response to changing demand and policy.

Perhaps, therefore, the least regarded aspect of the post-war higher education experience in the UK has been the significant role played by further education colleges (Parry 2003; Parry and Thompson 2002). Of course, those institutions that have focused on advanced (i.e. higher) further education, and which have been specially designated as such – the CATs in the 1950s and early 1960s, the polytechnics in the late 1960s and 1970s – have subsequently become universities in their own right, and have been discussed earlier in this chapter. The continuing role of the further education sector, and its large but changing roll-call of institutions, in providing local higher education opportunities is, by contrast, much less researched.

Parry and Thompson (2002: 79) show that, in the 10 years between 1989/90 and 1998/9, further education colleges in England accounted for between 9 and 12 per cent of all higher education enrolments (3–5 per cent of full-time enrolments, 19–25 per cent of part time), and between 33 and 40 per cent of all other undergraduate (i.e. below first degree) level enrolments (20–26 per cent full time, 39–50 per cent part time). They characterize the recent period as moving from a time of low policy, with little attention paid to the role of further education colleges in providing higher education, to a time of high policy, following the Dearing Committee's (National Committee of Inquiry into Higher Education 1997a) endorsement of this role. Their role is likely to both continue, given the contemporary emphasis in increasing participation in higher education, and be subject to further reinvention.

Small specialist colleges

Despite the post-war trend towards the massification of provision, with an increasing number of higher education institutions each recruiting more and more students, and with many mergers of smaller colleges into larger universities or polytechnics, significant numbers of small, specialist colleges have continued to pursue their particular remits.

Thus, many of the colleges of art and design founded in the nineteenth century and later continue as independent institutions. Indeed, two of them – the Royal College of Art, chartered in 1967, and the University of the Arts in London, founded through the amalgamation of several smaller colleges in 1986, and granted university status in 1993 – now enjoy university status in their own right. Four colleges of music, three of them based in London, enjoy the same status.

An analysis of English institutions of higher education in 2004–5 (Tight

2007) showed that 21 out of the total of 132 institutions were small, specialist colleges (indeed, several of the component parts of the federal University of London could be similarly classified). Focusing on agriculture, art, design, drama, food, music, speech and/or tourism, they typically had fewer than 1000 students enrolled.

Nurse education

The development and positioning of nurse education has followed a route somewhat similar to, but later than, that of teacher education. The inclusion of nurse education programmes in UK higher education institutions, initially only on a small scale, dates from 1957, with some of these courses gaining degree status from the mid-1960s onwards (Fitzpatrick et al. 1993).

Despite significant resistance from within the profession – where, as in the case of teaching, there are disagreements regarding the relative importance of practical and theoretical (or academic) knowledge – nursing courses linked to degrees increased in numbers during the 1970s. Colleges of nursing and midwifery became more closely associated with higher education institutions, and, in the 1990s, the Project 2000 policy signalled a move towards an all-graduate profession. This was followed by the integration of nurse education within the university system, with faculties or schools of nursing added to many, mostly newer, universities across the country.

'Odd' institutions

Two unusual institutions will be considered in this section, each very different from the other. The first, the Open University, founded by a Labour government, is the only UK university to eschew entrance requirements and to offer virtually all of its courses part time and at-a-distance. Though it may be said to have diverged from its original intentions, in terms of recruitment numbers it remains an undoubted success. The second, the University of Buckingham, supported by a later Conservative government, is the only UK-based university (as distinct, that is from the various off-shore activities of US universities) that is privately owned. By contrast with the Open University, and with all other UK universities, it remains tiny in size, and its success is highly debatable.

The Open University

The Open University represented the most notable of the innovations of the 1960s in nine main ways. First, it was not part of a national plan . . . Second, it was a political decision, whose academic plan was worked out later. Third, it did not come from the UGC in collaboration with the CVCP, local authorities and academics . . . Fourth, it had much opposition to contend with . . . Fifth, it is the largest single university institution . . . Sixth, in academic administration and in teaching technique it is unique in this country. Seventh, in the high predominance or part-time students it has the lowest student unit costs. Eighth, in several overseas centres the OU has been closely examined to ensure that it may travel. Ninth, its students have never been generally eligible for mandatory grants. (Stewart 1989: 116–17)

The Open University of the UK has been a much studied innovation, not least internally (e.g. Ferguson 1975; McIntosh et al. 1976; Rumble 1982; Sargant 1996; Tunstall 1974), and also much imitated internationally. It had its origins – like the campus universities, from which it took a rather different direction – in the coming together in the 1960s of related political and economic developments:

The concept of the Open University evolved from the convergence of three major postwar trends. The first of these concerns developments in the provision for adult education, the second the growth of educational broadcasting and the third the political objective of promoting the spread of egalitarianism in education. (Perry 1976: 1)

Originally known as the University of the Air, an advisory committee had been established soon after the Labour Party came to power in 1964. Two years later, a White Paper made clear the government's commitment:

The Government believe that by an imaginative use of new teaching techniques and teacher/student relationships, an open university providing degree courses as rigorous and demanding as those in existing universities can be established . . . The presentation of courses will variously involve a combination of television, radio, correspondence courses, programmed instruction, tutorials and practicals, short residential courses, and study and discussion at community viewing or study centres. (Secretary of State for Education and Science 1966: 3, 5–6)

Despite widespread opposition, a planning committee was set up in 1967, which reported in 1969. What had by then become known as the Open University would focus its attention on students who had been 'precluded from achieving their aims through an existing institution of higher education', using 'a fully integrated teaching system', mainly delivered at a distance rather than face to face, to provide 'a broadly-based higher education' rather than specialist degrees (Open University Planning Committee 1969: 5, 7, 16). Students would study part time, alongside their work and domestic responsibilities, and there would be no entrance requirements.

Working at speed, the Open University was duly chartered in May 1969, and began to enrol students scarcely more than six months later for a January 1971 start. It might have been aborted almost immediately, when the Conservative Party came to power in 1970, but the new Secretary of State, Margaret Thatcher, was persuaded to give it her backing. After that, it never looked back, enrolling 19,581 students in its first year, and then expanding rapidly year by year to assume the status of one of the world's 'mega-universities' (Daniel 1996; Open University 1972).

As with all such innovations, evaluations of the Open University were mixed, with much more enthusiasm evident, at least initially, internationally:

> . . . the Open University has succeeded to a remarkable degree. Approximately 20,000 new students have been admitted annually since 1971 – about a third lacking normal university [entry] qualifications – with the total student population vacillating around 55,000. The evidence to date (1981) suggests that about 50 per cent will obtain degrees in three to seven years, a figure comparable to that of American state universities but below that of more restrictive British institutions. Academic staff and teaching are probably as good as any found in Britain outside Oxbridge, and the OU degree is increasingly being regarded by employers as equivalent to that of conventional universities. (Cerych and Sabatier 1985: 27–8)

At home, while official reviews have been supportive (e.g. DES/Open University 1991), the verdict of outside commentators has often been less positive, with many arguing that the resources used could have been better expended elsewhere, and criticizing the higher non-completion rates and the middle-class status of most of its students:

> . . . whereas 39% of Open University students have fathers whose occupations were 'middle-class', this increased to 90% of students when their present occupations were considered. Therefore, while the Open University is undoubtedly used as a vehicle for enhancing upward social mobility, it is obvious that its students have already displayed a considerable degree of upward mobility by the time they enrol on their course of study. (Whitburn et al. 1976: 113–14)

Others were even harsher in their verdicts:

> What are the lessons of the establishment of the Open University? They are firstly that a university is an inappropriate institution to use to try to redress social class imbalance in educational opportunity. If you establish an institution with nearly all the attributes [of] a conventional university, then it will inevitably seek to assume more of those attributes. An 'open' university is in this sense a contradiction in terms. But it is an idea that only arises if higher education is identified with university education . . . This leads us to a second lesson, about the planning process itself. It is clearly insufficient to have the best of intentions. The Open University is another example of a universal law of social institutions, that the reverse of one's intentions will inevitably occur unless specific attempts are taken to achieve them; and what is more, the more radical the intentions, the more likely their reversal. (Pratt 1972: 82–3)

Today, however, it is probably true to say that the Open University is relatively safe in its status as a 'great British institution', like the monarchy and the National Health Service. Whatever its faults, it has affected, directly or indirectly, and usually enriched, the lives of millions.

The University of Buckingham

The origins of this 'odd' institution lie in mid-1960s' discussions among individuals concerned about the state funding and academic freedom of universities. The planning group initially considered providing courses for University of London degrees, then sought CNAA approval. A two-year accelerated, dense degree structure was planned, as compared to the standard English (and Welsh) three-year degree, with teaching also taking place during the long summer vacation. The first 'degree' course, in law, for the then self-styled University College's own licence, recognized by professional associations, was launched in 1976. Like the Open University, it was decided to follow the calendar rather than the academic year. Great emphasis was placed on tutorials, as at Oxbridge (Pemberton and Pemberton 1979).

Thirty years on, the University of Buckingham (chartered in 1983) remains an institution of only a few hundred students, the majority of whom are from other countries, studying a limited range of vocationally oriented programmes.

The picture in Scotland, Wales and Northern Ireland

While most of the institutional trends considered in this chapter have impacted on all parts of the UK, differences remain between the higher education systems and institutions of England, Scotland, Wales and Northern Ireland. Though there have been periodic trends towards centralization and standardization, both within the UK and, latterly, within the broader European community, in the most recent period, with growing devolution, the differences between the component parts of the UK have been magnified again. This section will, therefore, focus on how higher education in Scotland, Wales and Northern Ireland continues to differ from England.

Scotland

As the discussion so far in this chapter, and in Chapter 2, has indicated, Scotland has long prided itself on the distinctiveness of its higher education, and education, system, and, in particular, on its difference from that to be found in England. The system established in Scotland before the Second World War – four ancient universities, and a strong group of 'central' institutions and teacher training colleges – was maintained largely intact until the mid-1960s. Three new universities were then created: Stirling, a campus university and the only completely new foundation in Scotland, Strathclyde (the former Royal Technical College, which had been closely associated with the University of Glasgow) and Heriot–Watt (which, like Strathclyde, had been a central institution, but had gone through intermediary CAT status):

> As many universities were founded in Scotland between 1964 and 1967 as in the previous five and a half centuries. By 1970, when provision of places in England had reached 42 per thousand, the Scottish figure had advanced to 76. There has been a proportionate growth, too, in other sectors, the colleges of education in the sixties, the central institutions in the seventies, the further education colleges throughout. (Scotland 1982: 133)

There were no polytechnics designated in Scotland, though a number of the remaining central institutions – such as Napier College in Edinburgh, the Glasgow College of Technology, and Robert Gordon's Institute of Technology in Aberdeen – performed analogous functions. Indeed, at least one (Napier) adopted the polytechnic title before they were designated as universities, along with the polytechnics in England and Wales, in the early 1990s.

The greater rates of participation in higher education in Scotland, in part due to students leaving school for university a year earlier than in the rest of the UK, bolstered the historic image of Scottish education as a more democratic system (Davie 1961). This perceived image has, however, received a mixed assessment from Scottish higher education researchers:

> It is popularly believed that Scottish higher education is more socially open than the systems elsewhere in the UK, and so is able to become more open still. The claim about a tradition of openness is not without foundation for the period down to the middle of the twentieth century. The four ancient universities developed as community resources in the nineteenth century, and so higher education in Scotland never acquired the same intensity of social remoteness as came to characterise English higher education strongly influenced by the culture of Oxford and Cambridge. One cultural consequence was a belief that Scotland suffered less from the divide between vocational and academic education than England. In the twentieth century, there was never such an invidious binary line as in England, since most of the non-university colleges had distinct purposes with which they were quite happy until the 1980s . . . But, from another point of view, Scottish higher education is faced with a crisis of identity. The myths about its distinctiveness, however true they may have been for earlier periods, have become steadily less accurate as the twentieth century has progressed. (Paterson 1997: 30)

An alternative interpretation, however, sees the sustained higher participation rates in Scotland – albeit often at sub-degree level, and in further rather than higher education institutions – as evidence of continuing distinctiveness:

...a distinctive feature of developments in Scotland was the growth of HE provision in the FE colleges ... over the period 1985–1986 to 2000–2001, the numbers of students enrolled in HE-level courses in FE colleges increased by 141 per cent ... compared with a growth of 90 per cent for undergraduates in HEIs ... As a result, in 2000–2001, these FE college students accounted for 34 per cent of all undergraduate-level students in Scotland. These students are mainly enrolled on Higher National Certificate or Higher National Diploma courses, or shorter part-time programmes made up from Higher National units ... the age participation index ... stood at 27.9 per cent in 1990–1991 but had increased to 51.5 per cent by 2000–2001. On this measure, there is evidence of a relatively high HE participation rate in Scotland. However, it is clear that it is a participation rate to which HNC/D courses in FE colleges make an important contribution. (Gallacher 2006: 353)

Since devolution of certain UK government powers and roles, including those in higher education, to Scotland in 1999, the distinctiveness provided by higher participation rates and a somewhat different institutional mix has been extended further, most notably through the rejection of the policy on student fees introduced in England, following the recommendations of the Cubie Report (Independent Committee of Inquiry into Student Finance 1999).

Wales

Whilst the distinctiveness of education in Scotland and – if it is mentioned at all – Northern Ireland is universally recognised, 'England and Wales' has been the routine unit of analysis, with perhaps a footnote to acknowledge the special status of Welsh-language instruction. Certainly, the analysis of higher education follows this pattern, with only the most cursory acknowledgement of Welsh specificities. (Rees and Istance 1997: 50)

One way, however, in which the Welsh 'system' of higher education has remained distinctive from those in England and Scotland has been in the long dominance of the federal University of Wales within that system. This is no longer the only university in Wales: the University of Glamorgan was designated from the former Polytechnic of Wales in 1992; Cardiff went its own way in 2004; and, like London, its remaining major colleges now enjoy greater independence. However, it remains the major influence on the Welsh higher education landscape, and has even expanded through the accession of new university colleges in Cardiff, Newport, Swansea and Wrexham.

A second unusual feature of Welsh higher education, at least in the latter part of the post-war period, is – again in contrast to England and Scotland, and in this case Northern Ireland as well – the 'non-Welsh-ness' of its student body. In this respect it has become an adjunct to England, as this has been the source of most of its students:

> In common with the provincial universities in England, this [post-war] expansion inevitably led to a wider scope of student recruitment, necessarily leading to a dilution of the University's [the University of Wales'] distinctively Welsh character . . . Moreover, the further expansion which followed the Robbins Report also contributed to these trends. Hence, by the beginning of the 1970s, the University of Wales had more than doubled its size again, to some 15,400 full-time students (in 1973). Of these, the majority had a home residence in England. (Rees and Istance 1997: 53)

Not only that, but, in a reversal of this inward flow, most Welsh students themselves attended institutions outside Wales.

As with Scotland, however, the advent of devolution in 1999 has led to increased differentiation in higher education policy, not only from England but Scotland as well, as a further variant on student funding was developed: 'flexible top-up fees are to be introduced from 2007–2008, but Welsh-domiciled students studying at Welsh HEIs will receive a grant, which is not means-tested, equivalent to the difference between existing fees and the new levels to be introduced' (Rees and Taylor 2006: 372–3).

This development has caused a reassertion of Welshness, with more Welsh students (and/or their parents) seeing the value in staying to study within Wales:

> Of these Welsh-domiciled students, a substantial majority, over 60 per cent by 2002/2003, opted to study in Welsh HEIs, with the remaining 40 per cent mostly attending HEIs in England. Moreover, the longer-term trend has been a significant growth in Welsh-based study by Welsh-domiciled students. (Rees and Taylor 2006: 378)

Northern Ireland

> The principal contemporary feature of higher education in Northern Ireland is a high participation rate alongside an under-supply of places in the Province. (Cormack et al. 1997: 68)

Northern Ireland, like Wales, was long dominated in higher education terms by a single institution, though in its case this was a unitary university, Queen's in Belfast, rather than a federal body (though Queen's does trace its origins back to being part of an all-Ireland federal university experiment; see Chapter 2). Again, like Wales, many of its students have opted to study outside the province, in the Republic of Ireland, England or elsewhere, with the directions and size of the flows varying with the state of the economy and the religion of the students.

Currently, evidence indicates that Protestants are far more likely than Catholics to leave the province to study, and then be unlikely to return (Osborne 2006). Many also leave to study in other parts of the UK because of the relative lack of higher education places in Northern Ireland, and a consequent belief that their qualifications will not be good enough for entry.

The recent devolution of government responsibilities to the Northern Ireland Assembly holds out the prospect of further differentiation of practice in higher education, as in the cases of Scotland and Wales, but this has been too recent to make any judgement.

Diversity

> Diversity in higher education is generally agreed to be a desirable thing
> . . . A diverse higher education sector is one with the capacity to meet
> the varying needs and aspirations of those it serves: students, employers,
> purchasers of HE services, and the wider community . . . A diverse HE
> service should be able to provide choices of curriculum offer; choices as
> to the mode, pace and place of delivery; choices regarding the physical
> and intellectual environment available; and choices between a range of
> different institutional forms and missions. (Higher Education Funding
> Council for England 2000: 3–4)

> . . . whereas the diversified system of higher education in England and
> Wales is designed to meet a diversity of needs and functions without any
> status discrimination, it has tended to develop into a hierarchy of
> esteem in which the differentiation of function has become increasingly
> muddled and unclear. (Watts 1972: 40)

As these two quotations suggest, despite their difference in tone, the diversity among the universities and colleges that make up the UK higher education system has long been recognized. Most of the institutional classifications that have been devised to summarize and convey this diversity have been based chiefly on three factors: institutional history, nationality and designation. An example of this is the categorization offered by Scott (1995; see Table 5.1).

Scott's typology extends beyond higher education to include all post-compulsory education, so his final three categories can be ignored for present purposes. Though he considers the whole of the UK, the Scottish, Welsh and Northern Irish universities are simply lumped together in three separate categories. His remaining 14 categories (1–6, 10–17) focus on English higher education. Four of these categories (1, 2, 5, 10) refer to institutions that are for some reason unusual: the ancient collegiate universities of Oxford and Cambridge, the large federal university of London, Durham (old, collegiate) and Keele (post-war, and at that time still offering a four rather than three-year degree), and the distance teaching Open University.

Table 5.1 Scott's typology of British post-compulsory education

1. Oxford and Cambridge universities
2. The University of London
3. The 'civic' universities (e.g. Birmingham, Bristol)
4. The 'redbrick' universities (e.g. Exeter, Hull)
5. Durham and Keele universities
6. The 'technological' universities (e.g. Aston, Bath)
7. The Scottish universities
8. The Welsh universities
9. The Northern Irish universities
10. The Open University
11. The 'old new' universities (e.g. East Anglia, Essex)
12. The 'new new' universities (e.g. Anglia, Bournemouth)
13. Multi-faculty colleges (e.g. Bolton, Nene)
14. Liberal arts colleges (e.g. Bath)
15. Further/higher education colleges
16. Specialized colleges (e.g. Royal College of Music)
17. Higher education in further education
18. Further education
19. Adult education
20. The corporate classroom

Source: Scott (1995: 43–53).

Five further categories (3, 4, 6, 11 and 12) identify the successive waves of university foundation that have been discussed in this chapter:

- the 'civic' universities established in the major English cities in the late nineteenth century;
- the 'redbrick' universities founded in other cities in the early twentieth century;
- the 'technological' universities created from the former Colleges of Advanced Technology in the 1960s;
- the 'old new' universities set up on campus locations in the 1960s;
- the 'new new' universities, that is re-designated polytechnics and colleges recognized in the early 1990s.

The remaining five categories (13–17) relate to different kinds of college (though most of those in category 13 have since become universities).

Commonsense classifications of this kind have been largely confirmed by those who have applied techniques of multivariate analysis (e.g. cluster and factor analysis) to institutional statistics (see, for example, Dolton and Makepeace 1982; King 1970; Tight 1988, 1996). Thus, in the most recent of these analyses, Tight (1996: 75) identified 16 types of English higher education institution, with the key distinction from Scott's analysis being the separate identification of particular kinds of specialist college (e.g. arts, medical).

More recently, Universities UK (UUK) – the national body representing

universities in the UK (formerly the CVCP) – together with the body representing higher education colleges, the Standing Conference of Principals
(SCOP; since renamed GuildHE), has commissioned and published a series
of reports on patterns of higher education institutions (Ramsden 2003, 2005;
Ramsden and Brown 2002). These reports have charted changes over time
and between institutions in terms of level, mode and subject of study, student
characteristics and institutional finance. They have also looked at differences
between groupings of higher education institutions:

• between pre- and post-1992 universities, and generalist and specialist
  colleges in the 2002 report;
• between the emerging groupings of institutions created in a more
  market-oriented system in the 2003 report; that is, the Coalition of
  Modern Universities (CMU), the 1994 Group, the Russell Group, the
  generalist/specialist colleges (SCOP) and the remaining 'non-
  aligned' grouping.

Thus, for example, the 2002 report concluded that:

> There are, on many measures, differences between the post-1992 uni-
> versities and the other providers. Equally, it has been noted that the
> pre-1992 university sector is itself diverse, because of the differentiation
> between universities with medical schools and those without. (Ramsden
> and Brown 2002: 40)

The 2003 report found similarities between the 1994 and Russell groups of
universities, with the key difference being that most of the latter had medical
schools, and between the CMU and SCOP groups, with the 'non-aligned'
institutions lying somewhere between these two poles in terms of many
characteristics (Ramsden 2003: 51–2).

These kinds of classification are also reflected to a considerable extent –
because much of the data used is related to historical differences in institutional funding – in the institutional league tables that have come to
feature so widely in contemporary assessments of institutional worth, whether
reported in the national press or analysed in academic journals (e.g. Bowden
2000; Tight 2000).

Three, more recent, analyses would support the implication of these cat-
egorizations; namely, that there is considerable institutional diversity within
contemporary UK higher education. Thus, Taylor has concluded that 'It
is clear from this analysis of performance indicators that, in terms of
research profiles, financial turnover and student population, universities
have become more diverse since the end of the binary divide [i.e. since
1992]' (Taylor 2003: 283).

Second, Huisman et al. (2007) carried out a cross-national analysis
of institutional diversity, comparing 10 countries that belonged to the
Organization for Economic Co-operation and Development. The comparison covered student enrolments, forms of institutional control, disciplinary spread, degrees awarded and modes of study, and used data from

1996. They concluded that the UK higher education system was 'highly diverse'; indeed, the most diverse of the systems examined. A third analysis focusing on four key characteristics of 132 English higher education institutions in 2004/05 (Tight 2007) – their size (in terms of student numbers), the level at which students are studying, their mode of study and nationality – also demonstrated considerable institutional diversity. Underlying the evident variations in student numbers, level, mode and nationality were, it was suggested, three main explanatory factors: institutional age, location and strategy.

Institutional age, as well as being a key element in existing institutional typologies, explains much about their current state and status. Put simply, older institutions have had longer than newer ones to be successful, to grow and to occupy available market niches (otherwise they would no longer be with us). Thus, they tend to be larger than average, and to have more postgraduate and non-UK students. Newer institutions, in attempting to compete with those longer established, have perforce tended to focus more on those market niches less exploited by older institutions (or which they are willing to relinquish). Thus, they tend to have larger undergraduate populations, and to focus more on part-time and UK students (as encouraged by the present government's widening participation agenda).

There is also a clear locational factor in operation. This has two main forms of impact. On the one hand, institutions in larger cities (which also tend to be older) have more opportunities to recruit students locally, and thus tend to be larger than those in smaller towns. On the other hand, there is a specific London or metropolitan effect, which, because of its size and reach, permits an almost exclusive focus on particular market niches – such as postgraduate or part-time study, and the recruitment of non-UK students – by particular institutions. It is significant that a high proportion of the many small and specialist institutions in the English higher education system are located in or around London.

Third, institutional strategy mediates how particular institutions respond to the opportunities available to them, bearing in mind their age and location, and the strategies adopted by competing institutions (cf. the analysis provided in Curran 2000, 2001). Two broad strategies are identifiable: specialist and generalist. The first of these has been pursued by the many remaining specialist colleges and some of the component parts of the University of London, and has also been practised on a far larger scale – given the monopoly position it was granted by government – by the Open University. The second has been pursued in one way or another by all of the remaining institutions – the great majority of the system – who have pursued the large-scale, multi-faculty, multi-level vision of what most people in the UK today would understand a university to be.

An alternative perspective on these sorts of analysis – suggested by this last point – is that, while there is undoubtedly some degree of institutional diversity in English (or UK) higher education, there is not as much as one might either expect or wish for (cf. Watson 1998).

The system does contain a number of 'odd' institutions, including the Open University (part-time distance study), Birkbeck College (part-time face-to-face study), the University of Buckingham (small, private, postgraduate, non-UK students) and the University of the Arts (federal, arts, further and higher education). But these are relatively few in number. One might also point to the rather greater numbers of small, specialist colleges: of agriculture, art and so on. But these are not that significant in terms of overall size. Under different arrangements, they might all be amalgamated with their local universities or university colleges, as some have been – and as other colleges specializing in, for example, teacher education, medicine or nursing have been in the past – when they would no longer be noticeable.

And there are remaining differences between older and newer universities, with the older universities focusing more on full-time and postgraduate study, and the newer on both full-time and part-time and undergraduate study, with, in a few cases, significant further education provision as well. But it could be argued that these differences are not that great, and that all, or at least the great majority, are pursuing the 'large-scale [for the UK], multi-faculty, multi-level vision' of what a university is or should be. This commonality of vision is also evidenced by the majority allegiance to the importance of both teaching and research (see also Chapter 8), and to the maintenance of supposedly common standards of teaching and assessment (see Chapter 7). In a truly diverse system, such as, perhaps, the USA, one would expect to find many more institutions focusing solely on undergraduate level work, or solely on postgraduate study and research, and so forth.

So, paradoxically, the British or English higher education system may seem reasonably diverse or pretty much standardized, depending on the perspective you adopt in examining it.

6

Institutional management and relationships

Introduction

Like the preceding chapter, this chapter focuses on institutions. While Chapter 5 examined the development of the main types of higher education institution recognized in the UK, this chapter looks at the levels above, below and beyond this. As this suggests, the chapter is organized in three main parts.

The first part of the chapter discusses the national institutions – that is, funding bodies and employers', academics' and students' organizations – that have been critical to the operation of the higher education sector during the post-war period. The second part looks inside higher education institutions, considering their changing patterns of governance, management and leadership. The third part examines the relationships that universities and colleges have with each other, and with other institutions: nationally, internationally and locally.

Finally, the concluding section of the chapter reviews the arguments as to whether, over the post-war period, we have witnessed a shift from collegial to managerial ways of working in UK higher education institutions.

National institutions

Many national institutions have, of course, been involved in the operation and development of higher education in the UK since the war. As well as national and local government, and the representative and intermediary bodies established by them, they include employers' organizations (both general and those specific to higher education), trade unions and others. In contemporary parlance, they would be termed 'stakeholders'.

This part of the chapter examines the roles and records of some of the most influential of these national institutions. Thus, the first section focuses on three 'national' funding bodies – the University Grants Committee, the local education authorities and the National Advisory Body – each of which has now been superseded.

The second section moves away from funding bodies to consider the key national representative bodies within the higher education sector during the post-war period: notably the Committee of Vice-Chancellors and Principals, representing university leaders; the Association of University Teachers, representing academics; and the National Union of Students, representing students; and national admissions bodies.

Two other kinds of national institution are examined in other chapters: the research councils in Chapter 8, and organizations concerned with the validation of courses and institutions (notably the Council for National Academic Awards) in Chapter 7.

Funding bodies

The development and experience of three main 'national' funding bodies are reviewed here:

* the University Grants Committee (UGC), which had been established in 1919, and was abolished in 1989;
* the local education authorities, which oversaw the work of higher education institutions outside of the university sector in England and Wales, until this responsibility was taken from them in 1982;
* the National Advisory Body (NAB), which then assumed the role of the local authorities in England, until it was also abolished in 1989.

The organizations that replaced the UGC and the NAB are then outlined.

The University Grants Committee

The role and record of the University Grants Committee (UGC) has generally been fairly positively assessed, at least in print. This is, perhaps, because most of those who have reviewed its performance have been academics or academic administrators, who will have benefitted from its role as a so-called 'buffer' body between state and institution (e.g. Moodie 1983; Owen 1980).

The UGC was established in 1919, under the auspices of the Treasury, as a means of channelling needed government funds to universities and colleges. It consisted largely of senior university professors (see Chapter 2). Prior to the Second World War, 'its role was to advise on the distribution of recurrent and capital resources from government in the form of deficiency grants to university institutions' (Shattock 1994: 1). The initial arrangements were very hands-off, with institutions receiving block grants, which they were free to use as they saw fit, with little subsequent oversight or audit.

Immediately after the Second World War, however, with increased pressures on the universities and expansion in the offing, the need to significantly increase the sums available became coupled with both earmarking of grants and reportage on their use:

> . . . after World War II, the UGC reluctantly accepted the recommendations of a number of special committees of enquiry to initiate 'as a temporary measure' a system of earmarked grants for special fields. These sums of money, unlike the block grants, were to be accounted for in detail to the UGC, and any unspent balances were to be surrendered to the UGC at the end of the academic year. (Berdahl 1959: 143)

These, at first marginal, changes in funding arrangements, coupled with the continuing expansion of the higher education system, and thus the need for more and more public funding, may be seen, with hindsight, to have sown the seeds for the UGC's eventual demise, and the closer controls on state funding exercised in more recent years. This was, of course, not to be foreseen in the immediate post-war period, which was a time of expectation, and one where the critical role that the universities played in the national economy was increasingly appreciated (see Chapter 4):

> Thanks to cooperation and joint planning with the CVCP, the UGC was able to present the Treasury in 1945 with outlines for a ten-year university development plan which required substantially enlarged government grants. The Chancellor of the Exchequer agreed to an immediate doubling of grants and promised further increases after the reports of a series of committees of enquiry appointed by various government departments to investigate the national need for certain types of professional specialists. (Shattock 1994: 3)

Thus, 'by 1947 the UGC had already changed its role from a distributor of money to an agent of planning, even though the planning was of the simplest kind, depending on collecting estimates from universities and comparing them with "targets" set out in official papers' (Briggs 1969: 100). Its planning role steadily grew during the 1950s, with increasing numbers of institutions on its list, as first the University College of North Staffordshire was set up, and later the arrangements were made for the new campus universities that opened their doors in the 1960s (see Chapter 5). The Robbins Report (Committee on Higher Education 1963a) was to provide a further stimulus, such that it was argued at the time that 'The sheer number of universities has now meant that, from being a "buffer", the University Grants Committee is to be a signal box' (Armytage 1968: 93).

This growth in the number and complexity of institutions was paralleled within the UGC itself:

> One result of the growth of the university system and particularly the number of institutions was the enlargement of the UGC's machinery by the increase and importance accorded to discipline-based advisory sub-committees. These sub-committees were expected to advise the main Committee on the development of the subjects falling within their remit

and increasingly to rationalize existing provision. The normal form of UGC advice, however, was to encourage new developments in some areas and at some institutions, and to discourage them in others. (Shattock and Berdahl 1984: 477–9)

Nevertheless, the UGC at this time still operated in an essentially hands-off manner, keeping to a minimum the degree to which it interfered in individual university's affairs:

> Post-Robbins, the UGC continued to provide a broad framework within which individual universities organized their own affairs. For example, the UGC was responsible for establishing broad salary scales, determining the balance for junior and senior staff members in universities, prescribing formulae for unit construction costs of buildings, providing or withholding funds for expansion, approving the establishment of new universities, and 'indicating' what academic specialities different universities should strengthen or abandon. In principle, the powers vested in the UGC allowed it to intervene, in diverse ways, to structure the provision and organization of activities within universities. In principle, the potential for such interventions was virtually limitless. In practice, however, prior to the early 1980s, influence over resource allocation was exerted only at the margins. (Willmott 1995: 1007)

The benevolent relationship between the UGC and the universities was maintained while its funds came directly from the Treasury, and while the scope of the funding involved and the state of the national economy allowed these funds to be allocated for five-year planning periods:

> The success of the UGC rested on the fact that it enabled public money to be put responsibly in the hands of academics who would then distribute it according to academic criteria. The framework decisions – how many student places, and the balance between research and teaching and undergraduate and graduate students – were determined by ministers. But once those decisions were made, and finance for the cost of implementing policy agreed, academics could decide which institutions should get what and for which general academic purposes. Moreover, the UGC knew what sums were available five years in advance and could, therefore, tell universities what grants they would have over a whole quinquennium for such running costs as salaries. (Kogan and Kogan 1983: 42)

Those arrangements, however, gradually came to an end. First, the direct relation with the Treasury was removed in 1964, when the UGC was transferred to the auspices of the newly created Department of Education and Science (DES). Then, in the mid-1970s, the deteriorating state of the national economy, coupled with the increasing financial demands of the expanding higher education system, led to the abandonment of the quinquennial system:

... the greatest blow to the UGC was the loss of the quinquennial planning system. The quinquennial system stretched back to the creation of the Universities' Advisory Committee in 1908, although a regular sequence was not established until 1924–29, and represented an integral part of the network of procedures and conventions which had been created to preserve university autonomy within the framework of government funding. In essence, the system reflected a balance of advantage to the funding agency and the bodies funded. The universities were given a five-year promise of funds within which to plan their activities; the UGC, and by implication the Government, were given the opportunity to review university development across the board every five years and to set guidelines for the following five. (Shattock and Berdahl 1984: 486–7)

While the UGC continued its work, its involvement in implementing continuing cuts in funding, which was to peak in 1981, and its strategy of being increasingly selective in the allocation of the available funds, lost it significant support among the academic community (Kogan and Kogan 1983). It was finally wound up in 1989, to be replaced – though, as it turned out, only in the short term – by the Universities Funding Council (UFC):

The University Grants Committee, consisting largely, but not entirely, of university professors was replaced by the Universities Funding Council which had a much larger number of lay members from industry and commerce. The clear intention was to control expenditure and policy rather than simply sharing out funds between the universities. (Lawton 1992: 56)

The UFC lasted for only three years, being replaced by national funding bodies when the binary line was finally removed in 1992.

The local education authorities

For the first part of the post-war period, dozens of local education authorities (LEAs) in England and Wales exercised financial responsibility and control over higher education provision outside of the university system (in both Scotland, as the name 'central institutions' implied, and Northern Ireland, non-university higher education was coordinated on a 'national' basis). This sector of provision was initially referred to as advanced further education, but later was termed the local authority sector, and, subsequent to the removal of local authority control by national government, the public or polytechnics and colleges sector.

From the perspective of local government, the story of the post-war period in higher education is one of a steady loss of control over the institutions they had established and nurtured. From the perspective of central government, however, it is a story of a steady upgrading, rationalization and extension of provision, to create an alternative higher education sector alongside the universities, with which it would then be combined (see Chapter 4). Thus, in 1952 the government began to give direct grants to colleges with a high proportion of higher-level provision. In 1956, the Colleges of Advanced Technology (CATs) were established, though they remained under local authority control until 1962. Pooling of costs was introduced in 1959 in recognition of the uneven provision of higher education opportunities by local authorities – most, after all, did not have CATs, and some offered little or no higher education – with the remaining colleges organized in a hierarchy of regional, area and local. The polytechnics were created by amalgamating institutions towards the top of this hierarchy in the late 1960s and early 1970s, though they also remained under a degree of local authority control. Finally, the local authority sector became the public sector, with national control and financing, with the establishment of the National Advisory Body in 1982.

Up until then, in England, a system of 10 regional advisory councils (RACs) – and a variety of national advisory bodies, such as the National Advisory Council for Education for Industry and Commerce (NACEIC) – were used to coordinate and rationalize provision, and to link education and industry. They were not, however, generally well regarded:

> the RACs have never achieved a really satisfactory co-ordinative role in further education for a number of reasons. First, the universities have only been grudging participants . . . Secondly, the Government has revealed a somewhat dismissive attitude to the RACs . . . Thirdly the finance and staffing of RACs limit their effectiveness. (Regan 1977: 178)

The colleges operated by the local education authorities were of much lower status than the universities, comparing with them poorly on every index:

> In general, the teaching terms are longer under local authorities; the student–teacher ratio is worse; the hours of teaching are longer; the facilities for research (especially libraries) are more rudimentary; the students are sometimes less able; in general salaries are lower; super-annuation terms are notably less favourable – all these add up to substantial disabilities for the staffs of non-university institutions of all kinds. In all, the differences between universities and local authority colleges amount to a considerable difference in status, and this difference in status is related to the different methods of finance and control – just as the methods of finance and control are related to the high status of universities compared with other institutions. (Vaizey 1963: 163)

Though conditions have undoubtedly improved, these status differentials remain evident to this day (see Chapter 5).

Despite increased intervention by central government, and the removal of the CATs from local authority control, the LEAs strove to retain what influence and control they could over their local providers of higher education. This remained the case right up until the early 1980s:

The LEA are responsible for the general educational character of a polytechnic or college and for the place of the college in the educational system. They own the land and the buildings; they employ the staff and they are responsible for finance and development … Although the LEAs have, in retrospect, an excellent record in developing the polytechnics and the colleges there are surprisingly few cases of good mutual relationships between colleges and LEAs. Mutual mistrust and misunderstanding is more common. The most serious problems arise from the unwillingness of so many LEAs to retreat from detailed control and intervention and from the wide variations among the LEAs in attitudes to the resource needs of the colleges. (Matterson 1981: 107–8)

Not surprisingly, therefore, most of those who worked in the polytechnics and colleges, with aspirations for better conditions and enhanced status, welcomed their eventual removal from local authority control in 1982.

The National Advisory Body

The National Advisory Body for Local Authority Higher Education (NAB) was established for England in 1982, with a parallel body (the WAB) in Wales. It had a brief but intense existence. From the beginning, its powers were wide though its remit was a little uncertain:

In 1981 discussion was initiated on long-term arrangements for a 'central focus' to 'oversee the financing and management of higher education outside the universities'. As an 'interim' measure, arrangements were made to establish the National Advisory Body for Local Authority Higher Education, which started work at the beginning of 1982. In its initial, interim form NAB's remit covered only institutions maintained by local education authorities; later this was widened to include voluntary colleges. Its title was also altered to the National Advisory Body for Public Sector Higher Education to reflect its wider role. From then on, the AFE Pool was allocated on the advice of NAB. (Pratt and Silverman 1988: 11–12)

Great hopes were expressed at first regarding its potential influence: 'the NAB's creation has not only opened the way for more comprehensive planning and greater cross-binary co-operation. It has also given the public sector a powerful lobby' (Pratt and Lockwood 1985: 11). The NAB's main role was to build up the non-university sector of higher education as a rival to the universities, operating at lower unit costs and with a much greater emphasis on teaching. In this, it had some success, though it was also criticized:

The failure of the NAB as a halfway house between national and local control over the burgeoning public sector of higher education contributed in great measure to the DES' decision to remove polytechnics and colleges from the responsibility of the local authorities. (Shattock 1994: 151)

A fairer judgement might be that this was the direction in which matters were clearly then heading. By then, most of the polytechnics were as large, or larger, than an average-sized university, and clearly merited fully independent status. At the same time, there was a need and a logic in organizing their funding directly alongside that of the existing universities.

The NAB was replaced by the Polytechnics and Colleges Funding Council (PCFC) in 1989, which itself was then abolished three years later when a unified system of public funding of higher education was introduced. This was organized on sub-national lines, involving the Higher Education Funding Council for England (HEFCE), the Higher Education Funding Council for Wales (HEFCW) and the Scottish Higher Education Funding Council (SHEFC), as well as the continuing work of the Department of Education in Northern Ireland (DENI). This remains the arrangement today.

Other national organizations

In addition to the funding bodies, there are many other national organizations that have been, and are, involved in the operation of the higher education system in the UK. These include, most obviously, the representatives of institutions, academics and students. The most significant of these organizations, over the period as a whole – the Committee of Vice-Chancellors and Principals, the Association of University Teachers, and the National Union of Students – are briefly considered in this sub-section, along with national student admissions bodies, an example of institutional cooperation at a national level over a particular function.

The Committee of Vice-Chancellors and Principals

The Committee of Vice-Chancellors and Principals (CVCP) has been in existence throughout the post-war period, as the body representing the heads of the universities and university colleges. Its work has been paralleled during different parts of the period by other organizations representing the heads of other kinds of higher education institution. These have included the Committee of Directors of Polytechnics (CDP), which it effectively combined with in 1992; and the Standing Conference of Directors and Principals of Colleges and Institutes of Higher Education (SCDPCIHE), some of whose former members have also now achieved university status and joined the CVCP.

Not surprisingly, therefore, one of the key issues for the CVCP has been articulating a common position, when its membership has been continuously growing and has had increasingly disparate interests:

the Committee of Vice-Chancellors and Principals often encountered difficulties in representing the collective voice of institutional leaders who valued institutional autonomy above agreeing to a common line . . . The Committee of Directors of Polytechnics were much more tightly organized. (Kogan 2002: 51)

The demise of the UGC in 1989 left the CVCP as arguably the only national body that spoke for the universities, a position it has made some effective use of (Tapper and Slater 1997). However, the further massive expansion in its membership in 1992 has also made it an increasingly unwieldy lobbying group. One consequence of this has been the creation of more focused institutional groupings to lobby for their particular interests. These groups include: the Russell Group, representing the elite, research-led universities; the 1994 Group, including most of the other 'older' universities; and the Coalition of Modern Universities (CMU), representing many of former polytechnics and colleges with a greater focus on the teaching function. The remaining generalist/specialist colleges were represented by the Standing Conference of Principals (SCOP, the successor to SCDPCIHE), and there is also, intriguingly, a 'non-aligned' grouping (see also the discussion of diversity in Chapter 5).

Perhaps partly in response to these developments, the CVCP felt the need at the turn of the new century to 'rebrand' itself as Universities UK. SCOP followed suit shortly afterwards, and is now known as GuildHE.

The Association of University Teachers

The Association of University Teachers (AUT) is currently the only national union for academics and related staff. Not all academics choose to be members, of course, and there are other professional and learned societies that represent aspects of their interests.

The pre-war origins of the AUT reflect, as do those of many trade unions (though there were debates about whether the AUT should seek to be a trade union or a professional body), the desire to make use of the benefits of collective bargaining in a growing sector of employment (Perkin 1969a). Its early years reflect the struggle to engage with those responsible for funding (in this case the UGC, not the CVCP):

The driving force behind the founding of the AUT in 1920 was the desire to inject some order into the random salaries of UK academic staff which had emerged from the previous century reflecting different institutions', patrons', and professors' wealth and generosity. For the next 20 years the UGC strongly opposed any moves towards national salary standardisation . . . But by 1946 the UGC was recommending standard scales for professors, and in 1949 for non-professorial staff. (Wilson 2001: 252)

However, the UGC still betrayed some reluctance to become fully engaged, while emphasizing the problematic aspects of negotiating academic salaries and the special nature of the academic role.

> The relationship between the governing bodies of universities and their academic staffs differs in important respects from that between employers and employees, and makes inappropriate negotiating machinery of the normal type. After the salary review of 1954 the machinery for consultation was reviewed, and it was announced that the University Grants Committee would be ready to receive representations at any time as to changes in the basic salary framework for academic staffs of universities from the Committee of Vice-Chancellors and Principals or from the Association of University Teachers . . . We doubt whether there is any field of employment in which the settlement of rates of salaries raises issues more difficult and far reaching than those which arise over the remuneration of academic staffs. (UGC 1958: 32)

A formal salary negotiating machinery involving the UGC, the AUT and the CVCP was then instituted, though national bargaining rights were only finally established in 1970, following a report of the Prices and Incomes Board. While this remains the position today – bolstered by the recent absorption into the AUT of the National Association of Teachers in Further and Higher Education (NATFHE), which represented lecturers in the former polytechnics and colleges sector – the current pressures from employers are to move away from national to local bargaining agreements.

The National Union of Students

The National Union of Students (NUS) was established in 1922. Its pre-war origins and aims were rather different from what it was to become in the post-war period: 'The NUS owes its birth to the determination of young men, many of whom had fought in the [First World] war, to take part in a European youth movement' (Ashby and Anderson 1970: 64). Gradually, however, its early concerns with student welfare, and with the provision of cheap social and sporting facilities, became complemented by engagement with both student-specific and more general political concerns, most notably in the 1960s and 1970s (see Chapter 4).

This politicization led to some tensions within the organization, which had come to operate both nationally and through its component student unions (one for each higher education institution). Some of the local unions have opted, at various times and for various periods, to withdraw from national membership. There were also debates about the way in which the NUS was funded, and whether individual students could opt out of membership.

Most recently, however, the pendulum has swung the other way, with student unions becoming less interested in general political concerns, and more engaged with both the educational and graduate experience of their members: 'In England . . . a major change during the period [since the 1980s] has been the gradual depoliticisation of student unions and the repositioning of their action and activities' (Deer 2002: 74). Indeed, it might be said that, like universities and colleges themselves, many student unions have become more entrepreneurial in their operations.

National admissions bodies

The admissions function has been one of the key areas in which higher education institutions have come to see the sense of cooperating with each other. Before the first national admissions body was set up, prospective students would apply individually to all and any institutions and courses that they were interested in. This was not only time consuming for the students, departments and institutions concerned: it also meant that institutions would have very little idea of who would be enrolling with them until their courses started (which is still often the case, of course, at postgraduate level).

Increasing concerns over the handling and standardization of university entrance procedures were being expressed in the 1950s (Kelsall 1957). In response, the CVCP established an ad hoc committee to consider the matter in 1958, leading to the establishment of the Universities Central Council on Admissions (UCCA) in 1961 (Kay 1985). A national admissions scheme for the universities was introduced in 1964, though initially without the involvement of the elite institutions of Oxford, Cambridge and London. Application forms, school reports, dates for application and forms of institutional offer were all standardized, and limits were placed on the number of courses prospective students could apply to and the numbers of offers of places they could hold.

The polytechnics and colleges set up their own admissions system in the 1970s – the Polytechnics and Colleges Admissions Service (PCAS):

> The clearing-house systems of UCCA, and now of PCAS, are of interest because their methods presumably reflect the shared values and assumptions that govern admissions to higher education. Foremost amongst these, at the symbolic level, are the two principles of *competition* for places, and *selection* – by *academics*, the future teachers of those they select. (Fulton 1988: 19, emphasis in original)

UCCA and PCAS combined in the 1990s to form the Universities and Colleges Admissions Service (UCAS).

Governance, management and leadership

> Outside government there is no more fertile field for the practice of politics than a university. (Scott 1973: 88)

This part of the chapter focuses on a series of related themes affecting how institutions are governed, managed and led, and how this has developed during the post-war period. While these concepts are clearly closely related, indeed overlap in many ways, here governance will be interpreted as having to do with the formal arrangements existing for decision-making within universities and colleges; management with how these institutions are actually operated on a day-to-day basis; and leadership with their more strategic, medium to long-term direction.

Governance

Much of the attention paid to governance historically has been directed at the older universities, and the variations that exist in their constitutions, between different parts of the UK and different kinds of university.

> The constitutions of our universities are commonly summarised as follows. Oxford and Cambridge are autonomous societies, governed by academic men [sic] and without lay control. The Scottish universities since 1889 have been governed by Courts on which there is some lay representation, although responsibility for academic matters is delegated to the Senatus, which is composed predominantly of professors. The civic universities are governed by Councils composed predominantly of laymen, with some academic representation; though certain powers are delegated, as in the Scottish universities, to the board of professors (usually but not invariably called the Senate). (Ashby 1966: 98)

Not surprisingly, Oxford and Cambridge stand out as unusual, and as meriting special attention, in these analyses:

> Before the wave of new constitutions in the 1960s the only indigenous alternative pattern of faculty and subject organisation was that to be found in Oxford and Cambridge. There the division of responsibilities between colleges and university, whereby the colleges taught for university-run examinations but appointed their own staff, had led to a system in which the main subject areas were defined by the examination rubrics and in which the generality of teachers played a greater governmental role than in other universities. (Moodie and Eustace 1974: 70)

However, as Ashby noted, the Scottish universities offer an alternative pattern, as do both London and Wales, with their federal structures dividing responsibilities and powers between a central university and its component colleges (Livingstone 1974 – those these federations are, in a way, somewhat analogous to, and in part derived from, the Oxbridge pattern). Compared to them, most of the other 'older' universities – the old and new civics, the campus universities and former colleges of advanced technology – implemented a more standard pattern:

The characteristic structure of government in the unitary universities has five levels . . . In most universities the 'supreme governing body' is still the court . . . consisting of local notables, local government nominees, and representatives of various local bodies and institutions, of religious, professional and other organisations, of trade unions, and also of graduates, staff and, increasingly, students . . . The senior executive body, however, is council; it too has a predominantly lay membership, but it is both smaller and more active than court . . . The third major body is senate. Its chairman is the vice-chancellor and its membership almost wholly academic . . . The next level consists, typically, of the faculties . . . Traditionally, the next step beyond the sub-faculty has been to the department, a body very seldom legislated for at all, and left wholly to the discretion of its professor, who was responsible for the development and conduct of all teaching and research in his [sic] subject . . . Beyond, or beside, these 'levels' we have three university-wide organisations. The first of these, traditionally, is the convocation, the organisation of alumni (or graduates as they mostly are today) . . . Next there is the student organisation, usually the union or students' representative council, whose role is increasing . . . Finally, an essentially modern development, found chiefly at the newer universities, is the assembly of all staff. (Moodie and Eustace 1974: 52–5)

Since then there have, of course, been some changes. Departments, like universities, now tend to be larger bodies, with perhaps several professors. While some may have permanent heads, others elect their heads from among their number every few years. The role of the faculty is also more variable, almost replacing the department in some universities, wielding considerable power and influence between the department and the university in others, and having only a largely symbolic role in still others. The arrangements in the newer universities, the former polytechnics and colleges, also vary, but tend to exhibit tighter structures, more permanent positions and clearer line management, and, at the level of the governing body, greater involvement of external lay members.

Moodie and Eustace were writing at a time when the representation of ordinary academic staff in university had been improving, and the trend was then also towards greater involvement of students:

By 1970 . . . certain important governmental principles had been accepted by the Privy Council even if they had not all been enshrined in every charter. These principles are:

1. that general university government may be substantially in the hands of staff and that junior staff should have a significant part in it;
2. that senate should have a wide area of complete independence, a veto at least on academic and senior administrative appointments, and the right of consultation in financial matters; and

3. that it is proper, and perhaps necessary, to specify machinery of collective government at the 'subject' level.

To these may be added the most recent development, for all that it has not yet been consolidated in many charters, namely:

4. that students should have some share in general university government. (pp. 42–3)

Students are now commonly represented in university government at all levels, and, while the actual power they can wield is inevitably limited, they can play an influential advisory role. The involvement of ordinary staff representatives, by contrast, has declined in recent years, as the recommendations of the Jarratt Report (Committee of Vice-Chancellors and Principals 1985 – discussed later in this chapter) to introduce stronger management have impacted. Shattock (2002, 2003; see also Bargh et al. 1996) views these shifts in influence historically as fluctuations between academic- and corporate-dominated forms of university governance, arguing instead for what he calls shared governance. More recently, the Lambert Review (Lambert 2003; Shattock 2004) recommended further reforms in university governance.

Management

The organizational structure of the university is a combination of three frameworks, those of units, committees and officers, which are sometimes confused with the production, governance and administration functions. The fact that there are three frameworks and that they are not synonymous with those functions confirms the existence of complexity, fragmentation and the diffusion of authority within the university. (Lockwood 1985a: 34)

Universities are relatively unusual organizations, which in most cases have only recently adopted modern management practices. They had, after all, for much of their existence been relatively small institutions, with collegial patterns of operation that made any changes in practices slow, with academics supported by only a small administrative staff. More formalized and extensive institutional planning became common in the 1960s, with new universities being founded from scratch or from existing institutions (Lockwood 1985b). Only a decade or two later, however, national economic difficulties were to undermine the basis for such planning (see Chapter 4):

Financial uncertainty and constraint has not only affected the sums of money available to the universities, it has also reduced their planning horizons. The quinquennial system has been abandoned since the mid-1970s; from being certain of their funding over a five-year period, universities have found themselves working on annual budgets, sometimes not known until well into the year. (Pratt and Lockwood 1985: 8)

It was in these circumstances that the CVCP was pressured into investigating existing university management practices, and exploring how they might be improved.

The Jarratt Report

The 1985 Jarratt Report on university management consolidated the pressure for change by suggesting the centralization of executive control, the linkage between budgetary and academic considerations and the decentralization of accountable budgets to the lowest level. (Parker and Jary 1995: 324)

The Jarratt committee, led by an industrialist, was appointed by the CVCP in 1984, reporting in 1985 (CVCP 1985). It carried out efficiency studies of the management of six universities – Edinburgh, Essex, Loughborough, Nottingham, Sheffield and University College London – with particular foci on financial management, purchasing and buildings and plant. It was one of the first bodies in the UK to refer to students as 'the university's customers' (p. 9).

The Jarratt committee was, to say the least, highly critical of the universities and their working practices. The root cause of this was, in the committee's view, the unusual way in which academics were treated as employees:

Whatever the legal position may be, there is no doubt that a large proportion of the academic staff in universities either believe themselves to have security of tenure or act as though they have. Moreover, Senates in most universities believe that all academic staff should be treated as if they had tenure, whether or not they actually have. This in itself has inhibited change or even the discussion of change. (p. 10)

This was not a state of affairs that was conducive to the successful operation of universities and colleges at a time when public funding was declining in real terms, the UGC was becoming increasingly selective in the way it allocated available funds, and was expecting each university to be similarly selective. It was the committee's view that 'Government is coming to shape university development in a much more positive way than hitherto and this at a time when funding is not keeping pace with rising costs. This is likely to continue' (p. 14).

In this context, it was evident that the committee, well stocked with private sector representatives, were shocked when they discovered the reality of university planning at the time:

Long term planning is largely ignored ... There is no evidence of a thorough consideration of options and of means to arrive at objectives ... With the lack of strategic planning within universities and the short term planning horizons offered by the Government, it is not surprising to find little relation between long term objectives and the allocation of resources . . . A major omission is the lack of the systematic use of performance indicators . . . There is a general recognition . . . that the present committee structures for planning and allocation are not effective and need improvement . . . The responsibilities and accountabilities of heads of department are not always clearly defined . . . There is little formal accountability for the use of resources. (pp. 17–21)

Unsurprisingly, therefore, the committee recommended radical changes, and the adoption of private sector management practices:

No ideal planning structure can be laid down to fit the circumstances of every university but we offer the following as features which need to be present:

(a) It is important to bring the functions of planning, resource allocation and accountability together into one body in a corporate planning process.
(b) A planning and resources committee of strictly limited size reporting to Council and Senate . . .
(c) A series of bodies, each reporting specifically to the planning and resources committee, to deal with staffing, space, equipment and services.
(d) Care should be taken to find the best balance between effective central control and leadership and an appropriate degree of virement and incentive at budget centre level.
(e) Budget centres . . . should be large enough to ensure flexibility and redeployment . . .
(f) . . . [and be] aware of the full cost of their activities . . .
(g) There is a recognised need for reliable and consistent performance indicators. (p. 22)

Other recommendations included: the need for a clear division between academic and non-academic matters, with the latter (e.g. the operation of libraries and information technology, sports and social facilities, health services, careers advice, accommodation and marketing) becoming the responsibility of individual managers; the importance of regularly reviewing the size and frequency of committees; and the suggestion that it was time to transform vice-chancellors into chief executive officers:

The tradition of Vice Chancellors being scholars first and acting as a chairman of the Senate carrying out its will, rather than leading it strongly, is changing. The shift to the style of chief executive, bearing the responsibility for leadership and effective management of the institution, is emerging and is likely to be all the more necessary for the future . . . the use made of Pro-Vice-Chancellors will be increasingly vital. (pp. 26–7)

Academic departments were recognized as key units and budget centres, annual appraisal for individual academics was recommended, and the key managerial role of administrators was stressed.

Responses to Jarratt

The universities took the Jarratt Report very seriously, acting quickly at national level where this was possible, as in the adoption of performance indicators:

> The UGC and the Committee of Vice-Chancellors and Principals responded quickly to the Jarratt Report's recommendations on performance indicators by setting up a joint Working Group, which proposed a more detailed set of performance indicators than those suggested in the Jarratt Report. (Johnes and Taylor 1990: 7)

Performance indicators have been set and published regularly since then, though their impact on institutional strategy has not always been clear.

For most of Jarratt's recommendations, however, the response was in the hands of the individual universities. And, for the most part, they did respond, because they needed to do so in order to survive in a changing financial and political environment. Though the universities' responses took time to implement, they continue to have an impact:

> The Jarratt Report had long term effects on the internal management of institutions. Vice chancellors were to adopt the role of chief executives to whom deans and heads of department would report as line managers. The universities would create and work under a corporate plan that would be formulated by a small group drawn from the lay council and the senior academic management. (Kogan 2002: 57)

It was widely recognized, however, that responding to Jarratt represented a sea change in attitudes and practices within the universities, shifting these closer to those in the then polytechnics and colleges:

> Historically, there are two very different traditions of governance and management within UK universities. On the one hand, there are the 'old' pre-1992 universities established by royal charter, enjoying high levels of autonomy and traditionally run by and for the academic community. This was a collegial model, characterised by elaborate committee structures; slow, considered decision making; widespread consultation and high levels of academic staff involvement within institutional management ... The second key tradition arises from the 'new' post-1992 universities, the former polytechnics which acquired university status with the dismantling of the binary system. The former polytechnics had previously been run by local authorities before gaining their independence in 1987. Their approach to management was very different from the older universities, characterised by strong central control

and hierarchical models; line management was well developed for staff of all categories. (Taylor 2006: 252)

As, arguably, in the case of teaching, the tightly run polytechnic model has provided much of the template for the management of contemporary higher education institutions in the UK. But the former polytechnics have themselves also changed. McNay (1995) identified four models of universities as organizations, in terms of their positioning (from loose to tight) on the two dimensions of policy definition and control of implementation: collegium, bureaucracy, corporation and enterprise. In his terms, the latter part of the post-war period has seen the universities move from the collegium quadrant towards bureaucracy, while the former polytechnics moved from bureaucracy towards corporation; with both now seeking to move closer to the enterprise model.

These changes have involved the adoption of a variety of practices common in business and industry, though with varying enthusiasm and impact. For example, mission statements:

> It would appear that mission statements have been widely adopted by British universities, albeit most of them only relatively recently and probably only because they were required to do so as part of a strategic planning process itself a response to the demands of external stakeholders. For several of the 'new' universities, however, it was their establishment as a university which prompted the introduction of a mission statement. (Davies and Glaister 1996: 290–1)

Davies and Glaister also noted the tendency for the development of mission statements to be viewed as a matter for senior management only, with limited attempts made to communicate or use them once developed.

Changes in university management practices are continuing at the present time. Taylor examined the experience of four research-led, Russell Group universities during the first years of the twenty-first century. Each of them had undergone major organizational change, driven by the demands of improved administration, disciplinary change, external requirements and competition:

> All four universities have moved away from traditional Faculty and department structures towards new large 'super Faculties' with new large schools. Size of organizational unit was a crucial factor in the thinking of all four universities, implying efficiency of operation, enhanced managerial competence and potential for interdisciplinary collaboration in both teaching and research. In undertaking such restructuring, all four universities faced many fundamental issues, going to the core of academic life and organization ... In each case, the university concerned is treading a tightrope between the need for strong, authoritative central direction and a desire for devolved responsibilities and incentives. (Taylor 2006: 272)

While it was too early to judge how well these changes would succeed, it seems clear that continuing change in university organization is to be expected.

Leadership

The roles and characteristics of leaders in UK higher education institutions were of interest well before Jarratt reported. Thus, Collison and Millen (1969), using data drawn from *Who's Who*, showed that in 1935 68 per cent of vice-chancellors were from arts subjects, 19 per cent from science, 13 per cent from social science and none from technology. By 1967 there had been a shift away from arts and towards science, with respective proportions of 48 per cent, 41 per cent, 9 per cent and 3 per cent (p. 88). Virtually all, 95 per cent, of them had had predominantly academic careers in 1935, falling to 88 per cent by 1967 (p. 92). Half, 50 per cent, were members of the Athenaeum, a London gentlemen's club, in 1967 (p. 100). The great majority, 93 per cent, were aged 40 or over on appointment (54 per cent were 50 or over) in 1935, and 97 per cent (66 per cent) in 1967 (pp. 102–3).

Later research suggests that many of these patterns remain, and also that the labour market for leaders of higher education institutions is very much structured by institutional type:

> Our research data demonstrate some remarkably enduring character- istics in the career, educational and demographic profile of UK vice- chancellors. Vice-chancellors are typically males in their fifties . . . The vast majority, over 90%, are career academics appointed to their post after successful ascent of the higher education occupational hierarchy . . . One of the starkest results from our analysis is that there has been almost no movement from new to old universities. (Smith et al. 1999: 130–1)

Another clear and consistent finding of research is that the number of women working as senior managers or leaders in UK higher education remains small, and attitudes towards them are rather entrenched:

> the majority of our interviewees thought that gendered subjectivities, gender relations in the workplace and prevalent ideologies about gen- der roles were all important in either shaping their work as managers or in affecting how others regarded them and behaved towards them. (Deem 1999: 70; see also the discussion in Chapter 11)

Middlehurst surveyed leaders and managers in 'old' universities between 1986 and 1991, shortly after Jarratt had reported. The impact of that report is clear in how the leaders and managers viewed themselves, though Middlehurst argued that more needed to be done:

> The kind of leadership which is often projected as necessary for the academic world in response to the changes identified . . . is, in essence, a

transformational one where emphasis is placed on vision and a clear sense of direction, on building a corporate culture around common purposes, on political acumen, charisma and risk-taking. Top-down pro-active initiatives are seen as central to this process . . . Yet leadership . . . is crucially linked to the idea of 'taking people with you' and of building commitment, enthusiasm and trust in the directions and strategies proposed. This aspect of leadership has often been ignored in the rush to increase managerial efficiency, or to respond to government initiatives. (Middlehurst 1993: 82)

As well as noting the deficiencies in developing models of university management, Middlehurst identified the different arenas within which university leaders needed to operate:

In our study we identified three kinds of leadership that Vice Chancellors typically exercise: educational, academic and administrative . . . The first arena, that of educational leadership, has an external focus and takes place largely on an external stage. It is concerned with leadership in the realm of ideas and involves contributions to national and international policy debates . . . The second area, academic leadership, is concerned with establishing and promoting the academic direction and enhancing the academic performance of the institution . . . The third function, administrative leadership, is more directly concerned with the well-being, coordination and regulation of the whole institution. (p. 109)

She also identified the creation within the universities she studied of central management teams of the kind endorsed by Jarratt: 'One of the most notable features of changing styles of management in universities is the emergence of what can be loosely described as "senior management groups", which operate both apart from and in tandem with the formal committees' (p. 118).

Bargh et al. focused specifically on the role of the university 'chief executive', carrying out interviews and observations at 13 representative universities during 1995–97. They concluded that vice-chancellors had two key tasks: strategic planning and academic leadership, and that there was considerable overlap between these as well as divergence in the ways in which vice-chancellors went about their work:

. . . it is suggested that the vice-chancellor is not a manager or chief executive in the classical sense; while they now adopt a more managerial approach to many aspects of their work, the role is better conceived as a political one . . . The role, in formal terms, remains opaque and relies on a set of implicit and negotiated powers. (Bargh et al. 2000: 158)

By comparison with the central leadership of higher education institutions, relatively little attention has been given to the running of what Becher and Kogan (1992) referred to as the 'basic units'; that is, the component departments or schools that organize and deliver the academic activity of the university or college. This omission has occurred despite, or perhaps because of, the recent growth in the significance of departmental leadership: due to both the increasing size of departments and the increasing number of national initiatives – most notably the assessment of research and teaching quality – impacting at the departmental level. Not surprisingly, therefore, it is becoming more difficult to find academics willing, and with the requisite skills, to act as heads of department.

One notable recent exception to this lack of research is Knight and Trowler's study, which combines analysis of theory and practice with guidance. They couch their argument in the recognition that:

> ... leaders cannot hope simply to shape culture in the interests of organizational efficiency and effectiveness ... Neither can organizational policies be simply determined by the 'top team' with the expectation of unproblematic implementation on the ground. Organizational cultures are too localized, diverse, dynamic and rooted in extra-organizational structures, such as the disciplinary communities to which academics belong as well as to their departmental communities, for the levers of organizational change to be predictably effective. (Knight and Trowler 2001: 67)

Departmental heads, as the meat in the sandwich between the central university management and their academic colleagues, may opt, therefore – particularly if appointed for a period of only a few years – to take an essentially administrative rather than managerial approach.

Institutional relationships

The third part of this chapter examines the relationships that higher education institutions engage in, both with each other and with other kinds of institutions, and at all levels from the global to the local. Three main types of international relationship are considered: with the rest of the then British Empire, and later Commonwealth; within the European Community; and other international relationships. Focusing down then on the more local end of the global/local continuum, two other kinds of institutional relationship are examined: with local communities and with business. Finally, the institutional experience of economies of scale and mergers is considered.

International institutional relationships

At the international level, it is misconceived to simplistically view recent history through the lens of increasing globalization, though the contemporary impact of this trend is not to be denied. For, so far as higher education is concerned, there is a long history of transplantation of university models between countries (Ashby and Anderson 1966), a history which could be said to have begun with the multiplication of universities across Europe from the eleventh century onwards (de Ridder-Symoens 1992, 1996).

Three perspectives on international relationships are of particular relevance to UK higher education during the post-war period: those that took place within the British Empire, and latterly Commonwealth; those that, more recently, were located within the European community; and more general developments.

Empire and Commonwealth

> The Universities of Calcutta, Madras and Bombay were founded in 1857 on the model of its [the University of London] original constitution as were the Universities of the Punjab and Allahabad when they came into existence in 1882 and 1887 respectively. (Logan 1971: 18)

As an imperial power of long standing, it is no surprise that many of earliest international relationships entered into by UK higher education institutions were with institutions and individuals in other parts of the British Empire (and latterly Commonwealth). While independent universities were well-established by the early twentieth century in the 'old' Commonwealth countries (Australia, Canada, New Zealand, South Africa and – though now fully independent – the USA), this was not the case in many 'new' Commonwealth countries, notably in Africa. There the imperial power had been slow to encourage and support such developments (Nwauwa 1996), and aspirant students either went abroad to study – typically, of course, to the UK itself – or made use of the University of London's external degree system (Bell and Tight 1993).

Towards the end of the Second World War, as part of the huge surge of planning activity that took place at that time, two Commissions and one Committee were established to make recommendations as to the development of higher education in the then British colonies (Colonial Office 1945a, 1945b, 1945c). The University of London's external degree offered an obvious model for further development and application:

> At the present time, students of the University Colleges of Nottingham, Exeter, Southampton, Leicester and Hull sit for London external degrees. A similar evolution has already taken place in Ceylon, which was until recently a university college most of whose students worked for London degrees and is now a degree-granting university. The value of the London external degree in the development of higher education in different parts of the Empire is indeed well-recognised, and London examinations have been taken widely both by the 'private' student working in isolation and by students of the various colleges not yet of university rank. (Colonial Office 1945a: 39)

The result of these deliberations was the creation of an Inter-University Council for Higher Education in the Colonies. This would work as a cooperative association between the universities of Britain and the colonies, fostering the rapid development of colonial university colleges to independent university status. This development was couched in terms of general inter-university collaboration, involving staff visits, exchanges and secondments. While the University of London played the central role, a number of other UK universities were also involved, most notably the University of Durham, which had existing relationships with colleges in Barbados and Sierra Leone (Whiting 1932).

Though Africa was the main focus, the work of the Inter-University Council extended across the developing countries of the Empire:

> In 1955 the secretary of state for the colonies presented to parliament a report on the activities of the inter-university council over its first eight years. It records the state of the nine institutions which came under its influence: the Royal University of Malta; the universities of Hong Kong, Khartoum, and Malaya; the university colleges of the West Indies, the Gold Coast, Ibadan, and East Africa; and the college recently founded in Salisbury for Rhodesia and Nyasaland. It is a gratifying success story. Under the Colonial Development and Welfare Acts of 1945 and 1950 Britain had spent £7,750,000 on the nine institutions, nearly all of it on capital expenditure. The total contributions of the various local governments came to an even larger sum. There were in all about 800 staff and over 4,000 students, though student numbers . . . were not increasing fast . . . However, if quantity was disappointing, quality was not.
> (Ashby and Anderson 1966: 258)

The University of London alone entered into schemes of special relations with eight institutions in Africa and the Caribbean:

> The first was Gordon Memorial College in Khartoum, originally founded as a school by . . . Kitchener in 1898. For ten years after 1946 Sudanese students were permitted to take London degrees on the same basis as internal students and their teachers were permitted to suggest syllabuses and were appointed as examiners. Academic standards were raised and much was learnt by participating in the operations of an established university. The college became an independent university in 1956. The same special relationship was entered into with the University College of the West Indies in 1947, with the University College of Ibadan and the University College of the Gold Coast (later Ghana) in 1948, with Makerere University College in Uganda in 1949. The relationship lasted until 1961–3, by which time three further colleges were added: the University College of Rhodesia and Nyasaland in 1957–71, and the Royal College of Nairobi and the University College of Dar-es-Salaam in 1961–3. Altogether some 7000 London graduates were produced in this way.
> (Harte 1986: 252)

Much was made of the customised nature of the work, which allowed the colonial university colleges to vary the curriculum to better suit local needs and demands, introducing new subjects as required:

> The essence of the special relationship is that it is personal. It is not a uniform scheme but is developed separately for each college. The college works out in consultation with the University of London the arrangements which best suit its particular local conditions. (Inter-University Council for Higher Education Overseas 1955: 5)

These partnership arrangements lasted altogether for 24 years, from 1947 until 1970, when the last of the colonial university colleges attained independent status (Adams 1947, 1950; Carr-Saunders 1961; Maxwell 1980; Pattison 1984). The work involved was clearly both demanding and enervating:

> London did more than sponsor the university colleges; it took them into partnership. The University naturally retained control of its degrees, but teachers in the colleges had most of the privileges of teachers in the University's constituent schools; they could suggest syllabuses, were appointed University examiners and could register for higher degrees even if they were not London graduates. They learned how to manage the academic affairs of their own universities by participating in the affairs of an established university. The partnerships benefited both parties. (Pattison 1984: 167)

After 1970, the University of London seemed to lose interest for a while in its overseas role. Overseas registrations for the external degree were actually stopped in 1977, but then restarted in 1983 (Bell and Tight 1993). Closer relations with overseas institutions supporting external students are, however, once again on the agenda, and the numbers of external students have risen again to record levels (Jones 2008; Tight 2005). In a similar fashion, many other UK universities are now developing satellite campuses in other countries and/or relations with overseas institutions.

European developments

The European Union began to take an interest in higher education in 1971, shortly after the UK's accession, when the Ministers of Education of its component nations had their first meeting. At first, this interest was largely symbolic, focusing on what could be done through mutual agreement on student and staff exchanges, and recognition of qualifications. It became more concerted after 1983, with the COMETT programme, intended to promote cooperation between higher education and industry in training, introduced in 1986; and the ERASMUS programme, providing funding to enable student mobility, starting in 1987 (Baumgratz-Gangl 1996; de Wit and Verhoeven 2001; Smith 1996). While ERASMUS had an undoubted impact in developing the attitudes of the students involved, it substantially failed to achieve its target of getting 10 per cent of students to study abroad for a period (for an assessment from the student's perspective, see Chapter 10).

With the Single European Act and the creation of the internal market in Europe in 1992, supra-national higher education policy was to develop further. The LINGUA programme was designed to improve foreign language learning, while TEMPUS focused on encouraging mobility between eastern (then outside the European Union) and western Europe. SOCRATES was introduced in 1995 to continue and extend the work of ERASMUS and TEMPUS, alongside LEONARDO, which continued the work of COMETT and LINGUA.

More recently, the Sorbonne and Bologna declarations of 1998 and 1999 have sought to begin a process of harmonizing higher education practices and structures across the union. To date, however, this seems to have had a far greater impact outside the UK than within it, chiefly because the practices and structures chosen to harmonize around are very similar to those already existing in the UK (i.e. the three-tier structure of a relatively short first degree, followed by the master's degree and doctorate).

Other international developments

Two other international developments have been of key importance to UK higher education during the post-war period: the increasing numbers of students from other countries coming to study in the UK, and, conversely, the numbers of UK academics who have gone abroad to work.

Welcoming international students to Britain for study has a long history (see the broader discussion in Chapter 10), but there has been a significant shift in practice during the post-war period. Thus, in the first part of this period, as it had been pre-war, the emphasis was on students coming to study from the British colonies and Commonwealth countries. Such students were charged and ostensibly treated on the same basis as British students. During the latter part of the period, however, stimulated by the economic problems of the 1970s and 1980s, and the consequent pressures on higher education institutions to raise more funds from non-state sources, the emphasis has shifted towards charging international students higher fees and recruiting them from those countries that were prepared (usually on a family level) to pay the costs.

The trend for UK academics to go abroad to work, whether on a temporary or permanent basis, has somewhat paralleled the experience with international students. In other words, it has also been stimulated by the state of the UK economy, and the relative attractiveness of academic jobs in other countries, most notably the USA. This so-called 'brain drain' has been a feature, and a concern, throughout the post-war period. The reasons for it are easy to diagnose:

   . . . the reasons . . . for British scientists leaving . . . are: more opportunities . . . better pay and prospects . . . better facilities . . . frustration with the difficulties of getting research grants approved . . . aggressive recruiting . . . greater receptiveness of US industry to novel and untried ideas. (Advisory Board for the Research Councils 1985: para 8)

What is often overlooked, however, is the reverse process. Thus, historically, it has been common for graduates from the colonies and the British Commonwealth – who often, of course, would have received their higher education in the UK – to take up academic employment here. More recently, this inward migration of academics has come from a much wider range of countries. Indeed, in some disciplines (e.g. computer science, economics) – because of the much better paid opportunities outside academe – it is currently very difficult to recruit young UK academics.

Local institutional relationships

Shifting from the global to the local end of the continuum, there are two aspects of the relationships entered into by higher education institutions that are of particular relevance: those with the local community and those with business. Broadly speaking, these relationships have increased in significance as higher education institutions themselves have grown in size and numbers. Thus, Goddard et al. (1994) reviewed the various ways in which universities impacted on their local communities. They identified several different relationships: direct university employment (never more than 10 per cent of total local employment); local economic impact through purchase of goods and services by university, staff and students; technology transfer; vocational education and training; tourism; local student recruitment; and provision of continuing education, educational and cultural facilities.

The Organization for Economic Co-operation and Development took a similar view, but extended it further to suggest that these activities now constituted a 'third leg' or 'third role' for higher education, along with teaching and research, in much the same way that many US universities recognize the role of 'service':

> . . . universities have always made a wider contribution to the economy and society in the places which they are located – for example, through non-vocational education, research support for local firms, public lectures, concerts and access to museums and galleries. What is emerging now is a demand to recognise this activity as a 'third role' for universities not only sitting alongside, but integrated with, mainstream teaching and research. (OECD 1999: 10)

This is now also the perspective taken by the UK – though here the emphasis has been placed much more on third leg activities designed to stimulate the economy – and various incentive schemes have been created to encourage universities and colleges to do more in this respect.

Educational provision for the local community

For much of their history, as the discussion in Chapter 2 indicates, most UK higher education institutions have engaged to a substantial degree with their local communities in two main ways. The first of these was as their major market: thus, the universities and colleges established in the major cities in the late nineteenth century and early twentieth century were set up precisely to provide opportunities for local higher education, and to recruit local people. The second kind of relationship, starting again in the late nineteenth century, and involving the ancient universities of Oxford and Cambridge as well as more recent foundations, was through the provision of extramural or adult education classes.

Both of these relationships changed significantly during the post-war period. The largely local recruitment of many universities, colleges and, latterly, polytechnics, became less important as state support for full-time study was standardized in the early 1960s. This supported, and thus effectively encouraged, undergraduates – though not, of course, part-time students or mature students with family or other commitments – to study away from home (see the discussion of student accommodation and finance in Chapter 9). With the reduction and eventual removal of this support in the 1980s and 1990s, the financial attraction of studying close to home, particularly for students from poorer backgrounds, has been reinstated.

The extramural or adult education role of the established universities continued, indeed strengthened, during the first part of the post-war period. By the 1980s, however, it was coming under threat, as universities came under pressure to give greater priority to short updating courses for those in employment, and to accredit all of their provision, while massification undermined the social opportunity arguments that had originally been articulated to justify the universities' role in adult education. Thus extramural and adult education were rebadged as continuing education and then lifelong learning, and 'mainstreamed' within undergraduate provision as much as possible (see also Chapter 7).

Relations with business

For much of the post-war period the non-university institutions have arguably enjoyed a closer relationship with business, in both teaching and research, than the universities. That this has changed has been in large part due to the incorporation within the university sector of successive groups of institutions, most notably the former colleges of advanced technology (which brought in sandwich courses; see Chapter 7) and the polytechnics. The latter part of the period has witnessed more general encouragement from the government and national agencies for all higher education institutions to develop closer linkages, in both teaching and research, with business.

Thus, in the area of teaching, the 1980s (see Chapter 4) saw the launch of the PICKUP programme, a pump-priming scheme designed to get universities to offer more short post-experience courses, and the Enterprise in Higher Education initiative, an attempt to get higher education institutions to embed enterprise within their curricula. Meanwhile, in the area of research, a joint report by the Advisory Council for Applied Research and Development and the Advisory Board for the Research Councils (ACARD/ABRC 1983) recommended improvement of research links between higher education and industry.

The same period also witnessed the widespread development of science and industry parks by universities, the idea being that the co-location of particular types of industry – with firms often started by academics – with higher education brought mutual benefits. Their impact has, however, been assessed as relatively minor:

> . . . on quantitative criteria the significance of science parks has been much exaggerated. They will never represent more than a small proportion of high technology firms or jobs or floorspace, and they are but one (probably rather expensive) kind of university–industry research linkage. (Segal Quince Wicksteed 1988: vii)

The last decade has seen increased encouragement given to higher education institutions to become more entrepreneurial (Gray 1999). Some have gone so far as to identify 'entrepreneurial universities' (Clark 1998); that is, universities that not only seek to offer higher-quality teaching and research, but also to innovate and make profits, where possible, both from academic (e.g. business schools, post-experience provision, applied research) and non-academic (e.g. conferences, facilities) activities. Clark studied five European entrepreneurial universities, including Warwick and Strathclyde from the UK. He argued that such universities, if they were to be successful, needed to adopt particular managerial and incentivizing strategies:

> How do universities, by means of entrepreneurial action, go about transforming themselves? Five elements constitute an irreducible minimum: a strengthened steering core; an expanded developmental periphery; a diversified funding base; a stimulated academic heartland; and an integrated entrepreneurial culture. (Clark 1998: 5)

Most UK universities now have at least one central office working to try and stimulate, and then benefit from, entrepreneurial activities.

Institutional mergers and economies of scale

With increasing pressures on higher education institutions, particularly in the second half of the post-war period, to 'do more with less', it is no surprise that universities, polytechnics and colleges have been forced to look closely at their relations with each other. In the 1950s and 1960s, academics had clear ideas about the ideal and maximum sizes for higher education institutions – that is, a good deal smaller than they have become since – so that collegiality among students and staff could be safeguarded and promoted. Beyond that, much was achieved by cooperation between institutions. More recently, however, the 'bigger is better' view has come to dominate thinking. Hence, there has been a drive to secure economies of scale and scope through, for example, teaching larger classes:

> The situation now facing universities is that they are required to increase their student numbers with less than pro rata increases in resource inputs (and therefore cost). This threatens to impair the quality of the output of student-years, unless some real economies of scale are available. (Pickford 1975: 26)

One consequence of this trend has been the encouragement given to institutional restructuring, amalgamation and mergers. Rowley suggests there were up to 200 mergers involving a higher education partner in the UK in the 1970s and 1980s. These tended to share certain characteristics:

> Typically, *A* [the extant organisation] had 5,000–10,000 FTE (full-time equivalent) student numbers, while *B* [the merged institution] had fewer than 1,000. Their income ratio corresponded, at typically less than 10:1. In one-half of all examples, the distance between the partners was less than 10 miles, and the number of examples varied inversely with distance. In nearly every example, *A* had experience of operating in *B*'s geographical region . . . In 83% of examples, *B* was highly specialized in its academic portfolio. (Rowley 1997: 7)

As these figures suggest, it was particular kinds of institution that tended to get merged into larger institutions. Most, indeed, were colleges of education, pressured into these moves by the rapidly shifting policy of the period (see Chapter 4).

With two significant exceptions, no established university has ceased its independent existence in the post-war period. One exception is the University of Manchester Institute of Science and Technology (UMIST), which re-merged with the University of Manchester in 2004, having de-merged from it and been granted a separate charter in 1955. The other is London Guildhall University, the former City of London Polytechnic, which merged with London Metropolitan University, the former Polytechnic of North London, in 2002.

The New University of Ulster – which merged with Ulster Polytechnic to form the University of Ulster in 1984 – might be regarded as a third example, but the number of universities remained the same. The merger of the University College of Cardiff with the University of Wales Institute of Science and Technology (UWIST) in 1988 was somewhat similar, and also prompted by survival motives (Pritchard 1993; Shattock 1988, 2003). A few other institutions have suffered notable crises – for example, Thames Valley University over its quality assurance procedures in 1997–8 (Quality Assurance Agency

(QAA) for Higher Education 1998) – which for a period threatened their independent existence.

As the Manchester example suggests, however, there have also been examples of universities splitting in two to create more such institutions. This is shown by the division of Newcastle from Durham and Dundee from St Andrews. It can also be seen in the dissolution from the federal universities of London and Wales of Imperial College and Cardiff University respectively.

From collegiality to managerialism?

> How is it that these universities are able, despite their unpromising framework of government, to function virtually as self-governing societies? The answer lies in the direction of flow of business through the hierarchy of councils and committees. Major policy originates . . . at the level of departments and flows upwards to the Council as proposals to be approved: it never descends from the Council as directives to be obeyed. (Ashby 1966: 100)

> Managerialism, that is, the shift in power from senior academics and their departments to the central institution and the dominance of systems over academic values, resulted in part from institutions' need to meet new demands with fewer resources. (Kogan 2002: 57)

This final section considers whether it is the case, as these two quotations would suggest, that the various developments reviewed in this chapter – in the policies of national funding bodies and other national organizations; in the governance, management and leadership of individual higher education institutions; and in the relations between higher education institutions – set in their context of changes in underlying higher education policy, have caused, or at least paralleled, a move from collegiality to managerialism.

To begin with, we should recognize the mythic status of the idea of collegiality, bound up as it is with notions of a golden age in UK higher education at some time in the 1950s or 1960s (see the discussion in Chapter 11). This is not, of course, to say that there has never been any collegiality, but rather that the experience of it may have been limited to certain sorts of higher education institution and certain categories of academic staff and students. And we may also reject the necessarily pejorative connotations associated with managerialism, which would picture national and institutional managers as a kind of evil coterie hell bent on bringing academics to heel (though, again, there may be some truth in this point of view).

These reservations aside, however, virtually all of the evidence and argument is in support of a move from collegiality to managerialism, though the attitudes evidenced and explanations given are varied and nuanced. Thus, while some commentators view this development with regret, others regard it as a necessary change consequent upon massification, and yet others salute it as an essential freeing-up of innovative and entrepreneurial individuals and activities, enabling the maintenance and further development of the quality and international competitiveness of UK higher education.

Thus, Prichard contrasts the position in the pre-1992 and post-1992 (i.e. the former polytechnics and colleges) universities. In the case of the former:

> . . . despite the suggestion that the pre-1992 university to varying degrees resisted the managerial and market discourses, it is clear . . . that the demands of the HEFCE in the case of England have played a major part, together with the declining unit of resource, in provoking pre-1992 universities into deploying managerial practices – even if the label 'manager' was not attached to these processes. (Prichard 2000: 113)

Managerialism was, however, rather more full-blooded in the post-1992 universities, which had been used to local education authority control: 'It is this issue of strong central control worked out through the dictatorial practices of senior post-holders and "their" deans which many argue has become the hallmark of the post-1992 universities since incorporation in 1989' (pp. 115–16).

Taking a gendered perspective on the issue, Goode and Bagilhole identify a variety of stances taken by institutions and academics to managing change, ranging from resistance through collaboration to transformation:

> This research revealed distinctive stances towards the managing of an organization in flux, stances through which attempts were being made to preserve some of the earlier academic values and practices, within a regime imposed by a new entrepreneurial environment. The collaboration stance in particular [as opposed to the resistance and transformation stances] was characterized by an emphasis on competitiveness, self-sufficiency, hierarchical relationships and combative communication styles, over collegiality and staff development. (Goode and Bagilhole 1998: 161)

Deem and Brehony, tackling the issue head on, have identified the key features of what they term the 'new managerialism' in UK higher education:

> . . . changes to the funding environment, academic work and workloads (more students, a smaller unit of resource per student and pressure to do both teaching and research to a high standard); more emphasis on teamwork in both teaching and research, partly in response to external audit; the introduction of cost-centres to university departments or faculties; greater internal and external surveillance of the performance of academics and an increase in the proportion of managers, both career administrators and manager-academics, in universities . . . new managerialism as a general ideology is believed by both manager-academics and other academics and support staff to have permeated UK universities. (Deem and Brehony 2005: 225)

These features, in their view, have caused growing divisions within higher education institutions between 'manager-academics' (i.e. senior managers who used to be academics: it remains the case that, with the exception of specialist roles like information technology and estate management, senior managers in higher education are still predominantly former academics) and ordinary academics:

> The increased prominence of academics in management roles has also introduced a stronger divide between manager-academics and academics not in manager roles despite the fact that manager-academics have actually mostly previously worked as academics (and many continue to do so in an albeit more restricted manner). Management roles range from traditional heads of department (albeit with an enhanced role for performance management and quality control of teaching and research) through faculty deans (once a symbolic role, now often with a considerable amount of financial responsibility for faculty departments) to members of senior management teams such as Pro-Vice Chancellors and Vice Chancellors who determine the strategic direction of their institutions. (p. 226)

These changes and tensions are illustrated, for example, in the recent reorganization of four Russell Group (an elite group of research-led universities) institutions, driven by improved administration, disciplinary change, external requirements and competition: 'All four universities moved towards the establishment of a limited number of large multi-disciplinary Faculties or Colleges; in each case, a number of schools were established as a third tier of management' (Taylor 2006: 260).

We may conclude, then, with some limited exceptions, that managerialism is becoming the dominant *modus operandi* of UK higher education institutions, and it is difficult to see this trend changing in the foreseeable future.

7

Course design

Introduction

This chapter focuses on how institutions of higher education have designed and organized their courses during the post-war period. This is a topic, like many others, that has experienced changing fashions and the use of different labels. Whereas once we might have written or spoken of the syllabus and the curriculum, or of teaching and standards, now we are perhaps more likely to refer to learning and portfolios, or skill sets and quality.

In discussing course design, this chapter overtly takes the perspective of the institution, its component departments and lecturers. Essentially the same topic is considered, but from the perspective of the student, in Chapters 9 and 10. Thus, Chapter 9 focuses on the experience of undergraduate students, while Chapter 10 examines the experience of postgraduate, international and 'non-traditional' students.

This chapter is organized in three main sections. The first of these examines what might be thought of as the core element of higher education: the undergraduate curriculum (cf. Chapter 9). The second section then looks at other levels (sub-degree, postgraduate), types (professional) and modes (part time, sandwich, distance and e-learning) of curricular provision (cf. Chapter 10). The third section discusses changing practices and concerns regarding standards and quality. Finally, the chapter is briefly concluded by a discussion of the key question 'have standards changed'?

The undergraduate curriculum

This section is organized as a series of sub-sections that essentially follow the undergraduate's progression through the institution of higher education, examining how the institution responds at each stage. We start, therefore, by looking at the issues involved in student selection and enrolment, and how these have changed and developed over the post-war period. Learning, teaching and assessment practices, and curricular organization, are then reviewed. Finally, patterns of student success and dropout are explored.

Student selection and enrolment

> ... the concept of 'standards' embodied in admissions policies and procedures is one of the key elements in the value systems, internal and external, affecting higher education in Britain. (Fulton 1988: 16)

Throughout the post-war period, the selection and enrolment of under-graduate students has been largely a question of their level of performance, and qualifications gained, in their previous education (typically in secondary school or further education). Different (i.e. somewhat lower) standards have, at different times and in different institutions, been accepted from particular student groups (e.g. mature students), and alternative or equivalent qualifications have also been allowed (e.g. from international students or from home students following a vocational, rather than an academic, qualification route). But the basic process for the majority of student entrants has remained much the same, though the details have altered over time:

> Before 1951 admission to the *Degree courses* of the universities of England and Wales was theoretically based mainly on performance in the School Certificate examination, taken by grammar school pupils of about 16 years of age. To matriculate, i.e. qualify for admission, it was necessary to pass 'with credit' in five subjects, including English Language, Mathematics and a classical or modern language, though there was much variation between universities, and also additional faculty and departmental requirements. In practice many pupils stayed at school, studying in a narrower field of three or four subjects to take the Higher School Certificate two years later. Competition for places forced up the minimum standard of acceptance in some universities and in overcrowded courses such as Medicine. Those who passed the higher examination, however, were often able to secure exemption from the first year of university studies ... These examinations came to an end in 1950, being replaced the following year by the General Certificate of Education ... Minimum university entrance requirements (in February, 1953) are: passes in five or six subjects, of which two must be at the Advanced level. Candidates must pass in English language, a foreign or classical language, and Mathematics or an approved science. (Dale 1954: 1–2)

Just as the School Certificate and Higher School Certificate (which themselves had replaced university matriculation examinations, most notably that of the University of London – see Montgomery 1965) were phased out shortly before Dale was writing, so the General Certificate of Education (GCE) was replaced by the General Certificate of Secondary Education

(GCSE) from 1986. However, the Advanced (A) level (which has its origins in the University of London's intermediate degree examinations) currently still remains as the 'gold standard' of secondary educational performance, though buttressed somewhat by the introduction of the Advanced Supplementary (AS) level in 1989 (Kingdon 1991). The borderline between school and university education has been stabilized, at least for the time being – though attempts to broaden the school curriculum continue – so that advanced entry into the second or even later year of a degree course has become uncommon (except where students have followed an advanced course of further education, such as for a Higher National Certificate).

The general requirement for passes at particular levels in given subjects has been relaxed, though it remains on some courses (e.g. those seeking qualification as school teachers are still required to have GCSE passes in English and mathematics). Degree courses specializing in particular subjects typically require previous study of, and a certain level of qualification in, that subject (except in cases – for example medicine – where the subject is studied only at university level) and/or related subjects. Thus, for example, those seeking to study a science degree will typically be expected to have taken science A levels. And, of course, those courses and institutions that are in greater demand can set higher qualification targets or barriers, such that it is not unusual now for some to expect applicants to have, or be predicted to obtain, three or four relevant A levels with the highest possible grades (indeed, Oxford and Cambridge maintained their own entrance examinations for much of the post-war period).

The early part of the post-war period witnessed a growing recognition of the argument that the numbers entering higher education were being kept artificially low, and an increasing acceptance that there was no finite, limited 'pool of ability' (Furneaux 1961, 1963; Vernon 1963). This perspective underlay the work of the Robbins Committee (Committee on Higher Education 1963a; see also the discussion in Chapter 4), and later still became transformed further into the contemporary consensus: that the majority of the population are capable of benefiting from, and should have some engagement with, higher education.

As demand for higher education has grown, the more individualized selection of students (e.g. through extended interview) has been replaced by an essentially industrialized and national process (see the discussion of National Admissions Bodies in Chapter 6). More attention has also been given to the usefulness of school performance and other indicators for predicting success at university. Thus, the London School of Economics began investigating the use of psychological tests as early as 1945 (Himmelweit 1963).

Later, the National Foundation for Educational Research examined a test of academic aptitude (TAA) on behalf of the Committee of Vice-Chancellors and Principals (CVCP) (Choppin et al. 1973). Some 27,000 sixth-formers nationally took the test, and the subsequent performance of 7000 of them who entered UK universities in 1968 was assessed. The conclusions were, however, disappointing:

For most courses the best predictors of first-year performance as assessed by the university and of final degree results were GCE A-level grades . . . TAA appears to add little predictive information to that already provided by GCE results and school assessment in general. (Choppin et al. 1973: 63)

Similarly, in a Scottish study published in the early 1970s, Powell came to the conclusion that:

> . . . the levels of prediction obtainable on the basis of the school-level predictors presently used for university entrance are less than satisfactory but are unlikely to be markedly improved . . . The fact that most failure or drop-out was found to occur after only one year's attendance at classes makes it clear, however, that only improvement in the prediction of performance at this initial stage of the course would appreciably reduce 'wastage' of university resources. Yet this investigation holds no hope that any such improvements will be achieved. (Powell 1973: 77)

Hence, while school-leaving qualifications came to be acknowledged as a poor predictor of subsequent degree performance, they continued to be accepted as the best option available without devoting significant additional resources to the selection process (student 'wastage' is discussed further in this chapter in the sub-section on 'Student success and dropout').

From the institutional point of view, there have been two other main impacts of greatly expanded participation in higher education, and of increasing competition between institutions for the best or available students. One has been the closer attention paid to the marketing function, as higher education institutions have had to become more businesslike (Briggs 2006). The other has been the increased concern with student support, after they have been attracted to apply and are studying at the university. The contemporary consensus that the majority of the population are capable of benefiting from higher education is increasingly coupled with the view that, once admitted, it is the university's responsibility (rather than the student's) to do everything they can to ensure that students are retained and successful.

Learning, teaching and assessment

> . . . we doubt whether a teaching system which is based on small tutorials is necessarily expensive. (University Grants Committee 1964b: 116)

A 'typical' undergraduate course at a British university conjures up a set of familiar, almost emblematic pictures. The course will be founded on a single academic discipline: it will last three (or sometimes four) years; it will be taught by a combination of lectures and small group tutorials; and there will be examinations at the end of each year, consisting entirely of three-hour essay papers. Subjects with laboratory work will involve students doing standard set-piece experiments, often in rotation. These pictures are still generally valid: but we have come across numerous exceptions. (Nuffield Foundation 1975: 15)

From the institutional perspective, the impetus in the post-war period has been on whether and how to redesign and extend the conventional, accepted methods of teaching – lectures, seminars and tutorials, with laboratory sessions or fieldwork in particular subjects as well. These methods had a lengthy heritage, and had worked well enough when students were relatively few in number, and either well motivated or carefully selected.

Over the post-war period, however, the pressures on these practices have grown, with the demands to accommodate increasing numbers of students, make use of new learning technologies, and still enable each undergraduate to have a somewhat individualized experience (Gibbs and Jenkins 1992). Most recently, such initiatives have acquired the label of 'innovative', as opposed to 'traditional', learning and teaching, and become closely associated with government and funding body schemes (Hannan et al. 1999; Hannan and Silver 2000), and with the academic development movement. Indeed, the pendulum has now swung so far that it is old-fashioned to talk of 'teaching' and politically correct to refer only to 'learning'.

With continuing declines in the 'unit of resource', and in the ratio between numbers of staff and numbers of students, one obvious consequence has been larger class sizes. Outside of the most elite and well-resourced institutions, lectures, particularly on introductory courses in the first year, may now commonly be given to groups of several hundred. Many seminar groups are now of a size that lectures used to be, and tutorials may involve as many students as would previously have been designated a seminar group. In short, higher education has entered an era of mass production, or what some refer to as Fordism: 'Academics may not like it, but teaching has had to be transformed from a pre-Fordist artisan craft process into a Fordist organised mass production operation, at least in big universities and for undergraduate teaching' (Dearlove 1997: 68).

The potentially alienating effects of such operations, for both students and staff, have been mitigated to some degree by the widespread introduction of small group or individual activities, such as projects, presentations and dissertations. A whole raft of related learning and teaching strategies – for example, competency-based teaching, independent learning, peer tutoring, portfolio development, problem-based learning – have been developed and promoted to assist staff in these circumstances, though each has probably only been adopted by a minority of academics, and most particularly in specific disciplines or subject areas.

Most recently, online technologies have been used to provide alternative means of access to learning materials, to further encourage learning outside formal classes, and/or to provide mixed face-to-face/distance, or blended, learning environments (Conole and Oliver 2007). This has also compensated, to some extent, for the increasing necessity for many 'full-time' students to work part time, and their inability, as a consequence, to attend teaching sessions as regularly as they might otherwise have done. While relatively few courses – outside of the Open University and specialized postgraduate provision – operate largely or wholly on an online basis, it is now normal or expected that every higher education programme will provide at least basic guidance, lecture notes, reading lists and the like online.

The main trend in assessment practices during the post-war period has been an increasing balancing of the conventional, end-of-course, end-of-year or end-of-degree, unseen written examination with alternative forms of test (Brown et al. 1997; Cox 1967; Miller and Parlett 1974). This is not to say that conventional written examinations have been done away with – indeed, institutions and departments commonly retain policies to ensure that some minimum proportion of undergraduate assessment (at least) is by written examination – rather that more flexible types of assessment have been introduced alongside it (as they have in the school curriculum).

These alternative forms of assessment have included, most notably, project work and assignments completed during the course, sometimes involving groupwork, and, in certain subjects, multiple choice tests. At the same time, attempts have been made to make the criteria and purposes of assessment clearer, and to use the feedback process to change student learning practices in desired ways. Here, the ideas of closely aligning teaching, learning and assessment practices, and of providing timely formative, as well as later summative, feedback on performance, have been of key importance (e.g. Biggs 1999).

In the 1980s and 1990s, attempts were made by the government to encourage a much more skills-, competency- or outcomes-based approach to assessment, and to the higher education curriculum in general (Bennett et al. 2000; Jessup 1991; Stephenson and Weil 1992; Training Agency 1989). While this did lead to greater emphasis on work experience and work-based learning schemes, under the guise of making undergraduates more 'enterprising' or 'capable', and has been more recently supplanted by an emphasis on the developments of graduate skills or 'graduateness', the longer-term impact of such schemes is doubtful (Biggs et al. 1994; Coffield 1990; Cranmer 2006; Jones 1996; Jones and Little 1999).

There have been regular calls throughout the period to move away from the simple grading of degrees (i.e. the conventional first, upper second, lower second and third class designations) towards provision of broad profiles, giving more details of all that a student has studied and learnt, and their areas of strength and weakness (e.g. Klug 1977). While this, again, parallels moves in secondary education, it has yet to have a widespread impact on higher education. There have also been more general concerns expressed about academics' understanding and use of grading practices:

> There is no general agreement in higher education regarding how student performances should be graded, and no general understanding of the detail of how grades are cumulated into an overall index of

achievement. This presents those who use grades with an interpretive challenge, the scale of which is rarely appreciated. (Yorke 2008: 1)

In part, calls for changes in assessment practices have been motivated by a desire to both recognize, and give more appropriate credit for, the variability of students' ability and achievement. After all, in an increasingly 'massified' system, the more 'traditional' intentions of higher education – to produce well-rounded gentlemen or, in a few cases, prepare future academics – no longer apply:

> . . . staff expect few students to achieve excellence. Few students ever become critical or independent thinkers; few ever 'get on the inside' of a subject perspective or a professional orientation. Staff will tend to agree that their teaching and choice of content is oriented towards the standard of excellence which the majority will not achieve. (Percy and Salter 1976: 460)

Another major concern about grading is about what, if anything, interinstitutional (and, indeed, interdisciplinary) variability in degree results evidences, and what, if anything, should or might be done about it (this is discussed further in the section on 'Student success and dropout' in this chapter). For example, the Higher Education Quality Council (HEQC) examined this issue in the mid-1990s, concluding that:

> Variability in degree results cannot be regarded as unequivocal 'proof' of differences in standards . . . Between-subject comparability of degree awards does not and cannot exist because of the impossibility of deriving common yardsticks for assessing performance. The same problem applies to inter-temporal comparability. Viewed over time, degree standards are relative, not absolute . . . the fact that one university consistently awards a higher proportion of good degrees than another in the same subject may indicate better teaching, lower standards or some combination of these and other factors. (HEQC 1996c: 2–3)

Curricular organization

Just as student selection and teaching practices have changed – slowly and steadily, but not so dramatically that a lecturer from the 1950s would feel completely out of place in a 1990s' lecture hall – so the structure and organization of degrees has been subtly developed over time.

In the early 1960s, the Robbins Report (Committee on Higher Education 1963b, Volume II: 193–5) distinguished six types of first degree course: honours or pass degrees involving the study of one, two or three subjects. Since that time, the numbers of pass degrees – on which students could be registered from the start, as distinct from those awarded to students who had underperformed on honours degrees – have shrunk, as they were doing at the time Robbins was deliberating:

. . . pass degree courses offered for direct entry have decreased in number and . . . no new pass degree courses of this kind have been established in recent years . . . Preliminary years, from which appropriately qualified students are exempted, have been tending to disappear in recent years. (Committee on Higher Education 1963b: 207)

Robbins also noted the tendency for change in the content of degree courses, in order to keep them up to date, and for new courses to be established as knowledge developed:

> In pure and applied science many changes in first degree courses have occurred in response to the rapid expansion of scientific and technological knowledge and to the demand for more university-trained scientists and technologists. New knowledge has sometimes led to new first degree subjects, while in other cases it has required such sweeping changes in long-established subjects as to create virtually new courses and to alter the subdivision of old ones. Diversification within universities has also been an important factor, so that there are now more opportunities for studying certain subjects which were comparatively rare twenty years ago . . . Fewer new subjects had been introduced in the humanities and social studies faculties. There the changes were concerned more with broadening the treatment of subjects already taught and in combining them in different ways. (Committee on Higher Education 1963b: 201–2)

These trends have undoubtedly continued. The tendency for students to study more than one subject has, however, continued to diminish, as it was doing when the Robbins Report was being formulated. It was, and has remained, common for undergraduates to study related subjects in their first year, though differences in practice between Scotland and the rest of the UK were, and are, notable:

> Eighty per cent of first year students in England and Wales were taking examinable ancillaries or were involved in two-subject or three-subject courses; in their final year 75% will be on courses for which any examinable ancillaries they have had have been already completed. In Scotland no students were engaged in their first year in one-subject courses without ancillaries, and by their final year 64% of all students will be on courses in which ancillary subjects, if any, have normally been disposed of. (Committee on Higher Education 1963b: 213)

So, while the general pattern in England and Wales has been, increasingly, to register for, and complete, single-subject honours degree courses, more general degree structures have been the pattern in Scotland:

> First, the majority of students in Great Britain start and finish in honours courses. Second, the great majority of students in England and Wales are on one-subject honours courses, and this is equally true of students in the humanities, social studies, science and technology. By contrast, in

Scotland one-subject honours courses predominate only in technology. (Committee on Higher Education 1963b: 217)

The debate over the breadth and/or depth of university studies (as, indeed, of secondary education) has been a consistent theme of the post-war period, with – outside Scotland – a continuing disparity evident between rhetoric and practice (Jevons 1972).

Writing two decades after Robbins, Squires (1987: 129) noted that 'there has been surprisingly little direct discussion of the overall pattern and content of undergraduate studies in the UK'. He argued that there was a fundamental distinction between professional and academic courses:

Professional courses lead to a recognised professional qualification and licence to practice in one of the older well-established professions such as medicine, law and engineering, or in one of the newer professions or semi-professions such as pharmacy, social work, architecture, teaching, town planning, accountancy or management . . . With academic degrees, the direct, external manpower relationship is replaced by a much stronger internal relationship with academic structures and occupations. The student of history, English, sociology, mathematics or physics may or may not go on to use his knowledge and skills directly in a subsequent job; what is certain is that the way he studies the subject will reflect academic priorities and norms. (Squires 1987: 130–1)

Squires went on to recognize three other key dichotomies in the organization of the undergraduate curriculum: between breadth and depth, disciplines and interdisciplinarity, and theory and practice. He concluded that:

. . . higher education in the United Kingdom [sic: this statement is later qualified with reference to Scotland] today is largely *professional* education. Many degree courses are overtly professional anyway . . . But the argument has been that even 'academic' courses are professional in that they prepare students (ideally) for the academic professions. The pressures of professionalisation are felt not only in terms of the emphasis on expertise and depth, but in terms of the status of conventional disciplines and of what is called theory. (Squires 1987: 169, emphasis in original)

This pattern is then contrasted, rather unfavourably, with the broader, multidisciplinary patterns of study evident in, for example, the USA and Scotland, and at the Open University.

In a more recent, and more comprehensive, work, Squires (1990: 15–23) details 93 subject areas for first degree courses in the UK, from accountancy, banking and finance, through economics and pharmacy to veterinary medicine. He also noted that the details of what was provided varied significantly over time, as well as between institutions in the same subject or discipline (though some disciplines had a much more standardized curriculum than others).

One trend that has mitigated, to some extent, the increasing specialization of degree courses, noted by Robbins, Squires and others, has been the growing adoption of modular or unit course structures since the 1970s (Group for Research and Innovation in Higher Education 1976), often allowing for greater student choice:

> . . . multidisciplinary modular degree schemes . . . have a long academic tradition, [but] in their present form they are of recent growth in this country, although it could be said that some Scottish degrees have incorporated this pattern. They have been taken up notably by London University and the Open University, and have been growing to such an extent in polytechnics and other colleges in the CNAA system that they may become a distinguishing feature of this sector. (Lane 1975: 75, 78)

In the 1980s and 1990s, modularization was applied across whole institutions (e.g. Betts and Smith 1998; Bocock and Watson 1994). In terms of teaching and learning strategies, it had many of the characteristics of programmed learning:

> Essential characteristics of a fully modular scheme are as follows:
>
> 1. The material to be learned is organised in self-contained units of study, corresponding to uniform packages of timetabled hours . . .
> 2. Any student who has the necessary background may attend, so that the class is heterogeneous . . .
> 3. Each module is examined or assessed separately and the passes or grades obtained are accumulated by the student towards the award of the degree. (Lane 1975: 80–1)

Even more ambitious modular schemes have sought to develop national, and potentially international, credit accumulation and transfer systems (HEQC 1994; Toyne 1979). In practice, however, despite repeated initiatives, most modular applications have not been as fully developed as this. Indeed, their introduction has typically met a great deal of opposition (e.g. Seville 1997; Trowler 1998), and it has also long been argued that many of the benefits claimed are questionable (Church 1975).

Student success and dropout

Student success on degree courses – and its concomitant, dropout, wastage, non-completion or failure: the preferred term varies – has been a key concern throughout the post-war period, though the causes of this concern have varied over time. Long-standing concerns about failure rates have paralleled those about the variation in degree classifications between institutions and subjects (e.g. Dale 1959; Malleson 1958; Mountford 1957).

The University Grants Committee (UGC) (1958) collated data on the success or failure of students admitted to three or four-year degree courses in arts, pure science or technology in 1952. It found that, by the end of the

1955–6 academic year, 81 per cent had been successful, 3 per cent were still continuing their studies, 5 per cent had left for non-academic reasons, and 11 per cent had left having failed academically. The academic failure rate was highest in technology, at 16 per cent, compared to 13 per cent in science and 9 per cent in arts (p. 21).

Newfield (1963) reported on the degree performance of full-time UK students who entered in 1955 (n = c.6000). Overall, he found that in 1958 7 per cent of students gained first class degrees, 2 per cent undivided seconds, 20 per cent upper seconds, 20 per cent lower seconds, 13 per cent thirds and 22 per cent pass degrees (of whom 7 per cent had sat for honours degrees, and 15 per cent for pass degrees), while 5 per cent failed and 11 per cent did not sit their examinations (p. 118). The variations between university groups were not great, with the exception of the Scottish universities, where much higher proportions of students took pass degrees (65 per cent passing and 10 per cent failing). Differences by class and sex were also not great, though women got fewer firsts (3 per cent as compared to 8 per cent of men: p. 120). 'Good' (i.e. first or upper second class) degrees were commonest in the sciences (40 per cent), as compared to 35 per cent of arts and 33 per cent of technology students (p. 124).

The Committee on Higher Education report (1963b, Volume I) includes an analysis of 'wastage', based on UGC surveys. Without revealing the actual numbers or proportion of students who were thus classified, this analysis showed that 'Of those 1957 entrants in arts, science and technology who left without success by October 1961, 83% were recorded by their universities as leaving for academic reasons, among whom 16% failed their finals' (p. 125). Wastage was also shown to be lower at Oxbridge and higher at smaller universities, higher in science than in arts, and higher still in technology (pp. 128–9). It also varied from year to year: 'Only about half of students in arts, science and technology who leave without success do so in their first year at university, a quarter in their second year and a quarter in their final year' (p. 130). But these losses were by no means unmitigated: of those who left without success in 1955, 45 per cent had since gone on to further study, 8 per cent of them on degree courses (p. 137).

The Robbins Committee also turned their attention to the class of degrees obtained by undergraduates. In 1959, of those students graduating, 7.3 per cent gained first class degrees, 21.2 per cent upper seconds, 31.1 per cent lower seconds, 15.6 per cent other honours degree classifications, 24.8 per cent non-honours degrees (p. 140). They noted 'the diminishing proportion of degrees which are at pass or ordinary level' (p. 141), and the variability in degree classifications between disciplines:

> Within faculties, there are considerable differences in the spread of degree results between subjects . . . In humanities, 12% of graduates in classics obtained firsts compared with 7% in modern languages and 4% in history and geography. In science, comparable proportions are 14% in mathematics and 9% in geology; and in technology, 12% in

architecture and 7% in mining engineering and metallurgy. (Committee on Higher Education 1963b, Volume I: 145)

They also noted variations in student attainments between institutions, which could not be entirely explained by their different abilities and qualifications on entry:

> . . . the figures reveal wide differences in school leaving attainment, and these differences are broadly reflected in the proportions of entrants obtaining firsts and seconds, and in the proportions obtaining honours degrees. But the proportion of students obtaining firsts is much the same at Oxford and Cambridge, London and the larger civic universities despite the differences in entry qualifications, and it is much lower at the smaller than the larger civic universities, although the pattern of entry qualifications is similar. (Committee on Higher Education, 1963b, Volume I: 151)

Five years later, the UGC (1968) returned to the issue of student progress, focusing on students who would have been expected to complete their degrees in 1966. They found that 78 per cent completed their degrees in the expected period, 8 per cent did so after a further year, 1 per cent were still continuing their studies and 13 per cent left without obtaining a degree (p. 6). Completion rates were highest in arts and social studies, and lowest in engineering and technology; higher for women than for men; and higher for home than overseas students. Most of those who withdrew, 7 per cent, did so in the first year of study, with 4 per cent leaving in the second year and 3 per cent thereafter. Most who withdrew, 82 per cent, left for academic reasons, but there was a gender effect here, with 85 per cent of men leaving for such reasons compared to 69 per cent of women; and, while 25 per cent of women left for 'other' reasons, only 11 per cent of men did (p. 9).

A more psychiatric approach to dropout was expressed by Ryle, who worked in the Student Health Service at the University of Sussex. He considered students' physical and mental (especially) health as well as more mundane aspects:

> Evidence about the nature of the problems among students which are associated with wastage is fairly well documented and . . . reasonably consistent. Most writers agree that drop-outs include a significantly high proportion of those with personality or emotional problems. Estimates, where given, suggest that in Britain psychiatric illness may account for at least one-third of all wastage . . . clear identification of other relevant background factors is lacking. (Ryle 1969: 45–6)

Miller (1970: 13) quotes UGC figures showing that 15 per cent of arts undergraduates, 18 per cent of those studying science and 22 per cent in technology failed to gain a degree out of the 1952 entrants; but by 1957 the proportions had fallen to 12 per cent, 15 per cent and 21 per cent respectively. The proportion leaving without obtaining a degree in 1966 varied considerably between universities, from lows of 1.5 per cent at the Welsh National School of Medicine (i.e. one student: this detail of analysis would not be allowed today) and 3.4 per cent at Cambridge to highs of 40.5 per cent at St David's College Lampeter and 33.6 per cent at Heriot–Watt. The figure for all Scottish universities, 18.6 per cent, was above average, while that for England, 12.2 per cent, was relatively low (pp. 14–15).

Heywood offers an analysis, and extensive literature review, of UK studies of student wastage up until that time. He notes that the 'rate of wastage seems to have been relatively constant since 1950 (i.e. about 13–14 per cent)' (Heywood 1971: 192).

Bligh et al. (1980), using Universities Statistical Record (USR) data, examined the relationships between degree results, A-level scores, university type and discipline. While noting a relatively small, but significant, relation between A-level scores and degree results, they found considerable variations in degree classes by institutions and subjects. Thus, while 22 per cent of Oxbridge students in the physical sciences achieved first class degrees, only 1.5 per cent of those taking social sciences in the 'newer civic' universities did. Conversely, while only 3 per cent of those studying English in the then 'new universities' obtained a third class degree (and a further 1 per cent a pass or ordinary degree), the respective figures for physical sciences students in the 'ex-CATs' were 23 per cent and 20 per cent (p. 20).

More contemporary analyses of students' degree performance have become closely linked to debates on standards and quality, which are considered later in this chapter. One key change since the early part of the post-war period has been the improvement in degree results (i.e. classifications). Thus, one study of Higher Education Statistics Agency (HESA) data for 1995 graduates showed that 7.6 per cent of all degrees awarded were firsts, and 47.0 per cent 2.1s, meaning that the majority (54.6 per cent) of graduates now received 'good' degrees (Richardson and Woodley 2003: 482). While the proportion of firsts is very similar to that obtained in the analysis for the Robbins Committee, the proportion of 2.1s has more than doubled, with only a small minority (5.7 per cent) now getting the lowest classification of a third class degree. This has given rise to concerns, also felt within school education, about 'grade inflation' (Elton 1998).

Concerns over dropout have become more closely associated with the expansion of participation in higher education, and with the changed policies over student financing. Thus, Yorke surveyed former students from six institutions in the north-west of England, who had left prematurely during 1994–5 and 1995–6, using mail and telephone follow-up, achieving a 32 per cent response rate (2151 full-time and sandwich students, 328 part-time students). He concluded that:

> Three main influences on withdrawal dominate the responses of the full-time and sandwich students. Roughly equal in frequency of citation were the wrong choice of the field of study and financial problems, with

matters relating to the quality of the student experience a little further back. (Yorke 1999: 53)

Not surprisingly, the influences on part-time student withdrawal were found to be rather different, emphasizing the other demands on their time and attention: 'For the part-time students who responded to the surveys, the demands of employment were the most cited influence on withdrawal and were cited twice as often as the needs of dependants, the magnitude of the workload and financial problems' (p. 67).

Johnes and McNabb (2004) examined the records of about 100,000 students who passed through the central (old) university applications process in 1993. Their analysis stressed the importance of appropriate peer groups and the match between institution and student. In a smaller-scale study of 169 (23 per cent response rate) full-time students at two contrasting Scottish universities, Christie et al. confirmed that the reasons leading to withdrawal were complex, though they included an important financial element:

> Far from being a result of the academic weakness of the individual student, or simply the product of debt aversion, the study suggests that non-completion is a result of a complex range of factors including loneliness, isolation, poor course choice and financial problems. It is also clear that these problems are not unique to students who withdraw. (Christie et al. 2004: 631)

More recently, the National Audit Office (NAO) carried out a study of the national statistics on the issue in England for the House of Commons. It took an economic, indeed financial, perspective on the issue:

> Around 28,000 full-time and 87,000 part-time undergraduates who commenced their studies in 2004–05 were no longer in higher education in 2005–06. Substantially less value is gained from institution's investment in teaching undergraduates who do not complete their courses. (NAO 2007: 6)

Not surprisingly, the NAO found that part-time students and the less well-qualified were more likely to discontinue, which largely explained the variations in retention by subject and institution. While noting that 'the sector's performance on retention' had improved recently, and was good in international terms, it argued that more could be done by Higher Education Funding Council for England (HEFCE) and higher education institutions.

Other levels, types and modes of study

Other levels, types and modes of study have not received as much attention as full-time undergraduate study, perhaps not surprisingly given the latter's significance in overall higher education provision. Full-time undergraduate study, particularly when undertaken by 18 year olds entering straight from the school sixth form, is, in many ways, the 'gold standard' of higher education, and the image that probably comes to most people's minds in the UK when thinking about higher education.

Nonetheless, different levels (sub-degree, postgraduate), types (professional) and modes of study (part time, sandwich, distance and e-learning) have been the focus of policy and research concern, at different times and for different reasons, during the post-war period. In some cases, the issues raised overlap levels, types or modes of study. They will each be considered, in turn, in this section.

The sub-degree curriculum

Sub-degree level provision – that is, courses of higher education that do not lead, of themselves, to a first degree – has undoubtedly, compared to undergraduate study, received less attention than it has warranted. Substantial numbers of students have been enrolled in sub-degree level provision throughout the post-war period, though more commonly in non-university institutions than in universities themselves.

Compared to undergraduate study, however, this is a complicated level of provision; a kind of catch-all category for everything that is not a degree. For the purposes of this discussion, two main forms of sub-degree provision will be recognised, which have been largely separately organized, though recent developments have moved them closer together. First, there are certificate and diploma courses designed for young students who may not wish, or be able, to complete full degrees, mainly with a vocational rather than an academic intention, and often with employer support. Second, there are extramural, adult, continuing or lifelong learning (the preferred terminology has evolved over time) programmes targeted at older adults, and more often with a non-vocational, even leisure, intent.

Certificates and diplomas

For much of the post-war period, the mainstay of certificated sub-degree level provision has taken the form of higher national certificates and diplomas (part-time HNCs and full-time HNDs), and their Scottish equivalents (Venables 1955). Typically, these were two-year programmes, following on from ordinary national certificates and diplomas (ONCs and ONDs). The HNC was studied for while the student was in employment, not covering as wide a curriculum as the HND, but ostensibly being of the same level and standard. Sometimes HNCs and HNDs have been offered in parallel with degree programmes, to which they have enabled advanced standing, with the HND seen as equivalent to the first two years of a three-year degree programme.

The popularity of HNCs and HNDs has fluctuated over the period. Immediately following the war, enrolments increased rapidly:

The number of Ordinary and Higher National Certificates – the technician's qualifications – leaped upwards. In 1944 they only just exceeded the figure of 1939 (4,070 as against 3,999). By 1948 the number of Ordinary Certificates had more than trebled and that of Higher doubled; in 1952 nearly six times as many Higher National Certificates were gained as in 1938 – conclusive evidence that standards as well as numbers were rising. The range of demand increased; to meet this several new certificates were created. (Dent 1954: 135)

In the 1970s moves to upgrade the status of sub-degree level provision – and bring 'emerging professions' such as teaching and nursing more clearly within the ambit of higher education – by offering a different kind of qualification bore fruit. The Diploma in Higher Education (DipHE) was introduced, following the recommendation of the James Report (Department of Education and Science 1972). This, like the HNC and HND, was a two-year qualification (in its full-time mode), equivalent to the first two years of a degree programme, with a third year 'top-up' available if a full first degree was desired. Set against the 'gold standard' of the first degree, however, it did not really take off in the way desired.

After a decade and a half, Bruce et al. reviewed the DipHE experience. They identified that:

. . . three quite clearly distinguishable attitudes appeared towards DipHE curriculum development:

1. some polytechnics, aiming to open access to HE for a wider clientele than traditional students, attempted to develop genuinely new and radical approaches to HE,
2. some colleges of HE attempted to devise DipHE courses which were structurally innovative, allowing delayed choice before moving on to a BEd, BA, or BSc, and
3. some colleges used the DipHE as nothing more than a drop-out route for failing graduates – usually BEd students.

Commitment, therefore, ranged from mere lip-service to the new qualification, through desire for structural flexibility in pursuit of diversification, to a genuine desire to produce a radical alternative to conventional programmes which would allow much more open access to HE and encourage the development of more student-centred learning. (Bruce et al. 1989: 2)

Bruce et al. surveyed DipHE courses that recruited separately, or were linked to degree schemes, in 1984 and 1985, obtaining response rates varying between 39–53 per cent from a sample of 2252 students. Only 6 per cent of the students surveyed actually left with a DipHE, with 69 per cent progressing to a degree and 24 per cent withdrawing. They noted 'evidence of misunderstanding about the nature of the DipHE' and that 'the DipHE did not seem to have established a "clear identity" or to be held in high esteem by either students or employers'. Nonetheless, most respondents, 74 per cent, expressed satisfaction with their courses, and half, 49 per cent, felt that they had met their expectations (pp. 8, 9).

Recruitment to the DipHE continued to remain disappointing, certainly when compared with the HNC and HND:

> Of the 300,000 first year student enrolments in universities and colleges in 1992, less than 5,000 registered for the Diploma of Higher Education (of which half were student nurses) and only 2,000 registered from the previous year. BTEC Higher Diplomas and Certificates were faring better, but of the 79,000 initial enrolments (entirely in the former polytechnics and colleges), only 44,000 enrolled in the second year.
> (Robertson 1994: 296–7)

Arguments for the introduction of an alternative two-year qualification, to be called explicitly an associate or foundation 'degree', continued, linked to the desire to further expand participation in higher education. Foundation degrees were duly introduced in 2000. The 2003 White Paper (Department for Education and Skills 2003) gave the government's strong support to this initiative, as part of its policy of seeking to engage the majority of the population in higher education. Employers and institutions of higher education have now developed a range of foundation degrees, but the evidence on their success, when compared to conventional degrees, remains limited to date (Bowers-Brown 2006).

From extramural to lifelong education

The first half of the post-war period was also a time of expansion and increased recognition for what were then usually called extramural departments (Fieldhouse 1996; Kelly 1970; Raybould 1964). These offered adult education classes in a wide range of subjects, with literary, historical, political and environmental topics well represented. These would typically involve one evening meeting a week for a term, or a year, with no assessment or certification involved; though longer and certified schemes, some leading into degree programmes, were also offered:

> . . . the developments which have taken place since 1945, some of which are still gathering momentum, include the provision of an increasing number of courses with a strong vocational or semi-vocational purpose; the institution of extramural examinations and qualifications; the devotion of considerable resources to studies lacking any particular relevance to contemporary social affairs; the organising of many classes specially for university graduates and other students with a background of extended secondary, and often higher, education; a decline in the number of three-year courses, and a steady increase in the number of courses of less than one session's duration in which systematic private study is not a condition of membership; and organisational and administrative arrangements which put control of much of the work

wholly or almost wholly into university hands, with little if any participation by representatives of students. (Raybould 1964: 13–14)

By the 1970s, these arrangements – which in many areas could be characterized as offering leisure time learning for an ageing, and already well educated, middle-class audience – were coming under considerable pressure:

> . . . there was a growing expectation that university adult education should contribute to economic reconstruction and that this should take precedence over other aims. This led to a steadily growing emphasis on vocational training, post-experience courses and continuing professional education. (Fieldhouse 1996: 224)

For a time, liberal adult education was offered alongside shorter vocational courses in what had by then become departments of continuing education. Arguments were regularly made for the development of a coordinated system of provision – bringing closer together the work of the universities, the local education authorities and voluntary associations like the Workers' Educational Association (WEA) – including by the Russell Committee in 1973 (Department of Education and Science 1973) and the Advisory Council for Adult and Continuing Education in 1982 (ACACE 1982).

Over the decade between these two reports, the tenor of the argument was to change subtly. Thus, while the former recognized the importance of adults paying some of the costs of their education, but argued for greater 'educational leave', the latter proposed an educational entitlement for all adults and associated financial support. This idea was to resurface at the end of the century in the form of individual learning accounts, a national scheme providing limited funding for individuals for educational purposes, but these were soon discontinued due to fraud.

But the disparate aims, patterns and funding of liberal and vocational forms of education for adults made them difficult to organize alongside each other. In 1989, 'responsible body status', by which certain universities had been designated as providers of adult education, each with their own region, was abolished, and funding responsibility was transferred from the Department of Education and Science (DES) to the Universities Funding Council (UFC): 'This transfer of responsibility to the UFC ended the 65-year-old relationship between the 23 designated universities, the DES and the Inspectorate, and finally abolished the conditions of the adult education regulations' (Fieldhouse 1996: 228).

Adult and continuing education was henceforth both 'mainstreamed' – i.e. funded and organized alongside other forms of higher education – and accredited. While one consequence of this was the closure of the associated university departments, even the advocates of adult education recognized that the consequences were not all negative:

> It quickly became apparent that there might be two very important and positive effects of accreditation. One was that it forced universities to examine the quality of their continuing education programmes . . . The

second consequence which immediately began to show itself was that accredited courses attracted a younger and less well-educated clientele. (Fieldhouse 1996: 236)

The postgraduate curriculum

By comparison with sub-degree provision, much more attention has been given to the postgraduate curriculum, particularly during the second part of the post-war period. Much – at times, virtually all – of this attention, however, has been directed at postgraduate research study, rather than at taught master's courses (Knight 1997).

The Robbins Committee could justify this focus, at least at the time it was deliberating, in terms of the relative proportions of postgraduates studying for different purposes: 'Three quarters of postgraduate students (excluding students training to be teachers . . .) are engaged essentially in research, and this proportion has changed little in recent years' (Committee on Higher Education 1963b, Volume II: 218). They, nevertheless, recognized the recent growth in master's level provision, at that time mainly in the sciences, which was already starting to extend the time spent by some students in formal study, and which would grow in significance in subsequent decades:

> One of the major developments in science and applied science is the introduction of a MSc degree, granted on the result of a written exam-ination instead of (or in some cases, as well as) a thesis, after a course which normally lasts a year. (Committee on Higher Education 1963b, Volume II: 218–19)

Currently, only a minority of postgraduate students are studying for a doc-torate. Thus, the Higher Education Statistics Agency (HESA) statistics for 2006–7 (www.hesa.ac.uk) indicate that, of 128,390 higher degrees awarded, only 17,545 (14 per cent) were doctorates. In addition, 73,830 'other' post-graduate awards, including PGCEs, were made.

The 1980s and 1990s saw considerable attention given to the nature of the PhD, particularly in the social sciences, in the light of concerns about standards and practices as the numbers of research students increased (Burgess et al. 1994; Henkel and Kogan 1993; Tinkler and Jackson 2000; Young et al. 1987):

> By the mid-1980s it was evident that there were problems concerned with the submission and completion of the social science PhD, given that the proportion of candidates submitting a PhD thesis in four years was only 18.2 per cent of those who began their training in 1980. As a consequence the ESRC developed an institutional sanctions policy in universities and polytechnics. (Burgess 1994b: 3)

One key aspect of the debate about the doctorate was the perceived need to give greater attention to research training: 'While there has been little enthusiasm for "the American model" of the PhD, accepting research training as one objective has inevitably raised the question of structure and syllabus in the doctorate' (Becher et al. 1994: 53). Underlying this lack of enthusiasm, however, was a considerable variation in practices, and in views of what the PhD was for:

> There is no consistent view, either across disciplines or across institutions, about what constitutes an acceptable PhD thesis. Two key issues on which respondents disagreed concern the notion of originality and the nature of the written submission. On the former point, the more traditionally-inclined academics adopted a fairly strict interpretation of the requirement that a thesis should comprise an original contribution to scholarship in its field. In other words, it should not to any extent repeat work already done, and should ideally open up a new area for subsequent research. As against such a view, other respondents tended to regard the doctorate as having the primary purpose of providing advanced research training, leaving the fully-fledged research contribution to be made at the postdoctoral stage. (Becher et al. 1994: 108)

These variations in view impacted at all stages of the doctoral programme, and could lead to students, supervisors and their examiners having over-inflated expectations of what a doctorate could achieve:

> One underlying issue in the matter of tackling doctoral work is the relative absence of clear and distinct boundaries. In particular, it is difficult to pin down what are reasonable expectations of space and time, the amount of input required, the demands of examiners and the concept of standards. All these nebulous questions converge to test the resilience of the doctoral student during the final phase of his or her degree programme. (Becher et al. 1994: 126)

Another key element in the debate concerned completion rates. Young et al. studied practices in six universities on behalf of the Economic and Social Research Council (ESRC), interviewing academic and administrative staff. They found wide variations in submission rates, with, for example, the four-year submission rate for ESRC students registered in the years 1979/80 to 1984/5 ranging from just 4.5 per cent in one institution to a maximum of only 30.5 per cent in another (Young et al. 1987: 5). They concluded:

> We are persuaded that a measurable improvement would be likely to follow the more widespread adoption of the procedures and practices discussed in ... this report. Yet there were also indications that the diversity of academic and organisational circumstances between and within the six universities (and by extension, elsewhere in the university system) militates against the short-term adoption of such measures and thus against the widespread achievement of a radical improvement in submission rates. (Young et al. 1987: 2)

More recently, debate on the doctorate has moved on to consider the relative merits of the range of professional (sometimes, rather erroneously, termed 'taught') doctorates introduced from the 1990s onwards (Bourner et al. 2001). These have gained particular currency in certain subject areas, notably business and education. Typically targeted at mid-career professionals in employment, and therefore offered primarily on a part-time basis, professional doctorates have taken on elements of the 'American model', involving taught components with continuous assessment and a shorter research thesis.

The professional curriculum

> The professional bodies are organisations formed from the members of particular professions – by Royal Charter, by law or by articles of association – both to secure high national standards of professional service and to advance the interests of the profession. This is achieved by regulating conditions of membership, by asserting professional standards and codes of ethics, by advancing education and learning in the profession and by representing professional views to Government, industry and commerce or to overseas organisations. (Matterson 1981: 139)

The education of professionals has been a concern of universities and colleges throughout their history (Sutherland 2001; see Chapter 2), though the numbers of recognized professions and the nature of their relationship with higher education institutions have varied:

> ... professional education, training and qualification may be grouped into approximately four types: (1) the requirement of a university training including practical work spread over a prolonged period of time (doctors, veterinary surgeons, dentists); (2) a university degree or equivalent, with full-time or part-time education and training over an extended period (engineers, architects); (3) no full-time means of qualification, but a period of full-time sandwich courses (accountants, solicitors); (4) no full-time means of qualification, with education provided by evening classes, day release or correspondence tuition without the requirement of formal training. (Millerson 1973: 10)

Indeed, if we were to add to the professions mentioned by Millerson those others currently dealt with by universities – including, for example, teachers, nurses and other health workers, social workers and psychologists – it might be argued that most students, at both undergraduate and postgraduate levels, are following professional curricula (Becher 1994, 1999).

The relationship between profession and higher education institution is clearly mutually beneficial. Thus, university and college departments benefit from the associated recruitment, with courses that lead to entry into well-paid and respected professions being highly popular with students. As a corollary, they have to ensure that their provision meets the professional body's requirements, which involves some work and loss of autonomy (particularly in professions like teaching, where curricular requirements may change year by year).

The professional bodies, for their part, benefit from the preparation and screening process carried out by the higher education institutions. While their education and training could be organized in other ways – thus, some professional bodies provide their own training schemes, which often require and follow the successful completion of a relevant degree – most professional bodies work in liaison with universities or colleges.

Part-time study

Part-time higher education has long offered an alternative route to qualification for those students who have been unable or unwilling to study full-time (Hordley and Lee 1970; Raffe 1979). The growth in the numbers studying part time over the period – particularly outside the older universities, and at levels of study other than first degree – has reflected the opportunities and funding available for full-time courses, as well as the underlying state of the economy. Part-time higher education students have, in general, not been eligible for grants, had their fees paid, or been given other forms of state support, so have perforce had to rely on their own, or in some cases their employers', resources.

Though it was outside of its official remit, the Robbins Committee did give brief consideration to part-time higher education, seeing it mainly as a safety valve while full-time provision expanded to catch up with demand. It found that the majority, 85 per cent, of part-time day students attended college for one day a week in 1961–2, 14 per cent for less than one day a week. These would typically have been younger students studying at sub-degree level, and would have been given day release by their employers. By contrast, nearly half, 46 per cent, of part-time evening students attended three evenings a week – a major commitment – while 28 per cent attended on two evenings and 24 per cent on one evening (Committee on Higher Education 1963b, Volume II: 234).

More sustained attention was given to part-time forms of higher education by researchers in the early 1990s (e.g. Bourner et al. 1991; Smith and Saunders 1991; Tight 1991). They argued for the importance of part-time forms of provision in flexibly delivering study opportunities to diverse clients at a time of continuing expansion of the sector, while regretting the dominance of the full-time model, and the first degree, in policy-makers' thinking. Though these arguments have been regularly rehearsed since (e.g. Davies 1999; Schuller at al. 1999), little has changed in patterns of provision and support.

Thus, Boorman et al. (2006) surveyed the issues facing institutions offering part-time higher education for Universities UK, carrying out interviews at 26 UK higher education institutions. They found 'a complex mixture of different types of programme offering a variety of opportunities for students' (p. 5). While, at postgraduate level, part-time study could be seen as a clear alternative to full-time study, at undergraduate level it was usually the only alternative conceivable:

> The pattern of part-time study . . . is on the whole set flexibly to fit in with the student's availability, usually outside of normal working hours in locally accessible centres . . . The intensity of part-time study varies widely . . . It can also be varied to fit in with students' changing work or domestic responsibilities. (Boorman et al. 2006: 5)

The HESA's figures for 2006/7 (www.hesa.ac.uk) indicate that, of the 2,362,815 students then in UK higher education, 911,100 (39 per cent) were studying part time, a proportion which has remained fairly constant for some decades. This proportion varied with level of study, accounting for the majority, 57 per cent, of postgraduate students, as compared to one-third, 33 per cent, of undergraduates.

Sandwich courses

Sandwich courses – where periods of full-time study are interspersed, in a linked way, with periods of full-time work – are at least a century old (Venables 1959). Their underlying idea is to develop practical and academic understanding, and the interchange between them, at the same time:

> The first sandwich courses were introduced in the early 1900s, and the HND could be obtained by sandwich study at a number of colleges in 1956 (and still can). But the great achievement of the NCTA was to obtain academic recognition for sandwich courses. (Burgess and Pratt 1971: 35)

As Burgess and Pratt indicate, it was the work of the National Council for Technological Awards (NCTA) in the 1950s, with what were then the colleges of advanced technology (see Chapter 4), that successfully established sandwich provision – initially at certificate and diploma level, and subsequently at degree level when the Colleges of Advanced Technology (CAT) became universities – within higher education. There were varied ways in which the sandwich could be put together:

> Courses generally took one of two forms, depending on the arrangements for industrial training. In what the NCTA called 'sandwich' courses, the industrial and college periods were taken on alternate six months. On 'full-time' courses, the industrial training was taken for a full year, and later regulations ensured that this was during rather than before the course. When in 1961 the Ministry of Education introduced a classification of courses, both types of course were in the sandwich group, and became known as 'thin' and 'thick' sandwiches respectively. (Burgess and Pratt 1971: 30)

Sandwich provision was not, however, viewed as wholly positive in the 1950s and 1960s. Jahoda (1963) researched Diploma of Technology students at the then Brunel College, focusing in particular on the first industrial training period. She noted their comments on the equivalence or otherwise of what they were experiencing; that is, of the Dip Tech qualification, when compared to the degree, and of the CATs in which they were studying, when compared to universities (both issues that were soon to be resolved). She also encountered doubts regarding the lack of clarity of the role of industry in their education.

In the following decade, Smithers reported on longitudinal studies of sandwich course students at Bradford University (a former CAT). He also reported mixed views:

> . . . students entered sandwich courses with highly favourable attitudes to industrial training, but as their courses progressed they became somewhat less enthusiastic. The changes were mainly associated with the periods of industrial training themselves and they occurred among students on both thin and thick sandwiches and in various fields of study. (Smithers 1976: 127)

His tentative conclusion was that 'they have been something of a disappointment . . . The chief reason for disappointment is the acknowledged failure to bring the academic and industry parts into a satisfactory relationship' (p. 149).

These doubts were also shared, for related reasons, by many of the employers involved in sandwich provision, as a later study revealed:

> . . . sandwich courses are a mixed blessing in the eyes of many employers. They satisfy the need for work experience in undergraduate education but they create the problem for employers of providing that experience. Sandwich courses are not generally provided by the elite institutions and consequently are not perceived as attracting the best students. Further, the short period of the industrial placement is seen by some employers to disrupt work organization. (Roizen and Jepson 1985: 36)

Despite these continuing issues – and it has to be stated that both employers and students have reservations about other forms of higher education (i.e. full time and part time) as well, despite surveys consistently showing general satisfaction (see also Chapter 9) – the sandwich principle is now well established in the higher education sector.

Distance and e-learning provision

In another example of changing nomenclature, what was once known as correspondence tuition became distance education, and is now more commonly known as e-learning. Though educational technologists would argue that the distinctions relate to the more and more advanced technologies used in educational delivery, it may also be said that the underlying principles remain much the same. Correspondence, distance and e-learning are designed primarily for students who cannot attend educational institutions on a regular basis, but who instead have instruction and guidance relayed to them by post, telephone, radio, television and/or online. These techniques may, of course, be used in conjunction with a limited amount of face-to-face interaction – thus the Open University continues to offer summer schools and tutorial meetings in this form – or as adjuncts to conventionally delivered higher education.

Prior to the establishment of the Open University at the end of the 1960s, the leading provider of this form of higher education in the UK had been the University of London, through its external degree system. Apart from the course syllabuses and the examinations, however, the University of London actually provided very little in the way of distance support – with the exception of the BSc Econ degree, for which support was available through a Commerce Degree Bureau established after the First World War – leaving this role to private correspondence colleges and tutors.

Glatter et al. (1971) carried out a national survey of students enrolling on correspondence courses in 1967 for selected qualifications – including the University of London's external BSc Econ degree – achieving a response of 13,304 completed questionnaires (66 per cent). They also surveyed students who were known to have been studying for the qualifications in 1963 (2206 responses, 51 per cent). They concluded that most correspondence students lived in large conurbations, and so were not actually 'distant' from higher education opportunities, but had chosen to study in this way because they had 'positive expectations about features of the correspondence method' (p. 113). Vocational reasons for study were the strongest, and nearly all of the students were paying the costs of their study themselves.

Since then the Open University has become, and remains, the market leader in the UK for distance education, and now e-learning. While relatively few other universities and colleges became involved in distance education in the 1970s, 1980s and 1990s, with the principle exception of postgraduate programmes in business studies – where distance MBAs multiplied – all institutions of higher education now seek, and are expected to have, some engagement with e-learning (Cornford and Pollock 2003):

> The UK leader in eL [e-learning] remains the Open University. Its business depends on remote cost effective, well organised delivery of learning and, in the case of eL, good support for its tutorial model . . . Other HEIs [higher education institutions] now have similar high levels of engagement with eL. There are many examples of widespread deployment but they are distinctive: they are always within the specific structure and framework of the HEI and are integrated with local quality assurance and systems. (Slater 2005: 6)

These ambitions to engage with and exploit the possibilities afforded by e-learning reached a height in the foundation, with substantial funding, of the UKeU by the UK universities acting in a consortium at the start of the twenty-first century. The initiative was, however, short-lived:

> There are many people currently researching the reasons for the demise of the UKeU [United Kingdom eUniversity]. A possibly oversimplified explanation is that no-one actually had a primary interest in its success that was overriding. (Slater 2005: 8)

Standards and quality

In the immediate post-war period, few concerns were expressed about the standard of UK higher education (though there were concerns about, for example, the standard of the accommodation and equipment available). The first degree was, indeed, the 'gold standard', a relatively rare achievement that was highly regarded, if inevitably little understood, by the general public. There were few universities, and the system, such as it was, was dominated by Oxford and Cambridge, which had provided many of the (particularly senior) academic staff for the other institutions, and London, which oversaw the developing work of the university colleges through its external degree system.

With successive increases in the size of the UK higher education system – more students, more universities and more academics – a few concerns began to be raised about standards. There were, after all, naturally doubts about whether all institutions and departments could aspire to the quality of provision at Oxbridge, or even of the leading London colleges. And there were, from time to time, incidents or cases that provided support for these doubts. These concerns and doubts began to crystallize from the late 1960s onwards, taking a particular shape in the 1980s and 1990s in a demand for quality assurance.

This section focuses on two key aspects of this theme: first, the work of the Council for National Academic Awards from the 1960s to the 1990s; and, second, the 'quality movement', and its impact from the 1980s up until the present day.

The Council for National Academic Awards (CNAA)

> The CNAA's central concern was with standards, with the negotiation, approval and reapproval of courses through explicit validation procedures, with the quality of the student's academic environment. (Silver 1990: 90)

The CNAA was a fundamental part of the UK higher education system for three decades, between the 1960s and the 1990s, yet its existence and functions are probably little understood today among those studying and working in UK universities and colleges. The CNAA, established following the recommendations of the Robbins Committee (Committee on Higher Education 1963a), subsumed the National Council for Technological Awards (NCTA) and took on many of the roles exercised by the University of London's external degree system in the UK. In short, it validated higher education provision outside of the independent universities.

The CNAA both responded to the pressures being experienced by the external degree system, and steadily extended the approach of the NCTA, whose diplomas now became degrees in name as well as equivalence, to other subject areas. A key difference between its approach and that of the London external degree system was that the CNAA did not set the syllabus and examinations, but left that to the colleges themselves:

> The growing difficulties of the University of London's External degree system, with six times as many full-time students in the further education sector in 1961 as in 1957, with high failure rates, and the curriculum and examinations not subject to the control of the students' teachers, pointed to the need for alternative provision. The success of the National Council for Technological Awards (NCTA), created in 1955 to establish the Diploma in Technology, in raising standards of courses and colleges, giving college staff the power to devise courses together with control over teaching and examination, subject to external moderation, proved a compelling alternative. (Davis 1980: 31)

The practices and experience of the NCTA since its establishment in 1955 were a critical influence in the CNAA's early operations (Lane 1975):

> The NCTA did not itself conduct examinations or lay down syllabuses; this was left to the individual colleges (as with the national certificates and diplomas). Instead the NCTA had an inspectorial and supervisory role . . . The standards set by the NCTA were very high. In consequence the Dip. Tech. proved a notable success and became very acceptable to industry . . . This precedent was followed in art education when in 1961 the National Council for Diplomas in Art and Design was set up (equivalent to the NCTA) to administer a Diploma in Art and Design (equivalent to the Dip. Tech.). (Regan 1977: 180–1)

Another early influence on the CNAA was the experience of the established universities, to whom it naturally turned for much of the initial membership of the subject boards that conducted its validations. But these academics themselves had little experience of such a system (the NCTA had been limited to particular subject areas, while the London external system did not validate), which had to be quickly developed:

> The early history of the CNAA was dominated by university academics, who themselves (apart from the ubiquitous British system of external examiners) lacked any clear system of validation, formalized peer review or quality control. They, in the minds of officialdom, had a monopoly over the means of conducting legitimate academic discourse. They had

the credentials to conduct the examination, the maturity to administer the disciplines (both knowledge and power) that constituted the early CNAA. They and the CNAA officers virtually 'invented' a new academic panopticon. (Harrison 1994: 56)

The system that was developed was, indeed, highly bureaucratic. Getting a new degree programme approved in a polytechnic or college in the late 1960s or 1970s potentially involved several layers of government before the CNAA even became involved:

> Before a subject board can get down to the business of examining a proposal for a new degree course, other organs of the state have to give their blessing first. A college in England or Wales which wishes to offer a degree course . . . has first to seek the permission of its local education authority (usually a matter largely delegated by the authority to the college) and then the support of a Regional Advisory Council. If the proposal is supported regionally on the grounds of a need for the course, the matter is then sent for final decision to the Department for Education and Science, which considers the national need and the current level of provision, as well as the extra resources . . . that such a new course might entail. Only when this approval is given by the DES can the Council give its own academic approval, and in most cases subject boards do not give detailed consideration to a degree course until this whole process is completed or likely to be so. In Scotland most of the colleges offering CNAA courses are Central Institutions and approval for a new scheme is given by the Scottish Education Department. In Northern Ireland, the task is performed by the Northern Ireland Ministry of Education. (Lane 1975: 20–1)

The CNAA broke new ground in a number of ways, effectively establishing a modern pattern for course validation, and developing many of the processes that were later to be used throughout the higher education sector for quality assurance. Thus, it showed a keen interest in the institution offering the course, as much as in the details of the proposed course itself:

> From an early stage in its career, the Council saw the need to look at the environment in which a degree course was to be conducted. By this was meant not only the physical environment, in terms of the common facilities like libraries, student amenities and staff accommodation that might be expected to support all degree courses in a college, but the academic structure by which the staff could participate in policy-making and so exercise their full academic responsibility, and by which a college, acting collectively through its academic board, could help to uphold and maintain the quality of teaching and the standards of examinations. (Lane 1975: 26–7)

It also took a close interest in the broader student experience:

> While each university plans and validates its own degree programmes

in the light of a general awareness of policies, constraints and demands, the CNAA sets out general principles for first degree courses under its aegis. Many of these are couched in terms which would be unexceptional in universities . . . However, there are also two general principles which seem to signal a particular emphasis in the public sector. The first concerns the application of knowledge:

> The student must also be encouraged to develop the ability to see relationships within what he or she has learned, and to relate what he or she has learned to actual situations.

The second implies some breadth of study:

> The student must be encouraged to appreciate the nature of attitudes, modes of thought, practices and disciplines other than those of his or her own main studies. He or she must learn to perceive his or her own main studies in a broader perspective. As part of this process he or she must be enabled to develop an informed awareness of factors influencing the social and physical environment. (Squires 1990: 10–11, quoting CNAA 1986: 23)

A clear system of course and institutional validation emerged rapidly during the first decade of the CNAA's existence. All courses were expected to have specified aims, with strategies for teaching and assessment that delivered those aims. Considerable attention was also paid to 'the available or proposed necessary supporting resources, such as teaching accommodation, library facilities and other more specialised facilities where appropriate' (Whitburn et al. 1976: 153). A quinquennial pattern of institutional visits, reflecting the influence of UGC procedures, was established. Other patterns were also inherited:

> Naturally the legacy of London University work has been reflected in the design of CNAA degree proposals from a number of colleges involved in this transfer. In science, a typical example has been the preservation in some cases of the old 'London General' degree in the form of a three-subject first year (for example, physics, chemistry and mathematics), followed by two of these subjects studied for two years . . . Other colleges have drawn on the more recent London University model, the unit-based degree course. (Lane 1975: 42)

While this led some to accuse the CNAA of pursuing 'relatively conservative policies', that was arguably only natural for a new organization establishing itself in an uncertain terrain, particularly as 'both the Council and the colleges were under-powered in status and resource terms, which made an unfavourable climate for innovation' (Davis 1980: 40). Some significant innovations, such as the North East London Polytechnic's independent study scheme – in which each student was charged with developing their own degree programme, using available courses and project work (Percy et al. 1980) – were, however, supported and approved.

Over the first decade of its existence, the CNAA's work, and the spread of its disciplinary coverage, mushroomed:

> It is possible to see a number of processes taking place in the ten years since 1964, all adding to the complexity of the pattern of courses as it now exists in 1974. First of all, most external degree courses of London University have now been replaced by similar CNAA degree courses. Secondly, CNAA degrees have been substituted for many examinations previously conducted by professional bodies; and, thirdly, a number of new areas have developed based on some of the new syntheses and emphases of knowledge that emerge continuously as a historical process, in many cases assisted by a new vocational demand. (Lane 1975: 41)

The National Council for Diplomas in Art and Design merged with the CNAA in 1974. New DipHE courses were started experimentally in 1974 in association with the colleges of education.

Once its procedures had been clearly established and accepted, the CNAA was then able to begin a gradual loosening of its oversight of major institutions, moving towards partnership in validation by the end of the 1970s (CNAA 1973, 1979). Though they might at times have had reservations about some aspects of its work, the CNAA was intimately connected with the development of the polytechnics:

> ...whether the establishment of the CNAA facilitated individual polytechnic development, or whether the awarding of polytechnic status to individual colleges encouraged CNAA development and acceptance ... without such a vehicle as the CNAA, development of degree work would have been greatly impeded. The CNAA was an administrative necessity, and to this extent, facilitated the development of individual polytechnics. On the other hand, had not some colleges been elevated to polytechnic status and designated as 'the main centres for the future development of full-time higher education within the further education system', it is open to question whether their enthusiasm for developing degree work would have been quite the same. (Whitburn et al. 1976: 150)

More generally, the CNAA was the key vehicle for the development of the binary policy, which was announced shortly after its establishment:

> As an instrument of binary policy, the Council's record is an undoubted success. It has offered the academic base for the unparalleled expansion of degree and postgraduate work in the public sector colleges. In the UK as a whole, over 1,200 first degree courses, 45 DipHE courses and 423 postgraduate courses approved by the Council were running in 1980–81. In addition to the 120,000 students on first degree courses were 6,000 on CNAA DipHE courses, whilst 1,700 were following the Council's certificate of education courses and there were nearly 12,000 on CNAA postgraduate courses. (Pratt 1982: 118)

While the CNAA's very success was, of course, the instrument of its demise in 1992, with the elevation of the polytechnics and colleges it had played a crucial part in developing to independent university status, it has had a substantial legacy. A major part of that legacy is to be found in the drive to demonstrate and ensure quality across the higher education sector, initiated in the 1980s and continuing today.

The quality movement

Like all publicly provided services, UK higher education faces increasing pressure for accountability . . . These pressures reflect the greatly increased scale and cost of higher education, increasing consumer awareness and the ideological revolution that has led the Government increasingly to treat higher education as if it were a private good . . . As with many other professions, the traditional form of regulation in higher education has been self-regulation, by individual institutions and by the academic community collectively. We now have a mixture of self-regulation and external regulation, although self-regulation is still the principal mode. (Brown 2004: 3)

The concern with quality in the UK higher education sector, which began to be felt strongly from the 1980s onwards (see Chapter 4), was stimulated by government, public and internal concerns about coping with a massified system. Indeed, similar concerns were felt in other countries going through the same process. There were three main aspects of higher education affected: institutional management, which is considered in Chapter 6; research, considered in Chapter 8; and teaching and learning, the focus here.

The established means for ensuring the quality of teaching and learning in the universities was the external examiner system. By employing experienced academics from other universities, institutions were able to check that the quality of the work produced by their students – as evidenced in examination scripts and other assessed work – was on a par with that produced by students on similar courses at other universities. Typically, therefore, external examiners only concerned themselves with the outputs of the process; there was no direct assessment of the quality of the teaching and learning process itself. Nor, for that matter, were academics expected to engage in any form of teacher training.

Piper (1994) surveyed 757 course leaders (representing a 57 per cent response rate) and 645 external examiners (35 per cent), as well as interviewing 101 external examiners and administrators, in 1986/7. He argued that 'external examining may be regarded as an instance of a profession policing itself', while noting that there 'is evidence in the literature that the system falls short of the goal of maintaining parity between degree courses' (p. 233). He concluded that:

. . . the external examining system is not to be dismissed as an expensive cosmetic . . . It is a vigorous system involving a high proportion of the country's leading academics and the work is undertaken with great seriousness and care. It is a necessary function if there is to be a policy of parity between awards and it confers a number of incidental benefits. One might only ask that universities become a little less coy about enquiring into their own performance and more willing to produce and use the management data that all large organisations need if they are to be run purposefully. (p. 239)

Though Piper also noted that 'The most frequently heard comment from universities of all kinds was that the time and effort it required of academics were at best disproportionate to any gains accruing from it' (p. 99), it was clear at the time that more was going to be required. External examiners were still necessary, but not sufficient, for the modern climate of quality assurance:

> The external examiner system *remains* a crucial part of institutional quality assurance machinery because it provides an important external reference point. However, in the 1990s it is no longer the *only* means of ensuring the quality and standards of assessment processes and awards. (Williams 1997: 86; (original emphasis) see also Silver et al. 1995)

Matters moved quickly from the late 1980s onwards. The CVCP reported on academic standards in universities in 1986 (CVCP 1986), and an Academic Audit Unit was established by the higher education funding councils in 1990. The 1991 White Paper (DES 1991b) supplemented this with the Higher Education Quality Council (HEQC), which operated from 1992 to 1997 (Brown 2004).

> It is precisely because most of the 'traditional' universities are now unambiguously required to be mass higher education providers that they are being forced into a common system of 'three-tiered quality control' and assessment. The three-tiered nature of the system is an essential ingredient for a full-blown panopticon in higher education. Internal quality assurance systems, evaluated by external audit, are capped by a judgemental apparatus linked to the funding agency. (Harrison 1994: 56–7)

Particular interest was expressed in the franchising arrangements increasingly being used, both at home (e.g. with further education colleges) and overseas, by universities to offer courses through partner institutions, and in the idea of common specified graduate standards.

Assessment of a department's provision, involving a mixture of self-report and selective visits, was made on a three-point scale: excellent, satisfactory or unsatisfactory. Only 1 per cent of all departments in higher education institutions in England and Northern Ireland were found to be unsatisfactory:

> The overall outcome of the quality assessment exercise [1992–1995] was that 26 per cent of providers were excellent, 73 per cent were satisfactory

and 1 per cent were unsatisfactory . . . More UFC institutions claimed excellence and more were awarded excellence than PCFC institutions. (Williams 1997: 108–9)

This was, however, not enough. A more complex system was introduced, with departments producing extensive documentation, requiring a 'base room' to house it. Every department was then visited by inspection teams during the 1995/2001 period, with assessors observing a range of teaching sessions, and interviewing academics, students and other 'stakeholders'. Provision was scored out of 24 (out of 4 on six separate items), producing an overall average score of 21.12 over the period (Brown 2004: 93). Considerable criticism was levelled at the cost of the process, the scoring system employed, and the subsequent usage made of the scores awarded (Cook et al. 2006).

Part-way through this massive expenditure of time and effort, which again revealed little cause for concern, the HEQC was replaced by the Quality Assurance Agency (QAA) in 1997. By the end of the century, however, most parties to the process agreed that they were overdoing matters. A proposed new process of academic review was abandoned in 2001, and replaced by a more limited, institutional audit-based process, extolling 'lightness of touch'.

One other aspect of the quality movement, what has become known as academic development, is now, however, generally accepted and practised (if also somewhat resented). Historically, few academics, unlike school teachers, received any training in teaching (while at least those with doctorates had received some training in research), though a number of national and institutional schemes ran on a voluntary basis. From the late 1990s, HEFCE also made funds available for teaching quality enhancement, and a National Teaching Fellowship Scheme to recognize and reward excellent university teachers was instituted in 1999 (Trowler et al. 2005).

The increasing demands that academics should receive at least a basic teacher training were supported by the Dearing review (National Committee of Inquiry into Higher Education 1997a). This led directly to the creation of the Institute for Learning and Teaching in Higher Education (ILTHE), which was later absorbed by the Higher Education Academy (HEA) set up following the 2003 White Paper (Department for Education and Skills 2003). This also provided short-term funding for a series of subject-based Centres for Excellence in Teaching and Learning (CETLs). The Higher Education Academy (HEA) validates institutional academic development programmes, the successful completion of which is now normally expected of all new academics.

Have standards changed?

As the discussion so far may have suggested, a key issue, perhaps the key issue, in reviewing developments in course design over the last 60 odd years in the UK concerns whether standards have changed. Have they improved or been 'dumbed down' by the pressures towards massification? Is the level of achievement signified by the awarding of a degree of a particular class the same now as it was in 1946?

While these are undoubtedly key questions, they are also potentially dangerous to ask. Amis famously offered his answer in 1960 by asserting that 'more means worse' (Amis 1960). Ball responded 30 years later, during another of the periodic rounds of system expansion, by arguing that 'more means different' (Ball 1990). Both slogans could, of course, amount to much the same thing.

While most academics have avoided addressing these questions in public, especially when the awards given by their own institutions might be under debate, some researchers have provided qualified answers. Here are some selected from the research literature published in the 1990s. First, from a methodological point of view, Johnes and Taylor explored the usefulness of inter-university comparisons of non-completion rates, degree results, graduates' first destinations and research output. They concluded that such comparisons:

> . . . are of little value unless the inputs used to produce those outputs are explicitly taken into account. This can be done using regression models to estimate the output that each university *could be expected to produce given the inputs available to it.* Doubts were raised, however . . . about the value of using regression residuals to measure performance. In particular, it was shown that once inter-university variations in the inputs used were taken into account, the remaining 'unexplained' variation in each of the output measures was relatively small. (Johnes and Taylor 1990: 173, emphasis in original)

Second, here is a comment from Piper, in the context of his study of external examiners, on the impossibility of having an 'overall national standard':

> The purposes and justification of external examining have ultimately to be seen in the contexts and understandings of standards. There is not, however, and on the basis of the evidence available it would be difficult to envisage, an overall national standard for higher education (beyond what may be achievable in subject areas) which external examiners could be expected to help to sustain. (Piper 1994: 39)

Third, and almost in response, a comment from Court, suggesting that universities are benchmarking their standards against those of comparable institutions, set within a hierarchy of esteem:

> . . . there is evidence that higher education institutions – especially among the universities established before 1992 – are rethinking degree standards in terms of an academic standard related to the degrees of particular institutions, set in the context of the institution's tradition and reputation in teaching and research . . . Such a concept is a departure from the traditional, collegial nature of universities. In the days of

the elite higher education system, the honours degree gold standard was inclusive, in that it was supposed to represent a standard across all universities. (Court 1998: 118)

Fourth, and finally, here is Elton discussing the reasons for the observed upward drift in degree results in the latter part of the post-war period (such that a majority of students now graduate with at least a 2.1 degree):

> ... the most likely explanation ... is that the assessment instrument has been changed, through the inclusion of coursework (such that it now does not measure what it measured before), although the degree boundaries have been left unchanged. If this is so, then the effect reflects bad practice on the part of examiners rather than changes in student achievement. (Elton 1998: 35)

And my own answer, for what it is worth? Well, of course, standards have changed. How could they not do so, over a period of more than 60 years, at the start of which higher education was virtually a cottage industry, delivered by the elite for the elite; whereas now it is a major business, and we are getting close to educating half of the population to a higher level? How could they not, when in many disciplines assessment is a highly subjective matter, and the technology for assessment keeps changing? And how could they not, when academics are under increasing pressure to demonstrate that they are producing a quality product, and improved degree results will maintain or improve an institution's league table position?

But this does not mean that standards have uniformly gone down, or gone up. They probably have gone up, or gone down, in some subjects and in some places, but the pattern is undoubtedly complex. And other questions – such as the fitness for purpose of degrees and graduates – are probably rather more important.

8

Research and knowledge

Introduction

Research (and/or scholarship), along with teaching, comprises one half of what many have seen as the essential duality of higher education. The parenthetical reference to scholarship indicates that the nature and focus of the former half of this duality has changed over time, and that what it is called varies in terms of disciplinary and individual taste.

Both research and teaching rest inexorably on our changing understandings of knowledge. Teaching, from the perspective of the provider, has been considered in the preceding chapter (Chapter 7), while, from the perspective of the student, it is examined in the two chapters (Chapters 9 and 10) that follow. In this chapter, the focus is on research and knowledge, how they are understood and related to each other, the impact this has on the organization and practices of higher education, and how this has changed during the post-war period. The related issue of the idea of the university, and how this has changed, is considered in Chapter 12.

The chapter is organized in five main sections, considering:

- the place of knowledge and research in higher education
- the pattern of disciplines, their relationships and practices
- research funding and support, including, in the latter part of the period under consideration
- the impact of the research assessment exercise
- the relationship between research and teaching, and between these roles and other aspects of higher education.

The place of knowledge and research in higher education

The nature of knowledge and the nature of research are, of course, intimately bound together; with the former in essence the product of the latter, while the latter is typically driven by perceived inadequacies in the former. In organizational terms, within the university, both find expression through the pattern of disciplines, the subject of the following section. Here we focus on more general, cross-disciplinary, understandings of the nature of knowledge and research, and their place within higher education.

Historically, while universities and colleges have long served the function of disseminating knowledge and understanding – initially only to a select few individuals, but latterly to a substantial minority of the population, and perhaps soon a majority – their role in relation to research has not been so clear cut and established. Indeed, what may be called the 'classical ideal' of the university (see also Chapter 12), as advanced by Newman in the mid-nineteenth century (Newman [1852] 1976), saw the university as having no role in research (i.e. in the creation of new knowledge, as opposed to scholarship, or keeping up to date with thinking in one's field). After all, much of the post-Enlightenment development of science in the eighteenth century took place outside of the universities, and this continued to be the case, though to a decreasing extent, in the nineteenth century.

The classical ideal was under challenge at the time that Newman was writing (which is presumably why he was moved to write as he did), with the growing importance of science, the creation of new universities and colleges in the UK to spread access to higher education, and the development and diffusion of new university models in Germany and the USA. In these models, universities continued to play a key role in organizing and disseminating the growing body of knowledge, and took on the parallel role of creating further knowledge through research. However, while this new role was well established by the beginning of the twentieth century in the UK, it was by no means the case that active engagement in research was expected of all, or even the majority of, academics until well into the post-war period. Postgraduate study, whether for master's or research degrees, also remained a relatively small part of university activities until comparatively recently.

In the post-war period, the successive incorporation of new groups of institutions within the university sector (see Chapter 5) has affected the research role in a number of, not necessarily complementary, ways. Thus, while 'academic drift' (Pratt and Burgess 1974) has encouraged many newer universities, as well as aspirant universities, to seek to develop their research capacities so as to become more like older universities, some have also sought to champion alternative – for example, more applied or inter-disciplinary – approaches to both research and knowledge. Alternative approaches are, however, difficult to maintain in the longer term against a dominant, disciplinary (and funding) ideology; as, for example, universities like Keele and Sussex, which tried to redraw the 'map of knowledge', have found.

Conversely, as competition between institutions for available funding has increased, particularly in the latter part of the period (see the later discussion of the impact of the research assessment exercise), pressure has been placed on some of the newer university institutions to emphasize their teaching (knowledge dissemination roles) roles, and to support research only in specialized areas of particular strength. After all, not all of the institutions in a higher education system can aspire to 'world class' status in all, or even any, of their roles.

Even in the research-led universities, the pressure to deliver both high-quality teaching and high-quality research has led to the appointment of increasing numbers of 'teaching only' staff, typically specializing in the delivery of the early parts of the undergraduate curriculum. To some extent, this trend has balanced the continuing recruitment of 'research only' staff. While it used to be regarded as an early academic career stage, for many research – on a series of short-term and varied contracts – has become an alternative academic career (Collinson 2004; see also Chapter 11).

These recent trends have, however, resulted in (what is still seen as the core) 'research and teaching' academic staff becoming the minority of those employed in many universities, even though their influence remains strongest because of their core role and their more commonly permanent employment status. And, so long as they are successful, that influence is buttressed by the employment of others to carry out the more mundane teaching and research tasks.

Given this varied history and development, it may seem a little surprising, or perhaps an apt return to former practices, that recent analyses (Gibbons et al. 1994; Nowotny et al. 2001) have sought to challenge our understanding of knowledge and its creation, and to downplay the role of the academic. Thus, Gibbons et al. draw a dichotomous distinction between what they call mode 1 and mode 2 knowledge:

> By contrast with traditional knowledge, which we will call Mode 1, generated within a disciplinary, primarily cognitive, context, Mode 2 knowledge is created in broader, transdisciplinary social and economic contexts . . . The emergence of Mode 2, we believe, is profound and calls into question the adequacy of familiar knowledge producing institutions, whether universities, government research establishments, or corporate laboratories. (Gibbons et al. 1994: 1)

Others would, of course, refer to mode 1 knowledge as 'fundamental' or 'blue skies', and to mode 2 knowledge as 'applied', and view the distinction as being of long standing. Gibbons et al., though, would argue that the contemporary distinction is more deep-seated than that, relating to disciplinarity and social accountability:

> . . . in Mode 1 problems are set and solved in a context governed by the, largely academic, interests of a specific community. By contrast, Mode 2 knowledge is carried out in a context of application. Mode 1 is disciplinary while Mode 2 is transdisciplinary. Mode 1 is characterised by homogeneity, Mode 2 by heterogeneity. Organisationally, Mode 1 is hierarchical and tends to preserve its form, while Mode 2 is more heterarchical and transient. Each employs a different type of quality control.

In comparison with Mode 1, Mode 2 is more socially accountable and reflexive. It includes a wider, more temporary and heterogeneous set of practitioners, collaborating on a problem defined in a specific and localised context. (Gibbons et al. 1994: 3)

They link this accountability to the growth in targeted research funding, directed towards addressing issues identified by funders (i.e. by the government and its intermediaries, or by business and industrial sponsors):

Alongside the growing prominence of research an equally important shift has taken place in its character. Less and less it is curiosity-driven and funded out of general budgets which higher education is free to spend as it likes; more and more it is in the form of specific programmes funded by external agencies for defined purposes. This shift is also reflected in a changing view of university research. The emphasis has moved away from free enquiry to problem solving. (Gibbons et al. 1994: 78)

While Gibbons, Nowotny and their collaborators do have a point, it is probably rather overstated. The increased importance given in the UK, as in all developed nations, to the higher education of an increasing proportion of the population – couched in a policy language of knowledge economies, learning societies and widening participation – is enhancing the significance of the higher education sector (while, at the same time, making universities and colleges more commonplace). Engagement in knowledge production, of course, extends far beyond the university, but the universities still play the central role, and it is difficult to see how this could readily be replaced, or, indeed, why it should be.

The pattern of disciplines

In 1938–39, the largest faculties were those of arts and social studies with 44.7 per cent of the students; 27.3 per cent were in medicine and dentistry and 25.9 per cent in pure and applied science. By the end of the current quinquennium in 1966–67, the faculties of pure and applied science will contain 46.6 per cent of the students, arts and social studies 39.3 per cent and medicine and dentistry 11.6 per cent . . . the outstanding increase in the proportion of students studying pure and applied sciences has been due not so much to a falling off in the rate of increase in the arts and social studies as to a relative stability in the numbers of students studying medicine, dentistry, agriculture and veterinary science. (UGC 1964a: 83)

Studies of the different disciplines that structure study and research in higher education have taken a number of related approaches. Thus, there have been some generic studies, which have attempted to illustrate the overall development of patterns of disciplines over time (e.g. Abbott 2001;

Wagner 2001). In the latter part of the post-war period, and associated particularly with the name of Becher (Becher 1989, 1996; Becher and Trowler 2001), some studies have focused in particular on the internal structures and behaviours of disciplinary 'tribes' within their knowledge 'territories'. A further, and undoubtedly overall the most common, approach confines itself to the development of a particular discipline or subdiscipline. Since these are so common, and also often so detailed, only a limited number of examples will be referred to here.

Generic studies of disciplinary history often start from the classical or medieval, arts-based, curriculum of the trivium (grammar, rhetoric and logic) and quadrivium (arithmetic, music, geometry and astronomy; see, for example, Green 1969), and then trace developments from there. These developments include, most notably, the rise of the sciences in the late nineteenth century, and the technologies and social sciences in the first half of the twentieth century:

> Philosophy, anthropology, economics, history, played their discrete roles alongside psychology and sociology – all of them having established their academic bases and respectability in higher education at the end of the nineteenth century and in the early decades of the twentieth. Their history is basic to that of higher education in the twentieth century, and to that of education generally. (Silver 1983: 132–3)

In the post-war period, the relative decline of the arts disciplines has continued, in part associated with the decreasing relative importance of Oxbridge within the UK higher education system:

> Until the great upheavals that began about 1960 the arts were the core of university studies. Half the students in 1935 were in arts faculties. The picture was even more sharply marked at the universities of Oxford and Cambridge, whose arts students constituted respectively 80 per cent and 70 per cent of the entire student number. Philosophy, history, law, economics, the subjects relating to what humanity had done rather than the eternity it explored, dominated their outlook. (Carswell 1985: 8–9)

On the other hand, the science disciplines, with government support, continued to expand, at least for the first part of the post-war period. This expansion was associated with a redrawing of disciplinary boundaries and the development of new specialisms. Thus, the dichotomy between botany and zoology in biology was replaced by broad schools of biological sciences, and a concern with fields such as biochemistry, ecology, genetics and microbiology. This gave biological educators something of a dilemma of identity:

> Fundamental to the dilemma are, firstly, a concern to establish the biological sciences as rigorous, experimental sciences with the prestige and status of the physical sciences and secondly, the problem of defining the boundaries of this complex network of subject areas. (Waring 1979: 58)

From the 1960s onwards, however, the sciences declined in relative popularity, due to 'a general disillusion with science and the consequences of its application' (Dainton 1975: 37). The schools no longer produced sufficient numbers of well-qualified applicants for science degrees, and many university science departments struggled to recruit.

The social sciences also engaged in significant expansion after the Second World War, though this had much to do with their growing popularity with students. Jones (1963) surveyed all 25 departments in 1961/2 involved in social studies – which she defined as the linked fields of sociology, social administration and social work training – in the UK, and 196 (out of 223) of their members of staff. The responses she received conveyed a strong impression of a developing field:

> The views quoted . . . give some indication of the variety and complexity of the attitudes of university staff to their work, and of the considerable bitterness which exists in some quarters. Perhaps it is no greater than that existing in other developing fields of academic study – Psychology and Psychiatry spring to mind as subjects in which one can similarly find different schools of thought all busily denouncing each other's approach – and perhaps this is a sign of a lively and growing discipline. (Jones 1963: 26–7)

Since the institutional expansion of the 1960s and 1970s, however, the popularity of some of the social sciences has begun to diminish:

> The first wave of development of social science research which this country has ever known is now receding. It gathered momentum very slowly until the 1960s but then for a spell of fifteen years it was in full spate. There were only 212 university teachers in social science in 1938 but by the mid-70s the total was over 7,000. They became a very significant element in the universities, accounting for one in five of all academic staff, and in the polytechnics they were even more dominant. Alongside this increase in the teaching staff of higher education there grew up a substantial commitment to research funding by government which reached its peak in real terms in 1975/76; and more than half of these funds found their way into institutions of higher education. (Smith 1982: 150)

In more recent years, much of the continuing overall growth in social science numbers has been associated with the rise in importance of business and management studies. Yet this field, having emerged and rapidly established itself as of some significance – having had to overcome, in doing so, much mutual antipathy between academics and managers (Mosson 1965) – may also already have begun its decline. If so, some would see the seeds of this partly in a rather too enthusiastic apeing of existing university ideals by the academics concerned:

> The Oxbridge tradition of teaching not how to *do* certain kinds of work

but how to *be* a certain kind of person inclined the new management education toward, in one consultant's view, 'acculturisation for social roles at the expense of work itself'. Beginning with Henley, based on an archetypal country estate, such institutions spread a pastoral, gentry veneer over rising young executives. (Wiener 1981: 140, original emphasis)

For others, however, it was their adoption of US, rather than Oxbridge, practices that was of greater significance:

> The two elite schools which resulted from the [1960s] reforms, one in London and the other in Manchester, were inspired, and their educational structures deeply influenced, by American business schools' examples . . . London and Manchester adopted the two-years Masters programs; certain functional courses were taught (accounting, finance, law, economics, quantitative methods, psychology, organizational theory) in order to familiarize everyone in the program with business functions and managerial disciplines, but the courses also dealt with . . . management per se. The graduate schools at London and Manchester were . . . followed in the late 1960s and early 1970s by others which promoted management education, sometimes at the undergraduate (e.g. Bath), as well as graduate and postexperience levels of education. (Locke 1989: 177)

While the London school remains independent and strong, however, the Manchester school has been absorbed within the University of Manchester. The undergraduate level of business/management studies has continued to expand. In 2006–7, 310,255 students were registered on higher education courses in business and administrative studies – the most popular subject area recognized by the Higher Education Statistics Agency (HESA), accounting for 13 per cent of all students – and two-thirds of these were studying at undergraduate level (www.hesa.ac.uk).

Becher's work on academic tribes and territories, from the 1980s onwards, consciously built upon earlier disciplinary research. Becher (1989) interviewed over 200 academics in 12 disciplines in 18 elite universities in the UK and the USA (or, to be more precise, California). He focused on, among other things, the nature of the disciplines, specialization within them, community life, communications and careers. Applying the work of earlier researchers, he categorized the disciplines chosen in terms of 'four basic sets of properties: hard/soft and pure/applied in the cognitive realm; convergent/divergent and urban/rural in the social' (p. 153). He presented a picture of 'academic institutions made up of basic organizational units whose constituent faculty members have relatively little mutuality of research interest' (pp. 163–4), but concluded that:

> Paradoxically, the more it becomes necessary to recognize the academic scene as disjointed and compartmentalized, the more essential it becomes to turn towards an apprehension of that scene in its entirety.

The tribes, after all, share the same ethnicity; the territories they occupy are part of the same land mass. (Becher 1989: 171)

Becher later extended this research by examining six professions (1999 – for which he adopted a twofold technical/non-technical, procedural/processual typology), while his original study has also now been updated and extended (Becher and Trowler 2001). Delamont et al. have applied similar ideas in studying the transmission of disciplinary cultures between and across generations of academics:

> The social organization of academic socialization depends on the inter-generational transmission and inheritance of knowledge, skills and orientations: in short, of the academic habitus . . . there are significant cultural differences between different academic disciplines in the organization and construction of such transmission. Indeed, 'generation' itself is subject to different constructions in different cultural contexts. The nature of academic generations, and the character of transmission between them is subject to contrasting disciplinary definitions. (Delamont et al. 2000: 116)

Others have adopted the tribal approach in examining the history of particular disciplines or areas of study. Thus, Evans studied the discipline of English, noting the importance of myth, but also of the subdiscipline and the department:

> Most English People live their working lives as members of quite small groups which, like families, remain very constant over many years, and which, again like families, can be dominated by absent members, including the long dead. These groups may be organised in larger groups – English literature may be paired with English language or other entities in a school of some kind – and individuals may belong to various worldwide 'invisible colleges'. But basically the core sentient group is the department. (Evans 1993: 89)

He concluded his study on a metaphorical note, arguing for the perception, from within the discipline of English, of itself as a disorganized entity, when set against the imagined togetherness of others: 'The temptation to which I have yielded is to see English as the archipelago and other disciplines as land masses. I wonder rather whether *all* disciplines are not archipelagos which *others* see as land masses' (Evans 1993: 216, original emphasis). While this conclusion is probably apposite, it downplays the manner in which many disciplines – including, historically, English itself – tend to enjoy a period of comparative strength and importance.

Evans had earlier studied 'language people', a discipline that had emerged during the post-war period, and which became and remained strong, though mindful of its somewhat violent origins: 'Modern Linguists know that their subject emerged victorious from the struggle which destroyed Classics and they have an Oedipal fear of history's vengeful powers' (Evans 1988: 179).

To take one further example of a single discipline study, Cownie examined the case of legal academics, interviewing 54 academics in England in 2001–2. She concluded:

> . . . law is a discipline in transition, moving away from traditional doctrinal analysis towards a more contextual, interdisciplinary approach. When they talked to me, the legal academics I interviewed were evenly divided between those describing themselves as 'black-letter' (i.e. adopting a doctrinal approach) and those describing themselves as 'socio-legal/critical legal'. However, given the propensity of those adopting a socio-legal approach to stress the necessity for an understanding of cases and statutes before more theoretical analysis can be undertaken, and the equally strong comments made by the great majority of 'black-letter' lawyers about the importance of introducing contextual issues into their analysis, one could accurately characterise the dominant mode of academic law as 'concerned both with doctrine *and* with placing those doctrinal materials in their social context' . . . In embarking on the journey away from its purely doctrinal roots, academic law is cutting its closest ties with the legal profession, and bringing itself much nearer to the heart of the academy. (Cownie 2004: 197–8)

Beyond or between the disciplines lie those areas of study that have yet to achieve recognized disciplinary status: some of which will succeed while others fail. One example of such an emergent or contested subject area is, or has been, women's studies. Bird has sought to record something of the history of women's studies in the UK, noting its emergence in the 1960s and 1970s, its subsequent growth and decline, and its contemporary absorption into other disciplines, such as history and sociology. This cycle has been so marked that few free-standing women's studies degrees or departments are currently extant in the UK, though centres with this or similar titles, designed to coordinate continuing teaching and research in the area, still exist at a number of universities.

A somewhat similar fate – though it had been around for rather longer, and was, indeed, associated with the establishment of several older universities – has also befallen what was known for most of its life as adult education or extramural studies. At its peak, in the 1950s and 1960s, most of the established universities hosted large extramural or adult education departments, which were responsible for the provision of educational opportunities for adults not just within the university itself, but throughout their region. In the 1970s, these departments began to be transformed by pressures to provide more vocational and accredited courses, to which the label of 'continuing education' was attached. Latterly, this has again been renamed, this time as 'lifelong education', and, with the trends towards massification and accreditiation, the former adult education departments have almost all been shut down and their remaining work 'mainstreamed' throughout the university (see the discussion in Chapter 7).

Unlike women's studies, however, other areas of study have emerged in the post-war period and gone from strength to strength. One obvious example is that of computer science, which would probably now qualify as a discipline, having built on technological developments, and their associated and dedicated funding streams, to separate itself from other science and engineering disciplines (Clark 2006). In other cases, as already noted with the biological sciences, and also with subjects like medicine, new subdisciplines have regularly appeared through the splitting or merging or existing disciplinary territories and perspectives.

Research funding and support

The development of research funding and support in the UK during the post-war period, for both institutions and students, has essentially paralleled the development of the disciplines, though with some time lags built in. Throughout the period it has, however, given much higher priority to the demands of the hard sciences and medicine, given both their much higher costs and their greater immediate applicability to economic, technological and social needs.

For the first part of the period, a Department of Scientific and Industrial Research (DSIR – Melville 1962) oversaw the distribution of grants for scientific research, both in universities and in industry, and for postgraduate students. Separate medical and agricultural research councils had also been established for those fields in the first half of the twentieth century (see Chapter 2), and continued their work after the war.

By the early 1960s, there were doubts about the nature and extent of the DSIR's operation. Thus, in 1963, a Committee of Enquiry into the Organization of Civil Science recommended the dissolution of the DSIR, and its replacement by two new research councils: one for science and another for natural resources. Three years later, a Committee on Social Studies recommended the establishment of a further research council, the Social Science Research Council.

> The Science and Technology Act [1965] established four research councils – for science, for medicine, for agriculture and for the natural environment – together with an overarching Council for Scientific Policy which distributed a science budget between them. Very soon a fifth was added: the Social Science Research Council. (Carswell 1985: 59)

The DSIR was abolished at the same time, and the 'dual support' system – whereby funds for university research come from both the research councils and the funding bodies (i.e. the University Grants Committee (UGC) at this time, and, most recently, the Higher Education Funding Council for England (HEFCE) and its ilk) – which continues to this day, was formalized. This has been subject to significant strain at times, most notably during the 1980s following the cuts in university funding (ABRC/UGC 1982; see also Chapter 4).

Since then, the research councils, individually and collectively – acting through bodies such as the Advisory Board for the Research Councils (ABRC) – have exerted a major influence on research policy in the UK:

> Much of the visible politics of science spending in Britain revolves around the year-to-year budgets of the five research councils. Two of the five – the Medical and the Agricultural and Food Research Councils – date back to the first half of this [twentieth] century. The other three – the Science and Engineering Research Council (much the largest), the Natural Environment Research Council and the Economic and Social Research Council – began under the Labour government of the mid-1960s, though the first two had older roots. With the exception of the Economic and Social Research Council, long the poor relation, all the councils are large, complex organisations in their own right. They all sustain laboratories or support central establishments with long histories, as well as awarding grants for academic work elsewhere. (Ince 1986: 14)

There have been further changes in the number and identities of the research councils. Thus, as Ince indicates, the Social Science Research Council (SSRC) was renamed the Economic and Social Research Council (ESRC), as a result of the antipathy of the then prime minister, Margaret Thatcher, to the very idea of 'social science'. The various science research councils were reorganized and further split as a result of policy changes in 1993 (Chancellor of the Duchy of Lancaster 1993).

Currently, in addition to the continuing Medical Research Council (MRC) and National Environment Research Council (NERC), we have the Biotechnology and Biological Sciences Research Council (BBSRC), the Engineering and Physical Sciences Research Council (EPSRC) and the rather more prosaically named Science and Technology Facilities Council (STFC), formed in 2007 by the merger of the former Particle Physics and Astronomy Research Council (PPARC) and the Council for the Central Laboratory of the Research Councils (CCLRC). And, finally, in 2005, an Arts and Humanities Research Council was established, meaning that the ESRC was no longer the poor relation and that all of the main disciplinary areas now had their dedicated research council.

Along with the increasing recognition thereby given to the research function of the universities, another major development during the latter part of the post-war period has been – in line with general government policy (see Chapter 4) – the targeting of available funds more and more on particular topics and types of research: 'Increasingly, then, the funds available for the support of research in higher education became earmarked for research areas, or even specific topics, judged to be useful to industry or government departments' (Blume 1982: 25). This targeting has been further reified, from the mid-1980s onwards, by the development of the research assessment exercise (RAE), the subject of the next section of this chapter. The RAE has focused funding increasingly and selectively on the departments and institutions judged to be of the highest quality in particular disciplines and subject areas.

The increasing selectivity and targeting of the available research funds has also been associated with, though it does not wholly explain, a growth in both larger research projects and collaborative research. Thus, Smith (2001) notes that: 'Research, particularly in the life and natural sciences but also increasingly in other disciplines, has become an inherently collaborative endeavour' (p. 133). Smith studied relevant documents and carried out interviews with managers and research active staff in 15 higher education institutions for a HEFCE review. He identified three main models for collaborative research – interpersonal collaboration, team collaboration and corporate partnerships – involving increasing levels of formalization. He concluded that the models were integrally related, but that these relations were not well understood in management practice:

> Awareness of corporate and the larger team collaborations tends to be greater than the plethora of inter-individual collaborations. Corporate and team collaborations are usually associated with specific funding streams. They tend to have high visibility and (generally) are well aligned with broader institutional and research strategic objectives. Inter-individual collaborations tend to be much less formal, smaller in scale and more relevant to individual/disciplinary/professional research needs than corporate. Senior managers map such collaborations with much less precision. The paradox is that this model of collaboration forms the very foundations of the research system. Higher level collaborations are often impossible without this basic building block. Yet they are difficult to stimulate and manage; they are difficult to reconcile with the horizontal linkages that are the focus of corporate level partnership building. (Smith 2001: 154)

In terms of the funding and support for postgraduate student research, the post-war period has witnessed a steady growth in the numbers of studentships available, though with temporary cutbacks from time to time as economic circumstances have dictated. This growth has, in a similar way to the experience in undergraduate education, led to concerns about the quality of the training and support given by institutions to research students (particularly, of course, those funded by the research councils).

These concerns have impacted especially upon the social sciences, as the newest, least respected and, initially at least, least rigorous area of major research funding (see also Chapter 7). In the 1980s, the ESRC launched an inquiry into PhD submission rates (ESRC 1987), stimulated by worrying trends: 'ESRC's own data show that just under 4% of doctoral students submit theses within the three year maximum grant period; and the figures are 14.3% after four years and 24.8% after five years' (p. 1). The ESRC linked these concerns to a lack of consistency on the part of academics in their understanding of the purpose of research degrees:

> One of the striking findings in our inquiry has been the extent of confusion about doctoral degrees. We can record this only for the Social Sciences but we suspect it may extend to other fields. There has always been a tension between the training, learning and knowledge-generating elements but there seems to have been remarkably little debate or attempt to resolve the uncertainty. (ESRC 1987: 1)

In response, the ESRC has successfully strengthened the training component of the PhD, and developed a sanctions policy against universities and colleges judged as underperforming.

There have, however, also been more general concerns expressed about postgraduate education. The HEFCE commissioned its own report into the structure and funding of postgraduate education in the mid-1990s (HEFCE 1996b), which concluded that there was a need for greater clarity, and a standard nomenclature, so as to make sense of the increasing diversity of provision. It also argued for a strengthening of quality assurance, the development of institutional codes of practice for postgraduate research provision and the restriction of HEFCE funding for research students to institutions and departments that had a pervasive research culture.

This latter idea of the need for a 'critical mass' of doctoral research students has been criticized (Delamont et al. 1997) as perhaps being suitable to the laboratory sciences, but not a policy that could sensibly be implemented across all disciplines. It does, though, reflect the general trend in research funding and support, for both students and institutions (and, beyond research, more broadly throughout higher education as a whole). And it is a strategy that has been picked up in some, at least, of the social sciences, as well as some other disciplines, through the development of professional doctorate programmes designed to recruit and train cohorts of students, in contrast to the more conventional individual supervisory model.

The impact of the research assessment exercise

> For British academics, one very clear answer to the question of what is a discipline is those subjects defined in the Research Assessment Exercise (RAE) as Units of Assessment. For many of the British women that I interviewed, the RAE had marked the end of any separate involvement in Women's Studies, and an end to interdisciplinary work. (Bird 2001: 473)

The introduction of the research assessment exercise (RAE) in 1985/6, and its repeated use every few years since then, has been the main driver behind increasing selectivity in the distribution of research funding by the funding councils (i.e. the HEFCE, its parallel bodies and predecessors, the other part of the dual support system to the research councils). It has forced all institutions and academics to take research very seriously – even if they were not in a position to do much – and has shaped the structuring and development of universities, particularly those that have been more successful in the RAE over the last 20 years:

the RAE was one of a number of developments that converted research from a matter of individual professional responsibility to one of collective interest to institutions and departments. It triggered substantial changes in the management of the research function in universities and in academic professional culture. (Henkel 2000: 116)

The RAE was, of course, subjected to detailed and sustained examination by those it impacted on – that is, academics – right from the start. Thus, the 1989 exercise was criticized because the size of the subject centres (departments or groups of departments) reviewed appeared to have a positive effect on their rating, and because there was a 'vast disparity in the mean research rating between subjects' (Johnes and Taylor 1992: 86).

McNay (1997) concluded from his analysis of the 1992 exercise that institutions were responding to its demands by developing increasingly tight management practices. His later examination of the 2001 exercise led him to the view that: 'there were some issues of lack of clarity and consistency in the assignment of points for research quality among the various disciplines. There were differences in level of sampling and in how the final grade was constructed' (McNay 2003: 47). Research into professional areas appeared to be particularly disadvantaged by this system.

Sharp carried out a longitudinal analysis of the results of the 1992, 1996 and 2001 exercises. He found that not only had average ratings improved markedly over time, but that this varied between units of assessment (Unit of Assessment (UoAs-groups of subject centres). While this was due to some extent to the withdrawal of weak submissions, doubts were also cast over the validity of the RAE over time:

. . . the approach adopted so far in the RAEs has been wholly criterion-referenced, with the distribution of ratings in each UoA left to the Panel concerned . . . this latitude has led to inconsistencies between Panels in the usage of the rating scale. Panels seem to be developing different 'cultures' in respect of the proportion of 5 and 5* ratings [the highest ratings possible] awarded . . . This is a matter which needs to be addressed if the scale is to have credibility as a measure of research quality. (Sharp 2004: 216–17)

The RAEs were primarily interested in research that led, and led fairly quickly, to measurable outputs. This resulted, at one end of the research process, to discernible changes in publication and dissemination strategies (i.e. making them both quicker and more extensive). At the other end, it led to notably different strategies – even in the conventionally more individualistic disciplines of the arts, humanities and social sciences – for garnering and applying research funds: 'the importance of the RAE and its emphases on research output had created pressures for departments to become bigger, more senior and with more divisions on status, more structured, more specialised and more collective in their approach' (Henkel 2000: 134). In short, academics with track records of garnering significant research funds became a sought after and highly valued commodity.

Strategies also changed at the institutional level, with increasing attention paid to the playing of the RAE 'game' – which tended to change subtly between one exercise and the next as the rules (written and unwritten) were tweaked and lessons were learnt – and a growing ruthlessness in responding to its outcomes:

> Almost all of the 'old' universities had a pro-vice-chancellor responsible for research by the early 1990s. All universities evolved policies to improve performance. They had to consider the balance to be struck between teaching and research. At first, universities were reluctant to exercise selectivity in funding based on research performance and, indeed, many vired resources from high to low-rated departments. Only after 1996 was there substantial evidence of departmental mergers and restructuring to strengthen RAE performance. (Kogan 2002: 60)

Lucas interviewed institutional managers and academics in two universities (one older, one former polytechnic) in 1997/9, focusing on their departments of biology, English and sociology, and the impact of the research assessment exercise upon them. She found that a new logic had replaced the older patterns of the dual funding system. Though the national funding councils continued to fund institutions in a generic sense for research as well as teaching, individual academics and departments could only justify spending time on research where specific funds had been obtained:

> Academic time for research as well as the cost of research now has to be paid for by external funding. In the race to play in the main game of university research and to be successful in the RAE, therefore, the pressure is on to accumulate more and more material capital to support research work within universities. (Lucas 2006: 167)

This has not only re-emphasized the historical diversity and hierarchy of higher education institutions (see Chapter 5), but has privileged particular kinds of research; that is, those that will readily lead to measurable outputs:

> The RAE has served to increase the hierarchy and differentiation between universities, divisions created within university departments, steering and directing research efforts resulting in a homogenizing of research areas towards the mainstream, short-termism and lack of innovation, and also ensuring that research has become the prime motivator and mover within university departments detracting attention, resources and energy away from non-research activities, primarily teaching, and undervaluing applied and interdisciplinary research. The

differential valuing of teaching, administration and research, although perhaps always a feature of university life, has intensified and left many feeling demoralized. (Lucas 2006: 168)

The resulting and increasing emphasis placed on role divisions, noted earlier in this chapter, threatens to fragment the higher education community, destroying what many have seen as the essential synergy between research and teaching.

The relationship between research and teaching

The bulk of academic men [sic] believe, in principle, that the academic role should involve both teaching *and* research. (Halsey et al. 1971: 276)

The close relationship between research and teaching is widely assumed within higher education, whether it is actually practised or not. There have, of course, long been academics who have only taught, or who have only researched (and, for that matter, others who have only administered or, latterly, managed), and whose contracts specified this. Nevertheless, the supposed research/teaching relationship has been a key article of faith underlying much thinking about academe, at least within academe.

This belief can be traced back at least to the beginning of the post-war period that forms the focus for this book, though its purchase was not as strong then, with many academics focusing primarily on teaching:

Here, then, are the university's two aims: (1) *research* – patient and unremitting – including the cultivation of the spirit of research in even the youngest; (2) *teaching* – systematic and methodical, but also rich, stimulating and thought-provoking, so much so that again and again one finds the two aims merging and becoming temporarily indistinguishable the one from the other. (Truscot 1943: 49, original emphasis)

The Robbins Report, as in so many other things, provided one of the strongest statements of the indivisibility and critical importance of the research/ teaching relationship, firmly rejecting alternative views:

Most discussion of this subject clouds the issue by setting teaching and research over against each other as antithetical and supposing an opposition that exists only at extreme points, as if teaching were nothing but patient recapitulation and explanation of the known and all research were a solitary voyage to discover something that will be intelligible to a mere handful of persons. There is no borderline between teaching and research; they are complementary and overlapping activities. A teacher who is advancing his general knowledge of his subject is both improving himself as a teacher and laying foundations for his research. The researcher often finds that his personal work provides him with fresh and apt illustration which helps him to set a subject in a new light when he turns to prepare a lecture. (Committee on Higher Education 1963a: 182)

More recent analyses have recognized that not all academics need to be involved in both research and teaching all of the time – indeed, this is often impractical, with teaching and administrative demands often dominating term times – but that these roles can be shared in different ways within the academic community:

... for effective teaching in higher education to take place, someone, somewhere should have engaged in research. This does not imply that all teachers should engage in research. It does suggest that teachers corporately have a responsibility to assist in keeping alive the research tradition, but there is also only a minimal obligation to participate in the research enterprise. On the other hand, every teacher has a professional obligation to understand the key conversations going on in the research community. (Barnett 1990: 130)

Such a view, of course, brings to the fore notions of general academic scholarship. But it still rubs up against academics' self-identities:

While probably the majority of our respondents considered that the professional responsibilities of the academic included research, teaching and administration, the combination of research and teaching was what mattered for their sense of identity. (Henkel 2000: 184)

Hence the concern in contemporary debates with what has been called the research-teaching nexus, and with the development and encouragement of research-led teaching and learning (Zamorski 2002).

Henkel usefully broadens out the debate, by recognizing the existence of a third main academic role: administration or management. Indeed, as the discussion in Chapter 6 makes clear, this is a role of growing significance, and one that an increasing number of academics, as well as related professionals, are using to seek career advancement within higher education. To these three roles, others would add the more US notion of 'service', that is, work done for and with the community and industry (Macfarlane 2006). Despite the increased emphasis given to what have been termed 'third leg' activities (and regardless of the widespread demise of university adult education provision), this role has yet to be established on a par with research and teaching.

The recent trend towards the separate funding and assessment of research and teaching in the UK threatens to finally destroy their relationship, however well disposed individual academics may be towards maintaining and developing it. Coate et al. interviewed heads of department and carried out focus groups with other academic staff in four subject areas in eight universities as part of an HEFCE review. They concluded that:

...the challenges of promoting a synergistic relationship between teaching and research are compounded by the indication from our research that this synergy seems to be understood on an intellectual level but not from a managerial perspective. The day-to-day management of academic departments are often based on systems that treat teaching and research as distinct activities. When resources are limited, this can result in competition between teaching and research rather than synergy. It is clear that there are also strong external pressures driving teaching and research further apart. (Coate et al. 2001: 172)

Surprisingly, perhaps, the advocates of mode 1/mode 2 views of knowledge offer one way around this impasse, by arguing that, with the move towards mode 2, there is no meaningful distinction to be made between research and teaching:

Under Mode-2 conditions, the distinction between research and teaching tends to break down. This happens not only because the definition of who now qualifies as a research actor must be extended far beyond the primary producers of research, but also because the reflexivity of Mode-2 knowledge production transforms relatively closed communities of scientists into open communities of 'knowledgeable' people. (Nowotny et al. 2001: 89–90)

Most academics, however, tied to the day-to-day demands of their employers and clients, probably still do not see it in quite those terms.

9

The student experience I: full-time undergraduate students

Introduction

> The student's experience of the university is threatened by two internal phenomena – departmentalization and expansion. The civic universities in particular tend to be structured as collections of departments – and all too often a student's total university experience is conditioned by this circumstance . . . Expansion will alter the nature of the university and will diminish what students can derive from it. (Wilson 1965: 67)

Not surprisingly, given the central role of students in the life of higher education, a great deal of attention and research has been devoted in the post-war period to the student experience. Just as the student experience has changed over the period, with more students gaining differing kinds of experience of higher education, so the emphases placed on different aspects of that experience have also varied. For example, concerns over student accommodation, which had quasi-parental and moral overtones during the first part of the period considered, have much more of a practical, even entrepreneurial, flavour today. Similarly, the issue of student finance, having ceased to be of such importance (for most of those who gained entry, at least) with the adoption of a national grant system in the early 1960s, has re-emerged as an issue with the demise of that system at the end of the twentieth century.

This chapter focuses on the full-time undergraduate and sub-degree student experience – though it concentrates disproportionately on the former, as the latter have been less commonly studied – and is organized to reflect the process of being a student. Thus, the first section examines entry to higher education, while the last considers exit from higher education, and the sections in between look at the student's experience while in higher education. The sections are:

- the transition to higher education;
- teaching and learning;

- accommodation;
- social life;
- student finance;
- the transition to work.

A related analysis is presented in Chapter 7, which examines many of the same issues (i.e. course design) from the perspective of the institution.

In Chapter 10, the postgraduate and international student experience is considered, along with the continuing post-war issue of widening participation. Certain aspects of widening participation, in particular the relation between social class and participation, and the differing experience of men and women students, are given some consideration in this chapter as well.

The transition to higher education

> The Education Act, 1944, has formally abolished the policy of the 'educational ladder', introducing instead the policy of 'secondary education for all'. This involves, apart from increasing the provision, introducing a greater variety of forms of secondary education – and in such a way as to induce the public to attribute more or less equal standing to each. The difficulties of implementation are great and meantime the familiar competition for places in grammar schools and universities remains intense. Much work has still to be done to reduce the odds against individuals from families in the lower status categories of the population. (Floud 1954: 122)

The issue of the transition from school and/or further education to higher education – who gets to go to university or college, which institution they go to, what they study there – is clearly one of the keys to the whole student experience. It is discussed further in the context of the experience of particular, historically disadvantaged, social groups in the next chapter. In this chapter, the focus is on general patterns of transition for what are sometimes referred to as conventional or 'traditional' students – that is, full-time undergraduates, usually arriving straight from school at the age of 17, 18 or 19 – though, as will become apparent, many (probably most) general analyses draw attention to class differentials.

One of the earliest national studies during the post-war period to address the transition to higher education was carried out by Kelsall, who reported on applications to undertake full-time degrees and diplomas in the mid-1950s:

> Between May 1954 and the autumn of 1955 some 70,000 applications were received for admission in 1955–56 to full-time university courses leading to a first degree or first diploma [excluding Oxford and Cambridge] ... The 70,000 applications represented some 31,000 people, of whom 9,000 were women. About 18,000 of the applicants, or

60 per cent of the total, were known to have been admitted at the beginning of the 1955–56 session. (Kelsall 1957: 22)

Less than one-third of university applicants at this time, therefore, were women. More than half of all applicants were successful in gaining a university place somewhere, though this did mean that a large minority were not. This was a significant change from the pre-war experience, when university entry was relatively straightforward for those with the necessary entrance qualifications and financial support (Furneaux 1961). Over 80 per cent of the 'home admitted' were receiving some form of financial assistance to go to university, with the bulk of the remainder presumably receiving support from their families.

Perhaps surprisingly, just under one-third of applicants could be characterized as coming from working class backgrounds:

> ... excluding Oxford and Cambridge, about a third of the men amongst the home admitted and non-admitted had fathers in manual occupations. The corresponding proportion for women was 20–22 per cent, and for the two sexes taken together, 28–30 per cent. At Oxford and Cambridge Universities combined, the proportion of home admitted men whose fathers had been engaged in manual occupations was 12 per cent; for women it was 7 per cent, and for the two sexes together, 11 per cent. (Kelsall 1957: 22)

This pattern was confirmed by a study carried out in the early 1960s on behalf of the Robbins Committee:

> A quarter of undergraduates [in 1961/2] came from the families of manual workers: most (18%) coming from the families of skilled manual workers, and a few from semi-skilled (6%) or unskilled (1%) backgrounds ... There was little change between 1928–47 and 1961 in the proportions of students at university coming from working class backgrounds. (Committee on Higher Education 1963b, Volume II: 4)

Conversely, however, the great majority of students were from better educated families, even though only a minority then had parents who themselves had been to university:

> Three quarters of undergraduates in 1961/2 had at least one parent who had been to a selective school; and half came from families where both parents had been to such a school ... Only a fifth of undergraduates were 'second generation' students, in the sense of having at least one parent who was a graduate. (Committee on Higher Education 1963b, Volume II: 1–2)

The relative social exclusivity of Oxbridge, identified by Kelsall, was clearly evidenced:

> At Oxford and Cambridge 30% of undergraduates in 1961 came from maintained [i.e. state] schools, and over half (53%) from independent

schools. At other universities in England and Wales (excluding London), three quarters of the students came from maintained schools and only 12% from independent schools. (Committee on Higher Education 1963b: 8)

Most of those admitted to university were well qualified: thus, 97 per cent of students from England and Wales had sat advanced (A) level examinations, and almost all had gained two or more passes (p. 17). In a period when a national university application system had yet to be developed (see Chapter 6), three-quarters of undergraduates had applied to at least one university or college other than the one they attended (p. 40), and 39 per cent had applied to, and would have preferred to have attended, some other institution than their own. Not surprisingly: 'Of all students at universities in England and Wales other than Oxford and Cambridge, 13% would have preferred to go to Oxford and Cambridge' (p. 43).

The Robbins research also looked separately at students entering teacher training (full time) and advanced further education (full time and part time). The figures quoted on social and school background confirm – indeed, are expressed in terms of – a hierarchy of experience and choice. Thus, for teacher training:

About 59% of students in teacher training had at least one parent who had been to a selective school compared with 73% of students in universities . . . 13% had at least one parent with either a degree or a teacher's certificate, compared with 29% of students in universities . . . 54% of students in teacher training came from middle class homes compared with 71% in universities . . . Seventy nine per cent . . . had come from schools maintained by local education authorities, compared with 63% of students in universities . . . Only 11% had come from independent schools, compared with 25% of students in universities; and 10% from direct grant schools, compared with 14% of students in universities. (pp. 69, 71, 73)

And, for advanced further education:

More than half (57%) of all full-time students in [advanced] further education had at least one parent who had been to a selective school . . . 13% had at least one parent with either a degree or a teacher's certificate . . . More than half (58%) the full-time students in further education in 1961/2 came from middle class homes . . . Seventy nine per cent had been to maintained schools . . . Seven per cent had been to direct grant and 13% to independent schools. (pp. 90, 92)

While there was little difference evident overall, therefore, in terms of social and educational background, between teacher training and full-time advanced further education students, the former were mainly women and the latter mainly men (see also Phillips 1969).

There was, not surprisingly, a clear differential between teacher training, full-time advanced further education and university students in terms of prior qualifications. Nearly one-quarter, 23 per cent, of teacher training students had not attempted A level examinations, 18 per cent had but had not gained any passes; while 59 per cent had gained at least one A level, and 35 per cent two or more (Committee on Higher Education 1963b: 75). While over one-third, therefore, had the minimum university entry qualifications, only 13 per cent had applied to university (p. 77). Full-time advanced further education students were somewhat better qualified on average than those pursuing teacher training: while 57 per cent had gained at least one A level, 47 per cent had two or more (p. 96). Not surprisingly, then, a greater proportion, 26 per cent, had applied to do a degree at university, though a few, 3 per cent, had also applied to do a teacher's certificate (p. 125).

The social and educational differentials become further stretched when the evidence on those students studying part time (during the day or in the evenings) in advanced further education is examined:

> Some 37% of part-time day and 31% of evening students had at least one parent who went to a selective school . . . Only 4% of part-time day students and 6% of evening students had at least one parent who had either a university degree or a teacher's certificate . . . under half of part-time day (42%) and evening students (41%) in further education came from middle class homes . . . Almost 91% of part-time day and 88% of evening students had been to maintained schools . . . a higher proportion of part-time day students (21%) than of evening students (12%) held passes at 'A' level . . . The proportions with 2 or more 'A' levels were 17% for part-time day students and 10% for evening students. (pp. 127–9, 131)

Only relatively small proportions of part-time advanced further education students had applied to study a degree at university (5 per cent of evening students and 8 per cent of day students), while 2 per cent and 1 per cent respectively had applied to study for a teacher's certificate (p. 146).

So, while the Robbins research does demonstrate that there was scope for suitably qualified students from poorer social and educational backgrounds to aspire to what was perceived as the highest quality higher education (i.e. Oxbridge), it also clearly shows that the hierarchy within higher education – from Oxbridge through the other universities, teacher training and full-time advanced further education, down to part-time advanced further education – reflected that in British society as a whole. Watts (1972: 56) and Whitburn et al. (1976) confirmed the continuance of this hierarchy a decade later. The latter, in their study of polytechnic students, found that 'over half the students studying on degree courses indicated that their main reason for choosing to come to a polytechnic was the fact that they did not have adequate qualifications for university entrance' (p. 85).

In a smaller-scale study published shortly after the Robbins Report, Marris (1964) interviewed 416 students at four institutions: Cambridge, Leeds, Southampton and Northampton College (later City University). The students' responses indicated the constricted, almost automatic, nature of the 'choice' they had exercised in making the transition from school to university: 'Four-fifths of the students we interviewed at Cambridge, and two-thirds at Leeds and Southampton said they had never seriously considered any alternative to university . . . The Cambridge students had seldom considered any other university' (pp. 14, 16). Marris identified two class-based stereotypes of university student from his research:

> There is the upper-middle-class student who goes from public school to his father's old university. He sees his university career primarily as a means of qualifying for an occupation similar in status to his father's . . . By contrast, the working-class student is more influenced by his grammar school, and sees the university more as the final prize in the competition for education, whose vocational usefulness he takes for granted. (Marris 1964: 31)

Despite this constrained and stereotypical transitional behaviour, however, Marris concluded that the majority of students had little idea of what actually went on in universities: 'Most of the students certainly arrived at university only vaguely prepared, and seem at first to have waited passively for some inarticulate but great fulfilment' (p. 32).

Later studies have tended to confirm the poor preparation and lack of knowledge of those making the transition from school to higher education. Thus, Keen and Higgins (1990) surveyed 7169 sixth formers in 691 schools in England and Wales, revealing poor levels of knowledge about, for example, the numbers of different types of institution, grants and courses available, and entry requirements (see also Roberts and Higgins 1992). And Callender (1997), carrying out research for the Dearing Committee, found that: 'Overall, students were not very well informed about their institution before they attended. The majority (65%) knew about only one aspect of their institutions before starting – its academic reputation' (p. 26).

From the 1960s onwards, the opportunities to enter higher education, and the choices of institution and programme available, began to increase, with financial support provided to students as of right (first in the form of grants, latterly loans). These circumstances made the issue of choice much more important:

> . . . it is clear that England and Wales accord more attention than most countries to the need for choice in higher education: the emphasis on residential provision, the generous grants system, and the competition for places have all been important factors in allowing students to be mobile and encouraging them to devote considerable attention to their choice of institution. (Watts 1972: 217)

Tellingly, Watts concluded his analysis with the observation that 'it would seem that the justification for the vast expenditure required by the system of choice as it operates at present is at least open to question' (p. 219). The greater and more varied recruitment to higher education also had the effect of beginning to shift the perceived responsibility for ensuring that the student transition was as effective as possible more towards the institution, with increased attention being given to induction, counselling and what later came to be known as the first year experience (Simons et al. 1976).

Despite the greater amount and variety of choices available – and regardless of whether or not they were fully and consciously considered – the social and educational hierarchy remained strong throughout the 1970s and 1980s:

> Access to the university almost exactly parallels the academic hierarchy of the schools . . . The boy [sic] from a privileged school or from a privileged social background had a much higher chance than his unprivileged contemporary of gaining a place at university. These inequalities, however, were very largely a consequence of earlier decisions in the educational process . . . For those who survived in school as far as 18, therefore, the chances of going on to university were very similar. It is the earlier inequalities of access to selective schools and to the sixth form that are crucial. (Halsey et al. 1980: 178, 193)

This hierarchy was still clearly apparent in student choices and self-identities in the 1990s, as it is today. Thus, Ainley (1994) interviewed samples of students at 'Home Counties University' (Kent) and 'Inner City University' (East London): 'At Home Counties University, student interviewees placed themselves in relation to an elite minority of Oxbridge colleges above them, and also in relation to the rest of the elaborate hierarchy of institutions that has always existed but is being defined anew in the circumstances of a market-driven expansion of higher education' (p. 53).

The hierarchy was also reflected in the recruitment strategies of the institutions concerned (see also Chapter 7), with the transition into higher education in lower-status institutions effectively lasting for rather longer:

> At Inner City during the years of our study, students were deliberately over-recruited through clearing [the process of allocating students who had failed to get places at their chosen institutions] in order to 'put bums on seats', as everyone – students and staff – said, in exchange for grant-aided funding. Thus a certain percentage were regularly and predictably failed by the institution year after year. (Ainley 1994: 61)

In the mid-1990s, the difference in the transition undergone by full- and part-time students, noted by the Robbins research, remained evident; with the former embodying the sense of opportunities opening up, and the latter signifying an attempt to make the best of existing circumstances:

> It is quite clear that full- and part-time students had similar motives for entering higher education . . . They both wanted the benefits of a 'university/college education' but the younger, full-time students also valued the 'university/college experience' and the social life, independent living and associated activities which contributed to

their personal development and their transition into adulthood and employment . . . Consequently, full-time students chose their institution for a mixture of academic and subjective reasons . . . In contrast, the choices of part-time students were heavily constrained by their full-time jobs and familial ties. (Callender 1997: 33)

While location and accessibility have clearly always been of key importance for part-time students, with the recent shift in funding responsibility away from the state and towards the student, these factors are also becoming increasingly significant for many full-time students. Thus, Briggs (2006), in a survey of 651 students of accountancy and engineering at six Scottish universities – where local attendance has long been common – found that the three most important factors in influencing choice of where to study were academic reputation, distance from home and location.

Teaching and learning

Interest in the student experience of teaching and learning grows in strength from the time of the Robbins Report, with most attention being paid to how students were taught and to how they evaluated the experience.

The Committee on University Teaching Methods (1964; see also Committee on Higher Education 1963b, Volume II, Part IV) was established in 1961 by the University Grants Committee (UGC) to advise on current university teaching practices. Thousands of students and staff were questioned about their practices and preferences. Somewhat curiously, at least to the contemporary eye, the committee started its deliberations by considering the use students made of the long summer vacation. They concluded, rather disappointedly – but betraying a singular lack of not just knowledge but understanding – that: 'for a large proportion of students the long vacation is, academically speaking, time largely wasted' (Committee on University Teaching Methods 1964: 18–19).

In other words, the vast majority of students devoted hardly any 'vacation' time to study. The committee's main recommendation in response was the radical idea of changing the university year, so that it started in January rather than October, allowing both a less rushed selection of school-leavers and a more structured mid-year long vacation (an issue that came up again in the 1990s, in the light of the move by some institutions from a term structure to semesters: see Committee of Enquiry into the Organisation of the Academic Year 1993). While nothing came of this in general terms, it was pioneered at the end of the decade by the newly founded Open University.

Perhaps the most useful aspect of the committee's work was in documenting just what was expected of students, and how this varied by discipline and institutional type. In essence, they found that students (based on their self-reporting) worked a fairly conventional 40-hour week:

The median weekly hours of arts students are 10 under instruction and

25 in private study; those of students of pure and applied science are respectively 17 and 20 under instruction, and 20 and 19 in private study. Lectures, 7 hours, and discussion periods, over 2 hours, account for most of the teaching received by arts students. The longer hours spent under instruction by science students are mainly due to practical classes (pure science 8 hours, applied science 7 hours), but they also receive more teaching by lecture, particularly in applied science, and less in discussion periods. Weekly hours of instruction are shorter at Oxford and Cambridge than elsewhere by two hours, and longer in Scotland by about the same amount. (Committee on University Teaching Methods 1964: 114–15)

Despite criticism of the number and quality of lectures made in a submission by the NUS, the surveys showed that 'at all universities the majority of students appear to be satisfied with the time they are expected to give to lectures' (p. 49), though both students and their union were united in calling for more seminars and tutorials. Lecture audiences, however, remained relatively small:

The median size of lecture audiences is 19, but it is higher in Scotland (32) than elsewhere. As between the faculties it is highest in pure science (33) and lowest in humanities (15). Three lectures out of 10 are given to audiences of under 10. (Committee on University Teaching Methods 1964: 115)

Seminar and tutorial sizes were not much smaller at most universities, except at Oxford (where 61 per cent of tutorials involved just one student, and 94 per cent two or less) and Cambridge (32 per cent and 76 per cent respectively – p. 66). Examinations remained the dominant method of assessment, with other methods that now form staples of the undergraduate student experience (i.e. continuous assessment, projects, dissertations) referred to as 'experimental innovations' (p. 92). The Committee's main report concluded by arguing for the need for further study of, and training in, university teaching.

More than half, 58 per cent, of undergraduates prepared written work once or more per week, 16 per cent once a fortnight, 11 per cent less often, 14 per cent never (Committee on Higher Education 1963b, Volume II: 266). Nearly three-quarters, 73 per cent, had an official supervisor, while 11 per cent received no such advice (p. 268). Just over one-third; 34 per cent, met their supervisor once or more a week, 8 per cent once a fortnight, 16 per cent once or twice a term, 14 per cent less often (p. 269). Less than one-quarter, 22 per cent, thought that arrangements for academic supervision were inadequate (p. 271). Some 40 per cent had personal advisers, with 29 per cent expressing the view that such arrangements were inadequate (p. 273). While most undergraduates seemed fairly content with their teaching arrangements, therefore, a significant minority had reservations.

Students in teacher training received on average about 16 hours of teaching a week; 9 hours in lectures, 5 in practicals and 2 in seminars (p. 296). The majority, 78 per cent, wanted changes in these patterns (p. 301), with the most common requests being for fewer lectures and more seminars, practicals and fieldwork. Nearly two-thirds, 63 per cent, did no teaching practice during the sample week surveyed, 27 per cent a day or less (p. 310). Opinions on this were evenly split, with 47 per cent wanting more teaching practice and 51 per cent expressing themselves satisfied with the present arrangements (p. 311). Teacher training students spent on average a further 16 hours per week in private study, which, together with the 16 hours of teaching and an average of 3 hours per week in teaching practice, gave a working week of 35 hours, slightly less than the undergraduate average (p. 312).

Full-time advanced further education students, by comparison, worked slightly longer hours. They averaged 23 hours of teaching a week, including 10 hours of lectures, 9 hours of practicals, 2 hours of written exercises and 1 hour of seminars (p. 315). Most, 60 per cent, like teacher training students, wanted to see changes in these patterns (p. 321), with a general preference for more seminars and tutorials (p. 322). With an average of 19 hours per week spent in private study, their average working week amounted to 42 hours (p. 330).

Peers and Madgwick (1963) surveyed 433 students at two colleges of advanced technology (then advanced further education, but soon to become universities) regarding their attitudes and problems. There is a clear sense in their findings of their respondents comparing their experiences unfavourably with those of university students. Doubts were expressed about the credibility of the Diploma in Technology (the 'degree equivalent' qualification then offered in these institutions) and the sandwich education principle of alternating periods of relevant work with study, the place of general studies and the quality of facilities provided: 'there is a certain dissatisfaction in the minds of many students concerning the purpose to be served by the kind of training which they are undergoing . . . They resent the idea that they are to be turned out merely as technologists' (p. 89).

As well as the broad patterns of provision, interest was also being expressed at this time in the quality of teaching and learning, and in what might be done to enhance this: 'After techniques of explanation, and clarity of arrangement, the students most often mentioned the importance of a lecturer's interest in his subject, and his ability to make it interesting to his audience, so that they were stimulated to pursue it further' (Marris 1964, p. 49). Teaching in higher education remained essentially a craft, with a quality experience achieved in large part through not only the highly selective entry of learners, but also the small-scale and relatively intimate nature of teaching delivery:

The relatively rapid expansion of the 1960s has done little to modify the teaching milieu. The typical university department has no more than ten academic members and the situation remains, in this respect at least, perfectly compatible with the distinctive English idea of a university which provides for maximum solidarity between teachers and taught through the absence of a separate administration and an emphasis on close personal relations, achieved by means of tutorial teaching, high staff/student ratios, and shared domestic life. (Halsey et al. 1971: 80)

Mann, in an unusual study, examined the particular case of students' use of books, based largely on a survey sample of 763 students (77 per cent response rate) at the University of Sheffield in 1972. He came to a rather measured conclusion regarding student behaviour in this respect:

> . . . it can be asked if the students are not perhaps rather easily satisfied with the situation concerning books. Fifteen per cent of all students do not use a library for private study; 16 per cent do not borrow books from a library; 12 per cent spend no time in the week in a university library; 65 per cent had not used the Reserve-book Room during the past term; and 35 per cent had no books on loan from the university late in the Lent Term. Against this, a majority of students felt there were problems of obtaining books on loan for their work and a lack of multiple copies was noted, but overall only 18 per cent of all students felt that the university library stock in their subject was fairly or very poor. (Mann 1974: 192)

Whitburn et al. surveyed 9035 students studying in the then polytechnics. They found that students spent an average of 12 hours in lectures, 7 hours in group discussions and 13 hours in private study, giving a weekly total, 32 hours, rather lower than the figure for advanced further education found by the Robbins research a decade earlier (though full-time non-degree students were found to be averaging a slightly higher 37 hours a week: p. 95). When asked to rate aspects of their courses, the survey found that:

> in general, students were least prepared to give higher ratings to the methods of assessment used . . . Teaching methods received relatively negative ratings, while staff–student relationships and relevance to future career both enjoyed a high percentage of good assessments. (Whitburn et al. 1976: 96)

Roberts and Higgins (1992) surveyed 5858 second year undergraduates in 100 institutions in England and Wales in the autumn of 1990. Focus group interviews were carried out during the same period in 29 institutions. Though they remarked critically on the lack of training available to academics in teaching and management skills, student satisfaction levels were uniformly high.

Ainley's (1994) study of two contrasting universities in the south-east of England revealed differing attitudes towards study among their students. At the campus university: 'Knowing that they were neither exceptionally gifted nor exceptionally rich, the majority of Home Counties students played down their intellectual interest and appeared often indifferent to their course of study' (p. 55). By contrast, at the former polytechnic, 'in a world that is socially and environmentally galaxies removed . . . from the sheltered groves of Home Counties' modern academe' (p. 57), a more positive attitude was common:

Inner City students were more likely to feel that their courses of study were vocationally relevant. They particularly valued work placements and the projects they had undertaken on them, whereas for Home Counties students specific options in their courses, especially including individual project work, and years abroad, were held in equivalent regard. (Ainley 1994: 67–8)

Callender (1997) carried out a postal questionnaire survey in the UK for the National Committee of Inquiry into Higher Education in 1996/7, obtaining 1270 usable replies (63 per cent response rate). Like the research informing the Robbins Report, but in a much expanded and differently structured higher education system, this survey covered both full- and part-time students. While some 'experimental innovations' (as they had been seen in the early 1960s) such as projects and dissertations had by then been widely adopted, approaches to teaching were still fairly conventional: 'The four most widely used teaching methods to which the majority of both full- and part-time students were exposed were: lectures (98%); seminars and tutorials (91%); essays (82%); projects and dissertations (82%)' (p. 35).

Other teaching methods were only noted by a minority of students: these included practicals (49 per cent), computer-based learning packages (48 per cent), laboratory/workshop sessions (40 per cent), individual sessions with teaching staff (31 per cent), work experience (16 per cent) and work placements (15 per cent) (p. 36). Callender noted that '[b]y far the greatest variations in methods used were associated with the subjects students studied' (p. 35).

On average, full-time students spent 8 hours a week in lectures, 4 in seminars/tutorials, 6 on projects/practicals, 4 in other teaching situations, and 15 on independent study (total 37). While the overall figure was, therefore, similar to that found in the early 1960s by the Committee on University Teaching Methods, more of it was now spent in contact sessions and less in private study. By comparison, the average figures for part-time students were 5, 2, 3, 4 and 8 hours respectively (total 22) (Callender 1997: 37).

Those surveyed again expressed general satisfaction with their lot, while offering criticism about particular aspects of it:

Nearly three-quarters (73%) of students were content with the mix of teaching methods used on their course, one in ten were not . . . In contrast, students had much more mixed feelings about the size of their classes . . . Students were critical of the academic support they received from staff. Most serious of all was concern about the feedback they got on their work . . . just over seven out of ten students were either satisfied or very satisfied with the quality of their teaching while one in ten were either dissatisfied or very dissatisfied. (Callender 1997: 37, 39)

Assessment methods had developed since the 1960s, with other strategies now being widely used alongside examinations, though, again, there was significant variation between subjects: 'The majority of students experienced the following assessment methods at some stage during their course: essays (87%); written examinations (86%); projects/dissertations (81%); oral presentations (73%)' (p. 41). Another way in which the deliberations of the Dearing Committee had moved on from Robbins was in their concern with the development of key or personal transferable skills in higher education. Here the evidence on achievement was somewhat mixed:

> The majority of all students felt that all their skills had improved since starting their course, and especially their analytical (81%) and communication skills (69%). There was one exception – numeracy skills. Only one in three students thought that this skill had improved while the majority believed that it had stayed the same. (Callender 1997: 45)

The general satisfaction manifested by the students questioned was moderated by a concern with resource constraints, and in this context the age-based hierarchy of higher education institutions manifested itself again:

> . . . students studying at 'pre-1992' universities were more satisfied with both the academic and non-academic facilities available than were those at '1992' universities . . . The three most frequently cited changes students wanted to see were: more relevant/wider range of books in the library (12%); more time devoted to tutorials and individual teaching (9%); more communication between staff or departments and students (9%). (Callender 1997: 54, 56)

Bekhradnia et al. (2006) surveyed over 14,666 students in English universities (response rate 66%). The scheduled contact hours reported ranged between over 20 per week in the case of medicine to less than 10 for languages, historical and philosophical studies (para 7). Overall, students claimed to attend 92 per cent of these sessions. Time spent in private study also varied, but less so, from less than 10 hours per week in the case of mass communications to more than 16 hours in the case of law, architecture, building and planning. However, the authors argued that 'private study is a long way from compensating for the smaller amounts of teaching provided' in some subjects (para 11). Overall, they found that: 'The mean student workload for the entire sample was 25.7 hours. The mean for each subject grouping varied from 35.2 (medicine and dentistry) to 19.9 (mass communications and documentation)' (para 14).

  This average is somewhat lower than that found by the Dearing Report a decade previously. Considerable differences were also apparent in student workloads in the same subjects in different institutions. When given a series of optional 'priorities for further investment', a clear message emerged:

'students are more concerned with teaching quality (better facilities and class sizes) than quantity (contact hours) or the general environment (sports and social facilities, security)' (para 42). And, in general, students were satisfied with their experience, with only 11 per cent reporting that 'their experience has been worse than they expected' (para 46), with this proportion highest for those who had the least or most teaching: 'Sixteen per cent of students reported that they thought their course represented poor value for money, and non-EU overseas respondents were considerably less satisfied than others with the value for money received on their course' (para 53).

The generally positive student evaluation of their course experience throughout the post-war period has been born out, most recently, in the results of the annual National Student Survey administered to final-year undergraduates from 2005 (see www.thestudentsurvey.com).

Accommodation

> The notion that students should be in residence at the institutions where they study is relatively recent. The idea stems in part from the collegiate traditions of Oxford and Cambridge and is often justified in those terms. At the turn of the [nineteenth] century, however, the pattern of recruitment to universities, with the exception of Oxford and Cambridge, was predominantly local and most students lived at home. (Morgan and McDowell 1979: 5)

> There was a time, up to as late as the early 1980s, when most higher education institutions could have supplied confident and firm views relating to the role of student accommodation within their own particular university or college. What is more, those views would have tended to be similar between institutions and would have been shared on an almost consensual basis between all members ... In 1994 there are almost as many views on student accommodation as there are institutions. (Blakey 1994: 72)

Up until the 1970s, those working in higher education – or at least in universities and teacher training colleges; their less well-resourced colleagues in the further education sector simply could not entertain such ideas – betrayed an almost obsessive concern with student accommodation. This was part of the Oxbridge collegial ideal (see also Chapter 12), with religious or quasi-religious overtones, embodying the notion that learning, and in particular a suitable breadth of learning, was best achieved in a residential community, where students and academics from a range of disciplines would meet and interact socially as well as intellectually (Thoday 1957).

During the 1970s and 1980s, however – as with much else in political and social life in the UK generally – these attitudes changed, or at least became overlain with others (Rudd 1980). Students were no longer seen, at least not to the same extent, as children over whom some moral oversight must perforce be exercised, and there was no longer the same felt urgency to keep the sexes apart. The provision of accommodation by higher education institutions, while still seen as desirable and important, became more of a profit-making exercise, with – in the more desirable locations – student rentals viewed as only slightly less profitable interludes between the periodic bouts of conference business in the vacations.

In the immediate post-war period, however, the view was very strongly that communal living in halls of residence was greatly to be encouraged:

> . . . the university representatives whom we have met in the course of our visits and at our conferences in London have maintained that the further provision of Halls ought to be a prime object of university policy during the next decade. There is a strong and widespread feeling that the full advantages of a university education are not attainable by a student who does not spend at least part of his university career under conditions of community life; and our talks with representative students at many institutions have shown that they too share that feeling. (UGC 1948: 54–5)

In the mid-1950s, the UGC established a sub-committee on student accommodation (or halls of residence as they were known then), which clearly confirmed the orthodoxy: 'The evidence we have heard on the value of halls of residence in supplying the necessary accommodation for students in the form best suited to their needs makes us certain that the number of halls of residence should be considerably increased' (UGC 1957: 41). The following year, it noted the trend, 'perhaps as a result of the adoption of more liberal policies by award-making bodies', for more students to be studying away from home: 'In 1951–52 56 of every 100 students with homes in the UK went to a university more than 30 miles away; in 1956–57 62 did so' (UGC 1958: 25).

A few years later, the Committee on Higher Education (1963b, Volume I) also gave the subject its detailed attention. They started by mapping the patterns of student residence by sector of provision:

> In 1961/2 about a third of the full-time students in higher education were in residence, a quarter lived at home and the remainder (just over 40%) in some form of lodgings. The proportion in residence was much higher in teacher training (64%) than in universities (28%), and was lowest in [advanced] further education (6%). But the proportion living at home was much higher in further education (47%) than in universities (20%) or teacher training (20%) . . . The proportion of students in residence was higher in England and Wales (35%) than in Scotland (14%) . . . at Oxford and Cambridge and at the smaller English universities half of the students are in residence, in Scotland the proportion is an eighth, in London and the larger civic universities a

fifth and in Wales a third. (Committee on Higher Education 1963b, Volume I: 173–5)

The then trend towards increased numbers of students living in university or college accommodation was seen as clearly related to, indeed underpinned by, changes in government policy and student funding:

> The drift from home, which has intensified the pressure on lodgings and halls, has been in part the result of public policy. Local authorities in England and Wales now give grants to students whether or not they go to the local university. Moreover, grants to students living in lodgings or in residence are sufficiently high to impose no financial hardship on students who decide not to live at home even if their homes are within reach of the university . . . A smaller proportion of students now study at a university within 30 miles of their home (28% in 1961/2 as against 46% before the war), and of those students who do go to a local university (i.e. within 30 miles), fewer live at home (73% compared with 91%). (Committee on Higher Education 1963b, Volume I: 184–5)

The Robbins Committee was particularly concerned with two factors: how easily students could work (i.e. study) wherever they were living during their studies, and how long it took them to get to and from university. So far as the former issue was concerned, students living at home were most favoured, those in lodgings least – on average, 60 per cent of undergraduates usually worked in a room on their own in their living accommodation: 83 per cent of those living at home, 68 per cent in hall, 35 per cent of those in lodgings with board, and 55 per cent of those in other lodgings (p. 188). The journey to the university was also variable in time, with 23 per cent of undergraduates spending 30 minutes or more on it (p. 190), and between institutions:

> At Oxford and Cambridge, 93% of undergraduates live within a quarter of an hour's journey of the part of the university where they work. At London, the proportion is only 25%, at the larger civic universities and in Scotland about 40%, and at the smaller civic universities and Wales about 60%. (Committee on Higher Education 1963b, Volume I: 191)

Despite their endorsement of the general educational value of halls of residence, the Robbins Report was only too aware of the practicality of extending their availability beyond the ranks of the relatively privileged group of students who already enjoyed them: 'Those who stress the advantages of living in halls of residence often suggest that living in residence is particularly important for students from less favoured social backgrounds. All the evidence shows that such students are least likely to be found living in residence' (p. 194).

There were, however, also early critiques of the whole idea of halls of residence: 'In the residential planning of universities, formal halls are, I think, likely to increase the social distance between staff and students, because they tend to emphasize the hierarchy of authority, rather than the community of interest' (Marris 1964: 181).

In the following decade, Brothers and Hatch (1971) reported on their study of residence and student life, visiting 45 higher education institutions and undertaking eight detailed case studies. They noted the inability, in an expanding higher education system, of institutions to keep up with the demand for the supply of student residential places: 'in spite of the increase in residential places over the years, student demand for them usually exceeds supply. Undergraduates are increasingly going into lodgings rather than halls or other university-provided accommodation' (p. 60).

They appreciated, and took a measured view on, the arguments in favour of students living in halls of residence, noting:

> . . . the belief that residence was a means for enriching the students' experience of higher education. By living in a residential community he would, so the argument went, be drawn into relationships with a wider range of people, both students and staff, than if he lived at home or in lodgings, and he would have better opportunities, too, for taking part in and developing a variety of interests and activities. In particular, by providing an alternative focus to the department, residence could counteract the narrowing effects of intensifying subject specialization. (Brothers and Hatch 1971: 171)

But they also doubted, in practice, the ability of all halls of residence to match up to the remembered Oxbridge ideal:

> . . . there is great variation between different halls and colleges. Some do not give rise to any distinctive sub-culture or set of values but rather echo or amplify the wider student culture; others do promote certain norms and values, but these values are not necessarily or intrinsically liberal ones. Thus we cannot say that residence makes an essential contribution to a liberal education. (Brothers and Hatch 1971: 353)

A high point was reached in the 1970s, with moving away from home to study seen as desirable for all involved – students, parents and institutions. It had become a kind of right, at least for full-time university undergraduates, a part of growing up:

> Over British universities as a whole the proportion of students living at home has fallen from 43.9% in 1934–5 to 16.6% in 1969–70 . . . The prevailing belief in the importance of going away from home to university or college indicates the importance attached in Britain to what Weber called 'the pedagogy of cultivation' – cultivating the student for the style of life appropriate to the status group for which he is destined . . . The geographical mobility of degree students is part of this tradition, representing in effect a concept of the university or college as playing a central role in a complex *rite de passage* of separation, transition and incorporation, through which lower-middle-class and working-class students in particular are separated from their home

backgrounds and encultured into the values of an elite. (Watts 1972: 12–13, 89, original emphasis)

Morgan and McDowell (1979), in their study of student residence carried out just after Watts was writing, confirmed his general figures and showed just how quickly the balance of student housing options could change. They reported that, in 1974/5, 45 per cent of UK students were living in colleges or halls of residence, 37 per cent in lodgings or flats, and 15 per cent at home. Seven years previously, in 1967/8, the proportions had been 35 per cent, 47 per cent and 18 per cent respectively (p. 3).

From then on, the patterns changed again, as higher education institutions proved unable or unwilling to keep up with student demand for accommodation in an expanding system, more students themselves sought to live outside their institutions, and the private sector took a much keener interest in providing for the growing demands. The variety of living options available to students also increased:

> Looking at student accommodation today there is only a residual, traditional, catered halls sector, normally consisting of buildings where conversion to self-catering accommodation would not be feasible (or where such conversion will soon happen). Students now live in clustered, shared flats (sharing with between five and eight other students) with a communal kitchen and bathroom. Servicing is much less; cleaning has been reduced to exclude all but shared and communal parts. Although in the larger developments there will be on-site management, it has little or no responsibility for pastoral care . . . Student accommodation is priced increasingly at a rent level that not only pays for the actual running costs of the building but will, almost certainly, be paying for the capital construction of the building if the development is new or established complexes will be running at a financial surplus to cross-subsidize new accommodation development elsewhere within the institution. (Blakey 1994: 73)

In the matter of student accommodation, therefore, attitudes on the part of both students – if perhaps not, to the same extent, their parents – and higher education institutions would appear to have finally 'come of age'.

Social life

It seems curious that, while there has been so much research and writing over the years concerned with the student experience of teaching and learning, accommodation and employment, there has been so little investigation into what students do for the rest of the time; that is, in their social lives. One can understand possible reasons why this aspect of the student experience appears little researched, and also some of the potential risks involved, but it remains a key element of student life and development.

A search of the literature does reveal odd items of relevance. For example, there are a few collected (indeed rather manufactured) autobiographical recollections from the latter part of the period (e.g. Arksey et al. 1994; Tolmie 1998), serving in part to counteract the contemporary public image of undergraduates as idle and promiscuous heavy drinkers. One can also find fictionalized accounts of campus life in the 1960s – as well as other periods – in which students and their lives form part of the backdrop for the focus on academic intrigues and tragedies (and which tend to support the contemporary public image of students: see Tight 2006). And, at the end of the 1960s, there was a significant literature concerned with campus rebellions (for a retrospective account, see Fraser et al. 1988).

There are some earlier, perhaps somewhat more worthy, studies examining student membership of societies, clearly then seen as a key index of wider student engagement. For example, Whitburn et al. (1976) found that 34 per cent of degree students in polytechnics belonged to sports societies, 31 per cent to social societies and 27 per cent to subject societies, but expressed concern that 26 per cent (and 89 per cent of part-time students) did not belong to any society (pp. 98, 101).

And then there are those findings that can appear to the modern eye as oddities. Thus, in his survey, Marris (1964) found that: 'Just over a quarter of the students said their last discussion had concerned religion' (p. 92). Which is not something that you would imagine a researcher would ask today; and, if they did, that they would expect to find such a high proportion responding in this way (though here, of course, matters may be changing). Marris also acknowledged that social life at university had its pros and cons: 'Meeting people from a wide variety of backgrounds is one of the most worthwhile experiences the university can offer, but this social diversity is also a source of conflict and anxiety' (p. 101). There is a link here to the specialist literature on the psychological health of students, which flourished at about the same time (e.g. Ryle 1969).

Also writing at about the same time as Marris, Zweig interviewed 205 students at Oxford and Manchester universities, on behalf of *The Daily Herald*: a self-evaluation test was also administered. On the basis of the data collected, Zweig argued for 'the model student . . . the student as he sees himself at his best, the image to which he aspires' (1963: 190). This model student was characterized in a series of statements, amounting almost to a homily:

The model student should be co-operative, rather on the dominant side as a male but not aggressively so . . . should be self-confident . . . emotionally stable . . . sociable . . . try to be as carefree as he can . . . optimistic . . . voluntaristic . . . altruistically minded . . . orderly to a certain degree . . . as free from inhibitions as he can . . . 'a conforming individualist' . . . develop his imaginative faculties in order to get away from narrow specialization . . . be ready for compromise, except in fundamentals . . . be realistic . . . enthusiastic . . . economically sound . . . popular with his colleagues . . . self-disciplined . . . not be an 'angry young man' . . . interested in politics, but he should not take up politics . . . interested in religion, but he should not close the doors of agnosticism behind him . . . [have] a sexual code of his own . . . not disparage his elders . . . have a philosophy of life . . . have a level of aspiration transcending mere security, family life and a career. (Zweig 1963: 190–8)

While Zweig recognized that some might find this list 'too good to be true' (p. 198), he was clearly impressed by what he had found. Intriguingly, in discussing the desirability of freeing oneself from inhibitions, he noted that: 'The working-class student has many inhibitions bound up with his family and class origin, which keep him back or prevent him from reaching for the best' (p. 193). As well as sounding a mite patronizing, this would seem to fall into the trap, yet again, of blaming the less advantaged for the difficulties they experience.

Writing over 30 years later, Ainley (1994) indicated that, in many ways, relatively little had changed, except in terms of attitude and explanation. He made the point that concerns about social life at university or college would not apply equally to all students: 'Being older and local, Inner City students already had . . . social lives outwith the institution, though sometimes they were uncomprehending of if not in conflict with it' (p. 75).

The most comprehensive recent study of students' broader social lives during the post-war period is that by Silver and Silver (1997), who interviewed relevant staff and student representatives at 15 UK higher education institutions (and two US ones as a comparison) between 1993 and 1996, and also reviewed documentary sources. In addition to discussing student accommodation, student unions and other support services, and student political action, they consider how the student experience has changed during the post-war period. But, despite their concern with 'students as "real people"' (p. 2), there are clearly still many aspects of students' social lives into which they were not prepared to delve.

Student finance

Concerns over, and research into, student finance have fluctuated during the post-war period, and in a sense have now come full circle. In the immediate post-war period, a key issue was how to fund the number of ex-service personnel who wanted to enter higher education. Once that (relative) bulge had passed, the pre-war pattern of student funding (Whiteley 1933) – in which students might get varied amounts of funding from local authorities, scholarship and bursary schemes, charities, employers and/or their families – reasserted itself for a time. The 1960s, though, saw a move towards a standardized, national system of student finance (though administered largely through the local education authorities), involving the payment of students' tuition fees and the provision of a means-tested grant towards living costs.

That system then continued until the further expansion of the system undermined its viability, leading to, from the 1980s onwards, a reduction in the amount of grant provided, its replacement with a loan and the requirement for students to pay increasing tuition fees.

The Anderson Report (Ministry of Education 1960), which recommended the establishment of a national system of student grants and fees payment, could, in many ways, be seen as a far more significant document than the Robbins Report that shortly followed it. Indeed, there was some recognition of this in the Robbins Report itself:

> The pattern of the present system of awards, which came into operation in 1962/3, is set by the Education Act, 1962 and the regulations made under it. This system in turn stems from the Anderson Report. The basic principle of the system is that every student who is admitted to a university first degree course (or courses designated as 'comparable') and who has obtained two 'A' level passes in the GCE (or the equivalent) is entitled to an award from his local education authority. (Committee on Higher Education 1963b, Volume I: 215)

For nearly 30 years after the Education Act 1962, student finance ceased to be much of an issue, though there were concerns about the extent to which it increased in line with inflation, and where the means-tested element of the local authority grant was not paid to the student by their parents. The freezing of the grant and the gradual introduction of 'top-up' loans from 1990 (Department of Education and Science 1988), however, led to increasing concerns about students' funding arrangements (e.g. Roberts and Higgins 1992; Woodhall 1989). These concerns focused on the impact of debt on students (e.g. Pilkington 1994; Winn and Stevenson 1997), the variability of parental support (e.g. Christie et al. 2001), the impact on their studies of students working part time in order to support themselves (e.g. Ford et al. 1995; Leonard 1995; Moreau and Leathwood 2006), and the self-exclusion from higher education of potential students – typically from less advantaged groups – who did not wish to get into debt (Adnett 2006; Callender 2003).

Thus, Callender and Kempson interviewed 1971 students (59 per cent response rate), finding an average student income of £4907:

> . . . three-fifths of which came from various sources of student support (grant, parental or spouse's contribution, student loan or Access/ Hardship Funds), the remaining two-fifths from a range of other sources . . . Seventy per cent of students received a maintenance grant which averaged £1,726: of these, a third got a full grant, and two-thirds received a reduced one following an assessment of means . . . just over half of all students had borrowed from the Student Loan Company; the average loan being £1,243. (Callender and Kempson 1996: xiv–xv)

Most recently, Bekhradnia et al. (2006, para 35) found that 39 per cent of their undergraduate sample worked during term time. This appeared to have a negative, albeit only slight, impact on the amount of time spent in private study.

The Dearing Committee, set up with cross-party support, was intended to solve, at least in a political sense, the issues around student finance (National Committee of Inquiry into Higher Education 1997a; see also Chapter 4). It led to the establishment of a system of student loans and means-tested fees, but this system has been repeatedly tinkered with since (and the devolved administrations in Scotland and Wales have also adopted different policies). Currently, institutions of higher education are allowed to charge fees of up to £3000 per year, though in return they are expected to make bursaries and other forms of financial assistance available for students from less wealthy backgrounds. The pressures are already evident, however, for both increases in the fees universities can charge, and in the support made available to needy students. There are few signs, then, of the student finance system reaching a period of stability.

The transition to work

> Most students are just emerging from adolescence and are transients in higher education. Higher education is an interlude in their lives; in three or four years they will have passed through it. Very few see themselves as apprentice scholars or potential higher education teachers. (Percy and Salter 1976: 465)

The move from undergraduate study to employment has been one of the most researched aspects of the student experience in the post-war period, perhaps not surprisingly, given the continuing, indeed increasing, focus on the economic and vocational roles of higher education. This section is, therefore, the longest in this chapter. The main focus of attention in researching the transition to work has been on what sorts of occupations different kinds of students, and those specializing in particular subjects, went into. Some attention has also been given to how these outcomes fitted in with students' aspirations, and to what employers thought of their graduate recruits.

Political and Economic Planning carried out a questionnaire survey in 1954 of men who took a first degree in 1949/50: they received 4535 responses (a 66 per cent response rate), of which 3961 were used in their analysis. In terms of immediate occupational destination, they found that: 'nearly a quarter of the sample . . . had their first career job in Manufacturing Industry. A like number went into Teaching . . . 8.6 per cent . . . found jobs in the Civil Service, 7.5% . . . took up jobs in Commerce' (p. 60). In many cases – paralleling the evidence on students' lack of prior understanding of higher education (discussed in the section on The Transition to Higher Education) – there was little evidence of forward career planning:

> Half of these men did not decide, until they were embarked upon their

university studies, what work to do on graduating. Two out of three of them would acknowledge the influence of no one in deciding on this work, and, of the remaining third, the great majority were influenced by people – mainly parents – probably with limited knowledge of careers. (Political and Economic Planning 1956: 241)

Political and Economic Planning followed up this study by interviewing 134 managers in 51 firms and 594 graduates (1957), focusing on why graduates were employed, how they were selected, trained and used, and on what industry thought of higher education. They found that 'the numbers of university graduates on the strength, the academic standard aimed at in bringing in new graduates, and the regularity of the steps taken to assess need, run together with the size of the firm' (p. 215).

The Robbins Committee (Committee on Higher Education 1963b, Volume II), naturally enough, took a keen interest in the transition to work. Their survey, which looked at women as well as men graduates, and examined arts (i.e. arts, humanities and social sciences) and science students separately, found that in 1961/2:

Thirty nine per cent of all arts graduates entered school teaching; 9% went into industry and 11% into commerce and the law; 7% entered the public service; 24% entered a variety of occupations grouped together as other employment; and the remaining 11% stayed at university for further academic study or research . . . the main difference in the pattern of careers for men and women is that over half [55%] the women arts graduates entered school teaching, compared with under a third [30%] of the men. (Committee on Higher Education 1963b, Volume II: 150–1)

There were also marked differences of destination in terms of where the graduates had studied at. Thus:

A fifth of Oxford and Cambridge arts graduates in 1961/2 went into school teaching (the lowest proportion to do so from any university group), compared with a third from London, three fifths from Wales and over a half from Scotland. Conversely, a third of the Oxford and Cambridge arts graduates went into industry, commerce and the law (the highest proportion from any group to enter these occupations), compared with only 10% of arts graduates from Wales and 11% from Scotland. (Committee on Higher Education, Volume II: 156)

The patterns for science and applied science (i.e. engineering and technology) graduates were different, with less emphasis on teaching, and much more on going into industry or staying on at university. Just over a quarter, 27 per cent, of all science graduates went into school teaching, but only 3 per cent of applied science graduates. Conversely, 22 per cent of the former, but the great majority, 61 per cent, of the latter, went into industry. The respective figures for commerce and the law were 3 per cent and 1 per cent, public service 6 per cent and 8 per cent, other occupations 14 per cent and 11 per cent, and staying at university 28 per cent and 16 per cent (p. 158).

Just as with the arts graduates, the destinations of science graduates also varied by gender and university:

> Almost half (45%) the women science graduates became school teachers, compared with one fifth of the men . . . in science as in arts, the proportions of graduates from Oxford and Cambridge and from London entering school teaching are lower than from any of the other university groups, while the proportion from Wales is higher. (Committee on Higher Education 1963b, Volume II: 158, 162)

The Robbins Committee also considered the employment intentions of current undergraduates. In a survey of non-medical undergraduates, they found that 56 per cent said they had a fairly clear idea of the occupation they wanted to take up on going to university (p. 167). The most common occupations they had in mind were school teaching (29 per cent: 51 per cent of women, 20 per cent of men), research, development or production outside university (32 per cent: 13 per cent, 40 per cent), and professional services (25 per cent: 28 per cent, 23 per cent) (p. 169). More than half, 57 per cent, said that their intended occupation had been a major influence on their decision to apply for a university place, and 20 per cent that it had had some influence (p. 175). The great majority, 81 per cent, said that they had decided on all of the subjects they were going to study before going up to university (p. 176), though nearly one-third, 32 per cent, said that none of the subjects they were studying had been taught at school (p. 177).

Worryingly, only half, 50 per cent, reported receiving any advice on their university courses, with most of those who hadn't, 34 per cent, saying that they would have liked some (p. 178). Nearly one quarter, 24 per cent, of students in their final year had still not chosen their future occupation (p. 181). Over two-fifths, 42 per cent, had either applied or intended to apply for postgraduate study, 19 per cent of them (35 per cent of women, 14 per cent of men) for a school teaching certificate (p. 186). The same proportion, 42 per cent, reported that their course was directly related to their career intentions, a further 35 per cent that it was moderately so (p. 188). Over half, 56 per cent, said that they would choose exactly the same course again, 27 per cent a modified version, and 17 per cent a different course (p. 189).

These findings both help to build up a general picture of the transition to work in the first part of the post-war period, and to confirm some of the research on the transition to higher education discussed earlier in this chapter. Thus, we have a picture of substantial numbers of women graduates, those studying arts subjects, and those studying in Welsh and Scottish institutions going into school teaching; with, conversely, men, those studying science, and those studying at Oxbridge or London being more likely to go into industry or further study. While, in most cases, the subject being studied by undergraduates was related to their intended occupation, and a majority appear satisfied with their degree choice, a substantial minority would clearly have liked better advice, might have made a different subject choice if they had had this, and were unclear about their eventual occupation.

Hutchings focused specifically on science undergraduates, carrying out structured interviews with 2024 students in five English universities (Oxford, Cambridge, Imperial College, Leeds and Bradford). Like the Robbins study, he found a divergence in plans between those studying pure and applied sciences:

> In the sample as a whole, about three-quarters of the students interviewed said that they would like to stay on after getting their first degree in order to undertake further studies. In pure science subjects the PhD seemed to be regarded as the 'badge' of the fully trained scientist. The engineers and technologists, on the other hand, were more inclined to go straight into industry than to stay on at university. (Hutchings 1967: 9)

Kelsall et al. (1970) carried out a longitudinal study, using the results of a national postal questionnaire of 10,548 students who graduated in 1960. Thirty per cent of the men students had studied arts subjects (women 60 per cent), 15 per cent social sciences (10 per cent), 29 per cent sciences (22 per cent), 22 per cent technology (1 per cent) and 5 per cent other (7 per cent) (pp. 8–9). Half, 51 per cent, of the men and over one-third, 38 per cent, of the women entered full-time employment on graduation, with 73 per cent of men and 68 per cent of women engaging in some further study, either on a full- or a part-time basis (p. 16). By October 1966, 48 per cent of men (11 per cent doctorate, 4 per cent masters, 15 per cent teacher training, 18 per cent other professional training) and 53 per cent of women (3 per cent, 2 per cent, 34 per cent, 14 per cent) had obtained a further qualification (p. 27).

The main areas of first employment for the men graduates were 33 per cent in industry, 33 per cent education and 11 per cent public administration; for women the proportions were 8 per cent, 61 per cent and 14 per cent (p. 34). By 1966, these proportions had changed somewhat, with 36 per cent of the men then being employed in education (and 68 per cent of those women who were then working), 28 per cent in industry (5 per cent) and 10 per cent in public administration (13 per cent: pp. 46, 83). Of the women, in 1966 44 per cent were in full-time employment, 11 per cent in part-time employment and 40 per cent were housewives (p. 46). Some 11 per cent of the men worked overseas in their first job, and 15 per cent were working overseas in 1966 (pp. 74–5), figures indicative of the contemporary concerns about 'brain drain' (see also Chapter 4).

Kelsall et al. followed up this study, focusing this time on students' social backgrounds and progress. They noted that:

> graduates form a homogeneous group in relation to the rest of society, for they constitute only a tiny proportion of their age group. They are all, of course, graduates, they are all or have been in high-status

occupations, and as a group they exhibit similar marriage and family building patterns. (Kelsall et al. 1972: 59)

Kelsall et al. expressed particular concern about the fate of many women graduates, for whom school teaching, part-time work or housework continued to provide the main outlets:

From the evidence on women graduates we are again left in little doubt that human resources are being most ineffectively used; for highly educated women are, far more than their male counterparts, greatly restricted in their occupational achievements by prevailing conditions which bear little relation to their training and capabilities. (Kelsall et al. 1972: 140)

Bacon et al. (1979) took a different stance. Rather than focusing on students or graduates, and their aspirations or experiences, they surveyed employers' opinions of higher education, contrasting their attitudes towards university and polytechnic graduates. They sampled employers involved in interviewing final year students at six institutions, achieving 49 responses (a 56 per cent response rate). They found that the great majority 'think that universities produce better students both academically and intellectually' (p. 100), with one-third offering as an explanation the lower entry standards of polytechnics. They concluded that 'the most surprising and worrying finding was the lack of importance given to vocational training by employers' (p. 101), suggesting that this indicated that the then binary policy was failing.

Notwithstanding their preference for university rather than polytechnic graduates, employers were also known to have general doubts about the value of higher education: 'The main criticisms from industrial and commercial employers . . . relate to the lack of relevance of many degree courses, even in the vocational areas, and to the lack of a practical awareness of real-life problems and of an analytical capacity to solve them' (Hunter 1981: 33).

In one of the first of a substantial series of research publications stemming from projects based at Brunel University, Roizen and Jepson (1985) took a similar approach to Bacon et al. (1979), carrying out interviews in 139 organizations. As well as raising some doubts about employers' knowledge and expectations of higher education, their findings confirmed those of Bacon et al. on the continuing importance of a hierarchical view of higher education institutions:

Employers do for the most part, and with the exception of some particular courses and jobs, operate a rough stratification system, which considers most university graduates before most public sector [i.e. polytechnic and college] graduates (and for that matter, most Oxbridge graduates before most others). (Roizen and Jepson 1985: 96)

Boys and Kirkland (1988) followed Kelsall et al. (1970) in carrying out a limited longitudinal survey. They analysed data from two postal questionnaire surveys, one of final year undergraduates in 1982 (sample of 6000, 59 per cent response rate), and the second of the same group three years later (1584 answered both). They confirmed the tendency for graduates to take further, vocationally relevant courses shortly after graduation:

A high proportion of graduates had taken further courses after graduation leading to vocational or other qualifications. This applied to two-thirds of university graduates, compared with 50% of those from polytechnics and 43% from colleges. The majority of those taking such courses had done so in order to obtain qualifications relevant to particular careers. (Boys and Kirkland 1988: 26)

By the time of their study, it had become commonplace for major graduate recruiters to participate in what was known as the 'milk-round', visiting careers' events at a selection of higher education institutions to publicize employment opportunities and seek to interest suitable students. As with subsequent employment, an institutional hierarchy also operated here. Thus, Boys and Kirkland noted:

. . . the large institutional variation in the percentage of graduates who gained access to their first employer through the careers service at the institution at which they studied and/or through the 'milk-round' or other employer visits to those institutions. There was a clear institutional hierarchy: Oxbridge graduates at the top, followed by 'other universities', polytechnics and, with very small numbers, colleges. (Boys and Kirkland 1988: 41)

Their study again confirmed the relationship between subject studied and subsequent employment, with the institutional hierarchy intervening here as well:

Oxbridge was well represented in the financial sector and with large employers, while polytechnic graduates were well represented in industry and marginally more likely than their university peers to be working for medium or small organisations. College graduates were more likely to be working in education and for smaller organisations. (Boys and Kirkland 1988: 58)

The subject/employment relationship was, however, much closer for some subjects than others:

The extent to which graduates achieved the type of job aspired to as undergraduates varied more with the type of subject studied than with the type of institution attended . . . the most successful graduates in the sample were those who had studied law, mathematics or computer science, engineering, or commercial subjects. (Boys and Kirkland 1988: 69)

Or, in other words, the more vocational subjects, as well as, presumably, the more vocationally oriented students, achieved greater employment success.

Like most researchers, Boys and Kirkland concluded by establishing the overall satisfaction of most graduates with their experience of higher education: 'Generally speaking, graduates from all institutions and subject areas were satisfied with their period in higher education and confident that it would lead to advantages in the labour market, although in terms of salary these might be deferred' (p. 86).

Boys et al. (1988) studied the responsiveness of higher education to labour market demands, looking at six subjects (business studies, economics, electrical engineering, English, history and physics) in nine English higher education institutions. They carried out interviews with 304 staff, analysed relevant documentation and conducted a student survey (1094 responses from final year undergraduates, a 35 per cent response rate). Their research confirmed the importance of the subject/employment relationship at all stages of the higher education experience, adding to this an appreciation of the general as well as specific ways in which higher education could be seen as preparing students for employment:

> . . . differences in the level of importance attached to employment considerations at the time of entering higher education were related to differences in the level of certainty over careers paths at this stage . . . In all subject areas apart from engineering and business studies there were sizeable minorities who recognised the value of the degree in terms of acquiring general skills, rather than a particular occupation. (Boys et al. 1988: 125)

Many courses, of course, and particularly those that had clear vocational links, included elements of work experience. In these cases there was sometimes a mismatch between students' overall opinion of provision and their views of the linkage between work experience and academic study:

> Amongst students whose courses included work experience, levels of satisfaction were generally high . . . Satisfaction was much less marked when students were asked to comment on the relationship between work placement and the academic content of the degree course. (Boys et al. 1988: 127–8)

Not all students, of course, were so vocationally focused, with a substantial minority looking for something more than financial recompense: 'English undergraduates and historians were more likely to hold altruistic aspirations in their careers and less likely to want high extrinsic rewards, while the reverse was true of business studies graduates, along with economists and engineers' (p. 133).

Boys et al. also confirmed the earlier findings of the Robbins research, to the effect that many students did not decide upon their subsequent occupation until relatively late on in their studies. Indeed, their research suggested that the proportion in this state of uncertainty had grown to form the majority: 'Two or three months before completing their three or four year courses, only a minority of students had decided with any certainty on the type of job they would most like to do after graduation' (p. 134).

Squires (1990: 79–83) provides an analysis of USR data for 1986/7, showing 'the intake of graduates in 25 subjects or subject combinations into types of work which absorbed at least 1 per cent of the total for that subject in one year' (p. 78). This usefully shows the extent to which recruitment is more or less closely related to subject studied. In four of the 25 degree subjects identified – clinical medicine, pharmacy, clinical dentistry and architecture – only one type of work is identified: the professional fields of medicine, pharmacy, dentistry and architecture themselves. Clearly, such studies are very occupationally specific. Three types of work are identified for accountancy graduates – financial, accountancy and banking – nine each for computer studies and civil engineering, fourteen each for mechanical engineering and electronic engineering. At the other extreme, some degrees lead to very varied types of employment: 26 types of work are identified for human geography graduates, 27 for those who studied either combined languages or psychology, and 28 for history graduates.

Brennan et al. carried out questionnaire surveys of two cohorts of CNAA full-time graduates: 1982 and 1985 (10 per cent samples). They again confirmed the strength of the subject/occupation relationship, extending this to consider student orientations and social profiles as well:

> It is abundantly clear that there is a strong relationship between the character of graduate entry into the labour market (and subsequent labour market careers and experiences) and the character of higher education courses (distinguished in terms of such matters as subject area, course type, institution type and qualification type). It is also clear that there is a strong relationship between, on the one hand, student orientations and course type distinguished in terms of the extent of their vocational associations and, on the other hand, subsequent graduate labour market experiences. Moreover, the evidence suggests that because there is a strong relationship between student orientation and student social circumstances and characteristics – student 'social profile' – there is also a strong relationship between student social profile and eventual labour market experiences. (Brennan et al. 1993: 22)

They also noted again the substantial number of students who did not have a clear occupational focus: 'many students are not vocationally orientated in their decisions to enter higher education and in their choices of particular higher education courses . . . many students have far from a purely instrumental and extrinsic approach to higher education' (pp. 23–4).

And they confirmed the continuing importance of the institutional hierarchy: 'polytechnic and college graduates take longer to get jobs than their university counterparts . . . [and have] higher rates of unemployment' (p. 98). This was also seen to impact in other ways, as less advantaged students had a greater propensity to make more poorly informed course and career choices: 'Students from "less favoured" social and educational backgrounds show less evidence of well defined career orientations and choose courses with less direct links with the labour market' (p. 141).

By the time of these studies, of course, higher education had long ceased to be an elite activity, so the sheer numbers of graduates entering the labour market each year might have been expected to have had some impact on that market's behaviour. In this context, Brown and Scase (1994) examined the impact of massification on graduate careers, carrying out interviews with students at three contrasting universities and with recruiters in medium-to large-sized organizations. They found some evidence of impact in an increasingly competitive recruitment process: 'as recruiters more frequently express the need for charismatic rather than bureaucratic qualities in their recruits, the competition for credentials is inhibiting students' acquisition of personal and social skills' (p. 24).

Other findings, however, tended to confirm existing patterns:

despite increasing demands from employers for educational institutions to develop a broader range of personal and social skills that are under-developed and undervalued in most universities, when employers are recruiting for their fast-track graduate development programmes they continue to target students in the established universities. (Brown and Scase 1994: 25)

And, again, there were doubts expressed about employers' expectations, and the transparency of the higher education/employment interface: 'The idea that employers know what their human resource needs are, and that these can be defined and operationalized in educational terms is unsubstantiated' (p. 174).

Harvey et al. (1997) adopted a similar strategy, interviewing 258 managers and employees (graduate and non-graduate) in a range of organizations across the country. They stressed the changes that were taking place in graduate employment, the increased need for flexibility, and hence the development of a broader range of skills among graduates.

For the last decade or so, the Higher Education Careers Service Unit has been sponsoring research on graduates' early labour market experiences (Purcell and Pitcher 1996; Purcell et al. 1999, 2005). In the first of these studies, 5228 final year UK undergraduates completed questionnaires (42 per cent response rate), and focus groups were held at 10 universities (Purcell and Pitcher 1996). These researchers noted that:

Students' motivations in choosing their courses and expectations of what they will do next highlights the patterned diversity of the body of undergraduates in the UK, with more students from traditional [i.e. older] universities opting for further academic study, whereas students from new universities were more likely to pursue a vocational option. (Purcell and Pitcher 1996: 43)

They went on to identify:

three distinct categories of student: 'Hedonists' [61% of the sample], who had chosen their courses because they already enjoyed, or anticipated that they would enjoy, the subject matter of the course; 'Pragmatists' [29%], whose main reason was their clear career orientation or a belief that the course and degree would enhance their employment prospects; and "Fatalists" [7%], whose main reason was somewhat more passive. (Purcell and Pitcher 1996: 43 [11])

Purcell and Pitcher then tentatively postulated that there were also three 'core types' of graduate, though these groups were not directly linked to the student categories:

those who have developed a high order of written communication and analytic skills, those who have developed numeracy, IT and problem-solving aptitudes and those who are more generalist, having developed both sets of skills to a substantial degree, with a focus upon their *application* rather than their virtuoso specialist development. (Purcell and Pitcher 1996: 44, emphasis in original)

As with many surveys, they also found that most students were generally satisfied with their courses, with the skills they had developed, and with the advice they had received.

Purcell et al. (1999) looked at the experience of 2289 graduates who had been involved in the 1996 survey 18 months after graduation. They considered the effects on graduate career trajectory of degree subject (it helped to have done a vocational or numerate degree), gender (men were more likely to be in appropriate full-time employment, and were earning more), age (younger graduates did better in the labour market), university type (those from older universities did better) and degree performance (those with better class degrees did better). They noted that: 'Nearly half of those who had sought employment considered that they had experienced difficulty in obtaining appropriate employment' (p. iv). Taking a broad view of what constituted a graduate job, including both those that required a degree and those that made use of graduate skills and knowledge, they concluded that '89 per cent were in graduate jobs at the time of the survey' (p. v).

They then went on to identify another threefold typology, this time of graduate job seekers:

Career Planners, who had undertaken their courses with a clear view of where they wanted to get to – and who were most likely to be in an appropriate job and satisfied with their career development . . . *Adapters*, who had not thought ahead when choosing their course, or who had changed their minds about what they wanted to do . . . but who had considered their realistic options and had set about making the most of the opportunities available; and *Drifters*, who had not had clear ideas at the outset and were still experimenting with a variety of options or waiting for something to turn up. (Purcell et al. 1999 vi: emphasis in original)

In a further study, Purcell et al. (2005) examined the early career experiences of students who graduated in 1999, involving another large-scale survey, this time supplemented by 100 interviews. In general, their earlier findings were confirmed, with most of their respondents broadly satisfied and in appropriate full-time employment. Getting to that status, however, involved some transitional effort: 'Almost half the *Class of '99* who entered employment immediately following their studies were employed in non-graduate occupations, but this fell rapidly and by four years after graduation, 15 per cent of employed 1999 respondents remained in non-graduate jobs' (p. 3, original emphasis).

Concerns were expressed – as they were by Brown and Scase (1994) – about whether, in an expanding and changing graduate labour market, the benefits accruing to those who had 'invested' in degree studies were being maintained:

> . . . the rate of increase of the earnings of those who graduated in 1999 does not appear to have kept pace with earnings increases more generally in the economy. This may be particular to this cohort . . . or it may be the first indication that the graduate earnings premium is beginning to reflect a decline in the excess demand for graduate skills and knowledge. (Purcell et al. 2005: 3)

Brown and his colleagues also returned to their theme, arguing that a fundamental mismatch between the outputs of higher education and the requirements of the labour market had developed:

> Since the 1960s the proportion of students in higher education in Britain has increased at least fourfold and the proportion in managerial and professional jobs has more than doubled. Higher education has been transformed from the preserve of an elite to a mass pursuit. Many more people are in jobs labelled as managerial or professional. Despite this increase, the proportion of knowledge workers remains much lower than is often assumed and is well below the numbers required to absorb those leaving higher education. (Brown et al. 2004: 215)

Conclusions

The examination of the undergraduate student experience presented in this chapter might be criticized for adopting a systematic, process-oriented approach. In this, students are seen successively as inputs, subjects and outputs of a higher education system. While differentiated in many ways, this system behaves as if its key aims are the attraction of an adequate number of qualified entrants, the efficient satisfaction of student needs while they are in the system, and their rapid dispatch into the arms of appropriate employers once they graduate. Most would accept that the purpose of higher education is rather broader than this (see also the discussion in Chapter 12).

In particular, it seems odd that, while considerable effort has been devoted to tracing students' experiences, both socially and educationally, prior to coming to university, relatively little has been directed to their longer-term experience after leaving higher education. Longitudinal studies of the kind carried out by Kelsall et al. (1970) – which are, of course, both expensive and logistically difficult – are a partial exception to this rule, though they are limited by their quantitative survey approach, and by their focus on the vocational aspects of graduate life.

One recent, small-scale, qualitative approach to investigating the longer-term effect of degree study on graduate lives looked at the experiences of 18 former students who had studied a geography degree at one institution up to 20 years previously (Jenkins et al. 2001). They concluded that:

> The impact of a degree course and the interpretation a graduate places upon the course changes over time. Reconstructions take place all through life. Graduates may alter their view of a degree course from one minute to the next, and the big factor affecting these altered views is the different experiences of graduates after leaving college . . . Graduates will preserve much of their original individuality and background, and will then heighten their individuality in the light of their college relationships and interpretation of the course, which in turn is dependent upon relationships they form. Then, after graduation, with added work experience, a graduate's reflection on this particular course grows more and more individual and the variation between graduates grows larger still. (Jenkins et al. 2001: 158–9)

With the trends towards not just mass initial higher education, but also more students coming back to university as postgraduates, and to the development of a more general practice of lifelong education and learning, the importance of longer-term and repeated evaluation of the overall student experience can only grow.

10

The student experience II: postgraduate students, international students and widening participation

Introduction

This chapter picks up the threads of the preceding one, which focused on the full-time undergraduate and sub-degree student experience. Here, the focus, in the first two sections, is on the postgraduate and international (whether postgraduate or undergraduate) student experience. A third major section then considers the experience and impact of widening participation (to use the contemporary term) in higher education, an issue that runs through both chapters. Thus, in Chapter 9, considerable attention was paid to the comparative experience of men and women undergraduates, full- and part-time undergraduates, and those from different social groups. Here, specific attention is paid to the experience of women, mature and part-time students, ethnic minorities, lower socio-economic groups and the disabled.

Postgraduate students

Since they comprise a relatively small proportion of the higher education population, when compared to undergraduates and sub-degree level students, the postgraduate student experience has typically attracted less attention as either a policy or research concern. Postgraduate students were, however, given close consideration by the Robbins Committee, and this was subsequently followed up – as postgraduate numbers (following undergraduate numbers) grew – by both researchers and policy makers. Most of the concern and research has, however, focused on postgraduate research students, rather than those studying taught masters or other degrees, diplomas or certificates. It has also tended to focus on specific issues, such as completion rates and subsequent employment, rather than on the postgraduate student experience more generally.

When the Robbins Committee surveyed the scene, it noted that, in 1961/2, 17 per cent of all full-time university students were postgraduates. This proportion varied, however, in relation to the status and location of the institutions at which they were studying, ranging from 26 per cent at London, to 18 per cent at both Oxford and Cambridge, 16 per cent at the larger civics, 14 per cent at the smaller civics and Wales, and 11 per cent in Scotland (Committee on Higher Education 1963b, Volume I: 42). Just over one-third, 36 per cent, were studying for a PhD, 23 per cent for masters degrees, 18 per cent for higher diplomas, 18 per cent for Cert Eds, and, curiously enough (a reflection, perhaps, of somewhat less pressured times), 5 per cent were not actually studying for a qualification (p. 45). Barely one-quarter, 26 per cent, were then studying part time (p. 55). The proportions in receipt of public awards varied significantly by subject, amounting to 71 per cent of those studying science, 50 per cent in applied science and 37 per cent in arts (p. 238).

Interestingly, the Robbins Committee found that postgraduates, overall, came from less advantaged backgrounds than undergraduates:

> Sixty one per cent of those who were postgraduates in 1961/2 had parents who had been to a selective school, compared with 73% of undergraduates. Similarly only half as many postgraduates (12%) as undergraduates (22%) had a parent who was a graduate. This implies that the proportion of graduates proceeding to postgraduate study is higher among 'first generation' university students. (Committee on Higher Education 1963b, Volume II: 58)

Similarly, 61 per cent of postgraduates were from middle-class homes (compared to 71 per cent of undergraduates), and 68 per cent had been to a maintained secondary school (63 per cent undergraduates) (p. 59). There is a suggestion in these figures that those from more advantaged backgrounds had less need of postgraduate qualifications in their future careers, and this is born out by the data on where postgraduates had studied previously:

> . . . the proportion of postgraduates coming from Oxford and Cambridge is lower than the proportion of graduate output coming from these universities and . . . the reverse is true with regard to the University of Wales. At other universities the proportions are fairly equal . . . More than two thirds [68%; 77% of those doing PhDs, 78% of those doing masters degrees] of postgraduates were studying at the university from which they graduated. (Committee on Higher Education 1963b, Volume II: 65)

As it had for undergraduate students, the Robbins Committee also collected and analysed information on the amount of teaching contact postgraduates received, and on how much time they spent studying. The figures on contact time were, unsurprisingly, much less than those for undergraduates:

> Postgraduates receive on average about 5 hours of teaching a week, compared with about 15 hours in the case of undergraduates. Overall hours are divided into roughly 3 hours in lectures, 1 hour in discussion periods and 1 hour in practicals. (Committee on Higher Education 1963b, Volume II: 279)

These figures varied widely, however, depending on the qualification sought. Average teaching hours per week were only 1.9 hours for PhD students, 4.9 for masters degrees and 6.1 hours for Cert Eds, but rose to 12.6 for higher diploma students (p. 279). The great majority, 91 per cent, had been allocated to at least one supervisor (99 per cent of PhD students, 93% of masters degrees, 68 per cent on higher diplomas and 98 per cent of Cert Eds) (p. 286). Half, 51 per cent, met their supervisor once or more a week (55 per cent of PhD students), 17 per cent once a fortnight, 19 per cent once or twice a term, 3 per cent less than that, with 9 per cent having no supervisor (p. 288).

PhD students reported spending an average of 40.7 hours a week in private study, masters students 35.6, those on higher diplomas 23.6 and Cert Ed students 17.6. In addition, PhD students spent 1.9 hours a week teaching, masters students 0.7, higher diploma students 0.4 and Cert Ed students 0.1. This gave total working weeks of 44.5, 41.2, 36.6 and 37.0 hours respectively; as with undergraduate students, close to the 40-hour norm for a working week (p. 293).

Rudd and Hatch (1968) carried out a survey of those who embarked on postgraduate education in 1957/8: they received 2303 usable replies (67 per cent response rate). They were interested in completion rates and what students did following their postgraduate studies. As Robbins had found, most of their sample had studied at a limited number of universities: 'Altogether a third of them were at the larger provincial universities, a sixth were at Oxford or Cambridge, and over a quarter were in London' (p. 17).

Rudd and Hatch also noticed a bias towards the sciences in the recruitment – and, as Robbins had shown, the support – of postgraduate students, drawing attention to:

> ... the relatively high proportion of science graduates going on to graduate education even in 1957, at the beginning of the rapid expansion of government grants in this field. There were approximately equal numbers of graduates in arts and in science but more than two science graduates went on to graduate study for every one in arts. (Rudd and Hatch 1968: 20)

They found that, overall, 29 per cent had not achieved the qualification they were studying for. This proportion varied from 22 per cent of those studying technology, 25 per cent in science, 33 per cent in social studies, to nearly one half, 49 per cent, in arts. The figures also varied significantly in terms of qualification aim – 17 per cent of those aiming for a diploma, 46 per cent for masters and 22 per cent for doctorates – and in terms of mode of study, with only 11 per cent of those studying full time not achieving their qualification, as compared to 42 per cent of those studying part-time (pp. 32, 34).

As Kelsall et al. (1970) had found in their study of graduate destinations (discussed in Chapter 9 in the section on 'The transition to work), for a significant minority postgraduate study was associated with working in other countries: 'Of those who replied to our questionnaire, 15% were abroad when they completed the questionnaire and another 15% had been abroad for at least six months since 1957, but had returned to this country' (Rudd and Hatch 1968: 73). North America dominated as the destination, confirming the contemporary concerns about a 'brain drain' of Britain's most educated people (see Chapter 4).

These concerns were linked to dual perceptions of postgraduate, and particularly research, students as being of no great use to British industry and only valued by universities themselves. Thus, on the one hand, Rudd and Hatch found that: 'industry puts no greater value, even for its research and development staff, on time spent working for a PhD in a university than on a one year diploma followed by time spent in employment' (p. 144). And, on the other:

> Work and postgraduate study are most closely related for those in universities; in industry the relationship is considerably less close ... [resulting in] a picture of university education in Britain as something of a closed loop. At each stage the most able students tend to be creamed off and encouraged to take a purer and purer commitment to the advancement of knowledge and the academic way of life; they are put on to a route that will lead them back into the university as teachers. (Rudd and Hatch 1968: 160, 182)

Indeed, in 1966, one-third, 33 per cent, of those surveyed were employed in the universities (p. 57). The 1960s and early 1970s were, however, an unusual period, with the universities struggling to provide the new academic recruits demanded by their own expansion (Williams et al. 1974).

Rudd and Simpson returned to the topic of postgraduate students in the following decade, this time with a particular focus on research students and their supervision. On this occasion they carried out interviews with 800 full-time students and selected staff, and received completed questionnaires from 230 part-time students. Rudd and Simpson's study was contextualized within a perception of postgraduate education as a rapidly growing field, but one from which a significant proportion of students subsequently left the country:

> In 1938, when there were 50,000 full-time students in British universities, 3,000 of them were graduates (apart from those being trained for school teaching). By 1972 there were five times as many students but thirteen times as many graduate students – substantial growth by any standard. This must make graduate education one of Britain's foremost growth industries; and there can be few industries that have exported so high a proportion of their products – though it gets little praise on that account. (Rudd and Simpson 1975: 1)

Once again, the link between postgraduate study and university employment was demonstrated. Half, 50 per cent, of all of the research students (696) interviewed for the study said that they wanted to go into university teaching, and a further 12 per cent into university research (p. 44). There was also further clear evidence of only limited geographical movement between undergraduate and postgraduate study, as 'nearly three-quarters of the home students we interviewed were still at the university at which they had first graduated' (p. 60).

When they asked about topic of study, Rudd and Simpson found that almost all, 91 per cent, of the research students in the arts and social studies claimed they had been mainly responsible for choosing the general field of their research. In the case of the pure and applied sciences, however, just over two-thirds, 69 per cent, made this claim, with 23 per cent stating that the choice had been made mainly by their supervisors, and 6 per cent saying it had been agreed upon between them. In terms of the choice of the detailed topic of research, while 69 per cent of arts/social studies research students stated they were mainly responsible, 59 per cent of pure/applied sciences students said it had been their supervisor's choice (pp. 66–7).

Some dissatisfaction with supervision arrangements was revealed, with nearly half of the research students interviewed saying that they were not supervised as closely as desired during the critical initial stages of their research. The proportion was highest (55 per cent) for social studies students, and lowest (34 per cent) in the pure sciences (ibid.: 74).

Rudd (1985) returned to the postgraduate field again in the 1980s, this time focusing squarely on research student non-completion, the reasons for this, and the problems engendered by it. He carried out over 100 interviews with postgraduates who had withdrawn from 13 English universities in the period 1978/80. He concluded:

At the stage at which most students are deciding whether to enter postgraduate study, they know too little, for rational choice, about the options open to them . . . Most of those who fail to complete a degree lack any very strong wish to do so . . . The beginning of the road that leads to failure for many others is their choice of a research topic . . . Those students who believe they are receiving incompetent or neglectful supervision can find no remedy for this. (Rudd 1985: 114–15)

In response, he made a series of suggestions for changes in practice – in the selection and preparation of students, in the organization of supervision, and in form and level of the PhD – which fed into the policy discussions of the time.

In the early 1980s, this policy focus was continued when researchers working for the Policy Studies Institute carried out a series of studies on postgraduates for the Advisory Board for the Research Councils (ABRC) (Brown 1982; Whalley 1982). Heads of departments of engineering, science and social science in universities and polytechnics were surveyed (response rates of 88 per cent and 77 per cent respectively). The average department was found to contain between 30 and 40 postgraduate students, with their make-up and numbers varying between discipline and institutional type. The survey also covered demand issues, training arrangements, assessment and performance.

For research students, it found that:

> certainly the minimum period of enrolment and quite often even the reasonably acceptable extended period are exceeded by substantial numbers of PhD students before they submit a thesis: and . . . submission of a thesis does not necessarily lead to the awarding of a PhD. (Whalley 1982: 87)

All but two of the 110 taught postgraduate courses covered by the survey involved examinations, but only six relied wholly on examinations for assessment, with over half placing equal emphasis on the examination and a project or dissertation. The great majority, 87 per cent, of full-time students achieved their desired qualification (p. 101). Most departments, particularly those offering less vocationally oriented provision, were not well informed about the subsequent employment of their postgraduate students.

Former postgraduate students (1632 responses, 48 per cent response), 'good' graduates who did not go on to postgraduate study (699, 61 per cent) and employers (230, 66 per cent) were surveyed at the same time (Brown 1982). Of the former postgraduates, 86 per cent were men, and 87 per cent had studied at university, with 36 per cent studying for a PhD, 49 per cent for a master's degree, and 15 per cent for a diploma or other qualification (p. 11). At the time of the survey, 94 per cent of the men and 80 per cent of the women were in full-time employment, with 35 per cent working in research and 22 per cent in teaching (pp. 21, 22). While, on average, postgraduates earned more than the graduate sample, there were considerable variations. The great majority (75 per cent) of the postgraduates felt that their study helped them 'a great deal' or 'to some extent' in their subsequent employment, with almost the same proportion of employers (72 per cent) expressing the same view (pp. 63, 107).

The early 1990s saw a further flurry of research activity directed towards research students, on this occasion largely stimulated by a programme of funding established by the Economic and Social Research Council (ESRC) (Burgess 1994a). The focus of the research projects involved was squarely on the issues of major policy concern, namely the processes of supervision, the quality of both process and product, student completion rates and subsequent employment.

Thus, Parry et al. examined how academic research was conceptualized by interviewing PhD students and supervisors in social anthropology, development studies, urban studies and town planning. They stressed the significance of disciplinary or academic identity:

> The importance of academic identity is that it informs the way in which disciplinary work is conceived and carried out. Where disciplines, as in the case of anthropology, are strongly classified or, in other words, well insulated from other subject areas, we found that disciplinary identity

and academic loyalty to the subject area were strong . . . In the second-ary disciplines, urban studies, development studies and town planning, classification and framing were weaker as boundaries between different constituent subject areas were blurred . . . The different departments which we have studied were characterised by reliance upon preferred methods . . . whereas technicality indexes quantitative methods, indeterminacy indexes qualitative work. (Parry et al. 1994: 49–50)

Youngman (1994) was concerned with documenting what happens in supervision. He conducted 20 interviews with social science supervisors and students to construct a survey questionnaire, though this achieved a disappointing 106 responses (25 per cent). A key finding was 'the very limited supervision experience present in social science departments with only a third of supervisors having more than two completed PhD supervisions'. This was shown to have a significant impact on the supervision experience, as 'the more experienced supervisors engender a higher level of independence from their students, whilst at the same time maintaining the high guidance profile likely to be associated with success' (p. 101).

Pearson et al. (1993; see also Connor 1994) undertook a review of employer demand for doctoral students from the social sciences, interviewing over 750 employers and over 350 students. Confirming the earlier work by Rudd and Hatch (1968), they concluded that:

The small numbers, the fragmented nature of the opportunities and the high degree of substitution with other types of graduates and post-graduates means that the labour market for those with PhDs in the social sciences is largely invisible and that it is difficult to identify any significant explicit demand by employers outside academia for social scientists with PhDs (Pearson et al. 1993: 103)

In a contemporary study – but a broader one, ranging beyond the social sciences – Becher et al. (1994; see also Becher 1993; Henkel and Kogan 1993) focused on six contrasting disciplinary areas: economics, history, physics, sociology, modern languages and biochemistry. They interviewed 88 staff and 55 students in 16 institutions between 1987 and 1992. They were concerned to point out how matters had improved since Rudd's (1985) research, though they still had reservations:

The academic system has been concerned to improve its commitment to graduate students, through changes in the requirements of supervision and clarification in assessment practices. But there is evidence not only of excellent and committed work but also, in a minority of cases, of unacceptable negligence. Perhaps the most disturbing of our findings is the disjunction between what teachers think they are providing and the dissatisfactions of students. (Becher et al. 1994: 188)

At the same time, in the under-recruitment of doctoral students to the academic profession, and their poor financial treatment, Becher et al. detected 'a lack of that proper concern for research and graduate education' (p. 193) at a national level. Despite this concern, however – and this is one respect in which it diverted from the pattern set by the Robbins Committee – the Dearing Committee (National Committee of Inquiry into Higher Education 1997a) commissioned no research specifically on postgraduate students, and its report contained no significant analysis of their experience.

Delamont et al. (2000) followed up Parry et al.'s (1994) earlier work in interviewing 286 full-time PhD students, supervisors and departmental heads in 20 departments between 1990 and 1994. Like Becher et al. (1994), they also found some mismatches between student and supervisor understandings or expectations. Despite the continuing poverty of support for research students, however, they found that: 'The majority of the student informants saw the quest for a PhD as an opportunity to pursue a subject they loved: to spend three years full-time as apprentice researchers in "their" discipline' (Delamont et al. 2000: 47).

International students

International students – or, as they have been termed at different times, overseas, Commonwealth, colonial and/or foreign students – have been a feature of higher education within the UK almost from the start. Hence their experience, whether at sub-degree, undergraduate or postgraduate level, has also been a concern of providers, policy makers and researchers. From the late 1960s onwards, however (see Chapter 4), it has been the financial costs of, and/or profits to be made from, such students that has attracted most attention, as well as the implications of this for provision and practice.

Political and Economic Planning interviewed 287 'colonial' students in 1953, their enquiry having been stimulated by the rapid post-war growth in their numbers: 'their number is estimated to have been between 500 and 600 in 1939 . . . on January 1st, 1955, there were 10,200 colonial students in Britain, of whom 3,500 had arrived during 1954' (p. 1). These students came from:

> . . . every British colonial territory. In the academic year 1954–55 nearly one-third were Nigerians, about one-tenth came from the Gold Coast [Ghana], and a small group came from Sierra Leone and Gambia. The Far East – Malaya, Singapore, Hong Kong, Sarawak and North Borneo – accounted for over one-fifth of the total. The territories of East and Central Africa (but not Southern Rhodesia) sent about one-eighth, and so did the West Indies. Cyprus, Malta and Gibraltar, and Mauritius, Fiji and the Seychelles, and the remaining colonies make up the remaining one-tenth. (Political and Economic Planning 1955: 57)

Note that colonial students, by this time, did not include those from the old, 'white' Commonwealth, or from the newly independent Indian sub-continent (on which, see Singh 1963). Colonial students tended to be older than home students, nearly one-quarter were married, about one-third held a scholarship, one-fifth were student nurses, and just 'over a third are at universities and colleges, about one-eighth are at the Inns of Court, and the remainder are at other institutions' (Political and Economic Planning 1955: 63–4). Over half the total was studying in London, and, excluding the student nurses, only just over one-sixth were women.

Three-fifths said that their experience of Britain had not confirmed their previous impressions, many had problems with finding suitable accommodation and felt excluded from community life, while, among the Africans, nearly three-quarters had experienced colour prejudice (see also Carey 1956). Despite this, however, and the wish of some to have been studying at a higher status institution, most appeared to be reasonably content: 'some nine-tenths of the colonial students in the UK are pursuing the subjects of their choice, and . . . over three-quarters appear to be satisfied with their placement' (Political and Economic Planning 1955: 111).

The Robbins Report provides a useful mapping of the situation in the early 1960s:

> The proportion of full-time university students coming from overseas is now, at just over 10%, much the same as before the war . . . The less developed countries are responsible for the greater part of the increase in overseas student numbers, and students from these countries now form 70% of all overseas students, compared with 49% before the war. (Committee on Higher Education 1963b, Volume I: 253)

At that time, international student numbers were evenly split between undergraduate and postgraduate levels, with the Report noting that '47% of all overseas students are doing postgraduate work, the proportion being higher among foreign students than among Commonwealth students' (p. 255). While a minority, 13 per cent, were in receipt of awards from British public funds, most of those who held awards were funded by their own governments (p. 273).

Sen (1970) carried out a questionnaire survey of 2367 overseas students (41 per cent response rate), as well as 551 nurses, in 1964/5, following this up with 369 interviews. Some 42 per cent of the students surveyed were from Africa, 30 per cent from Asia, 18 per cent the Middle East and 8 per cent the West Indies (p. 14). They were evenly split in terms of financial support: a 'little more than half depended on private sources (including personal savings) with a little less than half having some form of grant or scholarship' (p. 33). More than two-thirds were at least 'quite satisfied' with their course, though problems with academic guidance, language and personal difficulties were noted (p. 73). A follow-up survey to the institutions at which they were studying found that:

> The wastage rate among students was 25.9 per cent. It is highest in colleges of technology and further education and lowest in colleges of

education. More than half of student withdrawals were voluntary, and about a third were due to poor achievement. (Sen 1970: 158)

With the continued expansion of the higher education system in the 1960s and 1970s, coupled with economic problems (see also Chapter 4), the subsidization of international students by the UK state became no longer politically tenable:

> ... for a long time access for overseas students to our higher education system on the same terms as for home students was regarded as part of Britain's global responsibilities, more particularly towards our colonies and the independent Commonwealth. After 1960 the mood changed ... As the number of overseas students grew and the value of the subsidy to them mounted, Britain became increasingly unwilling to treat overseas students on the same basis as home students and introduced fee discrimination. (Williams 1981a: 8)

Differential fees for international students were introduced in 1967, with voluntary quotas on institutional enrolment levels from 1977. These quotas were lifted when full-cost fees were brought in during 1980/1. Though this was soon followed by the introduction of a bursary scheme for international research students, the tenor had clearly shifted from seeing the higher education of students from overseas as a kind of post-colonial duty to viewing their recruitment as a source of additional income.

International students, like postgraduate students, were not spread evenly in geographical terms throughout the higher education system:

> ... in British universities ... an average figure of 11% for overseas students has been compounded of proportions of as much as 34% at the University of Manchester Institute of Science and Technology, 19% overall at the University of London, but only about 4% at Keele or Leicester universities. Within London University some individual schools such as Imperial College, the Institute of Education, London School of Economics, and School of Oriental and African Studies have had around a third of their students from overseas, and the School of Hygiene and Tropical Medicine as much as three-quarters. In polytechnics and further education colleges one has also encountered very high concentrations of overseas students, especially in the London area. (Williams 1981b: 27)

They were also concentrated in terms of level and subject of study:

> There is a similar contrast between *levels of study*. In the universities the number of overseas postgraduate students, at over 18,000 in 1978/79, was only slightly in excess of the number of overseas undergraduates. But the overseas postgraduates constituted 37% of the total student body at that level, whereas the overseas undergraduates were only 7% of all undergraduates. At postgraduate level overseas students seem to have been concentrated more heavily in taught courses than in research

degree courses. The distribution by *subject* is also uneven . . . At under-graduate level, overseas students are most numerous in engineering and technology where they constituted 21% of all students in 1977/78 . . . At postgraduate level [there are] . . . unusually high proportions in engin-eering and technology (57%), agriculture and forestry (56%) and medicine (44%). (Williams 1981b: 27–9, emphasis in original)

And international students were also clustered in terms of their nations of origin (a feature that has remained, though the nations sending the most students have altered as international relations and opportunities have fluctuated):

> There are also heavy concentrations among overseas students in terms of nationality . . . Malaysia and Iran jointly accounted for over a quarter of the total in 1978/79, and the top seven countries (Malaysia, Iran, Nigeria, Hong Kong, USA, Greece and Iraq) accounted for half the total. Until 1978/79 none of our eight partners in the European Com-munity had as many as one thousand students in UK public sector institutions. (Williams 1981b: 30)

With the renewed interest in the international student experience that the policy changes engendered, Blaug and Woodhall surveyed 1484 overseas stu-dents (57 per cent response rate) at 14 institutions in 1980. They found that:

> . . . the typical overseas student is (i) male (75% of all respondents) aged 30 or below (82%); (ii) studying for a first degree or a postgradu-ate degree in engineering and technology, science, or administrative and business studies, and (iii) likely to be studying a course in which more than half of all the students are overseas students . . . the typical overseas student is likely to be unmarried (72%) . . . The student tends to come from Asia (36%), Africa (16%), or the Middle East (16%), to be the son of a self-employed businessman, craftsman or farmer (40%) or a civil servant or other government employee (32%) . . . Nearly half of all students had a scholarship or grant of some sort (46%). (Blaug and Woodhall 1981: 241–2)

The policy changes of the 1970s and 1980s did, however, have a significant – though, in the overall scheme of post-war developments, temporary – impact on recruitment:

> Full-cost fees and the new emphasis on targeted scholarship support have between them had a considerable impact since 1980 upon enrol-ment levels and patterns. There has been a sharp decline in enrolment, in marked contrast to the rapid expansion of the two previous decades. Between 1979 and 1984 the number fell overall from 88,037 to 56,121. (Williams 1987: 114)

One other consequence of these changes was that the international student experience was increasingly reconfigured – as the 'home' student experience was to be at a later date – on a provider/consumer basis. Much more attention (and, on the part of the student, expectation) was then given to the quality of that experience, and how it could be improved. In this context, the UK Council for Overseas Student Affairs (UKCOSA) sponsored a series of studies in the mid-1980s (Shotnes 1986, 1987).

Kinnell (1990) and her associates reported on a study that surveyed international students at two universities, interviewing selected students and staff, in the late 1980s. The emphasis on the needs and expectations of the students was clear:

> On the basis of the survey of final-year overseas students, which had a representative flavour, their principal needs were for good quality rapport with their academic tutors, especially for a sympathetic listening ear and personal support in what was for many a difficult learning experience. Academically the need for good quality feedback on written work and other performance-based learning activity was keenly felt and strongly expressed. Related to this was the need for a more responsive course organization which paid more than lip-service to the strengths and weaknesses of overseas students and their individuality . . . Not surprisingly, overseas students were also very aware of their language difficulties and their need for practical help with written and spoken English. (Elsey 1990: 51)

In the most recent period, the other main emphasis in this area, in terms of both policy and research, has been European: concerning the experience of students on the ERASMUS (introduced in 1987), SOCRATES and related EU programmes. These could be either students from other European countries spending some time studying in the UK, or UK students studying elsewhere in Europe.

In general, evaluations of the ERASMUS programme have been positive (e.g. Maiworm et al. 1991; Maiworm and Teichler 1996; Opper et al. 1990; Papatsiba 2005; Teichler and Maiworm 1994, 1997), though it has probably achieved less than was intended. After all, the aims of the programme are both broad and ambitious:

> Study for some period in another European country is aimed to broaden academic experience, to contribute to personal development by means of acquiring new cultural experience, and also, in most cases, to improve foreign language proficiency. Last but not least, many students participating in the ERASMUS programme hope that competencies acquired during the study period abroad will later prove useful in the graduate's career. (Maiworm and Teichler 1996: 93)

The actual assessment, from extensive and repeated surveys of student participants is, however, slightly more measured and qualified:

> Most former ERASMUS students are employed in organizations which have continuous contacts with other countries . . . The majority of former

ERASMUS students consider themselves well qualified in the host country language . . . Many former ERASMUS students are convinced that
temporary study in another European country . . . has helped in obtaining employment . . . however, former ERASMUS students do not seem to
have above-average early professional careers. (Maiworm and Teichler
1996: 94–5)

From a specifically UK perspective, the experience of ERASMUS and similar
programmes has not been so well received. There is a greater demand for
study places in the UK from European students – due to the importance of
English as a world language, and the favourable perception of the UK teaching and learning environment – than there is from UK students to study
elsewhere in Europe:

> . . . it is the perception of local ERASMUS coordinators as well as
> the students that as far as directly academic issues are concerned UK
> students encounter more problems in studying abroad than do foreign
> students studying in the UK. UK graduates who have taken part in
> ERASMUS programmes are less likely to work abroad than other
> ERASMUS students, and are more likely to be dissatisfied with the jobs
> they have obtained relative to their qualifications. (Brennan 1997: 70)

Widening participation: experience and impact

The expansion in the numbers of university students has inevitably
increased the number of what are sometimes known as first generation
students, who have no close relatives with a first-hand knowledge of
university life. Such students have special problems, and for them it is
particularly desirable to spend a part or the whole of their university life
away from home so as to escape the daily reminders of differences in
outlook. (Brook 1965: 51)

What is now known as widening participation (Bekhradnia 2003) – and
used to be known as access, and before that simply as selection – can be
seen to underlie many of the analyses that have been referred to in this
chapter and the preceding one (Metcalf 1993). It reflects a concern to
ensure that the opportunities of higher education are available on an
equal footing to all, regardless of their characteristics (other than their academic abilities, of course, though arguably that is also now coming under
challenge).

The characteristics of actual and potential students who were seen as
important for equity in participation, and what it was felt could be done to
ensure this, have varied over the post-war period. For example, writing in
1961, Furneaux took a resigned view on what universities could do to
encourage greater participation by students from lower socio-economic
backgrounds:

Non-academic determinants, such as social-class membership, play a very important part in university selection, but not at the stage where the universities themselves select their students. All the important effects have already occurred by the time that a student enters the upper-sixth form. (Furneaux 1961: 101)

Watts (1972), in a small-scale interview-based study of Leeds school pupils, asked about their reasons for choosing to, or not to, apply for admission to Oxbridge. He noted that:

> . . . in distinguishing between the student bodies of different institutions, social class was the most important single criterion used, and . . . most of the pupils recognised that the social class differences between student bodies carried with them certain socialisation implications . . . the pupils who were deterred from applying to Oxbridge by its social class image and its socialisation pressures were deterred not by the effect they thought it would have on them, but by the feeling that their unwillingness or failure to conform to its norms would leave them lonely and isolated. (Watts 1972: 131)

Or, in short, they knew their place.

Writing some 20 years later, Egerton and Halsey still seemed inclined to admit defeat on equalizing social class participation, while arguing that gender inequality in higher education had been reduced:

> There have been three conspicuous features of the history of access to higher education since the beginning of the [twentieth] century: first, it has been a period of considerable expansion; second, studies have shown no diminution in relative social class inequality; and, third, there has been a significant diminution in gender inequality. (Egerton and Halsey 1993: 183)

Their analysis was confirmed in a related article (Blackburn and Jarman 1993).

Research carried out for the Dearing Committee updated this analysis, and added a commentary on the position of other more recently recognized widening participation groups – ethnic minorities and the disabled:

> Ever since the Report of the Robbins Committee was published in 1963, rates of participation in higher education have run ahead of most expectations and of expert predictions. The speed and scale of the expansion have been unprecedented within the UK and some outstanding achievements deserve to be recorded and celebrated. For example, the statistics show that within one generation the UK has achieved equal proportions of women and men in undergraduate HE and most ethnic minorities are now, if anything, slightly over-represented. There is, however, no room for complacency as some marked inequalities in educational opportunity remain. Social classes IV and V and disabled students are under-represented in higher education . . . Moreover, the

system has still to develop a strategy for lifelong learning. (Coffield and Vignoles 1997: 3)

Pugsley surveyed and interviewed pupils at 10 schools and colleges in south-east Wales, looking at the impact of institutional marketing and social stratification on choice. Focusing squarely on social class, she concluded:

> The data illustrate how university choices are mediated and reinforced by class based competencies. Earlier engagements with the education market and school choice by the middle classes ensures that their university choices are well facilitated. In contrast, those families who are unfamiliar with market discourse often find themselves choosing from a limited menu of options, with restricted access to A-level guidance and higher education choices. This can and does lead to disillusionment and disaffection with the . . . [higher education] sector and often results in a rejection of the system 'before it can reject me'. Clearly a marketized higher education sector merely replicates class-based inequalities, successfully polarizing rather than up-skilling the graduate workforce. (Pugsley 2004: 153–4)

In a more recent analysis, Reay et al. (2005) examined the overlapping roles of social class, race and gender in how potential students decided upon which higher education institution to attend. Their study focused on six schools and colleges in the London area, during the period 1998/2000, surveying and interviewing samples of students, parents and advisers. Their examination of national data confirms Egerton and Halsey's (1993) point that, while gender inequality seems to have been largely overcome, the position of lower class and ethnic minority students still gives cause for concern:

> In 1975–6 the ratio of female to male students . . . was 0.46:1 whereas by 1999–2000 this had reversed to 1.20:1 . . . While more working class and ethnic minority students are entering university, for the most part they are entering different universities to their middle class counterparts. (Reay et al. 2005: 3, 9)

In their analysis, Reay et al. draw a contrast between those for whom going to university, and a particular kind of university, is normal, unquestioned and assumed, and those for whom this is a conscious and difficult choice:

> Higher education choice takes place within two registers of meaning and action. One is cognitive/performative and relates to the matching of performance to the selectivity of institutions and courses. The other is social/cultural and relates to social classifications of self and institutions. (Reay et al. 2005: 19)

While these authors might disagree with Furneaux (1961) about whether there was anything that higher education institutions could do to change these choices, their assessment was that the existing assumptions and practices within different kinds of school had a major impact on students' higher education options:

> While both of these private schools provided protected worlds of 'already realised ends – procedures to follow, paths to take' the state students in the two large sixth forms, unless they were recognised as Oxbridge material, were likely to be negotiating a morass of choices they often felt ill-equipped to deal with. Even more disadvantaged were the predominantly working class students . . . involved in a process of finding out what you cannot have, what is not open for negotiation and then selecting from the few options left. (Reay et al. 2005: 59)

Reay et al.'s conclusion is, therefore – regardless of the contemporary concern with mass higher education and widening participation (see, for example, Higher Education Funding Council for England (HEFCE) 1996a; Metcalf 1993) – pessimistic, at least as regards social class:

> . . . despite the superficial noisy welter of innovation, at a deeper more impenetrable level certain structures of privilege remain impervious to change. These prevailing inequalities make the transition to higher education particularly difficult for mature working class students . . . who must fashion themselves in the image of the traditional higher education applicant, risking inauthenticity, or else restrict themselves to those universities, in a minority within the pre-1992 sector, with mature student friendly policies. (Reay et al. 2005: 106)

In addition to such general examinations of the issues involved in widening participation, many studies and initiatives have focused on particular groups within society. To the long-term concern with lower class and women students, other groups have more recently been added. At present, the most commonly identified groups of concern are women, mature (for a time, rather mystifyingly, also called 'alternative') students, ethnic minorities, those from lower socio-economic groups and those with a disability. In practice, of course, there is considerable overlap between the memberships of these groups. The changing position of these five groups are each now considered in turn.

Women

In 1965 the percentage of female undergraduates in the United Kingdom as a whole was 27.7: ten years later it had risen to 36.3: and in 1980–81, it reached 39.8. Particularly interesting in this increase is the case of medical faculties where special factors had kept the entry of women students low: a quota system had more or less openly been applied to keep female entrants at 10 to 25% of the total admitted. The system was abandoned in the early 70s: thus in 1962 female students were 24% of the total in medicine whereas in 1980 they were 38.65%. (Sutherland 1985: 7)

The post-war period has witnessed a steady rise in the relative participation of women in higher education in the UK, as restrictions on their involvement have gradually been dismantled. This rise accelerated from the 1960s onwards, associated with the development of the women's movement, which itself stimulated an interest in the history of women's education in general (e.g. Acker and Piper 1984; Deem 1980; Dyhouse 1995, 2006; Purvis 1991). Now that women make up the clear majority of students in higher education, it might be thought that their participation was no longer an issue – and that attention might be diverted, in particular, to the participation of working-class men – but they remain under-represented in particular disciplines and institutions, at higher levels of study, and, notably, among academic staff (see Chapter 11).

Earlier studies on this topic focused in particular on the experience of women who were successful in going to university, and their subsequent lives and careers. Thus, Arregger (1966) looked at graduate women, based on 1529 completed questionnaires (82 per cent response rate) from nine areas of England and Scotland. The occupational and employment patterns that she found were stark. Nearly three-quarters of her respondents, 73 per cent, were in paid work, with 58 per cent working full time. The clear majority, 55 per cent, were schoolteachers, with nearly two-thirds, 65 per cent, working in education altogether (pp. 12–13). While these figures may be partly explained by the marital and family status of the women concerned, only 25 per cent had no children (p. 11); so motherhood was clearly not a bar to full-time work for many, albeit in a profession better suited than most to this status.

Aiston (2005), in a retrospective study, surveyed women who had graduated from the University of Liverpool between 1947 and 1979, and were still living on Merseyside. She found that 'university-educated women were no longer rejecting marriage and motherhood on the same scale as their predecessors . . . by and large these women wanted to be graduates *and* wives and mothers' (p. 425, original emphasis).

Chisholm and Woodward also examined the experiences of women graduates, offering an analysis indicative of structural discrimination:

> Educational channelling and sex-role socialization at home and school result in girls and women entering a narrow range of occupations with lower aspirations and expectations for progress therein. Further, the existence of a sexually-segregated dual labour market is an important structural factor in the explanation of women's employment patterns: most work at a narrow range of tasks within a narrow range of occupations, in low-status badly-paid positions offering little opportunity for career progress. Women suffer both overt and covert discrimination in recruitment, promotion, salary and day-to-day interaction at work. Graduate women are no exception: most enter teaching or public service occupations traditionally dominated by women; they achieve less in purely career terms; they are discriminated against; and they appear to manage their careers less well than their male peers because of a

complex of structural and situational constraints, together with the effects of socio-psychological barriers which are reflected in women's typical lack of self-confidence in their abilities. (Chisholm and Woodward 1980: 163)

Thomas (1990) carried out interviews with 96 current students (evenly split in terms of sex) and staff in selected science and humanities departments at three higher education institutions. She was particularly interested in the relationship between gender and subject choice, arguing that 'our perceptions of the arts and sciences are shaped by notions of femininity and masculinity' (p. 36). As a consequence, the interleaving structures associated with gender, subject and career meant that: 'for most of the women, as for many of the men, the issue of choice (choice of subject and choice of career) was framed by questions of conformity and rebellion' (p. 176). Clearly, the continuing segregation, both horizontal and vertical, of the labour market means that it is easier for both women and men to make the subject and career choices expected of them by society (see also Chapter 9).

The Dearing Committee (National Committee of Inquiry into Higher Education 1997a) differed from the Robbins Committee (Committee on Higher Education 1963a) in commissioning research on groups of concern for widening participation. While the summary by the researchers concerned (Coffield and Vignoles 1997) of the position was more positive, the subject/gender imbalances noted by Thomas were still very evident:

> The evidence clearly shows that women are finally taking their place as equal participants in the undergraduate experience of HE and this constitutes a major success story in the struggle against exclusion. Less positively, women remain concentrated in certain subject areas, such as education and the humanities. (Coffield and Vignoles 1997: 9)

And, once the perspective was switched away from undergraduate level study, the position of women in other aspects of the higher education experience was shown to be more disadvantageous: 'Women are still very much under-represented on postgraduate research degrees and at all levels in the academic staffing hierarchy, particularly at the most senior levels' (p. 10).

A recent focus for research has been on women who have taken up places in higher education later in life, after a period of employment and/or child rearing. Thus, Pascall and Cox, using interviews, studied the experiences of 43 women returning to higher education:

> . . . these women saw education as a route out of being a housewife and of the low-paid part-time jobs that go with that role. They saw it as a source of identity when being a housewife failed to perform that function, and when motherhood could no longer be the centre of their daily lives. And they saw it as a means of independence when the support of the family system failed . . . Most also had faith in the possibility of career. (Pascall and Cox 1993: 76)

In a similar study, Edwards interviewed 31 mature women returning to higher education. She linked her analysis to the growing expectation that women should not merely be successful housewives and mothers, but should also succeed in paid employment and, in this case, in higher education as well:

> Women are under pressure to achieve success in each of the two greedy spheres by showing that neither suffers because of their participation in the other. They must show that their educational work is not affected by their family commitments, and that their family lives are not suffering because of their studies. (Edwards 1993: 63)

Further studies in this tradition include those by Lunneborg (1994) of 14 women studying with the Open University, and Webb's (2001) study of 92 first year students, which identified three key narratives of access denied, untapped and wasted potential.

While the increased participation of women in higher education is to be welcomed, it is clear that more still needs to be done:

> There may now be parity in the numbers of men and women under-graduate students, with double the proportion of women students than at the time of the Robbins Report in 1963, but major differences persist in their experience of higher education. In addition to differences in the proportions of women students between subjects, women out-number men as mature entrants and on access courses, but are under-represented on research degrees. (Woodward et al. 2000: 35–6)

Mature and part-time students

Mature and part time are distinct but strongly overlapping categories, which are discussed together here for convenience. The common theme is of difference from the kind of student – the full-time school-leaver – who has attracted most policy and research attention, and was the subject of the previous chapter. Mature students may, of course, study full time as well as part time, though, with their greater likelihood to have both family and work responsibilities, they are more typically part-time students. Conversely, young students, who tend to have fewer responsibilities, and more access to financial and other forms of support, are more likely to study full time.

The interest in mature students in higher education largely stems from the 1980s, when concerns about the changing age structure of the population became pronounced, and when a range of access schemes were set up to encourage their greater participation. But there is, of course, a much longer tradition of university involvement in adult education (see also Chapter 7), and research interest in part-time higher education (or advanced further education, as it used to be termed, as most part-time provision was outside the university sector) also has a longer, albeit patchy, history.

In a pioneering study, Hopper and Osborn surveyed and interviewed two small samples of adult students, totalling 295, in the mid-1960s and early 1970s. They noted that:

> . . . as a result of their educational and work experiences as well as their ambivalent self-identifications and generally low self-esteem, adult students are in marginal situations within their status groups and occupational roles. The upwardly and downwardly mobile are particularly likely to have experienced aspects of marginality. They were frequently subjected to a number of cross pressures from home, school and peers in adolescence. (Hopper and Osborn 1975: 110)

These pressures, coupled with their experience of 'doing' higher education at an unusual time in their lives, affected the very meaning of higher education:

> The return to education in adult life tends to be a form of instrumental adjustment, known as legitimate innovation, to the problems generated by an unusual set of life experiences which are manifest in high levels of feelings of relative deprivation and a series of contingent marginal situations . . . Marginality and feelings of relative deprivation affected the meaning which higher education had for them. (Hopper and Osborn 1975: 132)

Woodley et al. (1987) carried out a national sample survey of adult students (aged 21 or over) in the UK (achieving 5683 responses, a 46 per cent response rate) in 1980/1. The sample included students in universities, advanced further education and the Open University. They noted how the patterns of mature student participation tended to replicate those found in school-leavers: 'In terms of social class, the "working class", and particularly women within it, are massively under-represented among mature students on both qualifying and non-qualifying courses' (p. 169).

Bourner et al. (1991) surveyed 2876 students (achieving a 69% response rate) on 66 part-time CNAA-accredited degree courses in 1985. This was the kind of higher education provision on which one would expect to find many mature students, and this proved to be the case. As with the analysis of Woodley et al. (1987), the strength of other socio-economic structures was clearly in evidence:

> The average (median) age of the part-time students was 30. Almost two-thirds of them were male. The ethnic origins of the respondents were overwhelmingly UK/European. Most were married and in paid employment. Of those who were married, most had spouses in paid employment. Over 40 per cent of the respondents had children. Most of the respondents reported that both parents had left school at the age of 15. Compared with their parents, few of the respondents were engaged in manual occupations. The findings of this study are consistent with a picture in which taking a part-time degree course is part of a process of

upward social and economic mobility. There is also a suggestion in the findings that a significant proportion of the part-time students are members of families in which continuing education is perceived as a route to enhanced economic life chances . . . [and] that the students were continuing a process of upward socio-economic mobility started by their parents. (Bourner et al. 1991: 33)

Bourner et al.'s analysis fits squarely within the 'alternative route' tradition (Hordley and Lee 1970; Raffe 1979), where part-time higher education, usually in lower-status institutions, is seen as a means to social mobility, particularly for mature age men from lower socio-economic groups.

Brennan et al. (1999) also looked at the particular situation of part-time students. They surveyed nearly 6000 students in six selected universities, achieving a response rate of 36 per cent. Since part-time students are typically in work before, during and after their studies, the notion of higher education forming a transition to work (see the discussion of this for full-time students in Chapter 9) clearly needs modification for such students:

The many and various ways in which part-time students relate their courses to their careers, and indeed the extent to which they do this at all, make measuring the impact of higher education on their employability a difficult task. However, there appears at least general support from this survey for the notion that individual students do receive career benefits from their studies – especially if they are motivated to study by the prospect of those benefits. (Brennan et al. 1999: 31–2)

Callender, in research carried out for the Dearing Report, focused on the differences in this respect between part- and full-time students. She concluded that:

Full- and part-time students had very different plans once they had completed their studies. The majority of full-time students intended to get a job immediately after finishing their course and a further fifth wanted to continue studying. Over a third of part-timers planned to study for another qualification, and over a quarter intended to get a different job in a new type of work, or were undecided. (Callender 1997: 58)

As with women students, the contemporary verdict would probably be that the battle to engage more mature students in higher education has been largely won. After all: 'The majority of HE entrants are now officially "mature" i.e. over 21 years of age on entry and 30% are actually over 30. However . . . mature students are still concentrated in the post 1992 universities' (Coffield and Vignoles 1997: 12). But, and again as with women students, as the latter comment makes clear, more again needs to be achieved.

The most recent examination of part-time higher education students was for research sponsored by Universities UK (Callender et al. 2006; Ramsden

2006). Ramsden carried out an analysis of the available statistics, indicating that there were approximately one million part-time higher education students, or 40 per cent of the total, studying in the UK in 2003/4. The majority, 62 per cent, were women – the dominance of women students is now the case for both full- and part-time study – and half were aged between 30 and 49. The great majority were in employment, and were studying primarily for vocational reasons. They were more often to be found studying for sub-degree or taught postgraduate qualifications than for first degrees. The most popular subject areas for part-time study were subjects allied to medicine, education, business and administrative studies, and combined subjects. Most received no financial support and were studying locally.

Callender et al. (2006) surveyed part-time students' attitudes, finances and experience, carrying out an online survey of 2654 UK students. They confirmed that students were studying mainly for instrumental reasons, with their choice of course influenced by affordability, location and timing. The average cost of study was £1385 in 2004/5, with 59 per cent of this accounted for by tuition fees. Home and work responsibilities meant that most part-time students felt they could not devote enough time to their studies.

Ethnic minorities

The specific interest in ethnic minority participation in higher education is, like that in mature students, also relatively recent. It essentially stems from the time when a significant number of the children of post-war immigrants were of an age to be considering higher education. Much of the existing policy and research literature has concerned itself with whether ethnic minority students were participating in smaller numbers, relatively, than the majority population, and achieving different outcomes, and, if so, what might be done about this.

Brennan and McGeevor carried out one of the earliest large-scale studies of the employment of ethnic minority graduates, surveying 10 per cent of Council for National Academic Awards (CNAA) 1982 graduates. They found significant differences in employment patterns among Asian, Afro-Caribbean and UK European (i.e. white) graduates:

> For the Asian students, three clear concentrations emerge – Electrical and Electronic Engineering, Science and Pharmacy. Humanities appears to be particularly unpopular among the remaining courses. No such concentrations are evident for the Afro-Caribbean group . . . Thirty-seven per cent of the employed Afro-Caribbeans worked for local government or the public utilities. Thirty-eight per cent of the employed Asians worked for professional commercial companies. These two categories of employer together account for the employment of over 40 per cent of the employed UK European sample which divides between the two. (Brennan and McGeevor 1987: 12, 19)

Modood and Shiner examined Universities Central Council on Admissions (UCCA) and Polytechnics and Colleges Admissions Service (PCAS) application data for 1992 for UK citizens, employing logistic regression analysis to control for factors including A-level passes, resits undertaken and socio-economic characteristics. While ethnic minority participation did not, then, appear to be much different overall from that of the majority population, there were still some causes for concern in terms of their variable participation in different institutions within the higher education hierarchy:

> . . . the process of entry into the higher education system as a whole is not as discriminatory against certain ethnic minorities as would seem at first sight from an analysis of the (old) universities. The polytechnics were redressing the balance, at least in part. (Modood and Shiner 1994: 49)

Connor et al. (1996) followed up Brennan and McGeevor's (1987) interest in the transition of ethnic minority students to employment. They surveyed 272 1993 graduates (representing a 37 per cent response rate) at four universities, and carried out 25 interviews with graduates and 10 with recruiters. They found that: 'At every post-graduation career stage, ethnic minority graduates were less likely to be in permanent employment and slightly more likely to be unemployed than their white peers' (Connor et al. 1996: 54). Yet their analysis also indicated that ethnic minorities, in overall terms, were actually over-represented among higher education students, while concentrated in certain kinds of institution and subject:

> Ethnic minorities are well represented overall in higher education, relative to their position in the UK population, but their distribution across the sector is uneven, especially between institutions. Almost one in eight of all UK domiciled students at first degree level in 1994/95 were from ethnic minority groups, more than double their representation in the UK population . . . Ethnic minorities are better represented in the new (i.e. post-1992) universities, and particularly at a select few, where they account for over 30 per cent of UK domiciled undergraduates. Business studies and computer science are more popular degree subject choices for most ethnic minority groups than whites, while education is generally less popular. (Connor et al. 1996: ix)

Other researchers began to break down the patterns of overall ethnic minority participation to examine the differential experiences of particular ethnic minority groups within UK society:

> First, black students concentrate in some HEIs [higher education institutions], so that many HEIs have very small numbers of such students . . . Second, black applicants tend to apply for courses where competition is high (law, medicine) and hence A level requirements are high. Third, with the exception of Chinese and some groups of Asian students, black students often enter HE after 21 years of age as a result of

taking GCSEs after the age of 16. Finally – although this list is by no means exhaustive – black students often experience HE as isolating and discriminatory when they get there. (Bird 1996: 13: note that Bird here classifies all minority ethnic students as 'black')

Of course, it might well be said, in response to Bird's final point, that many majority population students also experience higher education as isolating, though probably not discriminatory in the sense that he means. As the studies confirmed that there was not, at least any longer, the expected pattern of discrimination, in overall terms, against ethnic minority entry to higher education, interest focused more and more on the experience of particular ethnic minority groups:

> Until 1990, the main debate concerning ethnic minorities and higher education centred upon an unsubstantiated impression that ethnic minorities were under-represented in higher education. Systematic data collection was instituted in the 1990s and it soon became clear that ethnic minorities, as a whole, are more successful in achieving university entry than white applicants . . . This is not to say that there is no issue of ethnic minority under-representation in higher education . . . gender differences exist, with Caribbean men and Bangladeshi women most likely to be under-represented. (Modood and Acland 1998: 158)

In their report for the Dearing Committee, Coffield and Vignoles reiterated these points, and added a concern regarding the over-concentration of ethnic minority groups in their local universities:

> . . . relative to their share in the population, ethnic minorities overall are now better represented in HE than whites . . . Satisfaction at this encouraging development needs to be tempered by the persistently low participation of specific ethnic groups in the pre 1992 universities, particularly Bangladeshis, people categorising themselves as 'Black-other' and Black-Caribbeans . . . More detailed research confirms that ethnic minority students remain concentrated in certain 1992 universities, predominantly those located in London and the Midlands, where they are the local institutions for large ethnic minority populations. (Coffield and Vignoles 1997: 6–7)

Whether this represents some kind of subtle institutional apartheid, with the more elite and residential higher education institutions seeking to discourage ethnic minority entry, or is instead the result of the collective choices of individual ethnic minority students to study within their comfort zone – as the evidence on mature students and those from lower socio-economic groups might suggest – is a matter requiring further investigation (see Shiner and Modood 2002). The feeling remains, however, that many higher education institutions could do more to encourage and support ethnic minority applicants and students:

The limited data on the experiences of ethnic minority students within HE indicate that many face overt discrimination and feelings of isolation, and that only limited attempts have been made by HEIs to provide targeted and appropriate support for these students. (Coffield and Vignoles 1997: 8)

Connor et al. (2003) returned to the study of ethnic minority students in 2002, interviewing a sample of over 1300 students (including over 700 from ethnic minorities) at 33 English higher education institutions. They emphasized 'the diversity of the ethnic student population . . . and the way patterns of participation, experiences within HE and outcomes vary substantially between the different minority ethnic groups' (p. ix). They found that, overall, minority ethnic students were more likely to be:

. . . on degree than sub-degree programmes than are White students . . . on full-time than part-time sub-degree programmes at HE institutions . . . better represented in certain subjects, in particular medicine/dentistry, computer science, law and business studies . . . better represented at new rather than old universities and HE colleges, in particular new universities in Greater London. (Connor et al. 2003: 123)

Lower socio-economic groups

Interest in the participation of lower socio-economic groups in higher education is at least as long-standing as that with regard to women (Archer 2003). This interest was in part an extension of a concern with the differential school experience of children from different social backgrounds. The 'classic' research of Jackson and Marsden (1966) in the 1960s has many parallels with the more recent analysis of Reay et al. (2005), discussed at the beginning of this section:

As the sixth-form course drew to an end thoughts began to concentrate on university or training college. The middle-class children had a fairly clear idea of where they were going, and of how to get there. The situation with working-class children was much more mixed. There was the small number whose parents were intent on thrusting them through to university despite all obstacles, and there was that larger number who drew from middle-class connexions a much clearer sense of possibilities. But by this stage many of even the most ambitious parents had, in a sense, been left behind . . . University and college were approached in a mood in which elements of sheer ignorance, general perplexity, or mere lack of initiative were hard to disentangle. (Jackson and Marsden 1966: 153–4)

Cotgrove (1958) surveyed 882 students (a 69 per cent response rate) at two London polytechnics in 1955. Most were already in employment and studying for vocational reasons. A split in terms of social origins was evident, with most of those studying full time and on higher education courses coming from middle-class families: 'although the expectation of occupational reward is the main motive for attending technical colleges, the main factor determining attendance is occupation' (p. 123). Only a minority had applied to study at a university, and most indicated they were studying at a technical college for financial reasons.

Abbott surveyed students who were at the universities of Edinburgh, Durham and Newcastle, achieving 1303 responses in total (response rates varying between 46 and 83 per cent). She concluded that:

> . . . it is clear that there has been no vast expansion of working-class students on the scale which was hoped or feared at the end of the 1940s . . . The failure of the working class to take advantage of educational opportunity and the reason for the corresponding expansion of lower middle-class students may be attributed to cultural factors at work at grammar school level. (Abbott 1971: 551–2)

Even for those working-class students who did make it to university, Abbott found that class nonetheless impacted on all aspects of the student experience:

> . . . the social classes are differentially distributed in faculties, i.e. in terms of work space – in residence – in terms of living space – and in societies and student organisation – or interest space. Indeed, it has been found that social and spatial distance are often closely allied, more working-class students living in digs rather than in halls; living out rather than in colleges; and living in spatially separate areas of the city . . . The spatial concentration leads to reduced social contact of the social classes and accentuation of existing social class divisions and cultural differences. (Abbott 1971: 554)

Much more recently, Robertson and Hillman reported on the position of students from lower socio-economic groups (and also on those with disabilities – a curious combined brief) for the Dearing Report. They again rehearsed the arguments about prior experience and expectations to explain the continuing social class patterns of participation:

> . . . it remains the case . . . that the social composition of higher education in the UK continues to reflect the advantages which accrue to people from higher socio-economic groups by reason of wealth, culture and prior educational success. For these social groups, entry to higher education has become an expectation and a 'natural' preparation for entry to positions of relative advantage in the labour market. On the other hand, the 'routinisation' of participation in higher education is largely absent as a feature of life for lower socio-economic groups and for those with disabilities. (Robertson and Hillman 1997: 34)

Robertson and Hillman went on to quote the figures for the age participation index by socio-economic group. Thus, while 8.4 per cent of the

18+ cohort in socio-economic groups I, II and IIIn (the higher socio-economic groupings) entered higher education in 1940, the proportion for groups IIIm, IV and V was only 1.5 per cent. By 1950, the respective proportions were 18.5 per cent and 2.7 per cent, and, by 1995, 45.0 per cent and 15.1 per cent (p. 40). While over the period as a whole, therefore, the proportion of the lower socio-economic groups participating in higher education had increased tenfold, those from higher socio-economic backgrounds were still by far the dominant student group.

Metcalf, reporting for the Council on Industry and Higher Education, came to broadly similar conclusions:

> . . . those from lower social classes are scarcely better represented in the 1990s than they were ten (and probably 20) years ago. Only nine per cent of young people in Britain entering higher education come from semi-skilled or unskilled family backgrounds, 29 per cent from junior non-manual and skilled manual family backgrounds but 61 per cent from professional and associate professional, technical and managerial families. (Metcalf 1997: 1)

Forsyth and Furlong surveyed 516 school-leavers in four socio-economically or geographically disadvantaged areas of Scotland in 1999, following this up with 44 interviews. They noted that:

> . . . for the vast majority of disadvantaged young people the labour market, and not higher education, was their post-school destination. This is simply because most such pupils tend to leave school before the final school year . . . this research confirms that the underrepresentation of disadvantaged young people in higher education is as a result of their lack of qualifications obtained at school, meaning that fewer apply, rather than because of any selection biases by institutions. (Forsyth and Furlong 2003: 221)

Thomas and Quinn focused in particular on working class students who dropped out from higher education, studying the experience of four post-1992 universities, and interviewing 67 'first generation' students. They concluded that:

> Parental education affects attitudes towards HE, the process of deciding to apply and enter higher education, transition, learning and teaching, social engagement and integration, and the decision to leave higher education. At all of these stages in the students' lifecycle, parents of first generation entrants can be perceived as supportive of their students, but the support tends to be non-directive and non-prescriptive. Parents appear to be broadly in favour of higher education and to encourage their children to participate, but they can only provide limited guidance about which courses or institutions to attend. (Thomas and Quinn 2007: 98)

The accounts provided by Metcalf (1997) and Forsyth and Furlong (2003) of the under-representation of disadvantaged groups in higher education could almost have been written by Furneaux, in placing the 'blame' squarely on their experience, and relative under-achievement, in their prior education:

> Only a low proportion of young people from lower socio-economic groups achieve the minimum entry qualifications for university . . . However, the likelihood of going to university for those who hold the minimum qualifications declines with class. (Furneaux 1961: 3)

Thomas and Quinn's (2007) analysis demonstrates how deep-seated and multifaceted the problem of working class under-participation is. It is in this aspect of widening participation, therefore, that higher education has improved the least, and where the pressures for improvement are currently most strongly felt (Bekhradnia 2003).

The disabled

Of all the widening participation groups that have been identified as being of concern in this section, the disabled have undoubtedly attracted the least attention. Much of this is down to the state only relatively recently starting to legislate against discrimination on grounds of disability, with higher education institutions only having been required to ensure that disabled students have access on equal terms during the last decade.

In a relatively early study, Gunn (1978) summarized the position at a time when only 0.2 per cent of the full-time student population had a physical disability: he concluded that more could be done to assist them. There have been a number of more recent studies of interest. Thus, Hurst (1993) studied disabled access to higher education, carrying out a series of interviews with students at a further education college specializing in disabled students, plus case studies of selected universities. Tinklin and colleagues (Tinklin and Hall 1999; Tinklin et al. 2004) have reported on disabled students' experiences in Scotland, and latterly England as well, making use of in-depth case studies of students and institutional surveys. And Fuller et al. (2004) have reported on the disabled student experience in a single English institution.

Part of the problem in responding appropriately to the needs of disabled students has been the lack of knowledge about how many there were, and what their disabilities and needs were. Robertson and Hillman's research for the Dearing Committee offered some basic statistics:

> There are currently 14,900 first year students in higher education who declare a disability. Of these, 11,500 are studying full-time and 3,400 study part-time. Of the students who study full-time, 72 per cent report a disability as dyslexia (2,000) or diabetes, epilepsy and asthma (6,200). A further 2,000 report a disability of blindness, deafness or mobility impairment (16 per cent). This latter group represents a much more significant fraction of part-time students (42 per cent). However, the

true extent of students with disability in higher education is obscured by the large number of 'not knowns' (33 per cent) and a significant proportion with 'not listed' disabilities. (Robertson and Hillman 1997: 69)

Disability, to a considerable extent, therefore, remains a hidden part of the student experience.

Conclusions

The whole tenor of this chapter – and, in a different way, the preceding one – has been on post-war progress in expanding the numbers of students of different kinds experiencing higher education in the UK: whether this has to do with the specific cases of postgraduate and international students, or, more generally, with widening participation of all kinds of student at all levels. Some consideration has also been given to the impact of this expansion, both on the students themselves and more generally. Given this focus, it seems only fair and balanced to conclude this chapter by offering a brief critique.

The move to a mass higher education experience may be critiqued on a variety of grounds, though, perhaps understandably, such criticisms are relatively little aired in practice at present. The issue of whether standards have changed was considered in the concluding section to Chapter 7. Here, I will raise two further issues: the impact on the meaning of higher education, and the pragmatic limits of 'massification'.

First, with both greater numbers and a greater proportion of the population – intended to rise above 50 per cent of the relevant age cohort in the foreseeable future – experiencing higher education, what impact does this have on its meaning? While the evidence on changing standards, discussed in Chapter 7, is simply not that straightforward, what does seem clear is that the nature of the higher education – excluding, perhaps, the most elite institutions – being experienced by students has changed. More students without proportionately more staff (and other resources) has meant less individual attention. And it also means that students do not feel as distinct and different, as privileged, a group as they once would have done.

One growing consequence of this last point is that, in a mass higher education system, a first degree, even a 'good' first degree, is often no longer enough. Graduates not only need to demonstrate that they have other qualifications and skills as well, but, increasingly, have to engage in further higher education during their careers if these are to develop satisfactorily. Thus, mass undergraduate education is leading inexorably to, relatively speaking, mass master's level education and even – witness the widespread development of professional doctoral programmes – mass doctoral education. In these ways, higher education is having to continually reinvent itself to remain truly 'higher'.

My second critique concerns the practical limits of mass higher education.

In Trow's (1989) formulation, beyond mass higher education lies universal higher education. There is little doubt that many, with the 'school-leaving age' effectively having been pushed up to 18 years old, would like to progress in that direction. But this would be to deny the reality of not just many people's abilities and wishes, but also the labour market. Despite the ongoing development of the knowledge society, and the transfer of many manufacturing jobs to cheaper labour economies in eastern Europe and Asia, there remain large numbers of low-skill/low-wage jobs in the UK economy for which a graduate education is not just unnecessary but probably also a disadvantage (see Mayhew et al. 2004).

Rather than seeking to entice more and more people, particularly young people, into higher education, and changing the nature of that higher education so that it may better accommodate them, therefore, perhaps we need to be improving post-16 education and employment opportunities more generally.

11

The staff experience

Introduction

This chapter considers the experience of higher education staff in the
UK since the end of the Second World War. It is organized in three main
sections. First, general discussions of the academic experience, both at particular times and in terms of how this has changed during the period in
question, are reviewed. Second, in the most substantive part of the chapter,
the survey evidence, of which there is a fair amount, on the academic experience is assessed. Third, more specific studies and information on different
groups of academics – notably women and ethnic minorities – and of
non-academic staff (a much less studied group) are discussed.

The changing academic experience

> . . . the war gave much more for intellectuals to do as intellectuals.
> Not only the scientists but the historians, economists, linguists, the
> philosophers, and other scholars, found hospitality in official circles,
> in the Cabinet Offices, in the Ministry of Information, in the Political
> Warfare Executive, in the BBC, in Military Intelligence, in the War
> Office Selection Boards, etc. (Shils 1955: 8)

> It has even been said that research is in danger of becoming a mon-
> opoly of the junior members of staff, since such part of the time of the
> senior men as is not devoted to teaching is almost entirely occupied by
> attendance at meetings of committees and by other administrative mat-
> ters. (University Grants Committee 1948: 49)

The golden age myth seems ever present, whether directly expressed or not,
in writing and thinking about academic life in the post-war period (see, for
example, Martin 1999). This myth – and my terming it a myth does not mean
that it has no elements of truth about it – states that academics were once

held in high esteem, well connected with the powers that be and enjoying a relatively leisurely and unpressurized existence, as a kind of elite priesthood. But then doubts began to be expressed, more and more demands were placed upon academics while university resources steadily reduced in real terms, and the special position of the academic was challenged. In the UK the final fall from grace is usually dated from the mid-1970s onwards: linked to international oil crises, the rise of Thatcherism and the aftermath of the 1960s (coincidentally, about the time that I was looking for my first academic post).

Just where the golden age is located in time does, however, vary depending on the authority consulted. For most now working in UK higher education, of course, if it was even considered, it would be located at a time before their career started, perhaps when they were students, perhaps well before then. For others, for example Annan, who definitely experienced what he was writing about, the golden age could be quite specifically dated:

> The years 1945–75 were the golden age of the don. The boffins had captured the public imagination: the stereotype of the absent-minded professor who had been transformed into the keen-eyed inventor in a white coat of radar and artificial harbours. The don rose in public esteem: became an indispensable back-room boy in Whitehall: became an advisor to politicians. (Annan 1990: 377)

For those who reached senior academic positions only in the 1980s or 1990s, the golden age started a little later (but still finished in the 1970s):

> Some senior academics depicted this earlier period [the 1960s and 1970s] as a golden age, in which individuals were free to pursue their own goals and at their own pace. Informants for our study contrasted an expanding academic labour market in the 1960s and the early 1970s with that of the 1990s. As one biochemist put it, at the time when he started people did not plan their careers. The idea of employment problems did not arise. (Henkel 2000: 167)

During this golden age, it was possible to argue for the importance of academics and academe in a way it would be difficult to imagine anyone doing (or being allowed to get away with) today:

> University teaching is the key profession of the twentieth century. In a world increasingly dominated by the professional expert, on whose competence, reliability and integrity not merely the functioning of our complex industrial society but the very survival of civilisation, if not of the human race itself, has come to depend, university teachers have become the educators and selectors of the other professions. (Perkin 1969a: 1)

It is not only the tone of Perkins' argument that strikes the modern-day reader as rather brash, however, but also his focus on 'university teaching' as the key role of the academic profession. Nowadays, as the Annan quote suggests, an equally high, indeed perhaps higher, profile would be given to the research role (see also the discussion of the relationship between research and teaching in Chapter 8).

Perkins' view of the academic as a professional, and of that profession as being rooted in the teaching role, is of long standing:

> The idea of the academic as a professional man was compounded of two traditions, that of the Scottish university teacher and the Oxbridge don. The former had the greatest influence on the faculty organisation of the newer universities, with the exception of Durham, which borrowed heavily from Oxbridge. (Rothblatt 1983: 134)

Spiritually, however, for many, perhaps most, academics south of the border, the Oxbridge ideal of the academic life was the one to which they aspired (a preference reflected in the dominance of Oxford, particularly, and Cambridge as the locales for academic novels: see Carter 1990; Delamont 1996; Wyatt 2000).

But, while the academic life may, once, have been relatively pleasant and something to be aspired to, at least in certain institutional settings – leading to the development of what Annan (1999: 304) has termed 'the intellectual aristocracy', groupings of senior academics linked by marriage or heredity – this is not to say that it was ever that well rewarded financially: 'The academic profession probably enjoys fewer direct financial rewards than any other with the exception of the Church' (Scott 1973: 64). And all the evidence is that such financial rewards as there were have steadily reduced in relative terms during the post-war period (Cradden 1998).

The golden age mythology has now been well and truly supplanted – if still yearned for by some – by a perception of academic life (on the part of academics) as being increasingly heavy in workload and challenging in content. Perhaps surprisingly, this conception dates back at least to the 1960s, when the pressures of post-war expansion were already being felt:

> The challenge to the present-day university teacher comes not only from the increased numbers of students and the diversity of their social and educational backgrounds, but also from the growth in the volume and complexity of knowledge. (Committee on University Teaching Methods 1964: 8)

This perception increased during the early 1980s, when work pressures were added to by budget cuts:

> One possible consequence of this was that the male collegiality was to an extent broken, with different staff identifying separately as managers, workers, academics, teachers, researchers or professionals. Staff also became segregated in other ways. Rather like the modules that they were soon to teach within modularization structures, some were defined as suitable for early retirement and voluntary severance; a few entered as

'new blood'; and numbers of short-term, temporary and part-time staff increased. (Hearn 1999: 132–3; writing about the 1980s)

The numbers of short-term, temporary and part-time staff, and indeed the number of specialist academic roles recognized – as a cursory examination of the job advertisements in the *Times Higher Education* or *Guardian Education* will confirm – have continued to increase since that time (Husbands 1998):

> ... the academic profession in Britain is fragmenting ... mass higher education has greatly reduced the faculty's political standing ... the university system has allowed itself to be downgraded by its own failure to recognise the implications of differentiation and the changed relationship between the state and higher education. (Shattock 2001: 27)

The idea of academic life as both challenging and under challenge is now endemic in writing on higher education, whether it focuses on the teaching (e.g. Trowler 1997, 1998), research (e.g. Sikes 2006) or administrative roles (e.g. Parker 2004), or on the job in its entirety (e.g. Beck and Young 2005; Bryson 2004). The processes involved and their effects have been variously characterized as 'casualization' (Bryson and Barnes 2000b), 'commodification' (Willmott 1995), 'feminization' (Goode 2000), 'industrialization' (Winter 1995), 'marketization' (Enders 2001), 'McDonaldization' (Hayes and Wynyard 2002; Prichard and Willmott 1997; Ritzer 1996) and, most popularly, 'proletarianization' (Ainley 1998; Dearlove 1997; Fulton and Holland 2001; Halsey 1995; Kogan et al. 1994; Wilson 2001).

Thus, Willmott, following Hearn, takes a very jaundiced view of the current state (or fate) of British academics:

> With the possible exception of an elite of 'high-flyers' working in the highest ranked universities and departments, academics are regarded, in the 1990s, principally as trainers of vocationally-oriented students and/or producers of knowledge to which it is possible to attach a value in terms of quasi-market league tables of research and teaching performance. (Willmott 1995: 1009)

Taking a comparative perspective, Enders comes up with a more measured appraisal, while still acknowledging a changing system under pressure:

> In the United Kingdom, with its high degree of institutional autonomy and professional collegiality, a series of reforms and initiatives has put the traditional distribution of power under strain. Recent developments can be interpreted as a threat to traditional patterns of institutional autonomy and bargaining. Here we observe a move toward a hybrid system with a growing impact of marketlike forces and greater governmental influence. (Enders 2001: 8)

Even within the UK, there are those who argue that the position is not as pessimistic as many of the authors quoted above suggest, and, indeed, that many contemporary academics not only accept their changed position – or, in

many cases, the position as it was when they started working as an academic –
but thrive on the challenges it throws up (e.g. Kolsaker 2008).

The survey evidence

Are these widely held beliefs about academic work – of a decline from a
'golden age' to present-day servitude or oppression – borne out by the evidence? Of course, all the authors so far referred to or quoted were making
use of evidence, not least their own experience and that of their colleagues.
There are, however, a series of national surveys of academic experience
available for the post-war period that allow a more dispassionate, distanced
evaluation.

The survey evidence dates mainly from the 1960s onwards, when the
Robbins Committee commissioned its own research and stimulated others to
follow this up. Most of this research (or, at least, that which will be referred
to in this section: there are also numbers of institutional studies) is based
on large-scale national questionnaire studies, allowing some comparisons
to be made both over time and, where the surveys were conducted as part
of international studies, comparatively. The evidence will be examined
chronologically.

Immediate post-war evidence

On the face of it, the evidence would suggest that the first decade or so of the
post-war period witnessed positive improvements in academic life, perhaps
laying the foundations for the golden age myth. The scientific research base
had been strengthened, rebuilding of war-damaged facilities was taking
place, student numbers were substantially up, and sufficient additional
resources were being pumped into the system to allow a proportionately
greater increase in academic staff numbers:

> In our last report we welcomed the improvement in the staff/student
> ratio, which had risen from 1:10.2 in 1938–39 to 1:8.0 in 1951–52 [out-
> side Oxford and Cambridge]. We attached importance to this for three
> reasons. The first was that it enables more individual teaching to be
> given to undergraduates . . . The second reason was that it enables uni-
> versities to take more postgraduate students . . . The third reason was
> that it enables university teachers to devote more time to scholarship
> and research. There has been a further increase in the staff/student
> ratio to 1:7.2 in 1956–57. (UGC 1958: 30)

However, a later examination of the same evidence by the Robbins Committee suggested that the evident improvement in the staff/student ratio during
this period was 'almost entirely due to the fact that the ratio in medical
faculties fell from 28.0 in 1938/9 to 7.3 in 1954/5, largely because of the

progressive conversion of part-time into full-time posts' (Committee on Higher Education 1963c: 3). But at least the staff/student ratio in other faculties was more or less maintained at its existing level, and in some areas had marginally improved.

The Robbins Report 1963

The Robbins Committee produced a separate appendix on 'Teachers in Higher Education' (Committee on Higher Education 1963c), drawing together existing information with the results of a diary-based survey carried out – in association with the Committee on University Teaching Methods (1964) – in 1962. This was organized in four main parts, focusing on teachers in universities, teacher training colleges and further education, before going on to estimate future needs. Curiously, while the sections on teacher training colleges and further education considered both full- and part-time staff, that on universities, in addition to excluding consideration of research-only staff funded by the research councils, ignored part-time teaching staff as well.

The survey of full-time university teachers was sent to 20 per cent of the national total (3498 staff, of whom 3098, or 89 per cent, replied). Its results indicated that full-time university teachers had a varied commitment to teaching: 'During a fortnight in February 1962, 9% of the staff did no teaching, 19% did up to 4 hours teaching a week, 54% did between 4 and 12 hours and 18% did more than that' (Committee on Higher Education 1963c: 2).

On average, full-time university teachers in 1961/2 reported working 40.5 hours per week during term (p. 56). One-third, 33 per cent, of their time in term was spent on teaching, preparation and correction, 28 per cent on research, 11 per cent on their own private study, 11 per cent on administration, 11 per cent on other work (advising students, examining, meetings) inside the university, and 6 per cent on work outside the university (extramural teaching, consulting, committees). The percentage distribution during 'vacation time' was very different, with research dominating: proportions of 8 per cent, 45 per cent, 15 per cent, 10 per cent, 15 per cent and 7 per cent respectively (p. 61).

> Members of staff taught on average for 7.6 hours a week, 6.1 hours on undergraduates and 1.2 hours on postgraduates, and 0.3 hours on combined classes of undergraduates and postgraduates . . . Postgraduate teaching is largely in the form of discussion periods, while undergraduate teaching is evenly spread between lectures, discussion periods and practicals. (Committee on Higher Education 1963c: 69)

The impression is created from this survey – ignoring the inevitable variations between disciplines and individuals that the figures mask – of a demanding, but by no means overdemanding, workload; one that allowed most full-time university academics a fair amount of time to pursue their own interests.

While the numbers of full-time university academic staff had increased, the proportion in the most senior grade had reduced: 'The percentage of teachers who are professors has declined from 22% in 1927/8 to 12% in 1961/2' (p. 12). There was a close relationship between holding a chair and overseeing a department. Thus, 74 per cent of heads of departments were professors, while 80 per cent of professors were heads of department (p. 17). Qualification levels varied: while 47 per cent of full-time university teachers had a PhD, 40 per cent had no higher degree (p. 20).

Student/staff ratios in teacher training colleges were higher, with 11.2 students per full-time teacher in England and Wales, and 16.4 in Scotland, in 1962/3 (pp. 92, 102). Their terms were also longer, and they taught for almost twice as many hours per week (an average of 13.2 in England and Wales, 15.0 in Scotland: pp. 101, 106) as their university counterparts. Training college staff tended to be less well qualified, with only 58 per cent of those in England and Wales, and 69 per cent in Scotland, graduates in 1961/2 (pp. 96, 104).

The further education figures in the report include those for institutions well on their way to university status, most notably at that time the Colleges of Advanced Technology (see Chapter 5). Given their subject emphasis, their student/staff ratios (using multipliers to convert part-timers) were relatively low, averaging just 6.8 (p. 111).

Halsey's 1964/5 survey

One of the key researchers into the UK academic experience during the post-war period has been Halsey, who – with his collaborators – was responsible for three national surveys carried out in the 1960s (1964/5), 1970s (1976) and 1980s (1989). The 1976 survey has not been so widely reported, so the focus in this chapter will be on the first and last of these.

The 1964 survey was sent to 2865 respondents who could be identified from the Robbins Committee sample, of whom 1408 (49 per cent – either Halsey had less 'pull' than Robbins, or the academic community was already tiring of being surveyed) replied. Further samples were then taken at the University of Sussex and three Colleges of Advanced Technology (Halsey et al. 1971: 508–10). While the Robbins survey had focused on getting an overall statistical picture, with particular emphasis on workload details, Halsey, as a sociologist, was more interested in academic status, attitudes, orientations and relations.

In their report, Halsey and his colleagues largely confirm the picture painted by the Robbins Report of a relatively privileged, elite academic staff. They go further, however, to portray the UK academic world as indeed enjoying a 'golden age' in the mid-1960s, using prose that is rather more upbeat than the dry statistics of the Robbins Report:

> Staff/student ratios in British universities are high and formal obligations light. There is freedom in the sense of personal autonomy of an

order to be found rarely, if at all, in other occupational groups. These conditions permit the essential elements of what is considered a 'gentlemanly' way of life. They also make professionalism possible in that, with assured income, both the self-respect of the university teacher and the pressure on him to work beyond the unexacting minimum of his formal duties derive in large measure from his reputation among his colleagues. Reputation largely, though not wholly, depends on professional standards. At the same time the material conditions permit yet a third possibility – entrepreneurship. (Halsey et al. 1971: 169)

They contrast the nature of the UK higher education system with that of the USA, stressing what is implicit in the Robbins Report, the relative emphasis placed on the teaching role:

Taking the evidence all together – an emerging national system of universities with a distinctive tradition and a standardised structure of career opportunities and rewards – there are consequences for the character of British academic life which may be contrasted with the typical conditions of university professors in the United States. In particular energetic and competitive research activity may be relatively subordinate to those norms of academic life which place heavy emphasis on teaching and devotion to students – activities which do not necessarily enhance professional reputations. Perhaps the outstanding difficulty of such a system is to maintain a high level of creativity. (Halsey et al. 1971: 199–200)

Somewhat in contradiction to this, however, was their finding that 64 per cent of their respondents 'leant towards' or were 'very heavily' involved in research, with only 36 per cent leaning towards teaching (p. 278); suggesting a split in both academic aspirations and duties.

Given the relatively generous level of resources then being provided by the state to what was still an elite, but expanding, system, it is not surprising that most of the academics questioned were pretty confident about the health of UK universities. Thus, fully 66 per cent, in a question on the effects of past expansion, answered 'it has not changed the quality of my students appreciably', while only 4 per cent expressed the view that 'the number of students admitted to the universities should remain about where it is now' (pp. 244, 249). Strikingly, 28 per cent favoured a 25 per cent increase in student numbers during the next decade, 40 per cent went for a 50 per cent rise; and 27 per cent opted for a doubling or more (reflecting and supporting, of course, developments that were already under way).

Halsey's other main interest – one might say obsession – was in the place of Oxbridge, and in particular Oxford (his own employer by then), within the system. The Oxbridge interest was then strong in terms of where academics had themselves studied or worked: 'Oxford and Cambridge influences are not confined within the walls of their colleges. A third of all British university teachers have at some time studied or taught in the two universities' (p. 218).

It was also evident in their preferences as to where they would like to work in the future:

> Nearly half, 47%, of those who indicated that they wanted to move universities would prefer a post at Oxford or Cambridge. Offered the choice between a university lecturership and college fellowship at Cambridge, a chair at Sussex, being a professorial head of department at Leeds, and a readership at London, the greatest number, though by no means the majority, 33%, opted for the first. (Halsey et al. 1971: 230–1)

Committee of Vice-Chancellors and Principals 1972

The CVCP sampled three survey weeks (normal, vacation, examination) in the 1969/70 academic year. A total sample of 7995 (out of 27,272) academics was surveyed. This survey found that the mean number of hours worked per week (a weighted average of the three survey weeks) was 50.5 hours, for 47 weeks a year. Of this, 37 per cent was categorized as undergraduate time, 5 per cent as graduate coursework time, 6 per cent as graduate research time, 24 per cent as personal research time, 19 per cent as unallocable internal time and 11 per cent as external professional time (p. 9).

Unfortunately, because of the different definitions used – notably the lack of separate recognition given to administration, which was largely incorporated within undergraduate and graduate teaching time – it is difficult to make a direct comparison with the findings of the Robbins survey eight years before. Two differences do, however, stand out: the apparent increase in the average working week from 40.5 to 50.5 hours, and the indication that this increase was chiefly due to a growth in teaching duties.

Williams et al. 1974

Williams and his colleagues focused specifically on pay, but their work has much to say about the academic experience at the time of their study more generally. Their surveys were carried out during the 1969/70 academic year, the same time as the CVCP study, involving questionnaires (2322 usable responses), interviews (1238) and interviews with applicants for advertised posts (611).

The picture they paint with their data is one of academics, working in the recently expanded UK higher education system, as being predominantly young, male and British:

> The academic profession is a young one: 63 per cent of university staff are under 40 years old, 26 per cent are under 30; only 13 per cent are over 50 . . . Women are a significant minority group amongst university teachers . . . Only 10 per cent of our sample were women, and this

falls to less than 9 per cent of university teachers, since women are concentrated in research grades, where they form 23 per cent of the total . . . In spite of rapid expansion, Britain does not import a significant proportion of its academic manpower . . . of our sample 93 per cent were UK citizens. (Williams et al. 1974: 24–5)

Williams et al. confirm Halsey's findings on the key role played by Oxbridge in educating academics, but break their figures down to show that this tendency is less strong in both Scotland and Wales, yet much stronger in Oxbridge itself:

. . . in 1969 just under a quarter of British academics had gained their first degrees at Oxford or Cambridge. However a third of professors had been to one of these universities . . . the Celtic fringes are particularly dependent on their own graduates: 47 and 43 per cent respectively of academics at Scottish and Welsh universities had got their first degree in Scotland and Wales . . . Oxford and Cambridge are also in-bred: 60 per cent of academics there are graduates of one or other of these universities. (Williams et al. 1974: 35, 38)

The level of qualifications held by academics had increased marginally since the Robbins survey in 1962: '51 per cent of the academic profession have doctorates, 23 per cent master's degrees and 18 per cent postgraduate diplomas . . . a third of the profession still have no qualification above a first degree' (p. 44).

One key finding of this survey concerned the problems experienced in the UK 'academic marketplace' in the 1960s, when the creation of several new universities and the expansion of those existing placed great pressure on the academic production line. This was so much so that an unusually high proportion of completing research students were finding academic jobs immediately (the universities were, in effect, working flat out in order to provide their own future staff):

. . . during the 1960s many universities experienced difficulties in recruiting adequate numbers of suitably qualified staff. There is by now widespread agreement that there was some deterioration in the purely academic qualities of recruits especially in the rapidly expanding social sciences. By the beginning of the decade of the 1970s the situation had changed dramatically. (Williams et al. 1974: 185)

But for those who were appointed during this period, it may indeed have seemed like a golden age.

People in polytechnics 1976

Whitburn et al. were responsible for the first national survey focusing on academic staff, as well as students, working in the then polytechnic sector.

Their survey covered 1479 staff and 125 research respondents in 1972/3. They found that:

> . . . the general profile of staff in the polytechnics and in the university sector tended to be very similar. The staff had comparable social class backgrounds, their educational opportunities had been very similar, they tended to have a similar age distribution and the majority of the staff in the polytechnics had had experience of the university tradition in that they studied for their degrees at these institutions. (Whitburn et al. 1976: 19)

Comparing their findings to those of Williams et al. (1974), however, it is clear that polytechnic staff were less likely than university staff to have studied at Oxbridge (only 10 per cent were undergraduates there), or to have a doctorate (16 per cent); but more likely to have a professional qualification (67 per cent) and prior experience of working in industry (29 per cent: Whitburn et al. 1976: 14, 15, 20).

Whitburn et al. found that polytechnic staff worked similar hours to university staff teaching similar subjects, as revealed in the CVCP (1972) survey. Their overall figure for the average number of hours worked per week, 35, looks low, but excludes two of the categories considered in the CVCP survey: unallocable internal time and external professional time (though there is no evidence provided as to whether polytechnic staff devoted a similar amount of time to these). However, the way that polytechnic staff distributed their time was different to university staff, with the former averaging 32 hours a week on teaching and administration (cf. 26 hours for university staff) and just 3 hours on research (cf. 11):

> . . . the figures give support to the popularly held view that in polytechnics more time is given to teaching than in universities and, conversely, much more of staff time in universities is allocated to personal research. On average, university staff had devoted 11 hours each week to their own research, compared with polytechnic staff who had spent only three hours in this activity. It should be noted that three hours for research is the norm granted by local education authorities to teachers at this level. (Whitburn et al. 1976: 25)

On average, polytechnic staff spent 24 per cent of their time on administrative work (included in teaching and administration in the overall figures just given).

Respondents were asked to rate various aspects of the facilities provided by their polytechnic:

> It appears from the assessment ratings that the main priorities must be the consolidation of undergraduate teaching through the provision of adequate teaching and library facilities, and then the further encouragement of research by the staff both for their own development and for the benefit of the local community. (Whitburn et al. 1976: 36)

While there were some indications of the 'academic drift' (Pratt and Burgess 1974; see also Chapter 5) to which the polytechnics would be subject in these responses, most respondents endorsed the continuation of a distinctive role for the polytechnics:

> When questioned about the future of the polytechnics (only a couple of years after their designation), 32% perceptively 'considered that the polytechnics would become increasingly like universities', though 62% 'did not think the polytechnics should become universities'. (Whitburn et al. 1976: 38)

Halsey's 1989 survey

By the time of his third, 1989, survey of university (2858 productively responded out of 5121) and polytechnic (1296 out of 2544) staff, the picture had changed substantially from Halsey's first survey in the 1960s. Staff/student ratios had risen, academic salaries had declined in relative terms; Thatcherism had changed the political landscape. The great majority, 72 per cent of university and 92 per cent of polytechnic, respondents stated that their faculty/department/school/unit had been reorganized in the past 10 years. Many more respondents than previously had considered leaving academic life permanently:

> ... senior common room morale is low. In 1989 as many as 37 per cent of university teachers and 39 per cent of their polytechnic colleagues had seriously considered leaving academic life permanently: the comparable percentage among university staff in 1964 had been 23. The underlying explanation was ... proletarianization. (Halsey 1995: 124)

Respondents wanted to rebalance their workloads. Thus, university respondents reported spending similar proportions of their time teaching undergraduates (26 per cent), in research (28 per cent) and in administration (24 per cent); but suggested an ideal balance of 22 per cent, 43 per cent and 12 per cent. For polytechnic respondents, the trends were similar if less ambitious: actual proportions of 43 per cent, 15 per cent (almost twice the proportion found by Whitburn et al. 1976) and 28 per cent; ideal proportions of 37 per cent, 30 per cent and 16 per cent (p. 186). Administration was clearly seen as a far greater bugbear than teaching, and polytechnics were becoming more like universities in their emphases.

But some things had not changed, including – though Halsey is inclined to exaggerate this – the importance of Oxford and Cambridge (see also Halsey 1982). Giving respondents the same four options for academic posts to move to as in 1964/5, Halsey found that:

> The attractiveness of the Cambridge position actually increased between 1964 and 1989 [with 40% now opting for it], and remains the most preferred of the four posts specified, despite the fact that it carries the

lowest salary and formally the lowest academic rank. (Halsey 1995: 141-2)

The International Study of the Academic Profession 1991/1993

In the most ambitious survey of academics to date, 19,472 questionnaires were returned from academics in 14 countries in the Americas, Australasia, Asia and Europe (Altbach 1996). About 10 per cent of these, 1948 (out of 3600 distributed) were from England, where 16 institutions were surveyed in 1992. Little effort was made in the project report, however, to make direct comparisons between the different countries and systems surveyed.

Fulton, who led the research in England (and who had earlier contributed to Halsey's research), commented on: 'the rather limited mobility of English academic staff . . . their apparently limited experience in higher education outside their own sector . . . surprisingly, however, experience of professional work outside higher education is quite wide' (Fulton 1996: 413). Perhaps the last point should not have been quite so surprising, given not only the substantial number of polytechnic (soon to be university) staff included in the survey (cf. Whitburn et al. 1976), but also the increasing size of 'vocational' departments (e.g. business, engineering, medicine) in the universities as well.

Along with what Fulton saw as a rather inward-looking perspective, however, came a higher level of qualification than found in previous surveys. By now, the great majority of university staff, 76 per cent, either had (70 per cent) or were working for (6 per cent) a doctorate; with proportions of 46 per cent among polytechnic staff and 39 per cent among those respondents working in the college sector.

At the core of the survey were the respondents' experiences of and views of teaching and research.

As elsewhere, for most academics the 'teaching load' is the defining element of their work situation. It is clear that in the polytechnics and colleges teaching dominates staff activities in term time: 56 per cent of staff in polytechnics and 62 per cent in colleges spend more than twenty-one hours per week on teaching – and even in universities the figure is 32 per cent. These figures . . . are higher than those in most of the (obviously) comparable countries in the international survey – and it is also the subjective experience of academics in each sector; many of the handwritten comments on the questionnaire confirm that teaching loads have increased sharply in recent years. (Fulton 1996: 413–14)

That may indeed have been their subjective experience, but it is not really supported by a comparison with earlier surveys (though much, of course, depends on the precise methodologies and definitions they used). Thus, the CVCP survey (1972) gives an average of 24 hours a week spent on teaching in term time by university teachers, as compared to Fulton's median of 18 hours; while Whitburn et al. (1976) suggest a similar average of 23 hours per week for polytechnic teachers, compared to Fulton's median figure of 25 hours.

If increased emphasis was being placed on teaching, this naturally impacted on the time available for research:

> The most striking feature of the research effort is how little time is now spent on research during term time, even in the universities, where median term-time research hours are only fourteen, and 45 per cent of staff have ten hours or less per week in which to pursue what can reasonably be called their central academic interests. (Fulton 1996: 415)

Yet the CVCP (1972) survey, 12 years earlier, suggested that university academics spent only 12 hours a week on research during term then.

These disparities apart, what is intriguing about Fulton's report are the positive and committed views expressed by his respondents, despite the evident pressures they were feeling:

> The survey revealed a paradox that appears to be common to a number of very different higher education systems in the 1980s and 1990s . . . On the one hand, the respondents make the positive statement . . . that their field is creative and productive; and on the other, they express a sense of personal strain, the widespread agreement that the profession's respect is declining and its influence insubstantial. (Fulton 1996: 419)

This strong sense of professional commitment extended to their views on the massification of higher education, even though this threatened to further increase their workload pressure:

> . . . a very large majority of members of the profession are now committed to the *principle* of mass higher education – in sharp contrast to faculty attitudes of thirty years ago. At the same time, the respondents' more detailed views on many aspects of their present work situation could be interpreted to mean that the *consequences* of mass higher education have not yet been fully accepted. (Fulton 1996: 435, original emphasis)

Yet, while truly mass higher education was not on the agenda then, most of Halsey et al.'s (1971) respondents had also responded positively to the idea of further expansion.

Association of University Teachers survey 1994

In 1994, the Association of University Teachers (AUT) carried out another diary-based exercise on the use of academic's time. They received 2605 diaries, representing a 22 per cent response rate. Their analysis showed an average working week in term of 54.8 hours, in vacation 51.3 hours. The proportion of time spent in administration during term and vacation was 32.8 per cent and 33.1 per cent respectively; on teaching 34.8 per cent and 17.3 per cent; and on research 20.3 per cent and 32.6 per cent. The predictable pattern of more teaching in term time, and more research in vacation, was again clear, as was the increasingly domineering proportion of time devoted to various types of administration throughout the academic year.

A specific feature of the AUT survey was the attention paid to changes in academic workloads over time:

> In overall terms, the surveys by Robbins, the CVCP and the AUT indicate an increase in the average hours worked per week by British academic staff between 1962 and 1994, from 40.5 hours (Robbins: term-time week), through 50.5 hours (CVCP: weighted working week throughout the year) to 54.8 hours (AUT: term-time). (Court 1996: 255)

It is interesting, though, that the greater part of this increase appears to have occurred in the 10 years between the Robbins and CVCP surveys – the time of the 1960s expansion – with relatively little subsequent change in the 20 years up until the mid-1990s.

Court draws particular attention to the impact of research and teaching quality assessment exercises on the day-to-day work of academics. The consequent growth in time spent on administrative activities may also, of course, be behind the pressures and strains reported by Fulton's respondents:

> One consequence of the development of this culture of assessment has been the growth of paperwork and administration required of academic and academic-related staff. This is reflected in the increase in administration since the Robbins survey – from 11 to 33 per cent in term-time – and the present predominance of administration in the use of time by academic and most academic-related staff. (Court 1996: 257)

Oshagbemi's job satisfaction survey 1994

Further evidence on academics' perceptions of their work patterns is provided by Oshagbemi, who administered a questionnaire to 554 university teachers at 23 UK universities, asking them to indicate their satisfaction regarding eight job elements on a seven-point scale:

> . . . respondents rated the satisfaction which they derived from teaching, research and their colleagues' behaviour highly . . . The ratings of the respondents on the satisfaction derived from their head of unit's behaviour, as well as of the physical conditions and working facilities in their universities, was rather lower. However, more than 50 per cent of the respondents were satisfied with each of these aspects of their job . . . The mean ratings of the satisfaction derived from the university teachers' administrative and managerial functions, their present pay and their promotions were low. (Oshagbemi 1996: 394–5)

What is again striking is that, while administration and pay rate lowly, most respondents appear to be surprisingly upbeat about most aspects of their work.

Henkel's study, 1994/97

Henkel – as part of a larger three-country study – interviewed academics and senior managers in seven selected disciplines in eleven universities. The focus of her study was on academic careers and identities changing in the light of national policies, with three such policies being given particular attention: teaching quality assurance, research selectivity and the Enterprise in Higher Education initiative (see Chapter 4). She noted how academic training had become a normal expectation, not just in terms of a doctorate providing evidence of research training, but also in terms of training in teaching:

> The doctorate had finally become institutionalised across the spectrum of disciplines as the foundation of an academic career. At least in the humanities and the social sciences the acquisition of teaching skills and experience had become a more explicit and formal component of their postgraduate experience. However, research or the production of knowledge remained central in the process of academic identity formation. It was now a more managed form of production, in more elaborately structured institutions, larger units. There were clearer and more limited time frames within which more tangible evidence of progress would be required. There were more rules and procedures. (Henkel 2000: 164)

Academic careers were becoming more difficult to attain and construct, with different strategies evident in the sciences and non-sciences:

> Most scientists appointed to their first university lectureships in the 1980s and 1990s had been through a protracted period of preparation. In two cases ten years elapsed between achieving their PhD and their first permanent university post . . . The language used in the interviews suggests that obtaining a permanent academic post in science in a university required efforts of heroic proportions, with high risks attached . . . The accounts given to us by academics in the humanities and the social sciences of the process of constructing a career were to some extent *post hoc* rationalisations of the processes through which individuals had gone. (Henkel 2000: 170–1, 175–6)

There were also disciplinary differences evident with regard to the place of research in the academic career: 'The ideal science career was to continue in research throughout . . . As far as the social sciences and the humanities were concerned, the majority of those who saw themselves primarily as researchers were in their first academic job' (p. 183).

The academics interviewed by Henkel were keenly aware of how their profession was changing, and many clearly had mixed feelings about at least some of these changes:

> ... almost all academics felt that the most profound change was in the scale of higher education ... Few of our respondents declared themselves to be unequivocally in favour of such expansion, although most were wary of rejecting the principle of mass higher education ... It is widely understood, however, that the challenges to academics were not simply a matter of numbers. They included changes in the characteristics of student populations. The range of abilities, and even more the range of age, expectations and motivations had widened. Not surprisingly the difficulties these presented were felt to be greater, and in some cases markedly greater, in the less prestigious institutions. Their cohorts contained more students who in a previous generation would not have entered higher education. (Henkel 2000: 213–14)

Compared to Fulton's (1996) analysis, Henkel seems to suggest, then, not only reservations about the consequences of mass higher education but a growing scepticism about the principle as well.

National Committee of Inquiry into Higher Education 1997

The Dearing Report imitated the Robbins Report in commissioning a survey into the experiences and expectations of academic staff (Casey 1997). By this time, however, the methodology of surveys had moved on, and Casey used the medium of the telephone to survey 809 UK academics in 1996/7 (achieving a 53 per cent response rate).

As well as survey methodology, attitudes were also continuing to change. In contrast to the relative optimism of Halsey's first survey, and the committed professionalism of Fulton's, academics were now more critical of many aspects of their working environments. Thus, many, following Henkel's findings, felt that the massification of higher education had led to a deterioration in the quality of the students they taught:

> Nearly half thought the quality of undergraduates had fallen [over the last five years], although only one in five thought that this was the case for postgraduates ... 'Pre-1992' university staff were much more likely to comment upon improvement, and less likely to comment on deterioration. (Casey 1997: 95)

Those questioned also tended to share the view that they were overworked: 'over one in five of those with teaching responsibilities found the number of teaching staff in their department much too low, relative to the number of students [43% stated that it was "on the low side"]; only one in three found it satisfactory or over-generous' (p. 98).

As Dearing was closely concerned with the student learning experience, and the ways in which it might be improved, the survey also focused on these areas. When questioned about how their teaching practice had changed during the previous five years, 61 per cent of respondents identified increased use of project work, 60 per cent more team/group-work, 59 per cent increased use of multimedia and 51 per cent more interactive coursework (p. 102). This naturally had an impact on assessment methods:

> The method[s] of assessment most frequently mentioned were projects and dissertations (97%), written examinations (93%), essays (82%) and oral presentations (76%). Much less common were multiple choice tests (30%) and work-based assignments (40%). (Casey 1997: 103)

There was some evidence that those working in '1992' universities (i.e. former polytechnics and colleges) made more use of more 'innovative' forms of teaching and assessment, though this may have been due to different subject emphases. Most of those questioned appeared well able to justify their use of assessment methods, and to identify what they were measuring:

> The majority of academics believe that the assessment methods that they use indeed, do measure 'depth of knowledge' (91%), 'the ability to think' (85%), and 'problem solving' (74%). They also recognise them as performing a wide variety of other functions, including 'diagnosing strengths and weaknesses' (65%), 'motivating students and giving them self-confidence' (61%), and 'testing the ability to memorise' (56%). (Casey 1997: 104)

Taking a more contemporary stance to Halsey's questions about the position of Oxbridge within the higher education system, Casey asked his respondents for their views on the equality of universities and the degrees they awarded:

> . . . very few [academics] now consider all universities to be equal . . . Nearly all think that first degrees are of unequal standard and that those of one university are 'better' than those of another. Staff at '1992' universities are less likely to adopt this view than those at 'pre-1992' universities but, nevertheless, the overwhelming majority of them appear to accept it. (Casey 1997: 106)

Though there was no attempt made to measure the amount of time that academics spent on different kinds of activity, specific attention was paid to the place of research in their working lives:

> Among those academic staff who do research, the median amount of working time spent on it is 20 per cent . . . those in '1992' universities . . . [spend] very much less time – 10 per cent . . . – on this activity . . . over half of those doing research claim to be doing some or all of it in their own time. (Casey 1997: 108)

While these figures are not so different from those of the immediately preceding surveys, they can be read as suggesting a steady reduction in the time available for this core academic activity. For Casey's respondents, research was being pushed increasingly into their evenings and weekends, as well as outside term time.

When asking about respondents' employment conditions, 'the survey found well over a quarter of all staff, and nearly all research staff, to have fixed-term contracts ... those academics who are, or have been, on fixed-term contracts have spent, on average, two thirds of their careers on a fixed-term contract' (pp. 116–17). Relatively little staff mobility was evident, either between institutions within the higher education sector, or between higher education and other sectors of employment: 'half of all academics had been employed in only a single institution ... Almost all staff had spent their entire career in higher education without interruption' (p. 118).

Respondents were also asked about their future plans: 'the survey asked respondents to state whether they thought it was likely that they would stay in the sector until they reached retirement age. Overall, rather over a quarter [27%] thought it was unlikely they would' (p. 121). This proportion is well below that found by Halsey in 1989 for either university (37 per cent) or polytechnic staff (39 per cent), however, and not much different from that found in 1964 (23 per cent); suggesting, perhaps, an adjustment of expectations to the prevailing environment.

The Working in Higher Education survey 1998/9

Shortly after Dearing had reported, Bryson and his collaborators carried out another survey of contemporary academic (and academic related) experience in the UK. Using both online and paper questionnaires, they assembled a total of 1586 responses (Bryson 2004; Bryson and Barnes 2000a, 2000b).

In an echo of the findings of Williams et al. (1974) – and more or less implicit in many of the other surveys – Bryson and Barnes found that: 'The academic workforce is predominantly male, white and full-time, particularly those with longer service and the contractual designation of teaching and research' (2000a: p. 180). On average, full-time staff worked 46.2 hours per week, 49.9 hours for teaching/research staff (p. 162). The latter figure for teaching/research staff is very similar to that found by the CVCP in their 1969/70 survey.

The responses to the Working in Higher Education survey also confirmed the mix of pressure and pleasure associated with academic work in the late twentieth century. Thus, on the positive side, most respondents (60 per cent) found their work challenging, and most (60 per cent) teaching and research staff preferred research. Most (68 per cent) reported being positively satisfied with job content, with this rising with job grading. Almost all, 95 per cent, said that they had a good working relationship with their colleagues. More than two-thirds, 68 per cent, had a sense of belonging to the academic community, and 58 per cent reported a strong sense of collegiality. A clear majority, 60 per cent, were proud to be a member of the profession, and 54 per cent felt loyal to their institution (pp. 164, 168–70).

On the debit side, however, most (60 per cent of teaching and research staff) disliked administration and bureaucracy. Half, 49 per cent, felt that workload 'interfered negatively with life outside work', with 24 per cent stating that it 'caused an unacceptable level of stress'. Nearly one-third, 29 per cent, stated that their basic salary was insufficient to meet their financial needs, while 64 per cent felt that their salary undervalued their work (pp. 164, 166).

Kinman et al.'s studies, 1998/2004

Kinman et al. carried out two questionnaire surveys of UK academics in 1998 (650 responses, 39 per cent response rate) and 2004 (844, 22 per cent). They focused, in particular, on job stressors, perceptions of changes in working conditions, working hours, psychological distress and the achievement or otherwise of Health & Safety Executive benchmarks. They noted that:

> Perceptions of job insecurity in the sector appear to have intensified in the 6 year period: 26% of respondents in 2004 indicated that they felt under personal threat of redundancy, compared with 19% of those sur-veyed in 1998. This proportion can be compared with levels of job insecurity amongst the general working population in the UK in the period . . . which have remained stable at around 12%. Almost half of the respondents to the 2004 study (48%) indicated that they had ser-iously considered leaving the university sector in the preceding 5 year period. (Kinman et al. 2006: 20)

Kinman et al.'s sample, therefore, were rather more pessimistic about their future in academe than those questioned by either Casey (1997) or Halsey (1995). And they clearly had their reasons: in 2004, most (62%) were work-ing in excess of the 48 hour weekly maximum set by the European Union, with 22% working more than 55 hours per week (Kinman et al. 2006: 23).

More specific studies

As well as studies and surveys that have focused on academic, or occasionally higher education, staff as a whole, there have been others that have focused on academics with particular characteristics, or on other, non-academic, kinds of higher education worker. The former have chiefly examined the position of women, and, to a lesser extent, ethnic minority academics and contract staff. The latter, rather less common, have explored the experiences and perspectives of at least some of the range of non-academic staff employed in higher education.

Women

> It is tempting to regard universities as hospitable places for women – places where academic excellence and the merit of an argument are the overriding values, places where there is a detached and impartial consideration of issues, and where argument is least likely to be *ad hominem* or *ad feminam*. Yet there has long been evidence to suggest that this is not so. (Davies and Holloway 1995: 11–12)

> HE has always been a white, male-dominated, hierarchical environment in which male norms abound. Women have had to fight for entry as students and academics, and for recognition that their academic qualifications and potential are as credible as those of their male colleagues. (Meehan 1999: 35)

Research and writing on the experience of women academics has become of particular significance in the second part of the post-war period (e.g. Howie and Tauchert 2002; Malina and Maslin-Prothero 1998; Morley and Walsh 1995, 1996; Sutherland 1985). These analyses tend to have one of two main foci. First, they set out to establish the under-representation of women in positions of influence within higher education, and, by contrast, their over-representation in less desired roles (e.g. Bagilhole 1993; Blackstone and Fulton 1975; Rendel 1975). Second, they seek to articulate what might be done about this, and to evaluate what progress has been made (e.g. Farish et al. 1995; Heward and Taylor 1992; Jackson 1990).

Thus, taking the first of these emphases, Rendel notes that: 'The proportion of women academics now is virtually the same as in the 1920s, and the proportion holding senior posts virtually the same as in the 1930s' (Rendel 1980: 143). Her statistics, derived from an analysis of the *Commonwealth Universities Yearbook*, indicate that, in 1951, 12.2 per cent of academics were women, ranging from 7.9 per cent at Oxbridge to 16.4 per cent at London and 17.6 per cent in the university colleges and 'young' civic universities (p. 149). In 1975, when, according to *Statistics of Education*, 11.5 per cent of academics were women, this proportion varied from 3.1 per cent in engineering and 7.2 per cent in science to 17.1 per cent in humanities and 17.6 per cent in education (p. 152).

By 1980/1, 'the . . . percentage of women in university teaching as a whole was 13.85' (Sutherland 1985: 9). The proportion, however, varied with location in the career hierarchy, with women making up only 2.6 per cent of professors, and 6.4 per cent of readers and senior lecturers, but 15.6 per cent of lecturers and assistant lecturers, and 34.2 per cent of research staff and others. Sutherland interviewed 60 women academics in her study. She found that:

> . . . for about half the group, university teaching had been a settled career for most of their working life to date. For others, it had been

an unforeseen and unexpected development. They had certainly not planned for it when they left secondary school. (Sutherland 1985: 22)

Her interviewees tended, though, to downplay the significance of discrimination within academic life: 'There is . . . little evidence of active discrimination against women in the experience of the group. Nevertheless, those who had achieved seniority did believe that there had certainly been prejudices in the past and they were somewhat astonished at their own success' (p. 26).

Morley, taking a somewhat more combative stance, noted that:

Research undertaken by the AUT indicates that:

* in all categories of staff women are concentrated in the lower-paid grades;
* fewer women than men are promoted;
* women are paid less than men on the same grade on a wage for age basis;
* the pay differential between women and men steadily widens as they get older. (Morley 1994: 194)

Halvorsen (2002) similarly notes the under-representation of women among senior, full-time and permanent academic positions, and among those returned to the research assessment exercises, and their lower than average salaries when compared to men at all grades. And Heward regrets that 'the continuing increase in the proportion of women among the undergraduate population had consistently failed to yield any change in the proportion of women above the lecturer grade' (1996: 12).

The gender gap in academic work is not, however, simply a matter of under-representation and pay, but also concerns the kind of work done. Thus, Barnes-Powell and Letherby (1998: 75) point out that ' "care work" within academic institutions is gendered', such that roles like personal tutoring are disproportionately taken on by, or left to, women staff.

Cann et al. surveyed the status of women staff in English colleges of higher education, the lowest tier of the higher education institutional hierarchy. They found even there:

. . . a consistent and entrenched pattern of male dominance on the college academic staff (of which men on average comprised 75%) . . . What was striking was the consistency of this across both voluntary and statutory sector institutions . . . the colleges in our survey showed a percentage of women students ranging from 60 to 85%, whereas the percentages of women academic staff ranged from a mere 15% to the highest proportion of only 34%. (Cann et al. 1991: 19–20)

As part of the Working in Higher Education survey of 1998/9 (discussed above), Goode (2000) carried out a gender-based analysis of the data collected. She began, following the second focus noted earlier, by reviewing the various initiatives that have attempted to improve equal opportunities and the position of women in the academy. She argued that there was still clearly a long way to go to break down the male-dominated pattern of academic life (which remains the standard conclusion of analyses in this area).

The position of women within the academy was indicated by their different ordering of concerns:

> Men and women shared concerns about maintaining quality in higher education, in a context of heavy workloads, and with too great a focus on outputs measured in quantitative terms. But there was a marked gender difference in the order in which these concerns were ranked, with women identifying casualisation as their top priority . . . For women, job insecurity superseded concerns about whether they felt enabled or frustrated in the performance of their academic work, and this would seem to be a rational reflection of their structural position in the institution. (Goode 2000: 265)

When asked about discrimination at work, the 'vast majority of respondents described some form of discrimination, and many cited more than one example' (p. 266); indicating, perhaps, an ability to be more open about this than Sutherland's (1985) respondents felt they could be. But there were again significant gender differences:

> Women were more likely to recount a broader spectrum of exclusion, painting a picture not only of a tenuous hold on job security, but a feeling of being completely undervalued and expendable . . . Men and women equally cited an 'alienating culture' as a form of systematic discrimination, although women were slightly more likely to refer to what they were describing as 'male', whilst men frequently used variants on the phrase 'if your face fits' . . . 'Informal networks' . . . were ranked highly as examples of discriminatory mechanisms in the responses of both men and women, and were identified by both sexes as characteristically male. (Goode 2000: 268–71)

Goode concludes that, though the academy is changing radically, and this has involved the employment of more and more women, it is not necessarily working to their advantage:

> The paradox for women, as they adjust to the changed milieu and their entry to it, is that the 'feminization' of higher education seems to be occurring in conjunction with its 'industrialization'. This is surely no coincidence. The proletarianization of the academic workforce is drawing in more women workers, but in this sense they can be seen to be gaining enhanced access to a deteriorating profession. (Goode 2000: 280)

Or, to put it another way, well-qualified men, recognizing the signs, are more likely to seek careers outside of academe.

Ethnic minorities

By comparison with women academics – though perhaps not surprisingly because there are far fewer of them – the experience of ethnic minority academics has been less researched and written about. Thus, when Heward et al. (1997) sought to interview both women and minority ethnic professors in law and biology, they ran into the problem of being unable to identify any minority ethnic professors in their chosen universities.

Within the research literature on women academics, there is an important sub-literature on black women academics (e.g. Mirza 1995; Ross 1996; Thompson 1998 – there are also smaller specialist literatures focusing on, for example, lesbian academics and women academics with disabilities). The general tone of this research concerns the double disadvantage faced by academics who are both women and black.

But there appear to be no larger-scale surveys of the experience of ethnic minority academics to compare with those of academics in general, or women academics in particular. When compared to the attention given to this topic in the USA, this absence is striking.

Contract staff

As with the case of women academics – though taking rather longer – an interest in the experience of contract researchers and teachers has developed only latterly in the post-war period. In part, this has been due to problems of definition, the heterogeneity of the staff included in this group, and the lack of data (Husbands 1998).

Varlaam (1987) carried out an analysis of Universities Statistical Record data on contract researchers for the Advisory Board for the Research Councils. She noted that, whereas the numbers of full-time academic staff in the UK had fallen by 5 per cent over the previous decade, the numbers of contract researchers had risen by 71 per cent (though the total numbers of the latter were only one-third of the former). Most (72 per cent) contract researchers were men, and aged between 25 and 49 (pp. 1–2). The pattern was one of considerable turnover: 'One third of researchers are recruited each year. Half of these leave during the course of the next two years; half remain into at least the third year' (p. 2).

Bryson and Barnes, as part of the Working in Higher Education Survey of 1998/9, had a particular interest in the increasing use being made of fixed term contracts (FTCs) in higher education:

> We have found a very widespread use of fixed term contracts in academic and related employment in higher education. Over half of the staff on teaching and/or research roles and one third of the staff on academic related roles are employed on FTCs. All the indicators are that the proportion of staff on temporary employment contracts will

increase unless there is some dramatic change in policy. (Bryson and Barnes 2000b: 233; cf. Husbands 1998)

Collinson interviewed 61 social science contract researchers, focusing on occupational identity. She concluded that:

Contract researchers are often marginalized within mainstream academia and dogged by inferior status and prospects, and financial insecurity. It is perhaps surprising then that they continue to make such a sustained and highly significant contribution to the research output of UK higher education and thereby bolster the financial well-being of the sector as a whole. The importance of their 'identity work' should not therefore be underestimated. (Collinson 2004: 326)

Here, once again, is evidence of the continuing mix of dedication and irritation exhibited by growing numbers of higher education employees.

Non-academic staff

By contrast with the attention paid to academics, non-academic staff have attracted relatively little interest until comparatively recently.

Thus, the AUT survey carried out in 1994 was unusual in not focusing solely on academics, but also looking at administrative, computer, contract research and library staff. While none of these categories averaged longer working weeks than the academics surveyed, they each exceeded the expected norm of the 35- or 40-hour working week. Thus, administrative staff averaged 48.2 hours in term time and 45.5 in vacation, computer staff 43.8 and 39.3, contract research staff 47.5 and 45.2, and library staff 42.3 and 40.5 (Court 1996: 250–4). These general trends were confirmed in the Working in Higher Education survey of 1998/9, where library and computing staff respondents were found to average 40.9 hours a week, and administrators 42.4 hours (Bryson and Barnes 2000a: 162).

Not surprisingly, general administration accounted for the major portion of administrative staff time: 40 per cent in term and 46 per cent in vacation. It also loomed large for both computer staff (26 per cent and 28 per cent) and library staff (35 per cent and 34 per cent); but was kept within reasonable bounds for contract research staff (12 per cent and 13 per cent), who reported spending an average of 56 per cent and 58 per cent of their time directly on project research (Court 1996: 250–4).

Unlike the Robbins Report, the Dearing Report did pay attention to the non-academic staff experience, and commissioned a report on this to parallel the one on academics (Whyley and Callender 1997). The research involved was, however, not as thorough or large-scale, with the survey of administrative and support staff in higher education carried out by conducting four focus groups with staff from eight institutions in the Midlands and South West. They comprised a mix of those who had entered higher education by chance or default (mostly computing and technical support staff), those who were pursuing a subject specialism (mainly librarians and administrators), and those who were in one of the new professional growth areas within higher education (the smallest and most recent group).

Like academics in the more recent surveys, these non-academic respondents felt that their workloads and pressures were increasing as well. But they also shared a sense that, partly through these increased workloads, they were making a more significant contribution to the academic enterprise as a whole: 'All of the administrative and support staff had experienced a significant increase in the volume of their work . . . [they] believed that they were playing an increasingly central role in higher education' (Whyley and Callender 1997: 175). Despite this sense of playing an enhanced role, non-academic staff, like academic staff, also tended to feel dissatisfied, but for a different combination of reasons: 'levels of dissatisfaction were . . . high for most staff and focused on a number of areas: lack of opportunities for progression; lack of recognition; pay; insufficient resources; lack of representation' (p. 177).

Whitchurch interviewed 35 senior and middle-level administrators and managers in UK higher education institutions. She contrasts the historically more managerial approach adopted in the former polytechnics and colleges with the civil service style of administration that existed in the older universities. In the contemporary university, however, a diversity of managerial approaches are used in partnership with others as necessary:

> Not only has the collective identity of professional administrators and managers diversified, but individuals also show themselves capable of adopting a range of voices and identities over time, and across the various projects with which they become involved, re-inventing themselves professionally as the need arises. Thus, the binary division between academic and other professionals in the university is being replaced by a mosaic community, in which administrators and managers, along with other professionals, are interleaved. (Whitchurch 2008: 88)

Conclusions

This review of the range of research that has focused on the higher education staff experience at national level during the post-war period reveals complex, indeed to some degree contradictory, patterns.

On the one hand, dissatisfaction with the changing demands of the job are regularly found by surveys, accompanied by perceptions of increasing workloads in general. But, on the other hand, academic respondents consistently recount their pride in their work and commitment to it. And, while the succession of surveys does indicate some increase in overall workload, they also suggest that it stabilized at about its present level – perhaps at around the level that most people, whether academics or otherwise, are prepared to bear – some decades ago.

Over the same time, the pattern of higher education employment has changed, and thus the experience of academic work has become more variable. The early post-war pattern of an academic workforce composed chiefly of full-time male lecturers, balancing a responsibility for (mainly) teaching and (increasing in importance) research roles, has been transformed. Not only has the workforce become increasingly feminized, though chiefly at lower levels, but growing numbers are employed on a research-only or teaching-only basis (though these designations do not necessarily mean precisely what they say), and/or on short- or part-time contracts.

To the many more job descriptions now current within higher education we may add the changing nature of the administrative or management function (see also Chapter 6). Here many of those in the growing range of non-academic roles are playing an increasingly important part in the direction of higher education institutions.

All of this reflects, of course, the move, from what was essentially a small-scale, craft-based, collegial organization, to a much more business-like, output-driven and customer-oriented operation. While this undoubtedly suits quite a number of those who now work within higher education, and the great majority are clearly able to get on with it – no doubt grumbling as they do so – it does help to explain the complexity of attitudes expressed to the researchers whose work has been reviewed in this chapter.

The modern-day academic is required to do many things that their predecessors would not have had to have done, and in many cases would not have been required at all. It is no longer so possible to focus on those aspects of the academic role that one is most suited to, or which one finds most conducive: a more multifaceted, considered and consistent performance is demanded.

12

The (changing?) idea of the university

Introduction

> The idea of an idea of a university is important. Without it, a university is utterly shapeless and possesses no means of distinguishing itself from any other kind of educational institution, the corporate classrooms, for example, appearing in giant firms. (Rothblatt 1997: 43)

If you have read this far, or perhaps more selectively, you may have formed (or had confirmed) the idea that the period since the end of the Second World War has been one of huge, and accelerating, changes in the higher education sector. Of course, there is much truth in this perspective, and it is one that can be applied to other sectors as well, but we should be careful of over-exaggerating it. For there is also considerable continuity within higher education, not least in terms of its underlying values: though this is not to say that these do not also change in their emphases. It might, thus, be argued that the history of higher education in the UK in the post-war period is as much about the efforts of academics and others to resist (often in indirect ways) changes they saw as inappropriate, as it is about the changes that did occur.

It seems appropriate, therefore, to conclude this book by reflecting on the continuity of values implied by the university. For, as has often been remarked, the university has proved to be one of the longest-lasting, most successful and adaptable institutions of all. Fundamentally, it remains an idea, and its history – while also being about student numbers, curricula, research and so on – is also a history of that idea. And it is a powerful idea, one which many thinkers and researchers have given a good deal of attention to.

Of course, at one level, all higher education research and writing may be said to embody, at least implicitly, one or more views on what the university is or what it should be (Tight 2003). But I am talking here about something much more specific and focused than that. Historically, it almost seems that, ever since the university was first established – or, perhaps more correctly, thought of – there have been debates about its purpose(s) and organization (though Rothblatt (1997: 5) dates these to the reaction against the revolutionary movements of the late eighteenth century). These debates appear to have been far more prevalent than those about almost any other institution you might think of, and they have often been closely contested. They have continued up until the present day, though varying in their fervour and emphasis over time.

Another feature of the attention paid to the idea of the university is that it varies from country to country (or system to system). Thus, while the main focus of this article is on the English idea of the university (as England is the dominant component part of the UK), differing national perspectives may be identified in other European countries – including, within the UK, in Scotland – in North America, and elsewhere. Though, at various times, national systems have borrowed elements of their ideas of the university from others, they have also tended to retain at least some of their differences, and thus maintain their own distinctive perspective.

My aim in this final chapter, therefore, is to offer a review and synthesis of the main trends in recent history regarding the English idea of the university – and the authors who have been concerned with them – and to put these trends into a broader context, both comparatively and in terms of other ideas of higher education more widely conceived. The state of the contemporary debate, and where it might be heading, will then be assessed.

The English idea of the university: a historical review

Like the Papacy and the Empire, the university is an institution which owes not merely its primitive form and traditions, but, in a sense, its very existence to a combination of accidental circumstances; and its origin can only be understood by reference to those circumstances. But the subsequent development of each of these institutions was determined by, and reveals to us, the whole bent and spiritual character of the age to whose life it became organic. The university, no less than the Roman Church and the feudal hierarchy headed by the Roman Emperor, represents an attempt to realize in concrete form an ideal of life in one of its aspects. (Randall [1895] 1936: 3)

Discussions of the nature of the university sometimes start from what might be thought of as first principles, looking to ancient antecedents in Greece and elsewhere, or to the medieval European foundations in Bologna, Paris and Oxford (Randall [1895] 1936; de Ridder-Symoens 1992, 1996). Here we start, fairly conventionally, with the mid-nineteenth century views expressed by Newman, so often quoted in this context (though McPherson (1959) usefully traces what he calls the 'classical ideal' back rather earlier), but also not infrequently misunderstood or taken out of context.

Newman's views were formulated at a time when he was involved with attempts to establish a catholic university in Dublin. As a former Oxford don, it was not surprising that he favoured an Oxbridge-style collegiate university system:

> The view taken of a University in these Discourses is the following: – That it is a place of *teaching* universal *knowledge*. This implies that its object is, on the one hand, intellectual, not moral; and, on the other, that it is the diffusion and extension of knowledge rather than the advancement. If its object were scientific and philosophical discovery, I do not see why a University should have students; if religious training, I do not see how it can be the seat of literature and science. (Newman [1852] 1976: 5, emphasis in original)

This idea of the university laid great emphasis on teaching (but did not necessarily reject research: Ker 1999), on studying a wide range of subjects in a communal, residential setting, and on developing the relationship between academics and students:

> It is a great point then to enlarge the range of studies which a University professes, even for the sake of the students; and, though they cannot pursue every subject which is open to them, they will be the gainers by living among those and under those who represent the whole circle. This I conceive to be the advantage of a seat of universal learning, considered as a place of education. An assemblage of learned men, zealous for their own sciences, and rivals of each other, are brought, by familiar intercourse and for the sake of intellectual peace, to adjust together the claims and relations of their respective subjects of investigation. (Newman [1852] 1976: 95)

Newman's idea of the university was also, in part, defined in opposition to other developments at that time, notably the establishment of the University of London as a purely examining body (Bell and Tight 1993; see also Chapter 2). In his conception of the university, examination, assessment and accreditation were unimportant; what mattered was the development of the minds of young gentlemen (as, perforce, women and the lower social classes were excluded at the time). For him, the university was not vocational in the narrow sense in which that term is now most often used; that is, concerned with the preparation of students for specific careers, but rather about the general inculcation of attitudes for life (for the narrow range or class of men involved). Thus, in a famous passage, he argued:

> I protest to you, Gentlemen, that if I had to choose between a so-called University, which dispensed with residence and a tutorial superintendence, and gave its degrees to any person who passed an examination in a wide range of subjects, and a University which had no professors

or examinations at all, but merely brought a number of young men together for three or four years, and then sent them away as the University of Oxford is said to have done some sixty years since, if I were asked which of these two methods was the better discipline of the intellect . . . which of the two courses was the more successful in training, moulding, enlarging the mind, which sent out men the more fitted for their secular duties, which produced better public men, men of the world, men whose names would descend to posterity, I have no hesitation in giving the preference to that University which did nothing, over that which exacted of its members an acquaintance with every science under the sun. (Newman [1852] 1976: 129)

Newman had only a limited opportunity to turn his idea of the university into practice, and it was clearly being both disregarded and overtaken by events at the time it was expounded. The development of the civic universities in the latter part of the nineteenth century in the major English industrial cities – Birmingham, Bristol, Leeds, Liverpool, Manchester, Sheffield – emphasized other ideas (Armytage 1955; Heyck 1987). These ideas, discussed at greater length later in this chapter (see also Chapter 2) in the context of the technical tradition, included the development and dissemination of useful knowledge, local recruitment and working closely (in teaching and research) with local industrialists.

Similarly, Newman's opposition (shared by many, both at the time and later) to the idea of the university as a federal examining body – as practised by London, Wales, the former Royal University of Ireland, and widely throughout the then British Empire – did not stop this strategy having a major influence on university development in Britain, right down until the present day (Rothblatt 1987). Indeed, that strategy may be said to have only effectively ceased in 1992, with the abolition of the Council for National Academic Awards (Silver 1990; see Chapter 7) – essentially a successor body to the University of London in its institutional examining role – though the University of London still maintains an external, examining arm for individual students (Tight 2005).

Yet Newman's more elite vision of the university has continued to influence – even, it might be said, to dominate – thinking, if perhaps not so much practise, in England and beyond (Rothblatt 1997; Wyatt 1990). If we move on to the point where the detailed discussion in this book starts; that is, to the mid-twentieth century – to the anticipation and aftermath of the end of the Second World War – it is evident, for example, in the ideas of Leavis about the university, though he did also acknowledge their vocational training function:

An urgently necessary work . . . is to explore the means of bringing the various essential kinds of specialist knowledge and training into effective relation with informed general intelligence, humane culture, social conscience and political will. Here, in this work, we have the function that is pre-eminently the university's; if the work is not done there it will not be done anywhere. (Leavis [1943] 1948: 24)

It is also clear in the influential writings of the academic who used the pseudonym Truscot (1943, 1945), and who contrasted what he felt as the rather dimmer reality of working and studying in civic (redbrick) universities to the Oxbridge ideal:

> Central to *Redbrick* was the critique of a university 'system' which gave Oxbridge all the advantages, including those of resources, residence and the networks that led to the most influential jobs and to privilege. Truscot traced with acerbic clarity the routes from Drabtown Municipal Secondary School for Boys to Redbrick University, and from public school to Oxbridge. He pointed to what later became known as 'merito-cratic' education by indicating the adaptations Oxbridge was prepared to make in order to deprive Redbrick of its potentially most able candidates. (Silver 2003: 65)

And it stands out in Moberly's work, where he sees the dissonance between the university idea and university practice (at least outside Oxbridge) as constituting a 'crisis'; and, in doing so, makes an early contribution to what would become a burgeoning crisis literature – at least in the UK and North America (Tight 1994):

> Many who are intimately connected with universities today are hampered by an uneasy sense of the discrepancy between profession and actuality in such respects as the following . . . First, the university professes to turn out 'rounded persons' with an understanding of themselves and of their place in the cosmos. But, in fact, a very large proportion both of stu-dents and of their teachers are narrow specialists with extremely limited horizons. Secondly, the university professes to stimulate a liberal and disinterested attitude to study . . . But, in fact, the common attitude is self-centred and utilitarian . . . Thirdly, the university professes to culti-vate objectivity and impartiality. In fact university teachers and their pupils, like other people, are commonly swayed by unexamined assump-tions . . . Lastly, the university professes to be a community and to derive from this fact much of its educational power . . . But for the majority of students in the non-residential universities at least, their university has been less an *Alma Mater* than a bargain-counter, at which certain speci-fic articles they require are purveyed. (Moberly 1949: 23–4; see also Oakeshott's (1948) critique)

Snow, while seeing the crisis in higher education as being chiefly about the insularity and increasing specialization of the disciplines, and in particular the science/humanities divide (which he referred to as the 'two cultures'), also wrote very warmly about the Oxbridge idea(l) of the university, both in his novels and his academic writing (Snow 1951, 1993 (1959/1964)).

The idea of the university so eloquently expressed by Newman, and so firmly associated with the practices of the ancient English universities of Oxford and Cambridge, continued to dominate thinking in England up until the 1970s (it still exerts great influence today, of course, but not so strongly).

It in essence provided the working assumptions for the Robbins Report (Carswell 1988; Committee on Higher Education 1963a; see Chapter 4), even though Robbins recommended that the planned expansion in student numbers should be achieved largely through an enlargement of the civic universities. And it most definitely informed the structures and practices for the new (campus) universities established in the 1960s, where, though not favoured by Robbins, more of that expansion did take place (Perkin 1991; see Chapter 5).

Perhaps the clearest, and most succinct, account of this university idea(l) at that time was offered by Halsey and his colleagues, though they (in my view falsely, as discussed further later) associated it with Britain as a whole rather than just England:

> . . . in Britain there is a distinctive idea of the university which serves also as an ideal. It is a traditional conception derived from the Oxford and Cambridge colleges (though not necessarily a description of them now or at any time in the past) . . . First, it should be ancient: second, it should draw its students, not from a restricted regional locality, but from the nation and internationally: third, its students, whatever their origins, should be carefully selected as likely to fit into and maintain the established life and character of the university: fourth, those who enter should be offered 'education' and not merely 'training'. This end necessitates, fifth, a small-scale residential community affording close contact of teachers with taught in a shared domestic life and, sixth, a high staff-student ratio for individualised teaching . . . A seventh criterion is that a university should be politically autonomous which tends to mean richly and independently endowed . . . Eighth and finally the internal affairs of the ideal university should be govern~ ~mocracy of its own academic members. (Halsey et al. 1°~

Interestingly, Halsey et al. recogn~ ~could be seen to have mythic qualities; whi~ ~ains its continuing attraction. But, in addition to allo~ ~s to indulge themselves in nostalgia for a vanished (or vanisl~ ~ golden age – as, indeed, Newman seems to have been doing in one of the quotations included above – this English idea of the university was dominant for at least two other reasons. First, it was only in the later post-war period that Oxford and Cambridge ceased to literally dominate the English higher education system; not only in terms of forming the acknowledged elite, but also in terms of staff and student numbers. Even when this dominance began to ebb, with the expansion in the size and number of the other English universities, the Oxbridge influence continued through its graduates providing so many of the staff, and particularly the senior staff, at the newer foundations (Halsey 1995). The second reason is of the 'grass is always greener' type; namely, that so many of those who had not been students, or did not work, at Oxbridge aspired to be or do so.

From the 1970s onwards, however, the English/Oxbridge idea of higher education began to come in for more sustained criticism (Minogue 1973). Thus, the transatlantic commentator Trow saw the continuing support for this idea as hampering the English higher education system in its transition from elite to mass participation:

> The Robbins Report (1963) helped to justify and chart the great expansion of British higher education in the decade and a half following up its publication. But this liberal and expansionist document has also served to limit the growth of British higher education by affirming the values and assumptions that define the English 'idea of a university'. Among these values are:
>
> (i)   the monopoly by state supported institutions of study leading to degrees;
> (ii) their commitment to high and common academic standards for the honours degree;
> (iii) a degree earned through full-time study over three years; and
> (iv) the costs of student maintenance and instruction being borne wholly (or nearly so) by the state. (Trow 1989: 55)

In an even wider critique, Scott (in another contribution to the 'crisis' literature), while harking back to Snow's identification of 'two cultures' in academe, also blames what he refers to as the 'traditional university' characterization for broader social and political ills:

> At least this characterisation of the traditional university helps to explain strange features of Britain's intellectual and university culture such as:
>
> • anti-intellectualism even among intellectuals and the suspicion/ absence of an intelligentsia
> • an enthusiasm for pragmatism and suspicion of over-abstraction
> • a continued commitment to the close and careful teaching of students
> • an obscure but evocative distinction between scholarship and research
> • an apparently almost unbridgeable cultural gap between science and non-science
> • an unnatural separation between 'human' and 'social' sciences
> • a high degree of independence from the state combined anomalously with an equally high degree of solidarity with established political society (Scott 1984: 4)

Yet the English, Oxbridge, idea of the university still remains influential, and Newman's ideas are still regularly called upon to justify or criticize positions or practices (e.g. Maskell and Robinson 2001; Smith and Langslow 1999; Smith and Webster 1997). This makes it all the more important to recognize that this is not the only idea of the university in town, not even in England and certainly not more widely, and that it has not been so for two centuries at least.

Alternative perspectives: (i) comparative

The English idea of the university may, therefore, be usefully compared and contrasted with alternative perspectives. Two sorts of alternative perspective will now be considered: those put forward in other countries or higher education systems (selected perspectives from Europe and the USA will be considered in this section), and those stemming from different stances on higher education, as well as or instead of, the university (the subject of the following section).

European perspectives

Perhaps the most important point to emphasize here is that the English idea of the university, as discussed in the previous section, is not, and was not, a British or UK idea. For there has long been an alternative, Scottish, idea of the university, one which has links with practices in continental Europe.

The Scots are justly proud that, while England for centuries only had two universities, Oxford and Cambridge, they had four: St Andrews, Glasgow, Aberdeen and Edinburgh (or five, since there were two separate foundations in Aberdeen, which did not amalgamate until 1860). Historically, more Scots participated in higher education, they started their studies earlier, and they followed a broader curriculum, akin to that advocated by Newman in Dublin (but less and less found in practice in English universities – see Chapter 7). There was also a greater flexibility in the ways in which higher education could be accessed (Bell 1973; McPherson 1973):

> In a reaffirmation of the genuinely democratic character of the universities, every effort was made to develop the traditional Scottish machinery designed to neutralise the inequalities of scholastic and family backgrounds. Junior classes, in which the Professor himself might teach the elements, enabled the intellectually gifted to 'catch up', and matriculation at sixteen and earlier was sometimes a counteractive to the counter-democratic influence of the sixth form. In this way, careers were opened to talents, scientific as well as philological, in accordance with the spirit of the nineteenth century, but, at the same time, lest this selection and fostering of talents would produce a flood of one-sided experts and bureaucratic specialists, general studies of a non-utilitarian kind were given pride of place in the curriculum, and, as in France, the path alike to science and to literature lay through compulsory philosophy. (Davie 1961: xvii)

Indeed, most of these trends are still evident today, with Scotland well ahead of the rest of the UK in terms of participation rates, typically recruiting its undergraduates a year earlier than in England, and maintaining at least some elements of the broader curriculum.

Within Europe more broadly, the English idea of the university is frequently contrasted with that originating in Germany, as it was establishing itself as a nation state in the nineteenth century. This perspective is particularly associated with Humboldt and the foundation of the University of Berlin (though, rather like Newman, he did not stay to oversee the university he helped to plan):

> Von Humboldt . . . declared that both teaching and research should take place, or, rather, teaching through research. He saw no inherent conflict between the two; in fact, he believed that teaching would stimulate *Wissenschaft* [learning]. Students and faculty members would enjoy a special relationship based on equality. Both would pursue *Wissenschaft*; this pursuit would be the means to *Bildung* [all-round education]. (Hofstetter 2001: 107, original emphasis)

Unlike the English idea, this stressed the critical role of research, which, in synergy with teaching, was seen as forming the core functions of the university. This view has assumed greater importance in the post-war UK, taking its contemporary form as the research/teaching nexus (see Chapter 8):

> The classical German university combines research and teaching in at least three different ways. First, the institution itself is conceived as having the dual purpose of teaching students and pushing back the frontiers of knowledge. German university professors are expected to do research as a normal part of their duties. Secondly, students are expected to learn by undertaking at least a limited amount of original research, and thereby learning procedures, habits and methods of work in a particular discipline . . . Thirdly, the best teaching is conceived as a kind of 'research'. True communication of knowledge involves a recreation of the processes which produced it, and this calls for more than rote-learning. (Pritchard 1990: 47)

Like the classical English (and the Scottish) idea, however, the German idea of the university also upheld the importance of a broad, general education – underpinned by ideas about the unity of knowledge – rejecting narrow vocationalism and advocating close interaction between staff and students. These beliefs were reaffirmed after the Second World War by Jaspers:

> The university is a school – but of a very special sort. It is intended not merely as a place for instruction; rather, the student is to participate actively in research and from this experience he is to acquire the intellectual discipline and education which will remain with him throughout his life. Ideally, the student thinks independently, listens critically and is responsible to himself. He has the freedom to learn [i.e. *lernfreiheit*, while the academics enjoy *lehrfreiheit*, the freedom to teach and research]. (Jaspers [1959] 1960: 19)

Another prominent European – in this case Spanish – thinker on the idea of the university, writing as the Second World War came to its close, was Ortega y Gasset. He appears much closer to the English idea in his writing, clearly regretting the impact of the rise of research and professional education on the university:

> Compared with the medieval university, the contemporary university has developed the mere seed of professional instruction into an enormous activity; it has added the function of research; and it has abandoned almost entirely the teaching or transmission of culture. (Ortega y Gasset 1946: 44)

His restatement of the university's mission aligns him closely with Newman, though the specific attention given to sociology is both a sign of the changing times and his own disciplinary career:

> The university consists, primarily and basically, of the higher education which the ordinary man should receive. It is necessary to make of this ordinary man, first of all, a cultured person: to put him at the height of the times. It follows then, that the primary function of the university is to teach the great cultural disciplines, namely:
>
> 1. The physical scheme of the world (Physics).
> 2. The fundamental themes of organic life (Biology).
> 3. The historical process of the human species (History).
> 4. The structure and functioning of social life (Sociology).
> 5. The plan of the universe (Philosophy). (Ortega y Gasset 1946: 58)

US perspectives

The USA is possibly the best example of a system whose idea(s) about the university, and about higher education more generally, have been influenced by and influenced those in other systems. Thus, while the earliest US ideas were, perforce, inherited from the colonial power, Britain, they were soon developed and expanded in the US context. The development of the land grant and state universities, and the special emphasis they placed upon the role of 'service', and, in the twentieth century, of mass participation in higher education, have been particularly influential (Bok 1986; Lucas 1994; Thelin 2004).

Conversely, the USA took German ideas about the importance of research in the university, leading to the creation of graduate schools (first at Johns Hopkins University, and then more widely). They also developed the PhD (and, more recently, the professional doctorate), which was then taken up by the German universities, and only later in the UK (Simpson 1983).

The admiration accorded in the early twentieth century by many Americans to the German idea of higher education is particularly evident in Flexner's writing, for whom English and US practices were poor by comparison:

> We are proceeding on the assumption that a university is essentially a

seat of learning, devoted to the conservation of knowledge, the increase of systematic knowledge, and the training of students well above the secondary level. This is, as we have discovered, not the current American idea of a university; it is not the English idea either . . . Hitherto, the English university has, like the American university, discharged three functions: part of it, much less than is the case in America, belongs to the secondary field; part of it has been devoted to 'service', but service at a far higher level than obtains in America; part of it concerns itself with genuine university activities. (Flexner [1930] 1994: 230)

Flexner was, however – like Newman – seeking to shut the stable door after the horse had bolted. The increasing expansion of the US university, particularly after the Second World War, and its continuing focus on the three missions of teaching, research and service was to lead to the creation of massive, state-wide systems of higher education, and the emergence of what Kerr famously characterized as the 'multiversity':

The multiversity is an inconsistent institution. It is not one community but several – the community of the undergraduate and the community of the graduate; the community of the humanist, the community of the social scientist, and the community of the scientist; the communities of the professional schools; the community of all the nonacademic personnel; the community of the administrators. Its edges are fuzzy – it reaches out to alumni, legislators, farmers, businessmen, who are all related to one or more of these internal communities . . . The 'Idea of a University' was a village with its priests. The 'Idea of a Modern University' was a town – a one-industry town – with its intellectual oligarchy. 'The Idea of a Multiversity' is a city of infinite variety. (Kerr [1963] 2001: 14, 31)

While Kerr's presentation serves as a reasonable account of contemporary US higher education practice, many US authors remain critical of the multiversity as an idea, tending to hark back, like the English and Europeans more generally, to an older idea of the university whose time has gone (e.g. Barzun [1968] 1993; Bloom 1987; Smith 1990, and other US 'crisis' authors). Thus, Wolff sets up a discussion of the ideal of the university by proposing four models:

The University as a Sanctuary of Scholarship
The University as a Training Camp for the Professions
The University as a Social Service Station
The University as an Assembly Line for Establishment Man

The first model is drawn from the history of the university; the second model reflects its present character; the third is a projection of present trends and thus is a prediction of the shape of the university to come; and the fourth is a radical critique of the university, an anti-model, as it were. (Wolff 1969: 3)

The multiversity could be seen, in these terms, as a combination of the first three models moving in the direction of the fourth, clearly not a prospect welcomed by Wolff.

Alternative perspectives: (ii) on higher education

In addition to the differences, and similarities, we have identified between the perspectives held on the idea of the university in different countries or systems, we may also recognize divergent views within higher education more broadly conceived. These begin to move us away from the simplistic equation between 'the university' and 'higher education', and towards an appreciation of the range of – sometimes conflicting or even contradictory – perspectives, or ideas, that may be accommodated (indeed encouraged) within a single system.

Three alternative perspectives of this kind are considered in this section, ordered in terms of their relative age. First, the technical tradition, dating to the nineteenth century, focusing on the preparation of the highly skilled worker; second, what I will refer to as the 'counter-cultural' movement, which arose in the 1960s and 1970s to challenge existing practices, both in higher education and more broadly; and, third, the technological developments that have impacted since the 1970s.

The technical tradition

> The ideological challenge to the university ideal is based on the idea that education is fundamentally an economic resource which should be employed in a way which maximises its contribution to the development of Britain as an industrial nation. (Tapper and Salter 1978: 149)

We have already noted that, following the medieval university foundations, the next major phase of university development in the UK – the establishment of the civic universities in the major industrial cities in the latter part of the nineteenth century – embodied a different idea of higher education. This technical tradition focused on the needs of the locality, of industry and business, and on providing alternative routes to qualification.

The entire history of British, and particularly English, higher education over the last two centuries could be understood as a contest between two ideas of higher education: the English (or Scottish) idea of the university, as symbolized and reified by Oxford, St Andrews, Glasgow et al., and the technical tradition. Indeed, this contest might be broadened to involve the whole of education, through the continuing debate over the relative status of academic and vocational courses and purposes, at all levels.

While the former, academic, idea sustained itself, and was re-emphasized in the 1960s with the foundation of the campus universities, the alternative, technical (and local; see Brown 1972; Marks 2005) tradition has had to be continually reinvented – in the older civic foundations of the late nineteenth century, in the newer civic foundations of the early twentieth century, in the colleges of advanced technology established in the 1950s, and in the polytechnics created in the 1970s (Armytage 1955; Jones 1988; Pratt 1997; Pratt and Burgess 1974; Venables 1955, 1978; see also Chapter 5). The reason for this continual reinvention has been what Burgess and Pratt have termed 'academic drift', an aspirational process through which all higher education institutions seek to become more like the older, 'traditional' idea of the university:

> . . . there is a process which continuously confuses the certainties of the contrasts we have been making, a process started and sustained by aspiration. For the last 100 years or more, colleges founded in the technical college tradition have gradually exchanged it for the alternative. In part this arose from a worthy pursuit of higher standards – but it always entailed the neglect of local needs, of social and industrial demand, of lower-level work and of the education of the working classes. The most famous example of the process was at Manchester, where the citizens in the nineteenth century founded Owens College as an avowed alternative to Oxford and Cambridge. When the college became the University of Manchester the city tried again, with the institution which became the College of Science and Technology. As this grew to be an institute of [the] university, the Royal College of Advanced Technology emerged at Salford, across the Irwell. Today, with the University of Salford well and truly chartered, the Manchester area is putting together its fourth institution of higher education – the polytechnic based upon John Dalton College. (Burgess and Pratt 1970: 5)

Of course, since Burgess and Pratt wrote those words, Manchester Polytechnic has become Manchester Metropolitan University, one of the largest higher education institutions in the country, and the process has started again through the development of yet other institutions in the further education sector.

Counter-cultural

The counter-cultural movement arose, peaked and then slowly declined in the 1960s and 1970s. At its heart was a critical assessment of western, developed society, and the desire to put in its place something freer, more open and flexible, and egalitarian (see, for example, Freire 1972; Illich 1973). Since, as a movement, it had a particular appeal for the young and certain kinds of intellectual (particularly those leaning to the left in political terms), it is no surprise that it had an impact on the university. This impact could take the form of student protest, or of critique of the existing idea of what the university should be, and how it should operate. For example, in the US context, Roszak launched this damning criticism:

'Service', by becoming a blanket willingness to do whatever society will pay for, has led the university to surrender the indispensable characteristic of wisdom: moral discrimination. So it is that the multiversity progressively comes to resemble nothing so much as the highly refined, all-purpose brothel Jean Genet describes in his play *The Balcony*. (Roszak 1969: 12)

The impact of the counter-cultural movement can also be detected in the intentions of the new university foundations of this period – and particularly the campus universities in England – to 'redraw the map of learning' (Daiches 1964). This was typically done by organizing the university, not in terms of conventional, discipline-based departments, but as a series of larger, interdisciplinary schools of study (a feature that is re-emerging today, but with more managerialist intentions: see Chapter 6). At the level of the degree, common foundation courses might be used (as at Keele), perhaps with some expectation that students would then take further courses in subjects outside their specialism. Interdisciplinary degrees were another strategy, often identifiable by the incorporation of the term 'studies' in their titles (see also Chapter 7).

A more radical impact was sought, and at least temporarily achieved, in cases where intellectuals inside and outside the university worked together to introduce entirely new subjects – or, at least, new perspectives on existing areas of study – into the academy. A prominent example of this was the creation of women's studies courses and departments (and it does seem significant that this is only the second time in this chapter that I am quoting a woman):

Undoubtedly, and as was recognised by my interviewees, the establishment of Women's Studies degrees belongs to a particular moment in history. It was a moment when radical politics tried to enter the academy, seeing this as one place among others for political activism . . . rather than overturning the system, either inside or outside the academy, knowledge was reined in and brought back into the intellectual and physical spaces that constitute traditional disciplines. (Bird 2001: 473–4)

As Bird recognizes, however, the women's studies movement has not had a significant long-term impact on the idea of the university. But, then, neither have any of the other developments that I have identified as counter-cultural, as conventional disciplinary patterns of organization – if, perhaps, not of management – have, over a period of just two or three decades, reasserted themselves.

Technological

The third alternative perspective on higher education I have identified for discussion in this section is the most recent. It differs from the long-standing technical tradition in not focusing on the end result or purpose of higher education, and from the counter-cultural movement in not aiming to overturn the established curriculum. Rather, the technological perspective seeks to alter the ways in which teaching is delivered and learning is practised, by making widespread use of new information and communication technologies.

Of course, at one level, the expectation is that all institutions of higher education will make increasing use of contemporary technologies – as they have always sought to do, albeit on occasion with some delay – either alongside and/or embedded within their existing 'courseware'. But the technological perspective on higher education has a more far-reaching agenda as well, which goes beyond arguing that an increasing amount of higher education is best delivered and experienced online, or at least in a mixed or 'blended' form, to suggesting that whole institutions, and perhaps systems, can be organized on this basis.

This is the land of the mega-university, making use of both economies of scale to deliver truly mass higher education, and of the flexibility and individualization which online learning can allow. The contemporary existence of the mega-university is undeniable:

> We define a mega-university as a distance-teaching institution with over 100,000 active students in degree-level courses . . . The definition of a mega-university combines three criteria: distance teaching, higher education, and size. (Daniel 1996: 29)

The only existing British example of the mega-university is the Open University (discussed in Chapter 5), founded at the end of the 1960s, though many national systems now boast at least one such institution. From the standpoint of the English idea of the university, however, what is interesting about the Open University is – alongside its innovations, in the British context, of open entry, modular provision, general degrees and predominantly distance delivery – the extent to which its founders felt the need to align themselves with prevailing views on academic standards, and make use of face-to-face provision wherever possible (Rumble 1982).

Another key reservation about the Open University, and similar examples worldwide, is that, in order to achieve the economies of scale on which their development is typically justified, a very standardized curriculum is required. This then limits the extent to which the other key characteristic of contemporary online learning – the ability to individualize the learning experience – can be achieved. While the Open University remains, therefore, the only British example of an overtly technological university, it is a constrained, and in some ways old-fashioned, example. And, though we have yet to see, certainly in the British context, the creation of a successful e-university – one high-profile, failed attempt notwithstanding (Slater 2005; see also Chapter 7) – all institutions of higher education are paying at least some, and most commonly an increasing amount of, attention to e-learning developments (e.g. Boezerooij 2006; Conole and Oliver 2007).

Contemporary perspectives

Despite the pressure exerted by advocates of the alternative perspectives on higher education just discussed, and the influence of comparative views on the university from other systems in a steadily globalizing world, the English idea of higher education retains a strong presence within the UK. It is still widely discussed as the model from which we should develop, or to which we should return, even if the visions are necessarily contested.

Perhaps the most widely read current English author working in this area is Barnett, whose work may be interpreted as an attempt to reformulate the classic idea of the university for contemporary times. Barnett defines higher education, and the institutions that provide it, in the following terms:

An institution of higher education justifies the title when it fosters educational processes of an appropriate kind . . . six conditions . . . together constitute such processes. *Higher* educational processes promote:

1. A deep understanding, by the student, of some knowledge claims.
2. A radical critique, by the same student, of those knowledge claims.
3. A developing competence to conduct that critique in the company of others.
4. The student's involvement in determining the shape and direction of that critique (i.e. some form of independent inquiry).
5. The student's self-reflection, with the student developing the capacity critically to evaluate his or her own achievements, knowledge claims and performance.
6. The opportunity for the student to engage in that inquiry in a process of open dialogue and cooperation (freed from unnecessary direction). (Barnett 1990: 202–3, emphasis in original)

Such an account – with its modern-day language (self-reflection) and presentation (bullet points) removed – would fit with little dissonance into one of Newman's discourses.

However, the most common form in which one encounters discussion of the English idea of the university in contemporary academic writing is one of wistful, critical regret. This recognizes that the English idea of the university is now, primarily, just that – an idea – but, nonetheless that it is an idea still earnestly supported and wished for by many. For example:

There is pressure from the economy for the education system to produce both manpower and knowledge relevant to the economy's needs.

However, the translation of such pressure into the ideological and political vehicles for educational change has faced its stiffest test in the case of the universities whose traditional values are unequivocally opposed to any such relationship. (Tapper and Salter 1992: 8–9)

Other writers have attempted to move the debate on by seeking to identify a sea change in the idea of the university. Thus, Bowden and Marton, harking back to the ideas of both Newman and Humboldt, have endeavoured to move beyond contemporary concerns with the 'research-teaching nexus' (see Chapter 8) to promote learning as the defining characteristic of the university:

> universities at different times prior to the twentieth century can be characterised as Universities of Teaching or Universities of Research. During the twentieth century, the conjunction of teaching and research has become the most distinctive aspect of the university and today's university could be styled as the *University of Teaching and Research.* We argue that . . . as we move into the twenty-first century, the university should be characterised as the *University of Learning.* (Bowden and Marton [1998] 2004: 4, emphasis in original)

The most influential current account along these lines, however, is probably that which argues that patterns of knowledge generation and use are fundamentally changing, challenging the role, and thus the very idea, of the university. Thus, Gibbons et al. (1994) present a dichotomy between what they term mode 1 and mode 2 knowledge; with the former representing the classic mode of disciplinary operation within the university, and the latter its more applied, transdisciplinary, heterogeneous, problem-based, extra-university equivalent (see the discussion in Chapter 8). This view may, of course, be criticized: for exaggerating the distinction between modes 1 and 2, for suggesting that this change has come about suddenly, and for not giving much guidance on what, if anything, universities might do in response. Some of the same group of authors have addressed the latter point in more recent writing:

> In a Mode-2 society, the future university will need to be more of a synergistic institution – in a double sense. First, it may be necessary to delineate, and so demarcate, its activities according to anachronistic divisions between research and teaching, scientific and social roles. This entails a commitment to being an open rather than a closed, a comprehensive rather than a niche, institution . . . Second, and much more difficult, the university will have to acquiesce in a process of de-institutionalisation, because in a Mode-2 society the boundaries between 'inside' and 'outside' make no better sense than those between research and teaching. (Nowotny et al. 2001: 91)

The problem with this formulation, though, is that it sounds both contradictory and still very difficult to implement. Perhaps a more measured trajectory across the same sort of territory has been suggested by Delanty:

the model of the university that prevailed in liberal modernity and which partly sustained the mass university of organized modernity is in decline today, for its presuppositions have been undermined by social change. The disciplinary structure of knowledge and the nation state no longer totally define the cognitive field of knowledge. Consensus on what constitutes knowledge has been replaced by dissensus, and culture, once preserved and reproduced in the university, is more contested than ever before. If the university is not to degenerate into technocratic consumerism by which students become mere consumers of knowledge and the university a transnational bureaucratic corporation legitimating itself by the technocratic discourse of 'excellence', it will have to discover another role . . . A new role and identity for the university is emerging around the democratization of knowledge. By democratization I mean the participation of more and more actors in the social construction of reality. (Delanty 2001: 6)

Delanty here appears to be using 'democratization' to cover much the same ideas embodied in the ideas of mode 1/mode 2 knowledge, while simultaneously moving beyond the demands for mass participation in university education to a formulation that envisages mass participation in something broader, 'the social construction of reality', both within and beyond the university. In doing so, he also takes a tilt at the contemporary discourse of the student as consumer, and the development of universities as multinational providers of higher education.

An alternative, perhaps more critical – or perhaps more tongue in cheek – formulation of the contemporary university idea is that of the McUniversity. This has clear links with the online-based mega-university, through its emphasis on standardized, indeed industrialized, forms of delivery and massification. The McUniversity has been McDonaldized; in other words, it has learnt lessons from the fast-food business (and from Weber), and has concentrated upon the provision of an efficient, calculable, predictable and controlled series of products to defined customers (Hayes and Wynyard 2002; Parker and Jary 1995; Prichard and Willmott 1997). It is presented as a rational response to the demands of providing mass higher education to an increasingly consumer-oriented clientele.

It would probably be difficult to conceive of an idea of the university that could be more depressing to, or far removed from, those brought up on Newman. But we can, however, at least note that the original advocate of the McDonaldization hypothesis has now moved away from its application to the university, arguing instead for their deMcDonaldization:

The spectacle of the deMcDonaldization of the university's everyday activities will not only be spectacular and attract students, but it will also serve to enhance dramatically the quality of the educational process. (Ritzer 2002: 32)

Conclusions

What conclusions might we draw from this discussion of the idea of the university? I will offer four.

First, the English idea of the university remains both a coherent and a highly influential model, particularly, of course, within the English system of higher education. Despite (or perhaps because of) its basis in an idealized version of an education that was only ever offered to a small minority at Oxford and Cambridge, and its founding text being the writings of a catholic priest in mid-nineteenth century Ireland, this idea still tends to be the model to which academics in England (and often elsewhere) turn when talking about what the university should be like.

Second, this English idea of the university has provided the focus for a great deal of discussion and debate over the years, enabling the presentation and contextualization of a wide range of variant or alternative models. Many of these, both those referred to in this article and others, are listed, in the form of prefixes to the term 'university', in Table 12.1.

Table 12.1 An alphabet of prefixes for the idea of the university

ancient	modern
blended	multi
campus	new
civic	online
collegiate	open
comprehensive	plateglass
distance	postmodern
e	post-1992
European	redbrick
examining	research
federal	romantic
global	service
industrial	teaching
ivory tower	technical
learning	technological
McDonaldized	utopian
mass	virtual
mega	western

Third, and perhaps more significantly, the English seem to have been able to hold on to this particular idea of the university, even though it has so little resonance with contemporary (or historical) policy and practice. It is now an ideal, one which few academics and even fewer students have ever experienced, but no less a powerful idea for that.

Yet, fourth, and finally, and as a corollary to that last point, how long can this idea of the university hold out as anything more than an ideal, or an elite experience, against the twin forces of, on the one hand, the increasingly overweening emphasis on the economic functions of the university (evident in the discussion of changing policy presented in Chapter 4), and, on the other, the standardization of higher education internationally, and particularly in the European context through the Bologna process (see Chapter 6)?

References

Abbott, A. (2001) *Chaos of Disciplines.* Chicago, IL: University of Chicago Press.

Abbott, J. (1971) *Student Life in a Class Society.* Oxford: Pergamon.

Acker, S. and Piper, D. (eds) (1984) *Is Higher Education Fair to Women?* Guildford: SRHE/NFER-Nelson.

Adams, W. (1947) Higher education in the British Colonies, *Universities Quarterly*, 1: 145–53.

Adams, W. (1950) Colonial university education, *Universities Quarterly*, 4: 283–92.

Adnett, N. (2006) Student finance and widening participation in the British Isles: common problems, different solutions, *Higher Education Quarterly*, 60(4): 296–311.

Advisory Board for the Research Councils (1985) *The Brain Drain: A Summary of the Findings from an Enquiry by the Advisory Board for the Research Councils.* London: ABRC.

Advisory Board for the Research Councils/University Grants Committee (1982) *Report of a Joint Working Party on the Support of University Scientific Research.* London: HMSO, Cmnd 8567.

Advisory Council for Adult and Continuing Education (1982) *Continuing Education: From Policies to Practice.* Leicester: ACACE.

Advisory Council for Applied Research and Development/Advisory Board for the Research Councils (1983) *Improving Research Links between Higher Education and Industry.* London: HMSO.

Ainley, P. (1994) *Degrees of Difference: Higher Education in the 1990s.* London: Lawrence & Wishart.

Ainley, P. (1998) Higher education in a right state: professionalising the proletariat or proletarianising the professions, in D. Jary and M. Parker (eds) *The New Higher Education: Issues and Directions for the Post-Dearing University*, pp. 133–50. Stoke-on-Trent: Staffordshire University Press.

Aiston, S. (2005) A maternal Identity? The family lives of British women graduates pre- and post-1945, *History of Education*, 34(3): 407–26.

Aldcroft, D. (1992) *Education, Training and Economic Performance 1944 to 1990.* Manchester: Manchester University Press.

Altbach, P. (ed.) (1996) *The International Academic Profession: Portraits of Fourteen Countries.* Princeton, NJ: Carnegie Foundation for the Advancement of Teaching.

Amis, K. (1960) Lone voices: views of the 'fifties. *Encounter*, 15(1): 6–11.

Annan, N. (1990) *Our Age: Portrait of a Generation*. London: Weidenfeld & Nicolson.
Annan, N. (1999) *The Dons: Mentors, Eccentrics and Geniuses*. London: HarperCollins.
Archer, L. (2003) Social class and higher education, in L. Archer, M. Hutchings, A. Ross, C. Leathwood, R. Gilchrist and D. Phillips (eds) *Higher Education and Social Class: Issues of Exclusion and Inclusion*, pp. 5–20. London: RoutledgeFalmer.
Archer, M. (1979) *Social Origins of Educational Systems*. London: Sage Publications.
Argles, M. (1964) *South Kensington to Robbins: An Account of English Technical and Scientific Education Since 1851*. London: Longman.
Arksey, H., Marchant, I. and Simmill, C. (eds) (1994) *Juggling for a Degree: Mature Students' Experience of University Life*. Lancaster: Unit for Innovation in Higher Education.
Armytage, W. (1955) *Civic Universities: Aspects of a British Tradition*. London: Benn.
Armytage, W. (1968) Thoughts after Robbins, in J. Lawlor (ed.) *The New University*, pp. 77–100. New York: Columbia University Press.
Arregger, C. (1966) *Graduate Women at Work: A Study by a Working Party of the British Federation of University Women*. Newcastle-upon-Tyne: Oriel Press.
Ashby, E. (1966) *Technology and the Academics: An Essay on Universities and the Scientific Revolution*. London: Macmillan.
Ashby, E. and Anderson, M. (1966) *Universities: British, Indian, African: A study in the Ecology of Higher Education*. London: Weidenfeld & Nicolson.
Ashby, E. and Anderson, M. (1970) *The Rise of the Student Estate in Britain*. London: Macmillan.
Association of University Teachers (1994) *Long Hours, Little Thanks*. London: AUT.
Bacon, C., Benton, D. and Gruneberg, M. (1979) Employers' Opinions of University and Polytechnic Graduates: *The Vocational Aspect of Education*, 31(80): 95–102.
Bagilhole, B. (1993) How to keep a good woman down: an investigation of the role of institutional factors in the process of discrimination against women academics, *British Journal of Sociology of Education*, 14(3): 261–74.
Ball, C. (1990) *More Means Different: Widening Access to Higher Education*. London: RSA.
Bargh, C., Bocock, J., Scott, P. and Smith, D. (2000) *University Leadership: The Role of the Chief Executive*. Buckingham: Open University Press.
Bargh, C., Scott, P. and Smith, D. (1996) *Governing Universities: Changing the Culture?* Buckingham: Open University Press.
Barnes-Powell, T. and Letherby, G. (1998) 'All in a day's work': gendered care work in higher education, in D. Maslina and S. Maslin-Prothero (eds) *Surviving the Academy: Feminist Perspectives*, pp. 69–77. London: Falmer.
Barnett, C. (1986) *The Audit of War: The Illusion and Reality of Britain as a Great Nation*. London: Macmillan.
Barnett, R. (1990) *The Idea of Higher Education*. Buckingham: Open University Press.
Barnett, R. (1999) The Coming of the Global Village: A Tale of Two Inquiries, *Oxford Review of Education*, 25(3): 293–306.
Barr, N. (1989) *Student Loans: The Next Steps*. Aberdeen: Aberdeen University Press.
Barr, N. and Crawford, I. (2005) *Financing Higher Education: Answers from the UK*. London: Routledge.
Barzun, J. ([1968] 1993) *The American University: How it Runs, Where it is Going*, 2nd edn. Chicago, IL: University of Chicago Press.
Baumgratz-Gangl, G. (1996) Developments in the internationalization of higher education in Europe, in P. Blumenthal, C. Goodwin, A. Smith and U. Teichler (eds) *Academic Mobility in a Changing World*, pp. 103–28. London: Jessica Kingsley.

Becher, T. (1989) *Academic Tribes and Territories: Intellectual Enquiry and the Cultures of Disciplines.* Buckingham: Open University Press.

Becher, T. (1993) Graduate education in Britain: the view from the ground, in B. Clark (ed.) *The Research Foundations of Graduate Education: Germany, Britain, France, United States, Japan,* pp. 115–53. Berkeley, CA: University of California Press.

Becher, T. (ed.) (1994) *Governments and Professional Education.* Buckingham: Open University Press.

Becher, T. (1996) The learning professions, *Studies in Higher Education,* 21(1): 43–55.

Becher, T. (1999) *Professional Practices: Commitment and Capability in a Changing Environment.* New Brunswick, NJ: Transaction Publishers.

Becher, T., Henkel, M. and Kogan, M. (1994) *Graduate Education in Britain.* London: Jessica Kingsley.

Becher, T. and Kogan, M. (1992) *Process and Structure in Higher Education,* 2nd edn. London: Routledge.

Becher, T. and Trowler, P. (2001) *Academic Tribes and Territories: Intellectual Enquiry and the Culture of Disciplines,* 2nd edn. Buckingham: Open University Press.

Beck, J. and Young, M. (2005) The assault on the professions and the restructuring of academic and professional identities: a Bernsteinian analysis, *British Journal of Sociology of Education,* 26(2): 183–97.

Bekhradnia, B. (2003) *Widening Participation and Fair Access: An Overview of the Evidence.* Oxford: Higher Education Policy Institute.

Bekhradnia, B., Whitnall, C. and Sastry, T. (2006) *The Academic Experience of Students in English Universities.* Oxford: Higher Education Policy Institute.

Bell, A. (1981) Structure, knowledge and social relationships in teacher education, *British Journal of Sociology of Education,* 2(1): 3–23.

Bell, Q. (1963) *The Schools of Design.* London: Routledge & Kegan Paul.

Bell, R. (1973) The growth of the modern university, in R. Bell and A. Youngson (eds) *Present and Future in Higher Education,* pp. 13–28. London: Tavistock.

Bell, R. and Tight, M. (1993) *Open Universities: A British tradition?* Buckingham: Open University Press.

Beloff, M. (1968) *The Plateglass Universities.* London: Secker & Warburg.

Benn, R. and Fieldhouse, R. (1993) Government policies on university expansion and wider access, 1945–51 and 1985–91 compared, *Studies in Higher Education,* 18(3): 299–313.

Bennett, N., Dunne, E. and Carre, C. (2000) *Skills Development in Higher Education and Employment.* Buckingham: Open University Press.

Berdahl, R. (1959) *British Universities and the State.* Berkeley, CA: University of California Press.

Betts, N. and Smith, R. (1998) *Developing the Credit-based Modular Curriculum in Higher Education: Challenge, Choice and Change.* London: Falmer.

Biggs, J. (1999) *Teaching for Quality Learning at University.* Buckingham: Open University Press.

Biggs, C., Brighton, R., Minnitt, P., Pow, R. and Wicksteed, W. (1994) *Thematic Evaluation of EHEI.* Sheffield: Employment Department.

Bird, E. (2001) Disciplining the interdisciplinary: radicalism and the academic curriculum, *British Journal of Sociology of Education,* 22(4): 463–78.

Bird, J. (1996) *Black Students and Higher Education: Rhetorics and Realities.* Buckingham: Open University Press.

Birks, T. and Holford, M. (1972) *Building the New Universities.* Newton Abbot: David & Charles.

Blackburn, R. and Jarman, J. (1993) Changing inequalities in access to British universities, *Oxford Review of Education*, 19(2): 197–215.

Blackstone, T. and Fulton, O. (1975) Sex discrimination among university teachers: a British-American comparison, *British Journal of Sociology*, 26: 261–75.

Blakey, M. (1994) Student accommodation, in S. Haselgrove (ed.) *The Student Experience*, pp. 72–81. Buckingham: Open University Press.

Blaug, M. and Woodhall, M. (1981) A survey of overseas students in British higher education 1980, in P. Williams (ed.) *The Overseas Student Question: Studies for a Policy*, pp. 239–63. London: Heinemann.

Bligh, D., Caves, R. and Settle, G. (1980) 'A' level scores and degree classifications as functions of university type and subject, in D. Billing (ed.) *Indicators of Performance: Papers Presented at the Fifteenth Annual Conference of the Society for Research into Higher Education 1979*, pp. 17–30. Guildford: Society for Research into Higher Education.

Bloom, A. (1987) *The Closing of the American Mind: How Higher Education has Failed Democracy and Impoverished the Souls of Today's Students.* New York: Simon & Schuster.

Blume, S. (1982) A framework for analysis, in G. Oldham (ed.) *The Future of Research*, pp. 5–47. Guildford: Society for Research into Higher Education.

Blyth, J. (1983) *English University Adult Education 1908–1958: The Unique Tradition.* Manchester: Manchester University Press.

Bocock, J. and Watson, D. (eds) (1994) *Managing the University Curriculum: Making Common Cause.* Buckingham: Open University Press.

Boezerooij, P. (2006) *E-Learning Strategies of Higher Education Institutions: An Exploratory Study into the Influence of Environmental Contingencies on Strategic Choices of Higher Education Institutions with Respect to Integrating E-Learning in their Education Delivery and Support Processes.* Enschede: The Netherlands, University of Twente.

Bok, D. (1986) *Higher Learning.* Cambridge, MA: Harvard University Press.

Boorman, S., Brown, N., Payne, P. and Ramsden, B. (2006) *Part-time Students and Part-time Study in Higher Education in the UK. Strand 2: A Survey of the Issues Facing Institutions.* London: Universities UK.

Booth, C. (1982) DES and Treasury, in A. Morris and J. Sizer (eds) *Resources and Higher Education*, pp. 25–57. Guildford: Society for Research into Higher Education.

Booth, C. (1999) The rise of the new universities in Britain, in D. Smith and A. Langslow (eds) *The Idea of a University*, pp. 106–23. London: Jessica Kingsley.

Bourner, T., Bowden, R. and Laing, S. (2001) Professional doctorates in England, *Studies in Higher Education*, 26(1): 65–83.

Bourner, T., Reynolds, A., Hamed, M. and Barnett, R. (1991) *Part-time Students and their Experience of Higher Education.* Buckingham: Open University Press.

Bowden, J. and Marton, F. ([1998] 2004) *The University of Learning: Beyond Quality and Competence.* London: RoutledgeFalmer.

Bowden, R. (2000) Fantasy higher education: university and college league tables, *Quality in Higher Education*, 6(1): 41–60.

Bowers-Brown, T. (2006) Widening participation in higher education amongst students from disadvantaged socio-economic groups, *Tertiary Education and Management*, 12(1): 59–74.

Boys, C., Brennan, J., Henkel, M., Kirkland, J., Kogan, M. and Youll, P. (1988) *Higher Education and the Preparation for Work.* London: Jessica Kingsley.

Boys, C. and Kirkland, J. (1988) *Degrees of Success: Career Aspirations and Destinations of College, University and Polytechnic Graduates.* London: Jessica Kingsley.

Brennan, J. (1997) Studying in Europe, in D. McNamara and R. Harris (eds) *Overseas*

Students in Higher Education: Issues in Teaching and Learning, pp. 62–75. London: Routledge.

Brennan, J., Lyon, E., McGeevor, P. and Murray, K. (1993) *Students, Courses and Jobs: The Relationship Between Higher Education and the Labour Market*. London: Jessica Kingsley.

Brennan, J. and McGeevor, P. (1987) *Employment of Graduates from Ethnic Minorities: A Research Report*. London: Commission for Racial Equality.

Brennan, J., Mills, J., Shah, T. and Woodley, A. (1999) *Part-time students and employment: Report of a Survey of Students, Graduates and Diplomates*. London: Centre for Higher Education Research and Information.

Briggs, A. (1969) Development in higher education in the United Kingdom: nineteenth and twentieth centuries, in W. Niblett (ed.) *Higher Education: Demand and Response*, pp. 95–116. London: Tavistock.

Briggs, S. (2006) An exploratory study of the factors influencing undergraduate student choice: the case of higher education in Scotland, *Studies in Higher Education*, 31(6): 705–22.

Brook, G. (1965) *The Modern University*. London: Andre Deutsch.

Brooke, C. (1993) *A History of the University of Cambridge. Volume IV: 1870–1990*. Cambridge: Cambridge University Press.

Brooks, R. (1991) *Contemporary Debates in Education: An Historical Perspective*. London: Longman.

Brothers, J. and Hatch, S. (1971) *Residence and Student Life: A Sociological Inquiry into Residence in Higher Education*. London: Tavistock.

Brown, C. (1982) *The Education and Employment of Postgraduates: Report of a Survey of Former Engineering, Science and Social Science Students and their Employers*. London: Policy Studies Institute.

Brown, G., Bull, J. and Pendlebury, M. (1997) *Assessing Student Learning in Higher Education*. London: Routledge.

Brown, I. (1972) The dispersed polytechnic, in T. Burgess (ed.) *The Shape of Higher Education*, pp. 205–25. London: Cornmarket Press.

Brown, P., Hesketh, A. and Williams, S. (2004) *The Mismanagement of Talent: Employability and Jobs in the Knowledge Economy*. Oxford: Oxford University Press.

Brown, P. and Scase, R. (1994) *Higher Education and Corporate Realities: Class, Culture and the Decline of Graduate Careers*. London: UCL Press.

Brown, R. (2004) *Quality Assurance in Higher Education: The UK Experience Since 1992*. London: RoutledgeFalmer.

Bruce, A., Cooper, A. and Doherty, G. (1989) *The DipHE Experience: Longitudinal Study (1983–87) of the 1983 Cohort of Students Registered on CNAA's Diploma of Higher Education Courses*. London: CNAA.

Bryson, C. (2004) What about the workers? The expansion of higher education and the transformation of academic work, *Industrial Relations Journal*, 35(1): 38–57.

Bryson, C. and Barnes, N. (2000a) Working in higher education in the United Kingdom, in M. Tight (ed.) *Academic Work and Life: What it is to be an Academic, and How this is Changing*, pp. 147–85. Oxford: Elsevier Science.

Bryson, C. and Barnes, N. (2000b) The casualisation of employment in higher education in the United Kingdom, in M. Tight (ed.) *Academic Work and Life: What it is to be an Academic, and How this is Changing*, pp. 187–241. Oxford: Elsevier Science.

Buchanan, R. (1966) The technological universities, *Universities Quarterly*, 21: 71–90.

Burgess, R. (ed.) (1994a) *Postgraduate Education and Training in the Social Sciences: Processes and Products*. London: Jessica Kingsley.

Burgess, R. (1994b) Some issues in postgraduate education and training in the social sciences, in R. Burgess (ed.) *Postgraduate Education and Training in the Social Sciences: Processes and Products*, pp. 1–10. London: Jessica Kingsley.

Burgess, R., Pole, C. and Hockey, J. (1994) Strategies for managing and supervising the social science PhD, in R. Burgess (ed.) *Postgraduate Education and Training in the Social Sciences: Processes and Products*, pp. 13–33. London: Jessica Kingsley.

Burgess, T. and Pratt, J. (1970) *Policy and Practice: The Colleges of Advanced Technology*. London: Allen Lane, The Penguin Press.

Burgess, T. and Pratt, J. (1971) *Technical Education in the United Kingdom*. Paris: Organization for Economic Co-operation and Development.

Callender, C. (1997) *Full and Part-time Students in Higher Education: Their Experiences and Expectations*. Norwich: National Committee of Inquiry into Higher Education, Report 2.

Callender, C. (2003) Student financial support in higher education: access and exclusion, in M. Tight (ed.) *Access and Exclusion*, pp. 127–58. Oxford: Elsevier.

Callender, C. and Kempson, E. (1996) *Student Finances: Income, Expenditure and Take-up of Student Loans*. London: Policy Studies Institute.

Callender, C. Wilkinson, D. and Mackinon, K. (2006) *Part-time Students and Part-time Study in Higher Education in the UK. Strand 3: A Survey of Students' Attitudes and Experiences of Part-time Study and its Costs 2005/06*. London: Universities UK.

Cann, J., Jones, G. and Martin, I. (1991) Behind the rhetoric: women academic staff in colleges of higher education in England, *Gender and Education*, 3(1): 15–29.

Carey, A. (1956) *Colonial Students: A Study of the Social Adaptation of Colonial Students in London*. London: Secker & Warburg.

Carpentier, V. (2004) *Historical Statistics on the Funding and Development of the UK University System, 1920–2002* [computer file]. Colchester, Essex: UK Data Archive [distributor], July 2004. SN: 4971.

Carr-Saunders, A. (1961) *New Universities Overseas*. London: George Allen & Unwin.

Carswell, J. (1985) *Government and the Universities in Britain: Programme and Performance 1960–1980*. Cambridge: Cambridge University Press.

Carswell, J. (1988) 'What Robbins took for granted', *Oxford Review of Education*, 14(1): 21–32.

Carter, I. (1990) *Ancient Cultures of Conceit: British University Fiction in the Post-war Years*. London: Routledge.

Carter, J. and Withrington, D. (eds) (1992) *Scottish Universities: Distinctiveness and Diversity*. Edinburgh: John Donald.

Casey, B. (1997) *Academic Staff in Higher Education: Their Experiences and Expectations*. Norwich: National Committee of Inquiry into Higher Education, Report 3.

Cerych, L. and Sabatier, P. (1985) *Great Expectations and Mixed Performance: The Implementation of Higher Education Reforms in Europe*. Stoke-on-Trent: Trentham Books.

Chancellor of the Duchy of Lancaster (1993) *Realising our Potential: A Strategy for Science, Engineering and Technology*. London: HMSO, Cmnd 2250.

Chisholm, L. and Woodward, D. (1980) The experiences of women graduates in the labour market, in R. Deem, (ed.) *Schooling for Women's Work*, pp. 162–76. London: Routledge & Kegan Paul.

Choppin, B., Orr, L., Kurle, S., Fara, P. and James, G. (1973) *The Prediction of Academic Success*. Slough: National Foundation for Educational Research.

Christie, H., Munro, M. and Rettig, H. (2001) Making ends meet: student incomes and debt, *Studies in Higher Education*, 26(3): 363–83.

Christie, H., Munro, M. and Fisher, T. (2004) Leaving university early: exploring the differences between continuing and non-continuing students, *Studies in Higher Education*, 29(5): 617–36.

Church, C. (1975) Modular courses in British higher education: a critical assessment, *Higher Education Bulletin*, 3(3): 165–84.

Clark, B. (1998) *Creating Entrepreneurial Universities: Organizational Pathways of Transformation*. Oxford: Pergamon.

Clark, M. (2006) A case study in the acceptance of a new discipline, *Studies in Higher Education*, 31(2): 133–48.

Coate, K., Barnett, R. and Williams, G. (2001) Relationships between teaching and research in higher education in England, *Higher Education Quarterly*, 55(2): 158–74.

Cockburn, A. and Blackburn, R. (eds) (1969) *Student Power: Problems, Diagnosis, Action*. Harmondsworth: Penguin.

Coffield, F. (1990) From the decade of enterprise culture to the decade of TECs, *British Journal of Education and Work*, 4(1): 59–78.

Coffield, F. and Vignoles, A. (1997) *Widening Participation in Higher Education by Ethnic Minorities, Women and Alternative Students*. Norwich: National Committee of Inquiry into Higher Education, Report 5.

Collinson, J. (2004) Occupational identity on the edge: social science contract researchers in higher education, *Sociology*, 38(2): 313–29.

Collison, P. and Millen, J. (1969) University Chancellors, Vice-Chancellors and College Principals: A Social Profile, *Sociology*, 3: 77–109.

Colonial Office (1945a) *Report of the Commission on Higher Education in the Colonies*. London: HMSO, Cmnd 6647.

Colonial Office (1945b) *Report of the West Indies Committee of the Commission on Higher Education in the Colonies*. London: HMSO, Cmnd 6654.

Colonial Office (1945c) *Report of the Commission on Higher Education in West Africa*. London: HMSO, Cmnd 6655.

Committee of Enquiry into the Academic Validation of Degree Courses in Public Sector Higher Education (1985) *Academic Validation in Public Sector Higher Education*. London: HMSO, Cmnd 9501.

Committee of Enquiry into the Governance of the University of London (1972) *Final Report*. London: University of London.

Committee of Enquiry into the Organisation of the Academic Year (1993) *The Review of the Academic Year*. Bristol: Higher Education Funding Council for England.

Committee of Vice-Chancellors and Principals (1972) *Report of an Enquiry into the Use of Academic Staff Time*. London: CVCP.

Committee of Vice-Chancellors and Principals (1985) *Report of the Steering Committee for Efficiency Studies in Universities*. London: CVCP.

Committee of Vice-Chancellors and Principals (1986) *Academic Standards in Universities: Universities' Methods and Procedures for Maintaining and Monitoring Academic Standards in the Content of their Courses and in the Quality of their Teaching*. London: CVCP.

Committee on Higher Education (1963a) *Report*. London: HMSO, Cmnd 2154.

Committee on Higher Education (1963b) *Higher Education, Appendix Two: Students and their Education*. London: HMSO, Cmnd 2154 II (two volumes).

Committee on Higher Education (1963c) *Higher Education, Appendix Three: Teachers in Higher Education*. London: HMSO, Cmnd 2154 III.

Committee on Higher Education (1963d) *Evidence*. London: HMSO, Cmnd 2154.

Committee on Manpower Resources for Science and Technology (1967) *The Brain Drain: Report of the Working Group on Migration*. London: HMSO, Cmnd 3417.

Committee on Manpower Resources for Science and Technology (1968) *The Flow into Employment of Scientists, Engineers and Technologists*. London: HMSO, Cmnd 3760.

Committee on University Teaching Methods (1964) *Report*. London: HMSO.

Connor, H. (1994) Doctoral social scientists and the labour market, in R. Burgess (ed.) *Postgraduate Education and Training in the Social Sciences: Processes and Products*, pp. 167–81. London: Jessica Kingsley.

Connor, H., La Valle, I., Tackey, N. and Perryman, S. (1996) *Ethnic Minority Graduates: Differences by Degrees*. Brighton: Institute for Employment Studies.

Connor, H., Tyers, C., Davis, S. and Tackey, N. (2003) *Minority Ethnic Students in Higher Education: Interim Report*. Nottingham: Department for Education and Skills, Research Report 448.

Conole, G. and Oliver, M. (eds) (2007) *Contemporary Perspectives in e-Learning Research*. London: Routledge.

Cook, R., Butcher, I. and Raeside, R. (2006) Recounting the scores: an analysis of the QAA Subject Review grades 1995–2001, *Quality in Higher Education*, 12(2): 135–44.

Cormack, R., Gallagher, A. and Osborne, R. (1997) Higher education participation in Northern Ireland, *Higher Education Quarterly*, 51(1): 68–85.

Cornford, J. and Pollock, N. (2003) *Putting the University Online: Information, Technology and Organizational Change*. Buckingham: Open University Press.

Cotgrove, S. (1958) *Technical Education and Social Change*. London: George Allen & Unwin.

Council for National Academic Awards (1973) *Procedure for the Validation of Courses of Study*. London: CNAA.

Council for National Academic Awards (1979) *Developments in Partnership in Validation*. London: CNAA.

Council for National Academic Awards (1986) *Handbook 1986*. London: CNAA.

Council for Scientific Policy (1968) *Enquiry into the Flow of Candidates in Science and Technology into Higher Education*. London: HMSO, Cmnd 3541.

Court, S. (1996) The use of time by academic and related staff, *Higher Education Quarterly*, 50(4): 237–60.

Court, S. (1998) The research assessment exercise: the basis for a new gold standard in higher education? In D. Jary and M. Parker (ed.) *The New Higher Education: Issues and Directions for the Post-Dearing University*, pp. 115–32. Stoke-on-Trent: Staffordshire University Press.

Cownie, F. (2004) *Legal Academics: Culture and Identities*. Oxford: Hart Publishing.

Cox, R. (1967) Examinations and higher education: a survey of the literature, *Universities Quarterly*, 21(3): 292–340.

Cradden, C. (1998) 'Old' university academic staff salary movement since 1949, *Higher Education Quarterly*, 52(4): 394–412.

Craft, M. (1971) A broader role for colleges of education, in J. Tibble (ed.) (1971) *The Future of Teacher Education*, pp. 7–38. London: Routledge & Kegan Paul.

Cranmer, S. (2006) Enhancing graduate employability: best intentions and mixed outcomes, *Studies in Higher Education*, 31(2): 169–84.

Cross, M. and Jobling, R. (1969) The English New Universities: A Preliminary Enquiry, *Universities Quarterly*, 23(2): 172–82.

Crouch, C. (1970) *The Student Revolt*. London: The Bodley Head.

Crouch, C. (1972) Britain, in M. Archer (ed.) *Students, University and Society: A*

Comparative Sociological Review, pp. 196–211. London: Heinemann Educational Books.

Curran, P. (2000) Competition in UK higher education: competitive advantage in the research assessment exercise and Porter's diamond model, *Higher Education Quarterly*, 54(4): 386–410.

Curran, P. (2001) Competition in UK higher education: applying Porter's diamond model to geography departments, *Studies in Higher Education*, 26(2): 223–51.

Daiches, D. (ed.) (1964) *The Idea of a New University: An Experiment in Sussex*. London: Andre Deutsch.

Dainton, F. (1975) A note on science in higher education, in R. Niblett (ed.) *The Sciences, the Humanities and the Technological Threat*, pp. 36–41. London: University of London Press.

Dale, R. (1954) *From School to University: A Study, with Special Relevance to University Entrance*. London: Routledge & Kegan Paul.

Dale, R. (1959) University standards, *Universities Quarterly*, 13: 186–95.

Daniel, J. (1996) *Mega-universities and Knowledge Media: Technology Strategies for Higher Education*. London: Kogan Page.

Davie, G. (1961) *The Democratic Intellect: Scotland and her Universities in the Nineteenth Century*. Edinburgh: Edinburgh University Press.

Davies, C. and Holloway, P. (1995) Troubling transformations: gender regimes and organizational culture in the academy, in L. Morley and V. Walsh (eds) *Feminist Academics: Creative Agents for Change*, pp. 7–21. London: Taylor & Francis.

Davies, P. (1999) Half full, not half empty: a positive look at part-time higher education, *Higher Education Quarterly*, 53(2): 141–55.

Davies, P. and Parry, G. (1993) *Recognising Access: An Account of the Formation and Implementation of the National Framework for the Recognition of Access Courses*. Leicester: National Institute of Adult Continuing Education.

Davies, S. and Glaister, K. (1996) Spurs to higher things? Mission statements of UK universities, *Higher Education Quarterly*, 50(4): 261–94.

Davis, M. (1980) The CNAA as a validating agency, in D. Billing (ed.) *Indicators of Performance: Papers Presented at the Fifteenth Annual Conference of the Society for Research into Higher Education 1979*, pp. 31–42. Guildford: Society for Research into Higher Education.

Davis, M. (1990) Technology, institutions and status: technological education, debate and policy, 1944–1956, in P. Summerfield and E. Evans (eds) *Technical Education and the State since 1850: Historical and Contemporary Perspectives*, pp. 120–44. Manchester: Manchester University Press.

Dearlove, J. (1997) The academic labour process: from collegiality and professionalism to managerialism and proletarianisation? *Higher Education Review*, 30(1): 56–75.

Deem, R. (ed.) (1980) *Schooling for Women's Work*. London: Routledge & Kegan Paul.

Deem, R. (1999) Power and resistance in the academy: the case of women academic managers, in S. Whitehead and R. Moodley (eds) *Transforming Managers: Gendering Change in the Public Sector*, pp. 66–83. London: UCL Press.

Deem, R. and Brehony, K. (2005) Management as Ideology: the case of 'new managerialism' in higher education, *Oxford Review of Education*, 31(2): 217–35.

Deer, C. (2002) *Higher Education in England and France since the 1980s*. Oxford: Symposium Books.

Delamont, S. (1996) Just like the novels? Researching the occupational culture(s) of higher education, in R. Cuthbert (ed.) *Working in Higher Education*, pp. 145–56. Buckingham: Open University Press.

Delamont, S., Atkinson, P. and Parry, O. (1997) Critical mass and doctoral research: reflections on the Harris Report, *Studies in Higher Education*, 22(3): 319–31.

Delamont, S., Atkinson, P. and Parry, O. (2000) *The Doctoral Experience: Success and Failure in Graduate School*. London: Falmer.

Delanty, G. (2001) *Challenging Knowledge: The University in the Knowledge Society*. Buckingham: Open University Press.

Dent, H. (1954) *Growth in English Education 1946–1952*. London: Routledge & Kegan Paul.

Department for Education and Employment (1998a) *The Learning Age: Higher Education for the 21st Century. Response to the Dearing Report*. London: DfEE.

Department for Education and Employment (1998b) *The Learning Age: A Renaissance for a New Britain*. London: The Stationery Office, Cmnd 3790.

Department for Education and Skills (2003) *The Future of Higher Education*. Norwich: HMSO, Cmnd 5735.

Department of Education and Science (1966) *A Plan for Polytechnics and Other Colleges: Higher Education in the Further Education System*. London: HMSO, Cmnd 3006.

Department of Education and Science (1972) *Teacher Education and Training*. London: HMSO.

Department of Education and Science (1973) *Adult Education: A Plan for Development – Report of a Committee of Inquiry Appointed by the Secretary of State for Education and Science under the Chairmanship of Lionel Russell*. London: HMSO.

Department of Education and Science (1978) *Higher Education into the 1990s: A Discussion Document*. London: HMSO.

Department of Education and Science (1980) *Continuing Education: Post-experience Vocational Provision for those in Employment*. London: DES.

Department of Education and Science (1984) *Demand for Higher Education in Great Britain 1984–2000*. London: DES, Report on Education No. 100.

Department of Education and Science (1985) *The Development of Higher Education into the 1990s*. London: HMSO, Cmnd 9524.

Department of Education and Science (1986) *Projections of Demand for Higher Education in Great Britain 1986–2000*. London: HMSO.

Department of Education and Science (1987) *Higher Education: Meeting the Challenge*. London: HMSO, Cmnd 114.

Department of Education and Science (1988) *Top-up Loans for Students*. London: HMSO, Cmnd 520.

Department of Education and Science (1989) *Universities in the Training Market: An Evaluation of the University Grants Committee PICKUP Selective Funding Scheme*. London: DES.

Department of Education and Science (1991a) *Education and Training for the 21st Century*. London: HMSO, Cmnd 1536 (two volumes).

Department of Education and Science (1991b) *Higher Education: A New Framework*. London: HMSO, Cmnd 1541.

Department of Education and Science/Open University (1991) *Review of the Open University*. Milton Keynes: The Open University.

Dobson, J. (1973) The training colleges and their successors 1920–1970, in T. Cook (ed.) *Education and the Professions*, pp. 49–68. London: Methuen.

Dolton, P. and Makepeace, G. (1982) University typology: a contemporary analysis, *Higher Education Review*, 14(3): 33–47.

Donaldson, L. (1975) *Policy and the Polytechnics: Pluralistic Drift in Higher Education.* Farnborough: Saxon House.

Dyhouse, C. (1995) *No Distinction of Sex? Women in British Universities, 1870–1939.* London: UCL Press.

Dyhouse, C. (2006) *Students: A Gendered History.* London: Routledge.

Economic and Social Research Council (1987) *The Social Science PhD: The ESRC Inquiry on Submission Rates.* London: ESRC.

Edwards, B. (2000) *University Architecture.* London: Spon Press.

Edwards, R. (1993) *Mature Women Students: Separating or Connecting Family and Education.* London: Taylor & Francis.

Egerton, M. and Halsey, A. (1993) Trends by Social Class and Gender in Access to Higher Education, *Oxford Review of Education,* 19(2): 183–97.

Ellis, T. (1935) *The Development of Higher Education in Wales.* Wrexham: Hughes & Son.

Elsey, B. (1990) Teaching and learning, in M. Kinnell (ed.) *The Learning Experiences of Overseas Students,* pp. 46–62. Buckingham: Open University Press.

Elton, L. (1998) Are UK Degree Standards Going Up, Down or Sideways? *Studies in Higher Education,* 23(1): 35–42.

Enders, J. (2001) Between state control and academic capitalism: a comparative perspective on academic staff in Europe, in J. Enders (ed.) *Academic Staff in Europe: Changing Contexts and Conditions,* pp. 1–23. Westport, CT: Greenwood Press.

Evans, C. (1988) *Language People: The Experience of Teaching and Learning Modern Languages in British Universities.* Milton Keynes: Open University Press.

Evans, C. (1993) *English People: The Experience of Teaching and Learning English in British Universities.* Buckingham: Open University Press.

Farish, M., McPake, J., Powney, J. and Weiner, G. (1995) *Equal Opportunities in Colleges and Universities: Towards Better Practices.* Buckingham: Open University Press.

Ferguson, J. (1975) *The Open University From Within.* London: University of London Press.

Fieldhouse, R. (1996) University adult education, in R. Fieldhouse, P. Baynes, R. Benn, W. Drews, J. Field, B. Groombridge, M. Hamilton, J. McIlroy, H. Marks, I. Martin, N. Sargant and V. Fieldhouse *A History of Modern British Adult Education,* pp. 199–238. Leicester: National Institute of Adult Continuing Education.

Fitzpatrick, J., While, A. and Roberts, J. (1993) The Relationship between Nursing and Higher Education, *Journal of Advanced Nursing,* 18: 1488–97.

Flexner, A. ([1930] 1994) *Universities: American, English, German.* New Brunswick, NJ: Transaction Publishers.

Floud, J. (1954) The educational experience of the adult population of England and Wales as at July 1949, in D. Glass (ed.) *Social Mobility in Britain,* pp. 98–140. London: Routledge & Kegan Paul.

Foden, F. (1989) *The Examiner: James Booth and the Origin of Common Examinations.* Leeds: University of Leeds Departments of Adult & Continuing Education.

Ford, J., Bosworth, D. and Wilson, R. (1995) Part-time work and full-time higher education, *Studies in Higher Education,* 20(2): 187–202.

Forsyth, A. and Furlong, A. (2003) Access to higher education and disadvantaged young people, *British Educational Research Journal,* 29(2): 205–25.

Franks, L. (1963) *British Business Schools.* London: British Institute of Management.

Fraser, R., Bertraux, D., Eynon, B., Grele, R., le Wita, B., Linhart, D., Passerini, L., Staadt, J. and Troger, A. (1988) *1968: A Student Generation in Revolt.* London: Chatto & Windus.

Frayling, C., Physick, J., Watson, H. and Myers, B. (1987) *The Royal College of Art: One Hundred and Fifty Years of Art and Design*. London: Barrie & Jenkins.

Freire, P. (1972) *Pedagogy of the Oppressed*. Translated by M. Ramer. Harmondsworth: Penguin.

Fuller, M., Healey, M., Bradley, A. and Hall, T. (2004) Barriers to learning: a systematic study of the experience of disabled students in one university, *Studies in Higher Education*, 29(3): 303–18.

Fulton, O. (1988) Elite survivals? Entry 'standards' and procedures for higher education admissions, *Studies in Higher Education*, 13(1): 15–25.

Fulton, O. (1990) Higher education and employment: pressures and responses since 1960, in P. Summerfield and E. Evans (eds) *Technical Education and the State since 1850: Historical and Contemporary Perspectives*, pp. 145–70. Manchester: Manchester University Press.

Fulton, O. (1996) The academic profession in England on the eve of structural reform, in P. Altbach (ed.) *The International Academic Profession: Portraits of Fourteen Countries*, pp. 391–437. Princeton, NJ: Carnegie Foundation for the Advancement of Teaching.

Fulton, O. and Holland, C. (2001) Profession or proletariat: academic staff in the United Kingdom after two decades of change, in J. Enders (ed.) *Academic Staff in Europe: Changing Contexts and Conditions*, pp. 301–22. Westport, CT: Greenwood Press.

Furlong, J., Barton, L., Miles, S., Whiting, C. and Whitty, G. (2000) *Teacher Education in Transition: Re-forming Professionalism?* Buckingham: Open University Press.

Furneaux, W. (1961) *The Chosen Few: An Examination of Some Aspects of University Selection in Britain*. London: Oxford University Press.

Furneaux, W. (1963) The two few chosen, and the many that could be called, in P. Halmos (ed.) *The Sociological Review Monograph No. 7: Sociological Studies in British University Education*, pp. 59–78. Keele: University of Keele.

Gallacher, J. (2006) Widening access or differentiation and stratification in higher education in Scotland, *Higher Education Quarterly*, 60(4): 349–69.

Gallie, W. (1960) *A New University: A D Lindsay and the Keele Experiment*. London: Chatto & Windus.

Galvin, C. (1996) A promotion of teacher professionality: higher education and initial teacher education in England and Wales, *Studies in Higher Education*, 21(1): 81–92.

Gibbons, M., Limoges, C., Nowotny, H., Schwartzman, S., Scott, P. and Trow, M. (1994) *The New Production of Knowledge: The Dynamics of Science and Research in Contemporary Societies*. London: Sage Publications.

Gibbs, G. and Jenkins, A. (eds) (1992) *Teaching Large Classes in Higher Education: How to Maintain Quality with Reduced Resources*. London: Kogan Page.

Glatter, R., Wedell, E., Harris, W. and Subramanian, S. (1971) *Study by Correspondence: An Enquiry into Correspondence Study for Examinations for Degrees and Other Advanced Qualifications*. London: Longman.

Goddard, J., Charles, D., Pike, A., Potts, G. and Bradley, D. (1994) *Universities and Communities*. London: Committee of Vice-Chancellors and Principals.

Goldman, L. (1995) *Dons and Workers: Oxford and Adult Education since 1850*. Oxford: Clarendon Press.

Goode, J. (2000) Is the position of women in higher education changing? In M. Tight (ed.) *Academic Work and Life: What it is to be an Academic, and How this is Changing*, pp. 243–84. Oxford: Elsevier Science.

Goode, J. and Bagilhole, B. (1998) Gendering the management of change in higher education: a case study, *Gender, Work and Organization,* 5(3): 148–64.

Gosden, P. (1983) *The Education System since 1944.* Oxford: Martin Robertson.

Gray, H. (ed.) (1999) *Universities and the Creation of Wealth.* Buckingham: Open University Press.

Green, V. (1969) *The Universities.* Harmondsworth: Penguin.

Green, V. (1974) *A History of Oxford University.* London: Batsford.

Group for Research and Innovation in Higher Education (1976) *The Container Revolution: A Study of Unit and Modular Schemes.* London: Nuffield Foundation.

Gunn, A. (1978) Helping the handicapped: university education for the disabled, in D. Billing (ed.) *Course Design and Student Learning: Papers Presented at the Society's Thirteenth Annual Conference 1977,* pp. 23–31. Guildford: Society for Research into Higher Education.

Halsey, A. (1982) The decline of donnish dominion? *Oxford Review of Education,* 8(3): 21–35.

Halsey, A. (1995) *Decline of Donnish Dominion: The British Academic Professions in the Twentieth Century,* 2nd edn. Oxford: Clarendon.

Halsey, A., Heath, A. and Ridge, J. (1980) *Origins and Destinations: Family, Class and Education in Modern Britain.* Oxford: Clarendon Press.

Halsey, A., Trow, M. and Fulton, O. (1971) *The British Academics.* London: Faber & Faber.

Halvorsen, E. (2002) Gender audit, in G. Howie and A. Tauchert (eds) *Gender, Teaching and Research in Higher Education: Challenges for the 21st Century,* pp. 9–19. Aldershot: Ashgate.

Hannan, A., English, S. and Silver, H. (1999) Why innovate? Some preliminary findings from a research project on 'Innovations in Teaching and Learning in Higher Education', *Studies in Higher Education,* 24(3): 279–89.

Hannan, A. and Silver, H. (2000) *Innovating in Higher Education: Teaching, Learning and Institutional Cultures.* Buckingham: Open University Press.

Harrison, M. (1994) Quality issues in higher education: a post-modern phenomenon? In G. Doherty (ed.) *Developing Quality Systems in Education,* pp. 52–67. London: Routledge.

Harrop, S. (ed.) (1987) *Oxford and Working-class Education.* Nottingham: University of Nottingham, Department of Adult Education.

Harte, N. (1986) *The University of London 1836–1986.* London: Athlone Press.

Harvey, L., Moon, S. and Geall, V. (1997) *Graduates' Work: organisational change and students' attributes.* Birmingham: University of Central England, Centre for Research into Quality.

Hayes, D. and Wynyard, R. (eds) (2002) *The McDonaldization of Higher Education.* Westport, CT: Bergin and Garvey.

Hearn, J. (1999) Men, managers and management: the case of higher education, in S. Whitehead and R. Moodley (eds) *Transforming Managers: Gendering Change in the Public Sector,* pp. 123–44. London: UCL Press.

Hencke, D. (1978) *Colleges in Crisis: The Reorganization of Teacher Training 1971–7.* Harmondsworth: Penguin.

Henkel, M. (2000) *Academic Identities and Policy Change in Higher Education.* London: Jessica Kingsley.

Henkel, M. and Kogan, M. (1993) Research training and graduate education: the British macro structure, in B. Clark (ed.) *The Research Foundations of Graduate*

Education: Germany, Britain, France, United States, Japan, pp. 71–114. Berkeley, CA: University of California Press.

Her Majesty's Inspectors (1992) *A Survey of the Enterprise in Higher Education Initiative in Fifteen Polytechnics and Colleges of Higher Education, September 1989–March 1991.* London: Department of Education and Science.

Heward, C. (1996) Women and careers in higher education: what is the problem? In L. Morley and V. Walsh (eds) *Breaking Boundaries: Women in Higher Education,* pp. 11–23. London: Taylor & Francis.

Heward, C. and Taylor, P. (1992) Women at the top in higher education: equal opportunities policies in action? *Policy and Politics,* 20(2): 111–21.

Heward, C., Taylor, P. and Vickers, R. (1997) Gender, race and career success in the academic profession, *Journal of Further and Higher Education,* 21(2): 205–18.

Hewett, S. (1972) The future of the colleges of education, in J. Lawlor (ed.) *Higher Education: Patterns of Change in the 1970s,* pp. 17–34. London: Routledge & Kegan Paul.

Heyck, T. (1987) The Idea of a University in Britain, 1870–1970, *History of European Ideas,* 8(2): 205–19.

Heywood, J. (1971) A report on student wastage, *Universities Quarterly,* 25(2): 189–237.

Hicks, D. (1974) The National Advisory Council on the Training and Supply of Teachers 1949–1965, *British Journal of Educational Studies,* 22(3): 249–60.

Higher Education Funding Council for England (1996a) *Widening Access to Higher Education: A Report by the HEFCE's Advisory Group on Access and Participation.* Bristol: HEFCE.

Higher Education Funding Council for England (1996b) *Review of Postgraduate Education.* Bristol: HEFCE (two volumes).

Higher Education Funding Council for England (2000) *Diversity in Higher Education: HEFCE Policy Statement.* Bristol: HEFCE.

Higher Education Quality Council (1994) *Choosing to Change: Extending Access. Choice and Mobility in Higher Education. The Report of the HEQC CAT Development Project.* London: HEQC.

Higher Education Quality Council (1995) *The Work of the Higher Education Quality Council.* London: HEQC.

Higher Education Quality Council (1996a) *Academic Standards in the Approval, Review and Classification of Degrees.* London: HEQC.

Higher Education Quality Council (1996b) *Guidelines on the Quality Assurance of Research Degrees.* London: HEQC.

Higher Education Quality Council (1996c) *Inter-institutional Variability of Degree Results: An Analysis in Selected Subjects.* London: HEQC.

Higher Education Quality Council (1997) *Graduate Standards Programme: Final Report.* London: HEQC (two volumes).

Himmelweit, H. (1963) Student selection: implications derived from two student selection enquiries, in P. Halmos (ed.) *The Sociological Review Monograph No. 7: Sociological Studies in British University Education,* pp. 79–98. Keele: University of Keele.

Hoare, A. (1991) Reviewing the reviews: the geography of university rationalisation, *Higher Education Quarterly,* 45(3): 234–53.

Hofstetter, M. (2001) *The Romantic Idea of a University: England and Germany, 1770–1850.* Basingstoke: Palgrave.

Hopper, E. and Osborn, M. (1975) *Adult Students: Education Selection and Social Control.* London: Pinter.

Hordley, I. and Lee, D. (1970) The 'alternative route': social change and opportunity in technical education, *Sociology*, 4: 23–50.

Howie, G. and Tauchert, A. (eds) (2002) *Gender, Teaching and Research in Higher Education: Challenges for the 21st Century*. Aldershot: Ashgate.

Huisman, J., Meek, L. and Wood, F. (2007) Institutional diversity in higher education: a cross-national and longitudinal analysis, *Higher Education Quarterly*, 61 (4): 563–77.

Hunter, L. (1981) Employers' perceptions of demand, in R. Lindley (ed.) *Higher Education and the Labour Market*, pp. 4–48. Guildford: Society for Research into Higher Education.

Hurst, A. (1993) *Steps Towards Graduation: Access to Higher Education for People with Disabilities*. Aldershot: Avebury.

Husbands, C. (1998) Assessing the extent of use of part-time teachers in British higher education: problems and issues in enumerating a flexible labour force, *Higher Education Quarterly*, 52 (3): 257–82.

Hutchings, D. (1967) *The Science Undergraduate: A Study of Science Students at Five English Universities*. Oxford: University of Oxford Department of Education.

Illich, I. (1973) *Deschooling Society*. Harmondsworth: Penguin.

Ince, M. (1986) *The Politics of British Science*. Brighton: Wheatsheaf Books.

Independent Committee of Inquiry into Student Finance (1999) *Student Finance: Fairness for the Future*. Edinburgh: The Stationery Office.

Inter-University Council for Higher Education Overseas (1955) *Inter-University Council for Higher Education Overseas 1946–54*. London: HMSO, Cmnd 9515.

Jackson, B. and Marsden, D. (1966) *Education and the Working Class: Some General Themes Raised by a Study of 88 Working-class Children in a Northern Industrial City* revised edn. Harmondsworth: Penguin.

Jackson, D. (1990) Women working in higher education: a review of the position of women in higher education and policy developments, *Higher Education Quarterly*, 44 (4): 297–324.

Jahoda, M. (1963) *The Education of Technologists: An Exploratory Case Study at Brunel*. London: Tavistock.

Jaspers, K. ([1959] 1960) *The Idea of the University*. London: Peter Owen Translated from the German by H. Reiche and H. Vanderschmidt.

Jenkins, A., Jones, L. and Ward, A. (2001) The long-term effect of a degree on graduate lives, *Studies in Higher Education*, 26 (2): 147–61.

Jepson, N. (1973) *The Beginnings of English University Adult Education: Policy and Problems. A Critical Study of the Early Cambridge and Oxford University Extension Lecture Movements between 1873 and 1907, with Special Reference to Yorkshire*. London: Michael Joseph.

Jessup, G. (1991) *Outcomes: NVQs and the Emerging Model of Education and Training*. London: Falmer Press.

Jevons, F. (1972) New university courses: breadth and balance, in F. Jevons and H. Turner (eds) *What Kind of Graduates do we Need?*, pp. 95–105. London: Oxford University Press.

Jobling, R. (1972) The new universities, in H. Butcher and E. Rudd (eds) *Contemporary Problems in Higher Education: An Account of Research*, pp. 325–34. London: McGraw-Hill.

Johnes, G. and McNabb, R. (2004) Never give up on the good times: student attrition in the UK, *Oxford Bulletin of Economics and Statistics*, 66 (1): 23–47.

Johnes, J. (1992) The potential effects of wider access to higher education on degree quality, *Higher Education Quarterly*, 46 (1): 88–107.

Johnes, J. and Taylor, J. (1990) *Performance Indicators in Higher Education.* Buckingham: Open University Press.

Johnes, J. and Taylor, J. (1992) The 1989 Research Selectivity Exercise: a statistical analysis of differences in research rating between universities at the cost centre level, *Higher Education Quarterly,* 46(1): 67–87.

Jones, C. (2008) *The People's University: 150 years of the University of London and its External Students.* London: University of London External System.

Jones, D. (1988) *The Origins of Civic Universities: Manchester, Leeds and Liverpool.* London: Routledge.

Jones, K. (1963) *A Review of University Social Studies Departments.* Manchester: University of Manchester.

Jones, S. (1996) Managing Curriculum Development: A Case Study of Enterprise in Higher Education, in J. Brennan, M. Kogan and U. Teichler (eds) *Higher Education and Work,* pp. 136–60. London: Jessica Kingsley.

Jones, S. and Little, B. (1999) Higher education curricula in the UK: the pushme-pullyou effects, in M. Henkel and B. Little (eds) *Changing Relationships between Higher Education and the State,* pp. 125–41. London: Jessica Kingsley.

Kay, R. (1985) *UCCA: Its Origins and Development 1950–85.* Cheltenham: Universities Central Council on Admissions.

Keen, C. and Higgins, T. (1990) *Young People's Knowledge of Higher Education: Findings of a Research Programme into the Perceptions of 'Traditional' Applicants.* Mansfield: Higher Education Information Services Trust (HEIST).

Kelly, T. (1970) *A History of Adult Education in Great Britain,* 2nd edn. Liverpool: Liverpool University Press.

Kelsall, K. (1957) *Report of an Inquiry into Applications for Admission to Universities.* London: Association of Universities of the British Commonwealth.

Kelsall, K., Poole, A. and Kuhn, A. (1970) *Six Years After: First Report on a National Follow-up Survey of Ten Thousand Graduates of British universities in 1960.* Sheffield: Sheffield University Department of Sociological Studies.

Kelsall, K., Poole, A. and Kuhn, A. (1972) *Graduates: The Sociology of an Elite.* London: Methuen.

Ker, I. (1999) Newman's *Idea of a University:* a guide for the contemporary university? In D. Smith and A. Langslow (eds) *The Idea of a University,* pp. 11–29. London: Jessica Kingsley.

Kerr, C. ([1963] 2001) *The Uses of the University,* 5th edn. Cambridge, MA: Harvard University Press.

King, J. (1970) The typology of universities, *Higher Education Review,* 2(3): 52–61.

Kingdon, M. (1991) *The Reform of Advanced Level.* London: Hodder & Stoughton.

Kinman, G., Jones, F. and Kinman, R. (2006) The well-being of the UK Academy, 1998–2004, *Quality in Higher Education,* 12(1): 15–27.

Kinnell, M. (ed.) (1990) *The Learning Experiences of Overseas Students.* Buckingham: Open University Press.

Klug, B. (1977) *The Grading Game.* London: NUS Publications.

Knight, P. (ed.) (1997) *Masterclass: Learning, Teaching and Curriculum in Taught Master's Degrees.* London: Cassell.

Knight, P. and Trowler, P. (2001) *Departmental Leadership in Higher Education.* Buckingham: Open University Press.

Kogan, M. (2002) The role of different groups in policy-making and implementation: institutional politics and policy-making, in P. Trowler (ed.) *Higher Education*

Policy and Institutional Change: Intentions and Outcomes in Turbulent Environments, pp. 46–63. Buckingham: Open University Press.

Kogan, M. and Hanney, S. (2000) *Reforming Higher Education.* London: Jessica Kingsley.

Kogan, M. and Kogan, D. (1983) *The Attack on Higher Education.* London: Kogan Page.

Kogan, M., Moses, I. and El-Khawas, E. (1994) *Staffing Higher Education: Meeting New Challenges.* London: Jessica Kingsley.

Kolsaker, A. (2008) Academic professionalism in the managerialist era: a study of English universities, *Studies in Higher Education,* 33(5): 513–25.

Lambert, R. (2003) *Lambert Review of Business-University Collaboration Final Report.* London: HM Treasury.

Lane, M. (1975) *Design for Degrees: New Degree Courses under the CNAA 1964–1974.* London: Macmillan.

Lawton, D. (1992) *Education and Politics in the 1990s: Conflict or Consensus?* London: Falmer Press.

Layard, R., King, J. and Moser, C. (1969) *The Impact of Robbins.* Harmondsworth: Penguin.

Leavis, F. ([1943] 1948) *Education and the University: A Sketch for an 'English School'.* London: Chatto & Windus.

Leonard, M. (1995) Labouring to learn: students' debt and term time employment in Belfast, *Higher Education Quarterly,* 49(3): 229–47.

Livingstone, H. (1974) *The University: An Organizational Analysis.* Glasgow: Blackie.

Locke, M., Pratt, J. and Burgess, T. (1985) *The Colleges of Higher Education 1972 to 1982: The Central Management of Organic Change.* London: Critical Press.

Locke, R. (1989) *Management and Higher Education since 1940: The Influence of America and Japan on West Germany, Great Britain and France.* New York: Cambridge University Press.

Lockwood, G. (1985a) Universities as organizations, in G. Lockwood and J. Davies (eds) (1985) *Universities: The Management Challenge,* pp. 24–45. Windsor: NFER-Nelson.

Lockwood, G. (1985b) Planning, in G. Lockwood, and J. Davies, (eds) (1985) *Universities: The Management Challenge,* pp. 164–88. Windsor: NFER-Nelson.

Logan, D. (1971) *The University of London: An Introduction,* 3rd edn. London: Athlone.

Lowe, R. (1987) Structural change in English higher education, 1870–1920, in D. Muller, F. Ringer and B. Simon (eds) *The Rise of the Modern Educational System: Structural Change and Social Reproduction 1870–1920,* pp. 163–251. Cambridge: Cambridge University Press.

Lowe, R. (1988) *Education in the Post-war Years: A Social History.* London: Routledge.

Lucas, C. (1994) *American Higher Education: A History.* New York: St Martin's Press.

Lucas, L. (2006) *The Research Game in Academic Life.* Maidenhead: Open University Press.

Lukes, J. (1967) The binary policy: a critical study, *Universities Quarterly,* 22(1): 6–46.

Lunneborg, P. (1994) *OU Women: Undoing Educational Obstacles.* London: Cassell.

Lynch, J. (1979) *The Reform of Teacher Education in the United Kingdom.* Guildford: Society for Research into Higher Education.

Macdonald, S. (1970) *The History and Philosophy of Art Education.* London: University of London Press.

Macfarlane, B. (2006) *The Academic Citizen: The Virtue of Service in University Life.* London: Routledge.

Maiworm, F., Steube, W. and Teichler, U. (1991) *Learning in Europe: The ERASMUS Experience.* London: Jessica Kingsley.

Maiworm, F. and Teichler, U. (1996) *Study Abroad and Early Career: Experiences of Former ERASMUS Students*. London: Jessica Kingsley.

Malina, D. and Maslin-Prothero, S. (eds) (1998) *Surviving the Academy: Feminist Perspectives*. London: Falmer.

Malleson, N. (1958) Student performance at University College, London, 1948–1951, *Universities Quarterly*, 12(3): 288–319.

Mann, P. (1974) *Students and Books*. London: Routledge & Kegan Paul.

Manpower Services Commission (1987) *Enterprise in Higher Education*. Sheffield: MSC.

Marks, A. (2005) Changing spatial and synchronous structures in the history and culture of learning: a Heideggerian analysis of the history of the English university, *Higher Education*, 50: 613–30.

Marriott, S. (1981) *A Backstairs to a Degree: Demands for an Open University in Late Victorian England*. Leeds: University of Leeds Department of Adult Education and Extramural Studies.

Marriott, S. (1984) *Extramural Empires: Service and Self-interest in English University Adult Education*. Nottingham: University of Nottingham Department of Adult Education.

Marris, P. (1964) *The Experience of Higher Education*. London: Routledge & Kegan Paul.

Martin, E. (1999) *Changing Academic Work: Developing the Learning University*. Buckingham: Open University Press.

Maskell, D. and Robinson, I. (2001) *The New Idea of a University*. London: Haven Books.

Matterson, A. (1981) *Polytechnics and Colleges*. London: Longman.

Maxwell, I. (1980) *Universities in Partnership: The Inter-University Council and the Growth of Higher Education in Developing Countries 1946–70*. Edinburgh: Scottish Academic Press.

Mayhew, K., Deer, C. and Dua, M. (2004) The move to mass higher education in the UK: many questions and some answers, *Oxford Review of Education*, 30(1): 65–82.

McDowell, R. and Webb, D. (1982) *Trinity College Dublin 1592–1952: An Academic History*. Cambridge: Cambridge University Press.

McIntosh, N., Calder, J. and Swift, B. (1976) *A Degree of Difference: A Study of the First Year's Intake of Students to the Open University of the United Kingdom*. Guildford: Society for Research into Higher Education.

McKinlay, R. (1991) *The University of Bradford: Origins and Development*. Bradford: Bradford University Press.

McNay, I. (1995) From the collegial academy to corporate enterprise: the changing cultures of universities, in T. Schuller (ed.) *The Changing University?*, pp. 105–15. Buckingham: Open University Press.

McNay, I. (1997) The impact of the 1992 Research Assessment Exercise in English Universities, *Higher Education Review*, 29(2): 34–43.

McNay, I. (2003) Assessing the assessment: an analysis of the UK Research Assessment Exercise 2001, and its outcomes, with special reference to research in education, *Science and Public Policy*, 30(1): 47–54.

McPherson, A. (1973) Selections and survivals: a sociology of the ancient Scottish universities, in R. Brown (ed.) *Knowledge, Education and Cultural Change*, pp. 163–201. London: Tavistock.

McPherson, R. (1959) *Theory of Higher Education in Nineteenth-century England*. Athens, GA: University of Georgia Press.

Meehan, D. (1999) The under-representation of women managers in higher education: are there issues other than style? In S. Whitehead and R. Moodley (eds)

Transforming Managers: Gendering Change in the Public Sector, pp. 33–49. London: UCL Press.

Melville, H. (1962) *The Department of Scientific and Industrial Research*. London: George Allen & Unwin.

Metcalf, H. (1993) *Non-traditional Students' Experience of Higher Education: A Review of the Literature*. London: Committee of Vice-Chancellors and Principals.

Metcalf, H. (1997) *Class and Higher Education: The Participation of Young People from Lower Social Classes*. London: Council for Industry and Higher Education.

Middlehurst, R. (1993) *Leading Academics*. Buckingham: Open University Press.

Miller, C. and Parlett, M. (1974) *Up to the Mark: A Study of the Examination Game*. London: Society for Research into Higher Education.

Miller, G. (1970) *Success, Failure and Wastage in Higher Education: An Overview of the Problem Derived from Research and Theory*. London: Harrap.

Millerson, G. (1964) *The Qualifying Associations: A Study in Professionalization*. London: Routledge & Kegan Paul.

Millerson, G. (1973) Education in the professions, in T. Cook (ed.) *Education and the Professions*, pp. 1–18. London: Methuen.

Ministry of Education (1950) *Challenge and Response: An Account of the Emergency Scheme for the Training of Teachers*. London: HMSO, Ministry of Education pamphlet no. 17.

Ministry of Education (1956) *Technical Education*. London: HMSO, Cmnd 9703.

Ministry of Education (1960) *Grants to Students*. London: HMSO, Cmnd 1051.

Minogue, K. (1973) *The Concept of a University*. London: Weidenfeld & Nicolson.

Mirza, H. (1995) Black women in higher education: defining a space/finding a place, in L. Morley and V. Walsh (eds) *Feminist Academics: Creative Agents for Change*, pp. 145–55. London: Taylor & Francis.

Moberly, W. (1949) *The Crisis in the University*. London: SCM Press.

Modood, T. and Acland, T. (1998) Conclusion, in T. Modood and T. Acland (eds) *Race and Higher Education: Experiences, Challenges and Policy Implications*, pp. 158–73. London: Policy Studies Institute.

Modood, T. and Shiner, M. (1994) *Ethnic Minorities and Higher Education: Why are they Differential Rates of Entry?* London: Policy Studies Institute.

Montgomery, R. (1965) *Examinations: An Account of their Evolution as Administrative Devices in England*. London: Longmans, Green and Co.

Moodie, G. (1983) Buffer, coupling and broker: reflections on 60 years of the UGC, *Higher Education*, 12(3): 331–47.

Moodie, G. and Eustace, R. (1974) *Power and Authority in British Universities*. London: George Allen & Unwin.

Moody, T. and Beckett, J. (1959) *Queen's, Belfast 1845–1949: The History of a University*. London: Faber & Faber (two volumes).

Moreau, M.-P. and Leathwood, C. (2006) Balancing paid work and studies: working (-class) students in higher education, *Studies in Higher Education*, 31(1): 23–42.

Morgan, D. and McDowell, L. (1979) *Patterns of Residence: Costs and Options in Student Housing*. Guildford: Society for Research into Higher Education.

Morley, L. (1994) Glass ceiling or iron cage: women in UK academia, *Gender, Work and Organization*, 1(4): 194–204.

Morley, L. and Walsh, V. (eds) (1995) *Feminist Academics: Creative Agents for Change*. London: Taylor & Francis.

Morley, L. and Walsh, V. (eds) (1996) *Breaking Boundaries: Women in Higher Education*. London: Taylor & Francis.

Mosson, T. (1965) *Management Education in Five European Countries*. London: Business Publications Ltd.

Mountford, J. (1957) *How They Fared: A Survey of a Three-year Student Entry*. Liverpool: Liverpool University Press.

Mountford, J. (1966) *British Universities*. London: Oxford University Press.

Mountford, J. (1972) *Keele: An Historical Critique*. London: Routledge & Kegan Paul.

Muthesius, S. (2000) *The Postwar University: Utopianist Campus and College*. New Haven, CT: Yale University Press.

National Advisory Body (1984a) *Report of the Continuing Education Group*. London: NAB.

National Advisory Body (1984b) *A Strategy for Higher Education in the Late 1980s and beyond*. London: NAB.

National Audit Office (2007) *Staying the Course: The Retention of Students in Higher Education*. London: The Stationery Office, HC 616.

National Committee of Inquiry into Higher Education (NCIHE) (1997a) *Higher Education in the Learning Society: Report of the National Committee*. Norwich: HMSO.

National Committee of Inquiry into Higher Education (1997b) *Higher Education in the Learning Society: Summary Report*. Norwich: HMSO.

Newfield, J. (1963) Some factors related to the academic performance of British university students, in P. Halmos (ed.) *The Sociological Review Monograph No. 7: Sociological Studies in British University Education*, pp. 117–30. Keele: University of Keele.

Newman, J. ([1852] 1976) *The Idea of a University Defined and Illustrated*. Oxford: Clarendon Press. Edited by I. Ker.

Niblett, R., Humphreys, D. and Fairhurst, J. (1975) *The University Connection*. Slough: NFER.

Noble, P. (1956) The 'redbrick' universities, *Twentieth Century*, 159: 99–111.

Nowotny, H., Scott, P. and Gibbons, M. (2001) *Re-thinking Science: Knowledge and the Public in an Age of Uncertainty*. Cambridge: Polity.

Nuffield College (1948) *The Problem Facing British Universities*. London: Oxford University Press.

Nuffield Foundation (1975) *The Drift of Change: An Interim Report of the Group for Research and Innovation in Higher Education*. London: Nuffield Foundation.

Nwauwa, A. (1996) *Imperialism, Academe and Nationalism: Britain and University Education for Africans, 1860–1960*. Portland, OR: Frank Cass.

Oakeshott, M. (1948) The universities, *The Cambridge Journal*, 2: 515–42.

Open University (1972) *The Early Development of the Open University: Report of the Vice-Chancellor, January 1969–December 1970*. Bletchley: Open University.

Open University Planning Committee (1969) *Report to the Secretary of State for Education and Science*. London: HMSO.

Opper, S., Teichler, U. and Carlson, J. (1990) *Impact of Study Abroad Programmes on Students and Graduates*. London: Jessica Kingsley.

Organization for Economic Co-operation and Development (1999) *The Response of Higher Education Institutions to Regional Needs*. Paris: OECD.

Ortega y Gasset, J. (1946) *Mission of the University*. London: Kegan Paul, Trench, Trubner & Co. Translated by H. Nostrand.

Osborne, R. (2006) Access to and participation in higher education in Northern Ireland, *Higher Education Quarterly*, 60(4): 333–48.

Oshagbemi, T. (1996) Job satisfaction of UK academics, *Educational Management and Administration*, 24(4): 389–400.

Owen, T. (1980) The University Grants Committee, *Oxford Review of Education*, 6(3): 255–78.

Papatsiba, V. (2005) Student mobility in Europe: an academic, cultural and mental journey? Some conceptual reflections and empirical findings, in M. Tight (ed.) *International Relations*, pp. 29–65. Oxford: Elsevier.

Parker, M. (2004) Becoming manager: or the werewolf looks in the mirror, checking for signs of unusual facial hair, *Management Learning*, 35(1): 45–59.

Parker, M. and Jary, D. (1995) The McUniversity: organization, management and academic subjectivity, *Organization*, 2(2): 319–38.

Parry, G. (1997) Patterns of participation in higher education in England: a statistical summary and commentary, *Higher Education Quarterly*, 51(1): 6–28.

Parry, G. (2003) Mass higher education and the English: wherein the colleges? *Higher Education Quarterly*, 57(4): 308–37.

Parry, G. (2006) Policy-participation trajectories in English higher education, *Higher Education Quarterly*, 60(4): 392–412.

Parry, G. and Thompson, A. (2002) *Closer by Degrees: The Past, Present and Future of Higher Education in Further Education Colleges*. London: Learning and Skills Development Agency.

Parry, O., Atkinson, P. and Delamont, S. (1994) Disciplinary identities and doctoral work, in R. Burgess (ed.) *Postgraduate Education and Training in the Social Sciences: Processes and Products*, pp. 34–52. London: Jessica Kingsley.

Pascall, G. and Cox, R. (1993) *Women Returning to Higher Education*. Buckingham: Open University Press.

Paterson, L. (1997) Trends in higher education participation in Scotland, *Higher Education Quarterly*, 51(1): 29–48.

Pattison, B. (1984) *Special Relations: The University of London and New Universities Overseas, 1947–1970*. London: University of London.

Pearson, R., Seccombe, I., Pike, G. and Connor, H. (1993) Employer demand for doctoral social scientists, *Studies in Higher Education*, 18(1): 95–104.

Peers, R. and Madgwick, P. (1963) Problems and attitudes in higher technological education, *Vocational Aspect of Education*, 15: 71–91.

Pemberton, J. and Pemberton, J. (1979) *The University College at Buckingham: A First Account of its Conception, Foundation and Early Years*. Buckingham: Buckingham Press.

Percy, K., Ramsden, P. and Lewin, J. (1980) *Independent Study: Two Examples from English Higher Education*. Guildford: Society for Research into Higher Education.

Percy, K. and Salter, F. (1976) Student and staff perceptions and 'the pursuit of excellence' in British higher education, *Higher Education*, 5(4): 457–73.

Perkin, H. (1969a) *Key Profession: The History of the Association of University Teachers*. London: Routledge & Kegan Paul.

Perkin, H. (1969b) *New Universities in the United Kingdom*. Paris: Organization for Economic Co-operation and Development.

Perkin, H. (1991) Dream, myth and reality: new universities in England, 1960–1990, *Higher Education Quarterly*, 45(4): 294–310.

Perry, W. (1976) *Open University: A Personal Account by the First Vice-Chancellor*. Milton Keynes: Open University Press.

Peston, H. and Peston, H. M. (1974) The further education and training scheme, in S. Mushkin (ed.) *Recurrent Education*, pp. 55–66. Washington, DC: National Institute of Education.

Peters, M. (1992) Performance and accountability in 'post-industrial society': the crisis of British universities, *Studies in Higher Education*, 17(2): 123–39.

Phillips, C. (1969) *Changes in Subject Choice at School and University*. London: Weidenfeld & Nicolson.

Pickford, M. (1975) *University Expansion and Finance*. London: Chatto & Windus/ Sussex University Press.

Pilkington, P. (1994) Student financial support, in S. Haselgrove (ed.) *The Student Experience*, pp. 55–71. Buckingham: Open University Press.

Piper, D. (1994) *Are Professors Professional? The Organisation of University Examinations*. London: Jessica Kingsley.

Political and Economic Planning (1955) *Colonial Students in Britain*. London: Political and Economic Planning.

Political and Economic Planning (1956) *Graduate Employment: A Sample Survey*. London: George Allen & Unwin.

Political and Economic Planning (1957) *Graduates in Industry*. London: George Allen & Unwin.

Powell, J. (1973) *Selection for University in Scotland: A First Report on the Assessment for Higher Education Project*. London: University of London Press Ltd.

Pratt, J. (1972) Open University! in T. Burgess (ed.) *The Shape of Higher Education*, pp. 67–85. London: Cornmarket Press.

Pratt, J. (1982) Co-ordination in the public sector: the Council for National Academic Awards, in M. Shattock (ed.) *The Structure and Governance of Higher Education*, pp. 116–32. Guildford: Society for Research into Higher Education.

Pratt, J. (1997) *The Polytechnic Experiment, 1965–1992*. Buckingham: Open University Press.

Pratt, J. and Burgess, T. (1974) *Polytechnics: A Report*. London: Pitman.

Pratt, J. and Lockwood, G. (1985) The external environment, in G. Lockwood and J. Davies (eds) (1985) *Universities: The Management Challenge*, pp. 1–23. Windsor, NFER-Nelson.

Pratt, J. and Silverman, S. (1988) *Responding to Constraint: Policy and Management in Higher Education*. Milton Keynes: Open University Press.

Prichard, C. (2000) *Making Managers in Universities and Colleges*. Buckingham: Open University Press.

Prichard, C. and Willmott, H. (1997) Just How Managed is the McUniversity? *Organization Studies*, 18(2): 287–316.

Prime Minister (1963) *Higher Education: Government Statement on the Report of the Committee Under the Chairmanship of Lord Robbins 1961–63*. London: HMSO, Cmnd 2165.

Pritchard, R. (1990) *The End of Elitism? The Democratisation of the West German University System*. New York: Berg.

Pritchard, R. (1993) Mergers and linkages in British higher education, *Higher Education Quarterly*, 47(2): 79–102.

Pritchard, R. (1994) Fissures in the federal structure? The case of the University of Wales, *Higher Education Quarterly*, 48(4): 256–76.

Pugsley, L. (2004) *The University Challenge: Higher Education Markets and Social Stratification*. Aldershot: Ashgate.

Purcell, K. and Pitcher, J. (1996) *Great Expectations: The New Diversity of Graduate Skills and Aspirations*. Manchester: Higher Education Career Services Unit.

Purcell, K., Pitcher, J. and Simm, C. (1999) *Working Out? Graduates' Early Experiences of the Labour Market*. Manchester: Higher Education Career Services Unit.

Purcell, K., Elias, P., Davies, R. and Wilton, N. (2005) *The Class of '99: A Study of the Early Labour Market Experiences of Recent Graduates*. Manchester: Higher Education Careers Services Unit.

Purvis, J. (1991) *A History of Women's Education in England.* Buckingham: Open University Press.

Quality Assurance Agency for Higher Education (1998) *Special Review of Thames Valley University.* Gloucester: QAA.

Quality Assurance Agency for Higher Education (2002) *QAA External Review Process for Higher Education in England: Operational Description.* London: QAA.

Raffe, D. (1979) The 'alternative route' reconsidered: part-time further education and social mobility in England and Wales, *Sociology*, 13: 47–73.

Raggett, M. and Clarkson, M. (eds) (1976) *Changing Patterns of Teacher Education.* London: Falmer Press.

Ramsden, B. (2003) *Patterns of Higher Education Institutions in the UK: Third Report.* London: Universities UK/Standing Conference of Principals.

Ramsden, B. (2005) *Patterns of Higher Education Institutions in the UK: Fifth Report.* London: Universities UK/Standing Conference of Principals.

Ramsden, B. (2006) *Part-time Students and Part-time Study in Higher Education in the UK. Strand 1: A Quantitative Data Analysis of 2003/04 HESA data.* London: Universities UK.

Ramsden, B. and Brown, N. (2002) *Patterns of Higher Education Institutions in the UK: Second Report.* London: Universities UK/Standing Conference of Principals.

Rashdall, H. ([1895] 1936) *The Universities of Europe in the Middle Ages.* London: Oxford University Press (three volumes). Edited by F. Powicke and A. Emden.

Raybould, S. (1964) *University Extramural Education in England, 1945–62: A Study in Finance and Policy.* London: Michael Joseph.

Reay, D., David, M. and Ball, S. (2005) *Degrees of Choice: Social Class, Race and Gender in Higher Education.* Stoke-on-Trent: Trentham.

Rees, G. and Istance, D. (1997) Higher education in Wales: the (re-)emergence of a national system? *Higher Education Quarterly*, 51(1): 49–67.

Rees, G. and Taylor, C. (2006) Devolution and the restructuring of participation in higher education in Wales, *Higher Education Quarterly*, 60(4): 370–91.

Regan, D. (1977) *Local Government and Education.* London: George Allen & Unwin.

Rendel, M. (1975) Men and women in higher education, *Educational Review*, 27: 192–201.

Rendel, M. (1980) How many women academics 1912–76? In R. Deem (ed.) *Schooling for Women's Work*, pp. 142–61. London: Routledge & Kegan Paul.

Richardson, J. and Woodley, A. (2003) Another look at the role of age, gender and subject as predictors of academic attainment in higher education, *Studies in Higher Education*, 28(4): 475–93.

de Ridder-Symoens, H. (ed.) (1992) *A History of the University in Europe. Volume I: Universities in the Middle Ages.* Cambridge: Cambridge University Press.

de Ridder-Symoens, H. (ed.) (1996) *A History of the University in Europe. Volume II: Universities in Early Modern Europe (1500–1800).* Cambridge: Cambridge University Press.

Ritzer, G. (1996) *The McDonaldization of Society*, revised edn. Thousand Oaks, CA: Pine Forge.

Ritzer, G. (2002) Enchanting McUniversity: towards a spectacularly irrational university quotidian, in D. Hayes and R. Wynyard (eds) *The McDonaldization of Higher Education*, pp. 19–32. Westport, CT: Bergin and Garvey.

Robbins, L. (1980) *Higher Education Revisited.* London: Macmillan.

Roberts, D. and Higgins, T. (1992) *Higher Education: The Student Experience – the*

Findings of a Research Programme into Student Decision-making and Consumer Satisfaction. Leeds: Higher Education Information Services Trust (HEIST).

Robertson, C. ([1930] 1944) *The British Universities*, 2nd edn. London: Methuen & Co.

Robertson, D. (1994) Proposals for an associate degree: the search for the 'missing link' of British higher education, *Higher Education Quarterly*, 48(4): 294–322.

Robertson, D. and Hillman, J. (1997) *Widening Participation in Higher Education for Students from Lower Socio-economic Groups and Students with Disabilities*. Norwich: National Committee of Inquiry into Higher Education, Report 6.

Robinson, E. (1968) *The New Polytechnics*. London: Cornmarket.

Robinson, E. (2007) 1966 and all that: a revolution in higher education that is yet incomplete, *Higher Education Review*, 39(3): 45–58.

Roizen, J. and Jepson, M. (1985) *Degrees for Jobs: Employer Expectations of Higher Education*. Guildford: Society for Research into Higher Education.

Rooke, M. (1971) *Anarchy and Apathy: Student Unrest 1968–70*. London: Hamish Hamilton.

Ross, C. (1996) Struggling for inclusion: black women in professional and management education, in L. Morley and V. Walsh (eds) *Breaking Boundaries: Women in Higher Education*, pp. 90–101. London: Taylor & Francis.

Roszak, T. (ed.) (1969) *The Dissenting Academy*. London: Chatto & Windus.

Rothblatt, S. (1983) The diversification of higher education in England, in K. Jarausch (ed.) *The Transformation of Higher Learning*, pp. 131–48. Chicago, IL: University of Chicago Press.

Rothblatt, S. (1987) Historical and comparative remarks on the federal principle in higher education, *History of Education*, 16(3): 151–80.

Rothblatt, S. (1988) London: a metropolitan university? In T. Bender (ed.) *The University and the City: From Medieval Origins to the Present*, pp. 119–49. New York: Oxford University Press.

Rothblatt, S. (1997) *The Modern University and its Discontents: The Fate of Newman's Legacies in Britain and America*. Cambridge: Cambridge University Press.

Rowley, G. (1997) United we stand: a strategic analysis of mergers in higher education, *Public Money and Management*, October/December, pp. 7–12.

Rudd, E. (1980) Halls of residence for students: a cautionary tale of decision-making, *Political Quarterly*, 51: 164–74.

Rudd, E. (1985) *A New Look at Postgraduate Failure*. Guildford: Society for Research into Higher Education/NFER-Nelson.

Rudd, E. and Hatch, S. (1968) *Graduate Study and After*. London: Weidenfeld & Nicolson.

Rudd, E. and Simpson, R. (1975) *The Highest Education: A Study of Graduate Education in Britain*. London: Routledge & Kegan Paul.

Rumble, G. (1982) *The Open University of the United Kingdom: An Evaluation of an Innovative Experience in the Democratisation of Higher Education*. Milton Keynes: Open University Distance Education Research Group.

Ryle, A. (1969) *Student Casualties*. London: Allen Lane/The Penguin Press.

Salter, B. and Tapper, T. (1994) *The State and Higher Education*. London: Woburn Press.

Sampson, A. (1962) *Anatomy of Britain*. London: Hodder & Stoughton.

Sandbrook, D. (2006) *White Heat: A History of Britain in the Swinging Sixties*. London: Little, Brown.

Sanderson, M. (1972) *The Universities and British Industry 1850–1970*. London: Routledge & Kegan Paul.

Sanderson, M. (ed.) (1975) *The Universities in the Nineteenth Century*. London: Routledge & Kegan Paul.

Sanderson, M. (1999) *Education and Economic Decline in Britain, 1870 to the 1990s*. Cambridge: Cambridge University Press.

Sargant, N. (1996) The Open University, in R. Fieldhouse, P. Baynes, R. Benn, W. Drews, J. Field, B. Groombridge, M. Hamilton, J. McIlroy, H. Marks, I. Martin, N. Sargant and V. Fieldhouse *A History of Modern British Adult Education*, pp. 290–307. Leicester: National Institute of Adult Continuing Education.

Schuller, T., Raffe, D., Morgan-Klein, B. and Clark, I. (1999) *Part-time Higher Education: Policy, Practice and Experience*. London: Jessica Kingsley.

Scotland, J. (1969a) *The History of Scottish Education. Volume 1: From the Beginning to 1872*. London: University of London Press.

Scotland, J. (1969b) *The History of Scottish Education. Volume 2: From 1872 to the Present Day*. London: University of London Press.

Scotland, J. (1982) Scottish education, 1952–1982, *British Journal of Educational Studies*, 30(1): 122–35.

Scott, J. (1973) *Dons and Students: British Universities Today*. London: The Plume Press.

Scott, P. (1982) Has the binary policy failed? In M. Shattock (ed.) *The Structure and Governance of Higher Education*, pp. 166–97. Guildford: Society for Research into Higher Education.

Scott, P. (1984) *The Crisis of the University*. London: Croom Helm.

Scott, P. (1989) The power of ideas, in C. Ball, and H. Eggins (eds) *Higher Education into the 1990s: New Dimensions*, pp. 7–16. Buckingham: Open University Press.

Scott, P. (1995) *The Meanings of Mass Higher Education*. Buckingham: Open University Press.

Scottish Executive (2003) *A Framework for Higher Education in Scotland. Higher Education Review: Phase 2*. Edinburgh: Scottish Executive.

Scottish Executive (2004) *The Competitiveness of Higher Education in Scotland. Higher Education Review: Phase 3*. Edinburgh: Scottish Executive.

Scottish Tertiary Education Advisory Council (1985) *Future Strategy for Higher Education in Scotland*. Edinburgh: HMSO, Cmnd 9676.

Secretary of State for Education and Science (1966) *A University of the Air*. London: HMSO, Cmnd 2922.

Secretary of State for Education and Science (1978) *Report of the Working Group on the Management of Higher Education in the Maintained Sector*. London: HMSO, Cmnd 7130.

Secretary of State for Education and Science (1987) *Review of the University Grants Committee*. London: HMSO, Cmnd 81.

Segal Quince Wicksteed (1988) *Universities, Enterprise and Local Economic Development: An Exploration of Links, Based on Experience from Studies in Britain and Elsewhere*. London: HMSO.

Sen, A. (1970) *Problems of Overseas Students and Nurses*. Slough: National Foundation for Educational Research.

Seville, A. (1997) The radical implications of modularity, in A. Seville and J. Tooley *The Debate on Higher Education: Challenging the Assumptions*, pp. 49–120. London: Institute of Economic Affairs.

Sharp, S. (2004) The Research Assessment Exercises 1992–2001: patterns across time and subjects, *Studies in Higher Education*, 29(2): 201–18.

Shattock, M. (1988) Financial management in universities: the lessons from University College, Cardiff, *Financial Accountability and Management*, 4(2): 99–112.

Shattock, M. (1994) *The UGC and the Management of British Universities*. Buckingham: Open University Press.

Shattock, M. (2001) The academic profession in Britain: a study in the failure to adapt to change, *Higher Education*, 41: 27–47.

Shattock, M. (2002) Re-balancing modern concepts of university governance, *Higher Education Quarterly*, 56(3): 235–44.

Shattock, M. (2003) *Managing Successful Universities*. Maidenhead: Open University Press.

Shattock, M. (2004) The Lambert Code: can we define best practice? *Higher Education Quarterly*, 58(4): 229–42.

Shattock, M. and Berdahl, R. (1984) The British University Grants Committee 1919–1983: changing relationships with government and the universities, *Higher Education*, 13: 471–99.

Shils, E. (1955) The intellectuals. I: Great Britain, *Encounter*, 4 (April): 5–16.

Shiner, M. and Modood, T. (2002) Help or hindrance? Higher education and the route to ethnic equality, *British Journal of Sociology of Education*, 23(2): 209–32.

Shinn, C. (1986) *Paying the Piper: The Development of the University Grants Committee 1919–46*. London: Falmer Press.

Shotnes, S. (ed.) (1986) *International Comparisons in Overseas Student Affairs*. London: UK Council for Overseas Student Affairs.

Shotnes, S. (ed.) (1987) *Overseas Students: Destination UK?* London: UK Council for Overseas Student Affairs.

Sikes, P. (2006) Working in a 'new' university: in the shadow of the research assessment exercise? *Studies in Higher Education*, 31(5): 555–68.

Silver, H. (1983) Expectations of higher education: some historical pointers, in H. Silver *Education as History: Interpreting Nineteenth and Twentieth-century Education*, pp. 173–238. London: Methuen.

Silver, H. (1990) *A Higher Education: The Council for National Academic Awards and British Higher Education 1964–1989*. London: Falmer.

Silver, H. (2003) *Higher Education and Opinion Making in Twentieth-century England*. London: Woburn Press.

Silver, H. (2006) 'Things change but names remain the same': higher education historiography 1975–2000, *History of Education*, 35(1): 121–40.

Silver, H. and Silver, P. (1997) *Students: Changing Roles, Changing Lives*. Buckingham: Open University Press.

Silver, H., Stennett, A. and Williams, R. (1995) *The External Examiner System: Possible Futures – Report of a Project Commissioned by the Higher Education Quality Council*. London: Quality Support Centre.

Simon, B. (1991) *Education and the Social Order 1940–1990*. London: Lawrence & Wishart.

Simons, H., Parlett, M. and Jaspan, A. (1976) *Up to Expectations: A Study of the Students' First Few Weeks of Higher Education*. London: Nuffield Foundation.

Simpson, R. (1983) *How the PhD came to Britain: A Century of Struggle for Postgraduate Education*. Guildford: Society for Research into Higher Education.

Singh, A. (1963) *Indian Students in Britain: A Survey of their Adjustment and Attitudes*. London: Asia Publishing House.

Sizer, J. (1988) British universities' responses to events leading to grant reductions announced in July 1981, *Financial Accountability and Management*, 4(2): 79–97.

Slater, J. (2005) *Spent Force or Revolution in Progress? eLearning after the eUniversity*. Oxford: Higher Education Policy Institute.

Smith, A. (1996) Regional cooperation and mobility in a global setting: the example of the European Community, in P. Blumenthal, C. Goodwin, A. Smith and U. Teichler (eds) *Academic Mobility in a Changing World*, pp. 129–46. London: Jessica Kingsley.

Smith, A. and Webster, F. (eds) (1997) *The Postmodern University? Contested Visions of Higher Education in Society*. Buckingham: Open University Press.

Smith, C. (1982) The research function in the social sciences, in G. Oldham (ed.) *The Future of Research*, pp. 150–70. Guildford: Society for Research into Higher Education.

Smith, D. (2001) Collaborative research: policy and the management of knowledge creation in UK universities, *Higher Education Quarterly*, 55(2): 131–57.

Smith, D., Bargh, C., Bocock, J. and Scott, P. (1999) New leaders at the top?: the educational and career paths of UK university vice-chancellors (1960–1996), *Higher Education Management*, 11(2): 113–35.

Smith, D. and Langslow, A. (eds) (1999) *The Idea of a University*. London: Jessica Kingsley.

Smith, D. and Saunders, M. (1991) *Other Routes: Part-time Higher Education Policy*. Buckingham: Open University Press.

Smith, P. (1990) *Killing the Spirit: Higher Education in America*. New York: Viking Penguin.

Smithers, A. (1976) *Sandwich Courses: An Integrated Education?* Slough: NFER Publishing Company Ltd.

Snow, C. (1951) *The Masters*. London: Macmillan.

Snow, C. (1993) *The Two Cultures*. Cambridge: Cambridge University Press (first published in two parts in 1959 and 1964).

Squires, G. (1987) *The Curriculum Beyond School*. London: Hodder & Stoughton.

Squires, G. (1990) *First Degree: The Undergraduate Curriculum*. Buckingham: Open University Press.

Stephenson, J. and Weil, S. (eds) (1992) *Quality in Learning: A Capability Approach in Higher Education*. London: Kogan Page.

Stewart, W. (1989) *Higher Education in Postwar Britain*. London: Macmillan.

Sutherland, G. (2001) Examinations and the construction of professional identity: a case study of England 1800–1950, *Assessment in Education*, 8(1): 51–64.

Sutherland, M. (1985) *Women who Teach in Universities*. Stoke-on-Trent: Trentham Books.

Swinnerton-Dyer, P. (1991) Policy on higher education and research: the Rede lecture, *Higher Education Quarterly*, 45(3): 204–18.

Tapper, T. and Salter, B. (1978) *Education and the Political Order: Changing Patterns of Class Control*. London: Macmillan.

Tapper, T. and Salter, B. (1992) *Oxford, Cambridge and the Changing Idea of the University: The Challenge to Donnish Domination*. Buckingham: Open University Press.

Tapper, T. and Salter, B. (1997) Who will speak for the universities? The Committee of Vice-Chancellors and Principals in the age of mass higher education, *Higher Education Quarterly*, 51(2): 113–33.

Tasker, M. and Packham, D. (1994) Changing cultures? Government intervention in higher education 1987–93, *British Journal of Educational Studies*, 42(2): 150–62.

Taylor, J. (2003) Institutional diversity in UK higher education: policy and outcomes since the end of the binary divide, *Higher Education Quarterly*, 57(3): 266–93.

Taylor, J. (2006) 'Big is beautiful'. Organisational change in universities in the United Kingdom: new models of institutional management and the changing role of academic staff, *Higher Education in Europe*, 31(3): 251–73.

Taylor, W. (1969) *Society and the Education of Teachers*. London: Faber & Faber.

Taylor, W. (1984) The National Context, 1972–82, in R. Alexander, M. Craft and

J. Lynch (eds) *Change in Teacher Education: Context and Provision since Robbins*, pp. 16–30. London: Holt, Rinehart & Winston.

Teichler, U. and Maiworm, F. (1994) *Transition to Work: The Experiences of Former ERASMUS Students.* London: Jessica Kingsley.

Teichler, U. and Maiworm, F. (1997) *The ERASMUS Experience: Major Findings of the ERASMUS Evaluation Research Project.* Luxembourg: Office for Official Publications of the European Communities.

Thelin, J. (2004) *A History of American Higher Education.* Baltimore, MD: Johns Hopkins University Press.

Thoday, D. (1957) Halls of residence, *Universities Quarterly*, 12(1): 45–56.

Thomas, K. (1990) *Gender and Subject in Higher Education.* Buckingham: Open University Press.

Thomas, L. and Quinn, J. (2007) *First Generation Entry into Higher Education: An International Study.* Maidenhead: Open University Press.

Thompson, S. (1998) Who goes there, friend or foe? Black women, white women and friendships in academica, in D. Malina and S. Maslin-Prothero (eds) *Surviving the Academy: Feminist Perspectives*, pp. 122–35. London: Falmer.

Thomson, A. (1973) *Half a Century of Medical Research. Volume I: Origins and Policy of the Medical Research Council.* London: HMSO.

Thomson, A. (1975) *Half a Century of Medical Research. Volume II: The Programme of the Medical Research Council.* London: HMSO.

Tight, M. (1988) Institutional typologies, *Higher Education Review*, 20(3): 27–51.

Tight, M. (1991) *Higher Education: A Part-time Perspective.* Buckingham: Open University Press.

Tight, M. (1994) Crisis, what crisis? Rhetoric and reality in higher education, *British Journal of Educational Studies*, 42(4): 363–74.

Tight, M. (1996) University typologies re-examined, *Higher Education Review*, 29(1): 57–77.

Tight, M. (2000) Do league tables contribute to the development of a quality culture? Football and higher education compared, *Higher Education Quarterly*, 54(1): 22–42.

Tight, M. (2003) *Researching Higher Education.* Maidenhead: Open University Press.

Tight, M. (ed.) (2004) *The RoutledgeFalmer Reader in Higher Education.* London: RoutledgeFalmer.

Tight, M. (2005) Re-writing history: the University of London as a global institution in the nineteenth, twentieth and twenty-first centuries, in M. Tight (ed.) *International Relations*, pp. 289–306. Oxford: Elsevier.

Tight, M. (2006) Higher education post-war: a novel history, *Higher Education Review*, 39(1): 17–33.

Tight, M. (2007) Institutional diversity in English higher education, *Higher Education Review*, 39(2): 3–24.

Tinkler, P. and Jackson, C. (2000) Examining the doctorate: institutional policy and the PhD examination process in Britain, *Studies in Higher Education*, 25(2): 167–80.

Tinklin, T. and Hall, J. (1999) Getting round obstacles: disabled students' experiences in higher education in Scotland, *Studies in Higher Education*, 24(2): 183–94.

Tinklin, T., Riddell, S. and Wilson, A. (2004) Policy and provision for disabled students in Scotland and England: the current state of play, *Studies in Higher Education*, 29(5): 637–57.

Tolmie, P. (ed.) (1998) *How I got my First Class Degree*, 2nd edn. Lancaster: Unit for Innovation in Higher Education.

Toyne, P. (1979) *Educational Credit Transfer: Feasibility Study.* London: Department of Education and Science, two volumes.

Training Agency (1989) *Enterprise in Higher Education: Key Features of the Proposals 1988–89.* Sheffield: Training Agency.

Training Agency (1990) *Enterprise in Higher Education: Key Features of the Proposals 1989–90.* Sheffield: Training Agency.

Trow, M. (1989) The Robbins trap: British attitudes and the limits of expansion, *Higher Education Quarterly*, 43(1): 55–75.

Trow, M. (1993) Comparative perspectives on British and American higher education, in S. Rothblatt and B. Wittrock (eds) *The European and American University since 1800: Historical and Sociological Essays*, pp. 280–99. Cambridge: Cambridge University Press.

Trow, M. (1996) Trusts, markets and accountability in higher education: a comparative perspective, *Higher Education Policy*, 9(4): 309–24.

Trowler, P. (1997) Beyond the Robbins trap: reconceptualising academic responses to change in higher education (or . . . quiet flows the don?), *Studies in Higher Education*, 22(3): 301–18.

Trowler, P. (1998) *Academics Responding to Change: New Higher Education Frameworks and Academic Cultures.* Buckingham: Open University Press.

Trowler, P., Fanghanel, J. and Wareham, T. (2005) Freeing the chi of change: the higher education academy and enhancing teaching and learning in higher education, *Studies in Higher Education*, 30(4): 427–44.

Truscot, B. (1943) *Red Brick University.* London: Faber & Faber.

Truscot, B. (1945) *Redbrick and these Vital Days.* London: Faber & Faber.

Tunstall, J. (ed.) (1974) *The Open University Opens.* London: Routledge & Kegan Paul.

Universities Funding Council (1989) *Report on the 1989 Research Assessment Exercise.* London: UFC.

University Grants Committee (1948) *University Development from 1935 to 1947.* London: HMSO.

University Grants Committee (1957) *Report of the Sub-committee on Halls of Residence.* London: HMSO.

University Grants Committee (1958) *University Development 1952–1957.* London: HMSO, Cmnd 534.

University Grants Committee (1964a) *University Development 1957–1962.* London: HMSO, Cmnd 2267.

University Grants Committee (1964b) *Report of the Committee on University Teaching Methods.* London: HMSO.

University Grants Committee (1968) *University Development 1962–1967.* London: HMSO, Cmnd 3820.

University Grants Committee (1984a) *Report of the Continuing Education Working Party.* London: University Grants Committee.

University Grants Committee (1984b) *A Strategy for Higher Education into the 1990s: The University Grant Committee's Advice.* London: HMSO.

Vaizey, J. (1963) *The Control of Education.* London: Faber & Faber.

Varlaam, C. (1987) *Contract Researchers in Universities: A Study for the Advisory Board for the Research Councils.* Brighton: University of Sussex, Institute of Manpower Studies.

Venables, P. (1955) *Technical Education: Its Aims, Organisation and Future Development.* London: G. Bell & Sons.

Venables, P. (1959) *Sandwich Courses for Training Technologists and Technicians*. London: Max Parrish.

Venables, P. (1978) *Higher Education Developments: The Technological Universities 1956–1976*. London: Faber.

Vernon, K. (2004) *Universities and the State in England, 1850–1939*. London: RoutledgeFalmer.

Vernon, P. (1963) The pool of ability, in P. Halmos (ed.) *The Sociological Review Monograph No. 7: Sociological Studies in British University Education*, pp. 45–57. Keele: University of Keele.

Wagner, L. (1982) The challenge of change, in L. Wagner (ed.) *Agenda for Institutional Change in Higher Education*, pp. 7–32. Guildford: Society for Research into Higher Education.

Wagner, L. (1998) Dearing is dead – Blunkett is born? The future funding of higher education, *Higher Education Quarterly*, 52(1): 64–76.

Wagner, P. (2001) *A History and Theory of the Social Sciences: Not All that is Solid Melts into Air*. London: Sage Publications.

Walford, G. (1987) *Restructuring Universities: Politics and Power in the Management of Change*. London: Croom Helm.

Walford, G. (1988) The privatisation of British higher education, *European Journal of Education*, 23(1–2): 47–64.

Waring, M. (1979) Biological science: integration or fragmentation? In W. Marsden (ed.) *Post-war Curriculum Development: An Historical Appraisal*, pp. 49–61. Leicester: History of Education Society.

Watson, D. (1998) The limits to diversity, in D. Jary and M. Parker (eds) *The New Higher Education: Issues and Directions for the Post-Dearing University*, pp. 65–81. Stoke-on-Trent: Staffordshire University Press.

Watson, D. and Bowden, R. (1999) Why did they do it? The conservatives and mass higher education, 1979–97, *Journal of Educational Policy*, 14(3): 243–56.

Watts, A. (1972) *Diversity and Choice in Higher Education*. London: Routledge & Kegan Paul.

Webb, S. (2001) 'I'm doing it for all of us': gender and identity in the transition to higher education, in P. Anderson and J. Williams (eds) *Identity and Difference in Higher Education: 'Outsiders Within'*, pp. 38–54. Aldershot: Ashgate.

Welsh Assembly Government (2002) *Reaching Higher: Higher Education and the Learning Country – a Strategy for the Higher Education Sector in Wales*. Cardiff: Welsh Assembly Government.

Whalley, A. (1982) *Postgraduate Education in Universities and Polytechnics: Report of a Survey of Heads of Department – Engineering, Science and the Social Sciences*. London: Policy Studies Institute.

Whitburn, J., Mealing, M. and Cox, C. (1976) *People in Polytechnics: A Survey of Polytechnic Staff and Students 1972/3*. Guildford: Society for Research into Higher Education.

Whitchurch, C. (2008) Beyond administration and management: changing professional identities in UK higher education, in R. Barnett and R. di Napoli (eds) *Changing Identities in Higher Education: Voicing Perspectives*, pp. 69–88. London: Routledge.

Whiteley, L. (1933) *The Poor Student and the University. A report on the Scholarship System with Reference to Local Education Authorities' Awards and Assistance to Intending Teachers*. London: George Allen & Unwin.

Whiting, C. (1932) *The University of Durham 1832–1932*. London: Sheldon Press.

Whyley, C. and Callender, C. (1997) *Administrative and Support Staff in Higher Education: Their Experiences and Expectations.* Norwich: National Committee of Inquiry into Higher Education, Report 4.

Wiener, M. (1981) *English Culture and the Decline of the Industrial Spirit, 1850–1980.* Cambridge: Cambridge University Press.

Williams, G., Blackstone, T. and Metcalf, D. (1974) *The Academic Labour Market: Economic and Social Aspects of a Profession.* Amsterdam: Elsevier Scientific Publishing Company.

Williams, L. (1987) Overseas students in the United Kingdom: some recent developments, *Higher Education Quarterly,* 41(2): 107–25.

Williams, P. (1981a) The emergence of the problem: editorial introduction, in P. Williams (ed.) *The Overseas Student Question: Studies for a Policy,* pp. 1–21. London: Heinemann.

Williams, P. (1981b) Overseas student in Britain: the background, in P. Williams (ed.) *The Overseas Student Question: Studies for a Policy,* pp. 22–46. London: Heinemann.

Williams, P. (1992) The UK Academic Audit Unit, in A. Craft (ed.) *Quality Assurance in Higher Education: Proceedings of an International Conference, Hong Kong, 1991,* pp. 141–59. London: Falmer Press.

Williams, R. (1997) The UK's eternal examiner system: its rise or demise? In J. Radford, K. Raaheim, P. de Vries and R. Williams (eds) *Quantity and Quality in Higher Education,* pp. 76–87. London: Jessica Kingsley.

Willmott, H. (1995) Managing the academics: commodification and control in the development of university education in the UK, *Human Relations,* 48(9): 993–1027.

Wilson, B. (1965) The needs of students, in M. Reeves (ed.) *Eighteen Plus: Unity and Diversity in Higher Education,* pp. 44–85. London: Faber & Faber.

Wilson, T. (2001) The proletarianisation of academic labour, *Industrial Relations Journal,* 35: 250–62.

Winn, S. and Stevenson, R. (1997) Student loans: are the policy objectives being achieved? *Higher Education Quarterly,* 51(2): 144–63.

Winter, R. (1995) The University of Life plc: the 'industrialization' of higher education? In J. Smyth (ed.) *Academic Work: The Changing Labour Process in Higher Education,* pp. 129–43. Buckingham: Open University Press.

Wit, de, K. and Verhoeven, J. (2001) The higher education policy of the European Union: with or against the member states? In J. Huisman, P. Maassen and G. Neave (eds) *Higher Education and the Nation State: The International Dimension of Higher Education,* pp. 175–231. Oxford: Elsevier.

Wolff, R. (1969) *The Ideal of the University.* Boston: Beacon Press.

Woodhall, M. (1989) Introduction: sharing the costs of higher education, in M. Woodhall (ed.) *Financial Support for Students: grants, loans or graduate tax?,* pp. 1–23. London: Institute of Education.

Woodley, A., Wagner, L., Slowey, M., Hamilton, M. and Fulton, O. (1987) *Choosing to Learn: Adults in Education.* Buckingham: Open University Press.

Woodward, D., Ross, K., Bird, J. and Upton, G. (2000) *Managing Equal Opportunities in Higher Education: A Guide to Understanding and Action.* Buckingham: Open University Press.

Wyatt, J. (1990) *Commitment to Higher Education. Seven West European Thinkers on the Essence of the University: Max Horkheimer, Karl Jaspers, F. R. Leavis, J. H. Newman, Jose Ortega y Gasset, Paul Tillich, Miguel de Unamuno.* Buckingham: Open University Press.

Wyatt, J. (2000) Persistent ghosts: romantic origins of the idea of university communities, in I. McNay (ed.) *Higher Education and its Communities*, pp. 13–28. Buckingham: Open University Press.

Yorke, M. (1999) *Leaving Early: Undergraduate Non-completion in Higher Education.* London: Falmer.

Yorke, M. (2008) *Grading Student Achievement in Higher Education: Signals and Shortcomings.* London: Routledge.

Young, K., Fogarty, M. and McRae, S. (1987) *The Management of Doctoral Studies in the Social Sciences.* London: Policy Studies Institute.

Youngman, M. (1994) Supervisors' and students' experiences of supervision, in R. Burgess (ed.) *Postgraduate Education and Training in the Social Sciences: Processes and Products*, pp. 75–104. London: Jessica Kingsley.

Zamorski, B. (2002) Research-led teaching and learning in higher education: a case, *Teaching in Higher Education*, 7(4): 411–27.

Zweig, F. (1963) *The Student in the Age of Anxiety: A Survey of Oxford and Manchester Students.* London: Heinemann.

Index

The Society for Research into Higher Education

The Society for Research into Higher Education (SRHE), an international body, exists to stimulate and coordinate research into all aspects of higher education. It aims to improve the quality of higher education through the encouragement of debate and publication on issues of policy, on the organization and management of higher education institutions, and on the curriculum, teaching and learning methods.

The Society is entirely independent and receives no subsidies, although individual events often receive sponsorship from business or industry. The Society is financed through corporate and individual subscriptions and has members from many parts of the world. It is an NGO of UNESCO.

Under the imprint *SRHE & Open University Press*, the Society is a specialist publisher of research, having over 80 titles in print. In addition to *SRHE News*, the Society's newsletter, the Society publishes three journals: *Studies in Higher Education* (three issues a year), *Higher Education Quarterly* and *Research into Higher Education Abstracts* (three issues a year).

The Society runs frequent conferences, consultations, seminars and other events. The annual conference in December is organized at and with a higher education institution. There are a growing number of networks which focus on particular areas of interest, including:

Access	FE/HE
Assessment	Graduate Employment
Consultants	New Technology for Learning
Curriculum Development	Postgraduate Issues
Eastern European	Quantitative Studies
Educational Development Research	Student Development

Benefits to members

Individual

- The opportunity to participate in the Society's networks
- Reduced rates for the annual conferences
- Free copies of *Research into Higher Education Abstracts*
- Reduced rates for *Studies in Higher Education*

- Reduced rates for *Higher Education Quarterly*
- Free online access to *Register of Members' Research Interests* – includes valuable reference material on research being pursued by the Society's members
- Free copy of occasional in-house publications, e.g. *The Thirtieth Anniversary Seminars Presented by the Vice-Presidents*
- Free copies of *SRHE News* and *International News* which inform members of the Society's activities and provides a calendar of events, with additional material provided in regular mailings
- A 35 per cent discount on all SRHE/Open University Press books
- The opportunity for you to apply for the annual research grants
- Inclusion of your research in the *Register of Members' Research Interests*

Corporate

- Reduced rates for the annual conference
- The opportunity for members of the Institution to attend SRHE's network events at reduced rates
- Free copies of *Research into Higher Education Abstracts*
- Free copies of *Studies in Higher Education*
- Free online access to *Register of Members' Research Interests* – includes valuable reference material on research being pursued by the Society's members
- Free copy of occasional in-house publications
- Free copies of *SRHE News* and *International News*
- A 35 per cent discount on all SRHE/Open University Press books
- The opportunity for members of the Institution to submit applications for the Society's research grants
- The opportunity to work with the Society and co-host conferences
- The opportunity to include in the *Register of Members' Research Interests* your Institution's research into aspects of higher education

Membership details: SRHE, 76 Portland Place, London W1B 1NT, UK Tel: 020 7637 2766. Fax: 020 7637 2781. email: srheoffice@srhe.ac.uk world wide web: http://www.srhe.ac.uk./srhe/ *Catalogue*: SRHE & Open University Press, McGraw-Hill Education, McGraw-Hill House, Shoppenhangers Road, Maidenhead, Berkshire SL6 2QL. Tel: 01628 502500. Fax: 01628 770224. email: enquiries@openup.co.uk – web: www.openup.co.uk

Related books from Open University Press
Purchase from www.openup.co.uk or order through your local bookseller

A WILL TO LEARN
BEING A STUDENT IN AN AGE OF UNCERTAINTY

Ronald Barnett

There is an extraordinary but largely unnoticed phenomenon in higher education: by and large, students persevere and complete their studies. How should we interpret this tendency? Students are living in uncertain times and often experience anxiety, and yet they continue to press forward with their studies. The argument here is that we should understand this propensity on the part of students to persist through *a will to learn*.

This book examines the structure of what it is to have a will to learn. Here, a language of being, becoming, authenticity, dispositions, voice, air, spirit, inspiration and care is drawn on. As such, this book offers an idea of student development that challenges the dominant views of our age, of curricula understood largely in terms of skill or even of knowledge, and pedagogy understood as bringing off pre-specified 'outcomes'.

The will to learn, though, can be fragile. This is of crucial importance, for if the will to learn dissolves, the student's commitment may falter. Accordingly, more than encouraging an interest in the student's subject or in the acquiring of skills, the *primary* responsibility of teachers in higher education is to sustain and develop the student's will to learn. This is a radical thesis, for it implies a transformation in how we understand the nature of teaching in higher education.

Contents
Acknowledgements – Introduction – Part 1: Being and becoming – Where there's a will – Being – Authenticity – Becoming – Part 2: Being a student – Travel broadens the mind – A will to offer – Voice – Dispositions and qualities – Part 3: Being a teacher – The inspiring teacher – A pedagogy for uncertain times – Space and risk – A critical spirit – Coda: Puzzles and possibilities – Notes – Bibliography – Subject index – Name index.

2007   208pp
978-0-33-522380-0 (Paperback)   978-0-33-522381-7 (Hardback)

FROM VOCATIONAL TO HIGHER EDUCATION
An International Perspective

Gavin F. Moodie

This book discusses current issues in vocational and higher education and the relations between them. As well as concentrating on the well developed English-speaking countries – the UK, US, Canada, Australia and New Zealand – the book also considers important developments in continental Europe: in particular:

- The Bologna process in higher education
- The Copenhagen declaration on enhanced European co-operation in vocational education and training
- The development of a European qualifications framework

From Vocational to Higher Education is key reading for university lecturers, those studying for higher degrees in higher education, managers and policy makers.

Contents
List of tables – List of boxes – Acknowledgements – Introduction – Comparing education – Defining 'vocational education' – Countries – Qualifications frameworks – European integration in vocational and higher education – Sectors – Relations between vocational and higher education – Student transfer between sectors – Summary and conclusion – References – Index.

2008 216pp
978–0–335–22715–0 (Paperback) 978–0–335–22716–7 (Hardback)

GENDER AND THE CHANGING FACE OF HIGHER EDUCATION

A Feminised Future?

Carole Leathwood and Barbara Read

A notable feature of higher education in many countries over the last few decades has been the dramatic rise in the proportion of female students. Women now outnumber men as undergraduate students in the majority of OECD countries, fuelling concerns that men are deserting degree-level study as women overtake them both numerically and in terms of levels of achievement. The assertion is that higher education is becoming increasingly 'feminized' – reflecting similar claims in relation to schooling and the labour market. At the same time, there are persistent concerns about degree standards, with allegations of 'dumbing down'. This raises questions about whether the higher education system to which more women have gained access is now of less value, both intrinsically and in terms of labour market outcomes, than previously.

This ground-breaking book examines these issues in relation to higher education in the UK and globally. It provides a thorough analysis of debates about 'feminization', asking:

- To what extent do patterns of participation continue to reflect and (re)construct wider social inequalities of gender, social class and ethnicity?
- How far has a numerical increase in women students challenged the cultures, curriculum and practices of the university?
- What are the implications for women, men and the future of higher education?

Drawing on international and national data, theory and research, *Gender and the Changing Face of Higher Education* provides an accessible but nuanced discussion of the 'feminization' of higher education for postgraduates, policy-makers and academics working in the field.

Contents
Acknowledgements – Introduction – The feminization thesis – The global context: Gender, feminization and higher education – Gender, participation and higher education in the UK – Institutional identities and representations of the university – Student identities, femininities and masculinities – Academic identities and gendered work – Academic practices: Assessment, speaking and writing – Academic practices: Curriculum, knowledge and skills – Conclusions: Re-visioning the academy – References – Index.

2008 224pp
978–0–335–22713–6 (Paperback) 978–0–335–22714–3 (Hardback)